The Complete Book of
GARDENING

The Complete Book of
GARDENING

A practical guide to a beautiful garden

Marshall Cavendish

PICTURE CREDITS

John Roberts, Ray Procter, R. J. Corbin, I.C.I., Fisons, M/C, Keith Paisley, D. Smith, Maxicrop, H. Smith, K. F. Ward, G. E. Hyde, R. G. Benfield, Barnabys, V. Stevenson, A. J. Huxley, Pamela Booth, E. Megson, D. C. Arminson, Ruth Rutter, L. Johns, Maurice Nimmo, Ianthe Ruthven, Animal Photography, Peter Hunt, V. Finnis, Picturepoint, P. Ayres, N. J. Prokter, J. K. B. Cowley, Amateur Gardening, Anthony Turner, John Hovell, Chilstone Garden Ornaments, C. Williams, B. Alfieri, C. Bevilacqua, A. F. Derrick, P. Becker, N.H.P.A., Murphy's Chemical Co., J. K. Burras, H. Angel, C. Reynolds, C. J. Dawkings, B. Furner, R. Perry, The Alpine Garden Society, Gerald Rodway, K. A. Beckett, Tourist Photo Library, J. E. Downward, I. Hardwick, P. Genereux, Miles Hadfield, H. R. Allen, D. J. Kesby, D. Woodland, J. Banks, D. Wildridge, C. Dawson, J. Markham, K. N. Sanecki.

Published by Marshall Cavendish Books Limited
58 Old Compton Street
London W1V 5PA

© Marshall Cavendish Limited 1968-1988

First printing 1973
This printing 1988

ISBN 0 85685 017 9

Printed and bound in Hong Kong by Dai Nippon
Printing Company

This volume is not to be sold in Australia,
New Zealand or North America

CONTENTS

INTRODUCTION

Gardening is one of the Western world's leading hobbies and leisure activities — and no wonder — for it seems to have all the virtues and none of the vices. It provides healthy and gentle exercise at a place of the utmost convenience and always at a time of your own choosing. It is the perfect relaxation from the pressures of the modern world. It is a creative hobby in which your personality can be expressed, based upon family needs and desires. It is economical, for it requires little special equipment and can, in fact, show a profit, through the provision of healthy and nourishing food which is fresher, cheaper and more delicious than any that can be bought.

Again, the smaller and more compact gardens of today, allied with the latest products of mechanical and chemical engineering, mean that gardening is easy, no longer a back-breaking chore. It can be enjoyed whenever you like and you are left with plenty of time to spend on other things.

Gardening today is easy, not only because of the aids available, but because of better understanding of the laws of nature. We have learnt not to fight but to co-operate, not to demand what is denied us but to accept that which is offered.

This is what our book is about. We aim to *explain* gardening. In simple terms and with the aid of many clear and helpful illustrations, we present the background picture of how and why a plant grows, what the soil needs to enable plants to develop quickly, easily and with the strength and health that so largely precludes attack by pests and diseases. We describe modern labour-saving methods of carrying out gardening tasks the easy way. We provide compact lists, compact descriptions of processes and compact tables of treatments. Here, we believe, is a book for the intelligent gardener, both man and woman, who uses brain power to save work, to speed results, to gain more for less work, to bring greater colour and increased productivity.

The glories of the garden: the masses of brilliant colour, the gracious and elegant trees above the grassy lawn, the limpid pool and the dainty but sturdy plants in the rock garden, the branches of the fruit trees bending under the weight of apples, pears and peaches, and the succulent joy of tender garden peas and crisp lettuce. These are all glories the gardener knows and they can be achieved with only a small expenditure of time, labour and cash so long as there is understanding of the processes involved and co-operation with the never-changing laws of nature.

Without extra expense and without extra work you can grow two crops where one grew before, you can beautify a drab plot, disguise an eyesore, cover a wall with brilliant colour, protect the house from the howl of the prevailing wind and increase the value of your property over the years while at the same time continuing to profit from it.

All this — and many more subtle pleasures which add depth and a new dimension to the true gardener's life — you can gain from your garden. But — and this but is important — you must learn to understand your garden, fit in with its patterns and accept its laws. Since you and your garden are in a real sense partners both in pleasures and labours, co-operation is essential. With co-operation you can work wonders.

We hope this book will help that co-operation along.

Chapter 1

GARDENING BASICS

Soil, of course, is the stuff from which your garden grows. It is not some inert substance you cannot change. Soil can be adapted to a hundred and one different requirements—and how you adapt it and treat it will very largely determine your success as a gardener.

All plants growing in the garden, as distinct from the greenhouse, the home, the pool or in pots and tubs, are dependent for their anchorage and their sustenance on the soil. So it is well to understand exactly what soil is and how it can be improved, adapted or altered to suit the special requirements of any plant. Soil may be defined as the natural medium for the growth of the land plants that cover most of the earth's land surface.

When the rocks of the earth's crust are subjected to the action of weathering agents such as frost, rain, and sunshine, they break down. The debris produced provides the mineral portion of the soil, but organic matter must be added to it. This takes place through plants beginning to grow on the rock debris. They drop their leaves or they die and decaying matter from them becomes incorporated in the ground as its organic constituent.

Soil types

Soils are not just deposited in their present position; they are largely the outcome of the deposits left by the plants and the animals they once supported and of the climate in which they develop and the type of rock that constitutes most of their solid or mineral matter. Not only are there broad differences among soils from different parts of the world as a result of differences in climate and nature of vegetation, but differences are found among neighbouring soils. It was John Evelyn, the diarist, who said in 1675 that he considered that there were no fewer than 179,001,060 different sorts of earth. The basis of this calculation is not recorded, but several hundred soils have already been identified and mapped in Britain.

The soils of the world are classified into a comparatively small number of major groups in rather the same way as plants are grouped into families. And, as each plant family consists of many different genera and still more species, so the major soil groups are divided into smaller units, of which the soil series is the most important for survey and mapping work. Most British soils come into the following five groups.

Brown earths which give most of the best garden soils in Britain, developed from a wide variety of rocks under fairly dry and warm conditions that favour the growth of deciduous forest; their colour is brown, yellow-brown or red. Having no natural lime they are generally slightly to moderately acid in reaction. Since they often have a friable, coarse-textured topsoil and a system of deep fine cracks they are generally well drained. But if you have one with a silty texture you will have to be careful not to cultivate it or water it too heavily for fear of panning the surface which leads to temporary waterlogging.

Gley soils are wet and in contrast to well-drained soils usually have a grey or blue layer somewhere in their profiles or they may have a variegated or mottled appearance.

The reason why plants grow poorly in such soils as these is not so much due to their excess of water but more to their lack of air; the roots of plants must breathe, just as other parts of the plant do, so that, aquatic plants excepted, they must rely upon air in between the particles of soil, if their roots are to survive. After rain these spaces fill with water and until this drains away the roots are unable to get air. The speed at which the water drains away varies greatly with different soils as also does the capacity of different kinds of plants to withstand immersion.

But the reason for the wet condition of a soil must be discovered before you can cure the trouble. Below are given the three main causes of wetness.

Poor penetration The rock underlying the soil may be more or less impermeable and prevent the free passage of water. Roots are swamped in wet periods and when followed by dry periods there is no reserve of water for the crippled root system to draw upon because the impervious rock does not store much water. Waterlogging is therefore followed by drought. This is one of the commonest causes of poor drainage and is found on soils overlying clays and shales.

A water table may be present in soils of low-lying land, resulting in the soil being saturated with water at a depth of a few feet or inches. The surface of this underground lake is known as the water table and it generally rises and falls following wet and dry periods. Provided that the fluctuation is not too great, a water table at about 3 feet below the surface of the soil can be an asset since the water will be available to the deeper roots. You can find out whether your soil has a water table near the surface by digging a hole or boring a hole with a post-hole auger about 3 feet deep; leave it open for a day and then see whether there is any water resting on the bottom of the hole. It is not only clay soils that are subject to this kind of wetness; sandy and loamy soils often have high water tables in low-lying areas such as the flood plains of rivers and estuaries.

When the water table rises during the winter the roots of perennial plants are killed and when it falls in the summer your plants are literally left high and dry and then suffer from drought.

Springs are more common than is gener-ally suspected because only the largest are seen at the surface; but large areas of land are waterlogged by subterranean springs.

You can usually tell whether a soil is well-drained or badly-drained by the colour of the soil; well-drained soil is an even colour of grey brown or brown and free from mottling, whereas defective drainage leaves definite symptoms in the soil. Well-drained soils are normally well aerated and have plenty of oxygen in them, but where the water stagnates the living organisms in the soil and plant roots use the dissolved oxygen as fast as it can be renewed, and some of the iron compounds which impart a yellow, brown or red colour to soils, lose part of their oxygen and cause grey or bluish colours to develop. When the water subsides air gets in again and the grey or bluish colours go brown again and so the soil becomes mottled with rust coloured stains, or even hard little lumps of rust. Spring water may deposit a heavy, chocolate-brown iron staining.

It is important to note the depth at which these symptoms occur because each inch above the waterlogged area means an inch of good heathy root run.

Podsolised soils are acid and have profiles consisting of very distinct layers. They are best seen on heathland overlying sandy or gravelly geological formations, in western Surrey, northern Hampshire, the New Forest and eastern Dorset, the Cornish moors and the heaths of the west Midlands especially in Cheshire and Shropshire.

The surface layer is often black and peaty, being rich in decaying plant remains. These produce acids which cause the washing out of iron and aluminium compounds from this and the next layer below. Under the dark-coloured surface layer lies one which is very pale brown, often almost white. This is because the iron, which normally colours a soil brown, has been washed out of it. Underneath this is a dark-brown to reddish-brown layer in which clay, iron and aluminium compounds and humus have been deposited. This is often cemented into a hard pan by the iron and organic matter. When you dig these soils the mixture of the bleached layer and the dark-coloured subsoil gives it an ashy appearance.

Extreme acidity and low nutrient content often characterise these soils; but by careful liming and the applica-tion of manures they can grow plants well, and, of course, many are ideal for rhododendrons and azaleas and other members of the *Ericaceae*. While their coarse texture makes for very easy working, moisture retention is usually a problem. Deficiency of potash is normal while manganese and boron deficiencies may result from over-liming. Where the garden has been recently reclaimed from heathland, generous manuring with nitrogenous manures is needed to speed up the decay of plant remains and

Gley soils are poor and waterlogged. so that oxygen cannot reach the iron content and so turn it red. This is 1 less apparent in the topsoil than in 2 the subsoil, which is more grey, 3 as shown by this profile.

magnesium compounds may have to be added.

Calcareous soils are naturally rich in lime (calcium carbonate) due to their development from chalk and lime-stone formations in downland areas of the south-eastern and southern central parts of England; they also occur in parts of Lincolnshire and Rutland.

You can generally see fragments or sometimes fairly large lumps of calcium carbonate in these soils and the presence of this substance makes them alkaline (the opposite to acid). This accounts for the fizzing (effervescence) when a small amount is treated with dilute hydrochloric acid.

When newly broken up they are almost always neutral to the surface and do not require liming. They are so alkaline that elements like iron, boron magnesium and manganese are less readily available to plants and symptoms of their deficiency can often be seen in many species.

Since many calcareous soils are only a few inches thick they lose their reserves of moisture in a very short time during dry weather, unless very large amounts of humus-forming manures are either dug in or added as a mulch.

The deeper calcareous soils have brown or reddish-brown sub-surface layers and make quite good garden soils, provided that you do not want to grow rhododendrons or most other members of the *Ericaceae* in them. They will also grow plums, apples and most of the soft fruits.

If the clay content is high you have a real problem soil to contend with and great skill is needed to cultivate them just at the right time, when they often

On calcareous soils the topsoil
1 often contains a high percentage of humus, and the subsoil
2 is almost all calcium carbonate.
3 *Left* **Calcareous soil** *right* **an organic soil.**
4 Surface layers of an organic soil.
5 The subsoil of an organic soil.

break down into an excellent tilth. But when wet, they are plastic and if cultivated in this condition the structure is destroyed and they are then liable to dry out into large blocks. Peat or well-rotted manure will help to prevent them from becoming like concrete, but it should always be worked into the surface and not buried deeply.

Organic soils are rich in humus and have a very dark brown or black colour. If they have over 50 per cent organic matter in a layer which is more than 15 inches thick they are classed as peat soils of which there are two main types, bog peat and fen peat. Bog peat consists of the residues of heather and mosses, particularly sphagnum moss. Bog peat is usually formed on an impervious rock formation which prevents water from draining away. So the natural vegetation decays very slowly in these badly aerated wet soils and peat is the result.

Given shelter, many garden plants will survive if the soil is limed, but it is not generally necessary to lime them to the point of neutrality, because many plants will grow well at pH values lower than would be possible in a mineral soil; in fact heavy liming may result in boron and manganese deficiences.

The other main type of peat soil is fen peat, which is composed of residues of

reeds, rushes and sedges and other water plants. This type of soil is usually formed at the edges of slow-moving or blocked rivers and streams. Such accumulations are generally much less acid and have pH values of about 6: the areas where they are formed may have been drained by rivers that have previously passed through limestone and chalk formations.

Some of the fen peat soils are among the richest in the country, being deep and very easily worked. Plants often produce rank, luxuriant, vegetative growth, owing to their naturally high content of nitrogen.

Phosphate content is often low and extra potash is generally required, but nitrogenous fertilisers are seldom needed in the richest fen peats.

Sandy, loamy and clayey soils The more usual way of classifying soils is on the basis of their texture. This is a property that depends on the relative amounts of the different sized particles that they contain. For example sand is the name given to coarse gritty particles that you can see quite plainly, whereas silt particles can be seen only with a microscope and a clay particle which is even smaller can be seen only with an electron microscope. All soils contain sand, silt and clay in varying ratios.

Texture is important because it affects the handling, drainage, aeration and nutrient content of the soil. Lime and fertiliser requirements are also keyed to texture. It can be assessed by hand. To do this take a handful of moist soil and rub a portion between your finger and thumb. Sand can be detected by the sensation of grittiness or roughness; the finer the sand the less the grittiness.

Silt has a floury or talcum powder-like feel when dry and is only slightly plastic when wet. Clay may feel smooth but the surface becomes polished when rubbed between the fingers and clay is sticky when wet. A true loam is smooth and not gritty, silty or sticky when moist.

Sandy soils These are warm and are most suitable for early vegetable crops. If less than 15 inches deep they cannot be recommended for fruits and shrubs. Soft fruits can be successfully grown in these soils provided they are mulched or irrigated. The only way to improve the soil is to add as much bulky humus-forming material as possible, and cow and pig manure are much favoured.

Fertilisers produce the best effect when they are applied in small quantities at frequent intervals during the growing season, but neither these nor the manure should be dug in too deeply. Sandy soils soon become acid and generally need frequent but small applications of lime.

Loamy soils A true loam has a well-balanced proportion of sand, silt and clay and is really the ideal texture as it is the easiest soil to look after. With good management most loams readily acquire and retain a good crumb structure and almost all plants grow well in them provided they are deep and in a good position.

Clayey soils These are very retentive of moisture and are sticky when wet. On drying they form hard clods, which are impossible to break down until they are moistened again. After long spells of hot dry weather they form deep, wide cracks which cause root rupture and loss of moisture. It is necessary to hoe regularly in order to fill in the cracks to

The colour of a soil is often an indication of its type.
1 Loamy sand.
2 One of the many types of clay.
3 A well-balanced loam.
4 A sandy clay loam.

provide a surface soil mulch. There is no quick way of improving clay soil. Artificial drainage may well be the first essential before any other form of improvement can be attempted.

Very thorough digging, or better still ridging in the autumn, will produce a frost tilth in the spring. Humus-forming materials are necessary to preserve the crumb structure so formed. Strawy stable manure is best, but a fine grade of peat when applied regularly can transform a heavy clay into quite workable soil in a few years. Gypsum can improve the structure of some clay soils when applied at the rate of 4–8 ounces per square yard. Clay soils are naturally rich in plant nutrients. These nutrients are not always readily available since roots tend to follow the cracks and fail to tap the nutrients in the soil lumps. Hence the proper use of fertilisers will produce still better results.

Clays are not always acid as is commonly supposed but when they are, large applications of lime are needed, at rates depending on the results of the soil analysis.

Soil testing
Broadly speaking soil testing includes any kind of examination to which a soil is submitted; for example, when you rub some moist soil between your fingers to assess its texture or dig a hole to see whether it is badly drained, you are

carrying out soil tests. But for most gardeners it means soil chemical analysis to find out whether their soil needs lime, and how much, and also whether it needs extra phosphates and potash.

You can test it yourself, using a test kit, or ask your county horticultural adviser to arrange to have it done for you, or send it to a private laboratory. Most soil test kits provide apparatus and chemicals for estimating the acidity, phosphates, potash and the amount of lime needed to correct acidity; some kits include a test for nitrogen, but it is very difficult to make a reliable prediction as to the amount of nitrogen that will be released during the season.

Whatever the method adopted the first thing to do is to get a sample of your soil. Collecting samples is not difficult, but it must be done properly if the tests are to give a reliable and accurate assessment of the nutrient status of your soil. Only about a tea-spoonful of soil is required for the actual test, but that spoonful must represent many thousands of pounds of soil.

Never just take one lump of soil but take a small amount of soil from at least ten different places in a plot, going down to a depth of 6 inches in beds or borders and 3 inches in the lawn. Do not pick places near manure, compost or similar heaps, or bonfire sites and hedges when sampling.

There are special tools for the purpose but most gardeners can make a V-shaped slit in the soil to a depth of 6 inches and take a thin slice of soil for testing. For the lawn a hollow-tine fork will cause the least disturbance.

The samples are then put into a clean plastic bucket and mixed together, saving about ½ pint of the mixture for the testing. If the sample is to be sent away for testing put it into a strong plastic bag and number each sample.

When the sample reaches the laboratory it will be dried in the air, ground up and sieved through a 2 mm sieve in order to remove stones and hard lumps.

The next step is to find out whether the soil is acid, neutral or alkaline. This is expressed in terms of the pH scale, which ranges from 0–14. Values less than 7.0 are acid, values above 7.0 are alkaline.

In the laboratory very accurate pH measurements can be made with a pH meter, which is an expensive instrument and is hardly practicable for most gardeners. There are, however, inexpensive indicator solutions that change colour according to the degree of acidity present in the soil.

A rough method of estimating pH in the open consists in placing a small quantity of fresh soil in a white dish and then pouring a little indicator solution on to it. The contact between the indicator and the soil is achieved by slowly rocking the dish to avoid breaking up the soil fragments and the formation of a muddy suspension.

After the soil has soaked up the indicator, the colour at the junction of the soil and the indicator should be used to assess the acidity. The colour should be checked with a colour chart provided with the testing kit.

Most soil test kits provide a more refined method of assessing pH, in which the soil is shaken vigorously with a clarifying agent (usually barium sulphate), distilled water and a soil indicator. On settling, a clear layer is obtained which may be compared with the colour chart. With a little practice an accuracy to within half a unit of pH can be obtained.

A pH assessment alone will not give an estimation of the lime requirement.

The amount of phosphates and potash that is readily available for plant use is found by carrying out the appropriate tests with one of the kits. A dilute acid is used for extracting the nutrients from the soil; the extract is treated with various reagents that produce colours or cloudy suspensions which may then be compared with charts or standard colours in glass tubes.

The estimation of the amount of fertiliser needed is the most difficult part of the operation; it depends on the nutrient content of the soil and the general requirements of the plants to be grown.

Generally autumn is the best time to sample and test. Not only is the soil in a more normal condition after the growing season, but if lime is needed it will have time to act during the winter.

pH

This is the measure used to indicate the active acidity of the soil. The term is based on the balance between the hydrogen ions and the hydroxyl ions and it is important to remember that a low pH figure indicates acid soil which for most crops requires correcting by the addition of lime. pH 7 represents neutrality. Below pH 6.5, the soil is acid and at pH 6, the degree of acidity reaches the point, where only acid-loving plants, such as heathers and rhododendrons will thrive. If the figure is up to pH 8, the alkalinity of the soil is such that certain essential foods are locked up and plants show signs of starvation.

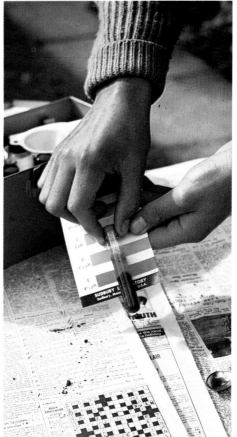

Testing the soil for acidity or alkalinity.
1 The sample of dry soil is put into a test tube using a clean spoon so as not to affect the chemical content.
2 The acidity testing solution supplied with the kit is carefully poured on to the soil sample. The tube is then corked to prevent the finger affecting the acidity of the sample. The tube is then well shaken.
3 The colour of the resultant solution is compared with the test card, and read off. The result here indicates pH 7·0.

The scale used is logarithmic, so that *p*H 5, is ten times as acid as *p*H 6, and *p*H 4, is one hundred times as acid as *p*H 6.

Simple and reasonably priced outfits are available to determine the *p*H value and it is advisable to take samples from various parts of the garden since the degree of acidity may vary. To raise the *p*H value (which means neutralising the soil acidity) lime is added. In general the lighter the soil, the smaller the quantity of lime required; a heavy clay soil needs about half as much again as a light sandy soil. As a rough guide, hydrated lime, applied at the rate of 8 to 12 ounces per square yard, according to the soil texture, every few years should be adequate, except, of course, where chalky soils are concerned which require no additional lime, or very acid soils, which would require more. The *p*H measurement is a useful check to be applied when the crops show signs of lime shortage.

It should also be remembered that excessive lime dressings over a long period produce deficiencies of various trace elements and encourage scab in potatoes on soils liable to produce the disease. Lime can be applied in hydrated form or as ground limestone or chalk. About 1 lb of hydrated lime is equal to 2 lbs of the other two forms. If spent mushroom compost obtained from farms using chalk in the casing soil is used in the garden as a mulch, the *p*H should be watched.

Lime and liming

Lime is strictly defined as a white caustic alkaline substance—quicklime; chemically, calcium oxide (CaO); made by heating chalk or limestone. But in gardening, lime means any calcium-containing material which is capable of correcting soil acidity.

Why lime is used The main reason for using lime is to reduce the acidity of a soil that is acid or, in other words, to sweeten the soil. Few plants will grow well in a very acid soil mainly because their intake of plant foods is reduced; phosphates, in particular, get 'locked up' in acid soils. There is often a shortage of calcium in very acid soils.

Aluminium and manganese, on the other hand, are often released in such large amounts that they can poison many plants. Tomatoes, beans and brassicas are particularly sensitive in this respect.

Lime encourages soil life The bacteria that convert ammonium salts to nitrates —one of the steps necessary before nitrogen-bearing foods can be used by the plant—are almost or completely inoperative in very acid soils. The organism which is responsible for fixing nitrogen in the roots of peas, beans and other leguminous plants operates most favourably when the soil is well limed, which is the reason why peas do not

thrive in really acid soils. But rhododendrons would be very sickly or even die in a soil limed for peas. Earthworms, too, thrive in well-limed soils; they make channels in soil improving the drainage of clay soils and compacted lawns (we know that wormcasts are unsightly but the good that worms do in improving drainage outweighs their harm).

Lime improves tilth Many clay soils, when limed regularly, become more porous and allow rain to drain away quicker, thus allowing you to get on to the ground earlier in the spring. It is possible to cure a really sticky clay soil by liming, but not all clays will respond since some are naturally limey. Lime has very little effect on the tilth of sandy and loamy soils.

Lime controls some diseases and pests Club root disease of brassicas flourishes in acid soils and can usually be controlled by liming, but it takes two or three years before it works fully. Slugs, leather-jackets or wireworms and several other soil pests are discouraged by liming.

How to tell whether soil needs lime The presence of spurrey, sheep's sorrel, corn marigold and other weeds that thrive in acid soils often indicates the need for lime, but these weeds are not very reliable indicators since they continue to grow for some time in soils that have been limed. If you see rhododendrons and blue hydrangeas growing really well in nearby gardens it is fairly safe to assume that your soil is naturally acid. But the only reliable method of finding out whether a soil is acid or alkaline is to carry out a soil test for lime. An old-fashioned way of telling whether a soil was limey was by pouring some dilute hydrochloric acid on to the soil to see whether it fizzed but this does not help very much; if a soil is rich in calcium carbonate it will react with the added acid and carbon dioxide gas which causes the fizzing. Lack of fizzing, however, is not a reliable indicator that lime is needed and, of course, this test gives no idea as to the amount of lime required to correct acidity in an acid soil.

How to test for lime The simplest do-it-yourself method is to buy some indicator papers from your garden supply centre and then take a sample of soil (see Soil testing). If the soil is dry, moisten it well with water (distilled water if possible) in a saucer but do not make it runny. After half an hour place a half-inch strip of test paper so that half of it lies on top of the wet soil and the other half against the side of the saucer. After 5 minutes compare the colour of the paper with the colour panels on the chart, which is sold with the papers.

And while we are talking of old-fashioned but useful techniques, let us have a quick look at a method of determining the texture rather than the acidity

or alkalinity of your garden soil. Take a sample of your soil, just a spoonful, and shake this up well in a glass or other clear vessel of water. Then set it aside to settle. If you have reason to believe that your soil differs in different parts of your garden then carry out the same test with more than one sample taken from other places.

After a time you will see that a number of definite layers have appeared. The stones are on the floor or base of the vessel and on top of these is a layer of sand. Loam having a proportion of sand forms the next layer. The clay content, light and powdery, will dissolve and do little more than colour the water, remaining in suspension for a very long time. Finally the humus will tend to float on the top of the water, or if the shaking has been vigorous, perhaps some will have sunk to form the top layer.

By this simple means you can make a very fair assessment of your soil's capabilities and requirements.

Soil reaction		Dressings of carbonate of lime		
		Sandy soil	Loams	Clay and peaty soil
		lb/sq yd	lb/sq yd	lb/sq yd
Slightly acid	*p*H 6·0	½	¾	1¼
Moderately acid	*p*H 5·5	1	1½	2½
Acid	*p*H 5·0	1½	2¼	3¾
Strongly acid	*p*H 4·5	2	3¼	4¾
Very acid	*p*H 4·0	2½	4	6

The above figures relate to carbonate of lime (ground chalk or ground limestone); if hydrated lime is used the dressings should be half of the above quantities.

For peaty soils and those that are naturally rich in humus you will have to increase the amount of lime even more. In fact, it is virtually impossible to correct the acidity of some of them; a few of the fenland soils are so acid that even after enormous quantities of lime have been applied, the soil still shows an acid reaction the following year. So, all you can hope to do is to correct the worst of the acidity. Fortunately such soils are rare.

If you feel that the whole business of determining lime requirement is too complicated and you know that your soil is acid, a good general rule is to apply ½ lb of hydrated lime per square yard on sandy or loamy soils, and ¾ lb per square yard on clay or peaty soils. On the other hand, you may be a precision gardener and will, therefore, want to know more exactly how much lime is required. For you, there is a special lime requirement test kit which gives more accurate guidance as to the amount of lime needed to correct the acidity of your garden soil or possibly to raise the *p*H value of your potting compost for a particular plant.

Soil test laboratories carry out a special lime requirement test by means of electrically operated *p*H meters and buffer solutions; this is the most reliable method.

Dangers of overliming Too much lime can be as bad as too little. Overliming may reduce the plants' intake of iron, causing yellowing of leaves. Deficiencies or iron and boron are also common in over-limed soils in the garden.

Alkaline conditions produced by liming favour the disease fungus responsible for scab on potatoes.

The danger of overliming is greatest in sandy soils so it is wise to add lime little and often to sandy soils, but there is rather less need to worry with clays and even loams.

Forms of lime Hydrated lime and carbonate of lime are the two forms most commonly listed in garden catalogues.

Hydrated lime comes from quicklime that has been treated (slaked) with water and is known chemically as calcium hydroxide. It is often sold under brand names.

It is a very fine powder which mixes well with soil particles and being slightly soluble in water is a most effective liming material where speedy benefits are wanted. It is an alkaline substance and is caustic and, therefore, likely to burn foliage if it blows on to plants during spreading.

When mixed with soil, hydrated lime combines with carbon dioxide and turns into calcium carbonate; this is the fate of all forms of applied liming materials.

Carbonate of lime or 'garden' lime as it is often called, is limestone or chalk that has been crushed to a gritty powder. Most garden limes are ground to pass through a ⅛-inch sieve.

The rate at which carbonate of lime works in the soil depends on how finely ground it is. Even the finest particles produced by grinding are not so fine as those produced chemically during the production of hydrated lime, but nevertheless they work quickly. The coarser particles act as a reserve and are longer lasting. Carbonate of lime does not burn plant foliage and is more pleasant to handle than hydrated lime; it is the best form to use in seed and potting composts.

Although insoluble in pure water, it does dissolve in soil water, forming calcium bicarbonate from which the calcium portion can be taken up by the clay and humus of the soil; some is also absorbed by plant roots, worms and other organisms.

This form of lime is less concentrated than hydrated lime and so you need

The presence of moss is often an indication of an over-acid soil.

larger amounts to reduce the acidity of an acid soil; but if you buy it in packs of 56 lb or over, it is cheaper than hydrated lime.

It is important to know that the acid neutralising value of any form of lime is expressed in terms of its content of calcium oxide (CaO). Carbonate of lime contains about 50 per cent CaO, and hydrated lime from 60 to 70 per cent CaO.

Other materials used in liming Marl is a clay rich in lime. This is obtained in many parts of the country from beds that are sufficiently near to the surface to be worked economically as in the new red sandstone formations in the north and west midlands, or the shell marls which occur in Norfolk. It is of particular value in sandy or peaty soils not only for its lime content but also for the clay which gives 'body' to this type of soil. Marling is an ancient practice which is still carried out in areas subject to severe wind erosion; the clay part helps to bind sand grains together and prevent them from blowing away.

Waste materials from the sugar beet, paper, tanning and cement industries often contain calcium carbonate and make useful liming materials. Some may be wet, lumpy and difficult to handle but, if available, nearly all can be a useful source of lime.

Oyster and other sea shells are mostly calcium carbonate. When free from salt

and ground finely they make useful liming materials.

Slags, which are waste materials from iron and phosphorus manufacture, contain calcium and magnesium silicates that are capable of reducing soil acidity

Dolomite lime is a natural form of calcium and magnesium carbonate which supplies two elements important for plant growth, calcium and magnesium, and which also provides the necessary neutralising effects. It is a useful form of lime to use on acid soils that are low in magnesium and is widely used in soil-less composts for potted and container grown plants.

Spreading lime Lime is not just magic out of a bag. To work properly it must be mixed thoroughly with the top-soil layers. To begin with the lime must be spread over the soil surface by hand from a bucket or a fertiliser distributor if the soil is firm and even. But do not dig it in because digging often shifts the surface lying lime simply into another layer below the soil surface.

It is best spread on a finely broken surface and then stirred about with the soil, using a hand or mechanical cultivator; when the soil is on the dry side, you cannot expect minute particles of lime to mix properly with clods.

When, in the first year after liming, results are disappointing—and this does sometimes occur—the cause is frequently the length of time needed for the dressing to become reasonably mixed into the top soil layer. If the lime fails to penetrate, seeds may be sown in what is locally and temporarily a too alkaline strip of soil. But if it has been dug some inches under, seedlings may be trying to grow in a thin layer of very acid soil and plants will grow poorly until the root system reaches the buried lime layer.

When to lime If your soil is very acid, the sooner lime is applied the better—as soon as the ground becomes vacant. Autumn dressing is often recommended so that rain can wash it into the soil.

But although lime is of use in certain sections of almost all gardens for certain purposes and at certain times, it should be clearly understood that the most useful soil for the average garden will be slightly acid, having a pH of about 6·5. This is for several reasons. In the first place the majority of garden plants grow best in this very slightly acid soil. Secondly, but vital, is the fact that although it is comparatively simple to alter the pH of a soil towards alkalinity by adding lime, it is much more difficult to lower the pH or make it more acid. The addition of relatively large quantities of acid grades of peat will help for brief periods, as will dosing with certain chemicals or proprietary products, but most soils with a high pH lie above basic layers of chalk or limestone, so that all moisture moving in the soil will be of an alkaline nature and impossible in normal circumstances to avoid.

On the other hand, all soil which is cultivated tends to turn gradually acid, so any new garden constructed on land on which crops have been grown for years will probably be slightly acid. This is largely because of the amount of organic matter, or humus, which has been added to the soil.

Humus

Humus is the term used to describe the organic matter in the soil. Its presence in adequate quantities is a vital factor in building up and maintaining soil fertility. Humus may consist of decayed vegetable or animal refuse, still showing traces of leaves, stems, stubble, bones, and so on, or it may have been completely broken down into a blackish, powdery substance.

Garden soil which has been regularly treated with humus, whether from the compost heap or from organic manures, has a rich dark colour. This factor is of benefit in itself, for dark soils, rich in humus, tend to warm up more quickly in spring, so promoting early seed germination and earlier cropping.

Humus aids fertility in two main ways. First, the organic matter stores nitrogen, which is converted into ammonia by the micro-organisms in the soil and released to the plants in the form of nitrate. Second, humus can hold and store considerable quantities of moisture. This moisture-holding capacity helps to break the soil down into crumbs, giving sufficient space for the retention of moisture, but allowing excess water to drain away. The good soil structure and aeration, obtained in this way, assist root development and, together with the water holding capacity, enable plants to stand up better to drought conditions. A humus-rich soil also produces the fine tilth necessary for seed sowing.

All cultivated soils lose organic matter and this loss is increased when the ground is limed. Some humus is left in the soil by plant residues, but this is not enough and the losses must be made good. The more rapid and thorough the cultivation, the more rapid the loss of humus. Where farmyard manure is available, it is still the easiest and most practical way of maintaining the organic content of the soil. It should be spread and dug into the ground as soon as possible, for some of the nutrients will be lost if it is allowed to stand in heaps exposed to the rain. In clay soils it should be dug in during the autumn.

The old-time gardeners dug manure into the second spit, but it is far better to incorporate it in the top spit within easy reach of the growing plants. Other manures (from pigs, rabbits, poultry, etc.) and spent mushroom compost can all be used to add humus. All gardens should have a compost heap where most of the garden refuse can be broken down (the roots of diseased plants and roots of persistent weeds such as bind-weed and couch grass should be burned).

Humus can also be added in the form of peat, leafmould, spent hops, seaweed, shoddy, straw, fish waste, or in prepared fertilisers made up from hoof and horn and bone meal. Blood and offal from a slaughter house can be an equally valuable source. The presence of adequate humus in the soil does not necessarily mean that fertilisers can be dispensed with.

While most crops benefit from high quantities of organic matter in the soil, some flowers, for instance nasturtiums, do better on poorer soils.

Fertilisers

Fertilisers provide plants with nutrients; they are commonly listed in catalogues under: Straight fertilisers, Compound fertilisers, Liquid fertilisers.

Straight fertilisers These are used to supply a specific nutrient. If you wish to make your spring cabbages grow away more quickly in the spring you could top-dress with Nitro-chalk. If your tomatoes are not ripening quickly enough in dull weather sulphate of potash could help. Straight fertilisers are either inorganic 'artificials' or 'organics'.

Artificials, which may be manufactured in factories, or are the purified salts from natural underground deposits, are more correctly known as inorganic fertilisers. They generally dissolve easily in water and when applied to moist soils act quickly. But this does not mean that they will be washed out of your soil.

Club Root on Brassicas can often be obviated by the addition of lime to the land to reduce acidity.

Both phosphates and potash are absorbed by soil constituents and so is nitrogen when applied as ammonium fertilisers. Nitrates, however, may be lost from the soil if applied during the winter or too far away from plant roots. Hence the need for top dressings.

Most inorganic fertilisers are fairly concentrated and we know exactly how much of each nutrient is present in any weight of fertiliser and so you can calculate how much fertiliser to apply to the soil to provide a desired quantity of any particular nutrient. But great care must be taken in handling them because being concentrated, overdoses are often harmful.

'Organics' are of animal or vegetable origin and their nutrients are locked away inside the complex structure of proteins and other materials. They must break down into soluble forms—nitrates or in some instances ammonia—before they can be used by plants. Since bacteria and other living organisms in the soil break these down, their effectiveness largely depends upon the soil conditions being satisfactory for the organisms; they are most effective when used in moist, well-aerated, well-limed soils. Many are fairly concentrated, but their nutrient content often varies from batch to batch.

Fine dusty particles break down much

Straight fertilisers in general use

Fertiliser and main nutrient supplied	Properties	When and how much to use	Fertiliser and main nutrient supplied	Properties	When and how much to use
Basic slag Phosphates 8–16% P_2O_5 (insol)	Slow acting inorganic. Active ingredient is calcium silico-phosphate which is an insoluble material; slow acting and long lasting. Its lime content makes it a useful fertiliser for acid soils that are also low in phosphates	Autumn or winter open ground 8 oz per square yard before sowing or planting. Not to be used with lime	**Magnesium sulphate** 10% Mg	Inorganic Coarsely crystalline soluble material. Tends to cake on storage. Used only where magnesium is lacking	Can be used at 1–2 oz per square yard or applied as a leaf spray $\frac{1}{4}$ oz per gallon of water
Bone flour Phosphates 27–28% P_2O_5 (insol) 1% N	Concentrated organic. Active ingredient calcium phosphate which is insoluble; being very finely ground it is fairly quick acting Has a very small amount of nitrogen. Useful for keeping home-made mixtures of fertilisers in dry condition	Open ground autumn or winter 4 oz per square yard before sowing or planting. Can be used in potting composts	**Meat and bone meal** Nitrogen and Phosphates 4–6% N 12–14% P_2O_5 (insol)	A good organic fertiliser for general use, which comes from waste meat, offals and condemned carcasses from slaughter houses. The mixture is steamed under pressure to remove fat and then dried at a high temperature to kill disease organisms. The nitrogen and phosphate content varies. The higher the content of bone the more phosphates it contains. These are insoluble in water and only slowly available to plants. The nitrogen portion works quickly in warm moist soils	Autumn or winter. Fork into open ground, 4 oz per square yard before sowing or planting. Safe to use in greenhouse borders and can be used in composts. Should be mixed with sulphate of potash to give a balanced feed.
Bone meal 20–25% P_2O_5 3–5% N	Concentrated organic. Active ingredient calcium phosphate, insoluble but releases its phosphates slowly over a long period Has a useful content of nitrogen which works quickly	Open ground autumn or winter 4 oz per square yard before sowing or planting. Can be used in potting composts 4 oz per bushel	**Nitrate of soda** Nitrogen 16% N	All the nitrogen is present as a soluble nitrate and is immediately available to plants as soon as it has dissolved in the soil moisture. If watered in its effects will be seen in a few days. It can destroy the crumb structure of some soils if large dressings are given too frequently	Spring and summer as a top dressing for green crops or plants that are growing very slowly after cold wet weather. $\frac{1}{2}$ oz per square yard at intervals of several weeks
Dried blood Nitrogen 7–14% N	Concentrated organic. Quick acting especially in warm, moist soils and it is one of the most rapid of organic fertilisers. There is a fully soluble form that can be dissolved in water and used as a liquid feed	Used as a top-dressing mainly for greenhouse plants throughout season. 2–3 oz per square yard	**Nitro-chalk** Nitrogen 21% N	A mixture of ammonium nitrate and chalk. It has some nitrate for immediate action and the ammonia comes into play somewhat later. The chalk present largely balances any loss of lime from the soil that may be caused by the ammonia part of this fertiliser. Its granular form makes it easy to spread It becomes pasty if left in air for long periods. The chalk content is so small that it does not make the soil alkaline	Spring and summer top dressing for many crops including lawns $\frac{1}{2}$ oz per square yard at intervals of several weeks
Hoof and horn meal Nitrogen 7–13% N	Concentrated organic. Acts fairly quickly in warm moist soils but long lasting. Available in a number of grades: Fine grade $\frac{1}{8}$ inch to dust as used in John Innes Base Fertiliser, acts quickly but hoof parings and other coarse grades very slowly	Open ground and greenhouse borders 4–6 oz per square yard John Innes Base Fertiliser for potting composts. Coarse grades are best for perennial borders			

more quickly than the coarse fragments in organic fertilisers. For example a fine grade of hoof-and-horn meal works very nearly as quickly as some inorganic fertilisers, while coarse particles break down slowly and release their nitrogen over a long period of time.

Synthetic organics such as Urea-Form are chemical combinations of urea and formaldehyde and are designed to give a slow release of nitrogen for several months. Their granules are almost insoluble and do not break down in the soil. The outer surface of each granule is gradually worn away in much the same way as you would suck a sweet. The process begins within a few days in warm moist soils and continues to release nutrients as the plants need them for long pre-determined periods. So, a 'one-shot' application may nourish plants throughout the growing season, whereas several applications of quickly available forms may be necessary.

Fruits and vegetables, properly fertilised with quickly available forms of

Brassicas suffering from manganese deficiency have stunted blue leaves.

nutrients are as healthful and tasty as those fertilised with slowly available forms; plants obtain their nutrients as simple chemicals through the roots. And these chemicals are exactly the same whether they come from an 'artificial' or an 'organic' fertiliser.

Compound fertilisers These contain two, or more usually, all three of the major nutrients nitrogen, phosphorus and potassium. These are the ones that are used by plants in the largest amounts and are, therefore, most likely to be deficient in soils. When you buy a fertiliser, therefore, you generally buy it for its content of these nutrients in order to give a balanced feed before sowing or planting.

You can make your own compounds by simply mixing together two or more straight fertilisers. The following are often made at home:

A fertiliser for general use:
Sulphate of ammonia 5 parts by weight
Superphosphate 5 parts by weight
Sulphate of potash 2 parts by weight

Analysis 8% N, 8% P_2O_5 8% K_2O.

John Innes Base Fertiliser for potted plants:
Hoof and Horn meal 2 parts by weight
Superphosphate 2 parts by weight
Sulphate of potash 1 part by weight

Analysis 5·1% N, 7.2% P_2O_5, 9·6% K_2O

Analysis When you buy a fertiliser you want to know how much of each plant food it contains and this information it given in the analysis provided with the fertiliser. The analysis states the content of nitrogen as N, phosphorus as P_2O_5 (phosphoric acid) and potassium as K_2O (potash). Plants do not absorb their plant foods in these forms, since nitrogen is an inert gas, pure phosphorus and potassium are very active chemically and burn if exposed to the air or water. So these elements can only be absorbed by plants when combined with other elements to form materials suitable for use in fertilisers. So the figures mean that the fertiliser contains the equivalent of the elements.

As an example, nitrate of soda contains 16% of nitrogen; what does the remainder consist of? The chemical name for nitrate of soda is sodium nitrate which is a chemical compound of nitrogen, sodium and oxygen. So there is about 26% of sodium and 58% of oxygen in this compound.

You are advised to read the labels very carefully and look for the analysis very carefully in order to save disappointment and money by avoiding 'miracle' or 'wonder-working' fertilisers bearing no guaranteed analysis.

Ready for use compounds Garden supply

1 Nitrogenous fertiliser is applied here in a ring around each plant.
2 The soil is scraped over with a cultivator to work in the fertiliser.

Straight fertilisers in general use

Fertiliser and main nutrient supplied	Properties	When and how much to use	Fertiliser and main nutrient supplied	Properties	When and how much to use
Potash nitrate Nitrogen Potash 15% N 10% K₂O	A mixed nitrate of sodium and potassium. Acts quickly. Useful two-in-one fertiliser for supplying potash as well as nitrogen in early spring crops that would make too much soft growth if nitrogen only was given. Useful for soils that are low in potash as well as nitrogen	Spring and summer, used as a top dressing for many crops. Apply 1–2 oz per square yard direct to the soil or mix 1 teaspoonful to one gallon of water two or three times during the growing period	**Sulphate of iron** Iron	When one part is mixed with three parts of sulphate of ammonia and sand it will kill moss, clover and broad-leaved weeds in lawns and freshen up the colour. Can be used for correcting iron deficiency in acid soils, but is ineffective for this purpose in limey soils. It should be powdered finely	Used in lawn sands
Potassium nitrate Nitrogen Potassium N 12–14% K₂O 44–46%	This is a pure concentrated fertiliser that is used mainly in liquid feeds. It is suitable for all greenhouse plants when dissolved in water	Mix 1 teaspoonful to one gallon of water and apply regularly as a liquid feed	**Urea-form** Nitrogen 38% N	Synthetic organic. A combination of urea and formaldehyde which is sold under a trade name—which in spite of its high analysis, will not burn plants. Although mainly insoluble in water its nitrogen is gradually converted by soil bacteria to a form which is available to plants, and will feed plants continually for several months from one application. It is non-corrosive and will not rust fertiliser spreaders and other equipment	Use at any time of year before sowing or planting in the open or in the greenhouse. The slow release action of this fertiliser encourages durable healthy turf and reduces the danger of burning the lawn 1–2 oz per square yard. Can be used in place of hoof-and-horn in soilless composts 1 part by weight of Urea-form 2 parts by weight of super-phosphate 1 part by weight of sulphate of potash
Sulphate of ammonia Nitrogen 20·6% N	When applied to the soil the ammonia part is held by the clay and organic matter and is preserved from immediate loss during wet weather. When the soil is warm enough the ammonia is quickly turned into nitrate by soil bacteria. But this conversion is very slow when the soil temperature drops below about 42°F (5°C) When mixed with sand is called lawn sand. Repeated heavy dressings may make the soil too acid for good growth but acid forming property is an advantage to chalky soils	Spring and summer direct to soil at ½–1 oz per square yard. Or dissolve 1 teaspoonful in 1 gallon of water and use as liquid feed Often mixed with superphosphate and sulphate of potash but do not mix with lime			
Superphosphate of lime Phosphate 18–19% P₂O₅	This contains phosphates that are soluble in water and it acts quickly, being particularly suitable for seed beds and root crops. It does not supply lime in spite of its name	Can be used at any time at rate of 1–2 oz per square yard before sowing or planting. Used in John Innes Base Fertiliser to supply phosphates	**Wood ashes** Potash	Freshly made wood ashes contain potassium carbonate, which is soon washed out by rain water unless the ashes are protected. Ashes from prunings and other young plant material are richer in potash than old stumps. Heavy dressings may cake the surface and spoil the tilth of clayey soils. Do not give large dressings to chalky soils because ashes may make them more alkaline	Autumn or winter in open ground. 4–8 oz per square yard well ahead of sowing or planting
Sulphate of potash Potash 50% K₂O	The best form of potash for most garden plants. Acts quickly. It is held by the clay and humus in soils until required by plants. To correct potash deficiency quickly dissolve 1 oz in a gallon of water and wet soil thoroughly. Always use for gooseberries, red currants and other soft fruits in preference to muriate of potash	Generally used in combination with other fertilisers and raked in before sowing or planting at any time of the year ½–1 oz per square yard	**Soot** Nitrogen 1–7% N	Contains nitrogen mainly as ammonium sulphate and therefore acts rapidly. Since fresh soot contains substances harmful to plants it is best left under cover for three months before use. Light and fluffy soot contains more nitrogen than the heavy dense type. Most soots supply useful amounts of trace elements	Spread over soil after digging and then rake in at rate of 4–6 oz per square yard. Can be used as top dressing for brassicas at the same rate

shops offer for sale a wide variety of materials for feeding garden plants and lawns. Some of these products are much more expensive than others. They vary in price because of:

Nutrient content Fertilisers with a high percentage of plant nutrients cost more per pound than those containing a small percentage of nutrients. So always find out from the supplier what the guaranteed content of nitrogen phosphoric acid and potash is. The plant nutrient content of a compound is often indicated by its grade—a series of three numbers separated by dashes. The numbers show the percentage of nitrogen, phosphoric acid and potash, in that order, contained in the product.

Form Pelleted or granular fertilisers, and soluble fertiliser concentrates cost more than powdered fertilisers. But the granular form may be more convenient for you to use.

Powdered fertilisers often contain a lot of very fine dusty material which may blow away or be objectional to use on a windy day. They may become damp more easily and may cake and fail to spread properly through your fertiliser spreader.

Granular fertilisers are not as dusty as powdered fertilisers and they do not cake so easily; they flow freely through fertiliser spreaders. The granules roll off plant foliage, reducing the danger of fertiliser burn.

Ingredients Nitrogen is the most expensive ingredient in a fertiliser compound. Slowly available forms derived from organic sources and Urea-Form are more expensive than the quickly available forms. So, the more nitrogen a compound contains—especially slowly available forms of nitrogen—the more expensive the product is.

Added materials Products that contain added trace elements, pesticides or herbicides cost more than plain fertilisers. Fertiliser/weed killer combinations are generally prepared for use on lawns. These combinations can be quite satisfactory if:

(a) the best time for applying the fertiliser and the best time for applying the weedkiller are the same.

(b) the nutrient content and the weedkiller concentration of the mixture are adjusted so that each is applied at the proper rate.

Package size Fertilisers sold in small containers cost more per pound than the same product in larger packages.

Liquid fertilisers are simply fertilisers in solution; if you mix 1 oz of sulphate of ammonia with 1 gallon of water you have a very weak solution containing nitrogen. You can make up feeds to your own prescription, using concentrated chemicals such as potassium nitrate, ammonium phosphate and urea, but this does require a fair amount of technical knowledge and it is usually more convenient to purchase one of the ready-made products which are of two main types:

Concentrated liquids that have to be diluted with water according to the maker's instructions. Mixtures of solid chemicals for dissolving in water. These are the cheapest since you do not have to pay for the cost of transporting the water.

Liquid compound fertilisers are much more expensive than solids, as they have to be manufactured from purer materials. But they are popular for the ease and speed with which nutrients can be applied in balanced form to meet the changing needs of plants at different stages of growth and weather conditions. Also feeding and watering is done in one operation—a distinct advantage when there are large batches of plants to be dealt with.

But they are not necessarily better than solid feeds, merely more convenient, and of course liquid feeding is essential when using certain forms of irrigation equipment.

Some facts to remember when using fertilisers

Never guess at amounts; overdoses can be harmful or even fatal to plants; too little may be ineffective. Either weigh on household scales or buy a special graduated gardener's measure.

A match box will do if you have no scales available. When full a standard match box will hold:
½ oz of superphosphate.
¾ oz of sulphate of ammonia, bone meal, many compounds.
1 oz of sulphate of potash.

Potash deficiency in potatoes is indicated by blueing of the leaves.

How to cure deficiencies with straight fertilisers

Plant food	Plants most susceptible to deficiency	Deficiency may occur in these soils	Fertiliser to use	How to apply fertiliser
Nitrogen	All plants especially brassicas and other leafy plants	Wet, acid, very sandy and thin soils	INORGANIC: Nitrate of soda, nitro-chalk, potash nitrate, sulphate of ammonia. ORGANIC: Hoof and horn meal, dried blood	When plants are growing
Phosphorus (Phosphates)	All plants: fruit, flowers, vegetables and shrubs	Very wet areas strongly acid soils. Some peaty soils	INORGANIC: Basic slag, superphosphate of lime. ORGANIC: Bone meal	At sowing or planting
Potassium (Potash)	All plants especially potato, beans, gooseberry, apple, currants	Light chalky; badly drained; or very sandy soils	INORGANIC: Sulphate of potash, muriate of potash. Potash nitrate	At sowing or planting in top dressing
Calcium (lime)	All plants	Only in very strongly acid soils	Lime (see Lime)	Before planting
Magnesium	All plants: especially potato, cabbage, carrot, apple, gooseberry, tomato, Solanum (winter cherry)	Wet areas and seasons. Very sandy soils. Soils over-manured with potash fertilisers	Magnesium sulphate (Epsom Salts) Magnesian limestone	Broadcast in fertiliser or spray leaves Broadcast
Boron	Brassica crops, celery, beetroot, carnations	Very limey; Very sandy or overlimed soils	Borax (sodium tetraborate)	Mixed in pre-planting fertiliser
Iron	Apple, plum, pear, cherry, raspberry, currants, strawberry	Very limey or overlimed soils	Iron chelate. (Fe-Edta, sold under trade names)	Leaf spray or soil application
Manganese	Potato, brassica crops, peas, dwarf and runner beans, onion, carrot, celery, apple, plum, cherry, raspberry	Very limey; overlimed or on many peaty soils	Manganese sulphate	Leaf spray
Copper	Vegetables and some fruits	Some peaty soils and sandy reclaimed heathland	Copper sulphate (Blue stone) Copper oxychloride fungicide	Broadcast before sowing or planting Leaf spray
Molybdenum	Cauliflowers	Very acid soils	Usually cured by liming. Sodium molybdate may be applied	Before planting

Always follow the instructions on the label of the container when using proprietary compounds.

Always scatter them as evenly as possible otherwise patchy growth will result. Distributors can be used for lawns and large beds.

You can buy dilutors for liquid feeds which meter the correct amounts.

Always rake fertiliser into the top 2 or 3 inches of soil or rotary cultivate, but do not bury deeply. Slow acting ones are best mixed thoroughly with the top 6 inches by raking or rotary cultivation.

Never apply liquid fertilisers to dry soil or composts. Always water first.

Keep fertilisers in a dry place and keep the tops of the containers closed up; always keep bags off the floor.

Do not allow fertilisers to touch leaves or flowers—they may scorch.

NPK

These are the chemical symbols for the three plant foods that are needed in the largest amounts by plants, and are the ones most likely to be deficient in soils. When you buy a fertiliser you generally buy it for its content of these plant foods. Hence the value of a fertiliser depends upon its analysis which should be stated on the bag or other container.

N stands for nitrogen which is a gas and cannot be absorbed by plants in this form; it is taken from nitrates which result from the chemical combination of nitrogen with oxygen.

P stands for phosphorus, which is a chemical element that catches fire when exposed to air; so plants cannot take it up in this form. Plants get their phosphorus from soluble phosphates which are a combination of this element and oxygen. Unfortunately an archaic expression is still used to denote the content of phosphorus in a fertiliser—this is P_2O_5—which is commonly called 'phosphoric acid'.

K stands for potassium, the Latin name of which is *Kalium*. Since potassium is a metal that bursts into flame when it comes into contact with water it cannot be used by plants in the raw state. It is taken up from soluble potassium salts in soils.

The word potash, the chemical name of which is potassium oxide—K_2O, arose from the old custom of concentrating the solution of ashes, which contain potassium, in pots. The plant food content of a compound fertiliser may be indicated by its grade—a series of three numbers separated by dashes. The numbers show the percentage of nitrogen, 'phosphoric acid' and potash, in that order, contained in the compound.

Manure

Manure may be defined as any substance applied to the soil to make it more fruitful—a term which may also be applied to fertilisers; so really it is without precise meaning. But we generally think of a manure as a bulky,

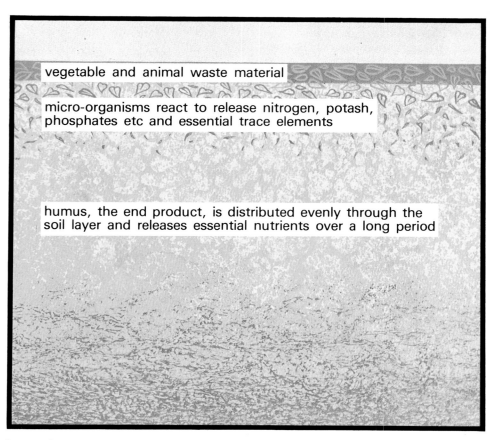

vegetable and animal waste material

micro-organisms react to release nitrogen, potash, phosphates etc and essential trace elements

humus, the end product, is distributed evenly through the soil layer and releases essential nutrients over a long period

humus-forming substance that is formed from animal or vegetable origin or in other words, it is a 'natural' manure.

Some bulky manures are inconvenient to handle, usually smelly and expensive to buy. So, will we get better plants, more nutritious vegetables and fruit, and do a better job of conserving soils if we use organic manures instead of relying solely on factory made or 'artificial' fertilisers that supply plant foods alone? The answer is that bulky organic manures add to the content of organic matter, which plays a vital role in building and maintaining soil fertility. Every time you dig, hoe or cultivate a soil you let more air in. Then the soil organisms become more active and these break down organic matter, which is their food, and soils often lose their structure and become more difficult to work and soils on sloping ground often erode.

When first applied, the fibrous material opens up all soils making them more porous, better aerated and drained. Small animals and minute organisms break them down and in so doing produce waste products that bind and cement small particles together to form clusters and in some soils porous crumbs. These have large spaces between them that hold moisture yet allow surplus water to run away. The minute spaces within the crumbs hold moisture and plant foods available for plant use. A soil with a good crumb structure does not fall to paste when rained upon nor does it crush easily when cultivated.

Humus is one of the end products of

Humus is one of the end products of decay. It absorbs many times its own weight of water thus helping sandy soils to hold moisture better. Substantial amounts of plant foods—nitrogen, phosphates, potash and others including trace elements—are produced in the process of decay. These become available to plants at a slow steady rate over a long period.

decay. It absorbs many times its own weight of water and this helps sandy soils to hold moisture better—an effect that is most noticeable in dry periods. Close-grained soils, either silts or clays, which tend to pan or are difficult to work, are much improved. Garden compost, farmyard manure and most other organic manures also supply substantial amounts of plant foods—nitrogen, phosphates and potash and many others including trace elements. But being formed from plant and animal residues they differ from most factory-made fertilisers because their nutrients are not in a form that can be used by plants. For example the nitrogen may be part of a complex protein molecule and as such it cannot be absorbed by a growing plant as it stands. As the material begins to decay the resident nitrogen in its proteins undergoes chemical change and is eventually converted into ammonium and nitrate forms that may be absorbed by plant roots. While these forms of nitrogen are exactly the same, whether they come from an inorganic fertiliser or a manure, they are released at a slow and steady rate over a very much longer period. This long-lasting effect is now being imitated in some of the newer synthetic organic fertilisers.

As 'natural' manures are long lasting in effect they are not exhausted as quickly as inorganic fertilisers, and generally leave useful residues for crops that follow. This is important to remember when planning vegetable rotations; cauliflowers and many other vegetable crops thrive in soils generously manured with organic manures, while others prefer the residues from a previously well-manured crop—a fact that leads to economy in the use of bulky manures.

Apart from the incorporation of manures in the soil before planting or during the life of the plant these materials are of great value when used as surface mulches. Mulches are like a blanket in retaining moisture. Water vapour from the soil surface diffuses very much more slowly through a loose mulch than it does from the bare soil surface. A wet bare soil can easily lose ½ inch of rain in a week, whereas a mulched soil will take about six weeks to lose this amount.

Mulches usually allow water to penetrate soils more easily, the raindrops trickle slowly through the fibrous material and do not compact the soil as badly as they do when falling on bare soil. So mulches are of particular value to silty soils that are subject to surface panning through heavy rain. On such soils even a very light mulch will break the force of rain and prevent compaction and, by protecting the surface from exposure to rain, lessen the chance of cracking.

The best-known organic manure is farmyard manure, but rotting plant remains, usually called composts, are manures too, and undecomposed materials like straw may be included (see Compost heaps). Organic wastes from industrial processes, town refuse and sewage sludges are also offered as organic manures.

All organic manures are not perfect. Some may have a bad effect on plants. For example straw, sawdust and even very strawy farmyard manure. These contain only a very little nitrogen but a lot of carbon and hydrogen, in the form of carbohydrates such as cellulose. But the attacking organisms need supplies of nitrogen while they feed on the carbohydrates and if extra nitrogen is not applied, they will take it from the soil and rob the plants.

This effect can be overcome by adding extra nitrogen to materials of this kind or by allowing them to undergo a partial decay before they are mixed with the soil.

Farmyard manure (FYM) Foldyard manure and dung are names used to describe a mixture of the excreta of farm animals and the straw or other litter used in yards or stalls to absorb the urine and to keep the animals clean.

If you live in a livestock-producing rural area it is easy to get a load of manure delivered to your garden. The average 3-ton lorry usually holds about 5 cubic yards of manure which is sufficient for about 500 square yards of soil so that may be too much for your garden and it is necessary to share the load with a neighbour; a cubic yard weighs anything from 10 cwt to 15 cwt according to the amount of straw contained and the age of the manure. The main trouble, of course, is getting the manure into your garden. You need a gate at least 7 feet wide for lorry or tractor and trailer access otherwise the manure has to be dumped outside the garden and barrowed in rapidly to prevent it from becoming a nuisance to passers-by.

Town gardeners are hindered by the problems of access and the high cost of transport. Even so, many town gardeners do buy FYM, either directly through manure contractors or through garden centres. Composted farm manures that are sold in bags are an obvious alternative to the fresh bulky material direct from the farm.

Quality Like all organic manures farmyard manure can vary in many ways from load to load, in contrast to inorganic fertilisers that have a fixed and definite composition.

The type of animal producing the dung has a big effect on quality. The dung (the solid excreta) of horses is the richest in all nutrients and it is drier than that of cows or pigs, so that the bacterial changes during rotting are much more rapid and a greater amount of ammonia is produced. Horse manure when stacked soon begins to steam showing that fermentation is going on; so it is called a 'hot' manure, specially suitable for mushrooms and for greenhouse work.

Pig dung is the next richest, followed by cow dung; both of these are much wetter than horse dung and in consequence heat up more slowly and are referred to as 'cold' manures.

So far as nutrients are concerned, farmyard manures are weak; for example you need about 50 lb of horse manure to supply as much nitrogen as there is in 1 lb of sulphate of ammonia. The average analysis of most farmyard manures is about ½ per cent nitrogen, ¼ per cent phosphates and ½ per cent potash. All animal manures contain in addition useful amounts of magnesium and calcium and are very good suppliers of trace elements, together with other substances which are believed to have growth-promoting properties.

Quality also depends upon the kind of litter used for bedding. The most commonly used litter is straw, which absorbs about three times its own weight of urine and of course provides additional humus-forming matter. Peat moss is an even better absorber of urine and makes a manure which is easily spread and mixed with the soil. Sawdust and wood shavings are poor absorbers of liquids and are very slow to break down in the soil.

Benefits of manure In view of the foregoing you may well think that in a space age it is an archaic practice to use farmyard manure at all. But the results of experiments with good quality products show that it is the yardstick for comparing all other organic manures. In addition to its content of plant nutrients it is a humus supplier and for every ton you buy you will get about 3 to 5 cwt of organic matter which soon becomes humus in the soil and gives all the benefits associated with humus (see Humus). It supplies its nutrients in a slowly available form and, therefore, has a long-lasting effect; the benefits of a single dressing can last for 3 or more years.

Using farmyard manure If you have some ground ready when the manure comes in, you will lose less of your manure by digging it in right away; but it is often a question of getting a load when you can and storing it until the ground becomes vacant. If you buy a ton of manure now, you will only have about ½ a ton in six months time because the microbes change parts of the manure into carbon dioxide and ammonia gases which blow away in the wind; nutrients are also washed out of the manure during heavy rain, forming the brown liquid which you often see round the bottom of a dung heap.

While in the heap it is best kept under cover and always kept trodden down tightly to exclude air, and if the drainings can be collected in a bucket or tank a great waste of precious plant nutrients can be avoided.

A mulch of peat around Runner Beans not only keeps the roots cool and moist, but also provides food.

In very dry weather, moisten the heap periodically. By stacking fresh manure straight from the stable or piggery for a few months the product is improved; you get a better balance in nutrient content, the nitrogen part becomes slower-acting and is less likely to burn seedlings or the delicate roots of tender plants. The well-rotted manure is much easier to spread and mix in with the topsoil. You can tell if it is well rotted by the absence of unpleasant smell and even texture of the product—the straw part will no longer be recognisable. Fresh manure is much more difficult to spread and mix; if you intend to sow or plant soon after an application you have to bury it deeply otherwise it interferes with operations needed for preparing a plant bed.

Deeply buried manure does not give the best results; ideally it is spread on well-broken soil and then worked in to a depth of 3 or 4 inches with a cultivator, then turned with a spade or fork. Take care not to turn the soil completely upside down, but rather at an angle wide enough just to cover the surface material. Manure covered with slabs of wet soil merely prevents humus formation. By mixing it with 3 or 4 inches of topsoil, hard crusts which prevent seedlings from pushing through easily, are obviated. To do any real good to soil that is low in humus it is essential to cover the soil with a layer thick enough to obscure the soil beneath it; this will need at least 10 lb of well-rotted manure per square yard. For vegetables this is done every 3 years before you plant crops such as brassicas that respond to generous dressings of manure.

Well-rotted farmyard manure can be applied at any time of the year before sowing or planting, but fresh or 'long' manure as it is called, is best dug in during the autumn or early winter so as to allow it to break down and lose its caustic nature in time for spring plantings.

For mulching during the summer the manure is useful for suppressing weeds and retaining moisture; when dug in at the end of the season it adds to the humus content of the soil.

Since large dressings of farmyard manure supply appreciable amounts of plant nutrients you can reduce your fertiliser dressings by half if 10 lb of well-rotted farmyard manure per square yard has been added.

Composted manures There are a number of products derived from fresh animal manures that are sold in bags under brand names. Large heaps of the fresh manure are allowed to decay under cover for several months during which time the coarse material is broken down and the heat of decomposition drives off much of the moisture.

The resultant dark brown spongy manure is applied at the rate of 6 to 8

A cultivator handles manure easily.

ounces per square yard and is lightly forked in or mixed with the topsoil by means of a rotary cultivator.

These products are clean and convenient to handle.

Soil composts These are balanced mixtures designed to support healthy and active plant growth throughout all stages of propagation, pot and container culture and other forms of simulated growth conditions. They are also, on occasions, used for mixing into outside planting positions in order to give trees, shrubs and plants a good start.

There were at one time innumerable, highly individual soil composts, especially where potting was concerned, but some years ago the John Innes Horticultural Institution at Bayfordbury in Hertfordshire, decided to seek some standard formulations.

After considerable work and research by Mr. W. J. C. Lawrence, a series of standard potting and propagating composts was developed, making it clear that apart from certain modifications in special cases, such standard mixtures would work efficiently for an extremely wide range of plants. And they came as a very welcome simplification of what had been a highly complex, not to say hit and miss process; satisfactory for the skilled gardener, perhaps, but certainly not for those with little experience.

Five composts were devised, three for

the various stages of potting, and one each for seed sowing and propagation by cuttings. The primary ingredients are partially sterilised loam – steamed at 200°F (93°C) for twenty minutes, essential in order to destroy pests, diseases and weed seeds – granular peat with a minimum of dust, and coarse river sand up to ⅛ inch aggregate; with nutrient materials in the form of hoof and horn, ⅛ inch grist (13 per cent nitrogen), superphosphate of lime (16 per cent phosphoric acid) and sulphate of potash (48 per cent pure potash) and, finally, ground limestone or chalk.

For potting composts Nos. 1, 2 and 3, the basic formula is:

7 parts by loose bulk of medium loam – partially sterilised
3 parts of granulated or moss peat
2 parts of coarse sand.

It is important to note that in each instance the measurements are by *loose bulk* and not by weight. The fertilizers and limestone or chalk are measured by weight, not by bulk.

These materials are mixed most efficiently by placing them in three complete layers, one upon another, and then turning this flat, sandwiched heap over, working from one end to the other and shovelling from ground level throughout. The heap should be turned at least twice – out and back – for maximum success.

Fertilizer mixed in the ratio of:
2 parts by weight of hoof and horn
2 parts by weight of superphosphate of lime
1 part by weight of sulphate of potash plus ¾ oz of ground limestone or chalk, making sure to mix all thoroughly throughout.

This complete mixture is suitable for most basic potting in small to medium pots, for delicate and hothouse plants and those which are not to be kept for any length of time.

Plants other than delicate and hothouse, when requiring a shift beyond the 4 or 4½ inch pot stage, should be potted into John Innes No. 2; made by adding twice the amount of combined fertilizer and chalk to each bushel of loam, peat and sand. John Innes No. 3 comes from adding three times the amount of these materials and is suitable for the more robust and long-standing plants requiring, perhaps, shifts into 8 inch pots and beyond.

Compost made up for plants objecting to lime should obviously have the chalk or limestone omitted; it should be reduced where lime is present to any extent in the loam used in the basic formula. Ideally, this should not be so, with loam with a pH of 6.5, the kind to use if possible.

The John Innes standard seed sowing mixture consists of:

2 parts by bulk of loam – partially sterilised
1 part by bulk of peat
1 part by bulk of sand

to each bushel of which is added only 1½ oz superphosphate of lime and ⅜ oz ground limestone or chalk. The loam and peat may have to be rubbed through a ½ inch sieve to make them sufficiently fine for seedling growth.

Certain plants require special composts; orchids, for instance, are traditionally potted in a basic mixture of osmunda fibre, sphagnum moss and charcoal.

Where many tiny alpines are concerned, extra grit in the compost is often required in order to allow them very adequate drainage, essential to many of them, especially in their early stages.

Sometimes commercial growers handling plants, trees and shrubs in containers for immediate planting, use a 90 per cent peat, 10 per cent soil compost for general expedience, nutrients being supplied in balanced liquid form.

Using the compost Well-made composts from vegetable wastes may contain more nutrients and more organic matter than good farmyard manure.

If you know that your soil is very low in humus, about 10 lb per square yard should be mixed with the topsoil for a year or two and in subsequent years give 5 lb per square yard.

Seaweed One of the oldest manures known is seaweed, which is widely used for improving the soils of gardens and farms in coastal districts. The different weeds vary in plant food content; the long broad-leaved species, which is usually found just below the low water mark, is richer than the bladder wrack (*Fucus*) found between low and high tides. It is gathered all the year round but the richest harvest is thrown up by spring tides, or during storms.

About three-quarters of seaweed is water, the remainder being humus-forming material. It contains about ½ per cent nitrogen and up to 1½ per cent phosphates and about 1–1½ per cent potash. Since seaweeds have no roots they obtain all their nutrients from the dissolved substances in the sea, which is constantly being enriched by drainage from the land. So they absorb very large

1 Leaves collected in the autumn can be composted to form leafmould.
2 The site is prepared for a compost heap with a layer of old hedge clippings to ensure drainage and aeration. Wire netting surrounds the heap.
3 Pea haulms, cabbage stumps, egg shell and general garden rubbish are added in a thick layer. The sides of the heap must be kept firm.
4 Sulphate of ammonia is lightly spread over the heap at the rate of ½ ounce per square yard to encourage decay and hasten decomposition.

quantities of nutrients and are, therefore, an excellent source of trace elements.

The actual organic matter consists very largely of alginic acid which, unlike the cellulose which you get in farmyard manure, rots readily in the soil and is an excellent soil conditioner. The other carbohydrates and simple sugars found in seaweed also decompose readily in the soil.

It is best dug into the soil immediately after spreading to prevent it from drying out into a hard, woody mess. The usual rate of application is 10 lb per square yard. Seaweed is particularly suitable for sandy soils in view of its comparative freedom from fibre, thus allowing rapid humus formation. Freedom from weed seeds and disease organisms is an additional advantage of this manure. Its content of common salt is not usually harmful to plants when the manure is used at the normal rates of application.

Dried seaweed products Whole seaweed dried and ground is now available under brand names. Thus prepared the natural product can be transported inland economically and is four to five times as concentrated as wet seaweed or farmyard manure. The product is dry and pleasant to handle and is sold in small packs. Some manufacturers reinforce their products with fertilisers to give them a higher plant food content and to overcome the tendency of dried seaweed temporarily to tie-up nitrogen in the soil.

The best results are obtained from dried products to which fertiliser has been added when they are applied to the surface of the soil during winter cultivation and left for a few weeks to break down; this time varies according to weather and soil conditions, but about four weeks is sufficient in most instances. A reasonable dressing is 2–4 ounces per square yard.

Products reinforced with NPK fertilisers are sold by some manufacturers and are intended to overcome the initial 'tie-up' of nitrogen in the soil. These can be used in the spring and summer on growing plants, at the rate of 2–4 ounces per square yard, for all crops.

Dried seaweeds are also used in soil composts and in topdressings for lawns. The usual rates of application already quoted may seem to be rather low for a bulky organic manure whose main function is to supply humus, but seaweed preparations contain alginates which stimulate the soil organisms to greater activity that results in better tilth formation in heavy soils and greater water-holding properties in sandy soils.

Their trace element content is most valuable and makes this class of manure one of the best and safest means of providing soils with nutrients that are needed in very small amounts.

Spent hops The residue after hops have been extracted with water in the brewery is usually sold to haulage contractors who supply commercial growers with the entire output from many breweries and in consequence the amounts available for gardeners is somewhat limited. Much of the output is purchased by fertiliser manufacturers who reinforce the spent hops with concentrated fertilisers in order to raise the food content.

In the fresh wet state straight from the brewery, spent hops contain about 75 per cent water, about $\frac{1}{2}$ per cent of nitrogen, $\frac{1}{4}$ per cent phosphates and traces of potash. But since the moisture content varies considerably so does the

1 Peat is used as a mulch for Strawberries, and is forked in after picking.
2 Chrysanthemum cuttings rooted, *right,* in a seaweed meal compost, and *left,* without the meal in the compost. Although it is not usual to grow cuttings in such a compost, there is the advantage that food is available if potting-on has to be delayed.
3 French Beans, *left,* grown with the addition of a seaweed compost, germinate better and are pest free.

plant food content. So an analysis based on the dry matter is the best figure. On this basis the nitrogen content ranges from 2–3 per cent and the phosphate content is about 1 per cent. If you are able to get a good supply of spent hops locally you can improve the plant food content by adding ½ cwt of National Growmore fertiliser to every ton of hops. The fertiliser should be sprinkled over the hops and the heap turned over twice to ensure even mixing.

You cannot, as a rule, get small quantities of spent hops; they are usually sold by the lorry-load which may weigh several tons. If you have large areas of shrub borders to mulch or a very large vegetable garden you will need a lorry load to do any real good.

Hop manures are proprietary products prepared from spent hops and reinforced with fertilisers. They are sold in bags together with instructions for use in the garden.

Spent hops are regarded mainly as humus suppliers and are used in the preparation of ground for planting and also for mulching established plants. The best results are obtained when they are incorporated thoroughly with the top 6 inches of soil at the rate of 10 lb per square yard during the winter. For mulching purposes spent hops are very effective in keeping down weeds and retaining soil moisture in shrub borders and soft fruit plots, provided the ground is covered really thickly. If you apply a layer 4–6 inches thick it will last for two years before rotting noticeably. The material gives off an objectionable odour after application but this usually disappears after 2–3 weeks. Although spent hops are slightly more acid than most soils they are used with great success for practically all trees and shrubs except for some of the outstanding lime-requiring plants. The fire hazard from burning cigarette ends is low since spent hops do not burn readily when used as mulches.

Spent mushroom compost The material left after a mushroom crop has been cleared from the beds in which the spawn was planted usually consists of a mixture of well-rotted horse manure and the soil which was used for covering the beds before planting the mushroom spawn. Peat and chalk is often used in place of soil in which case the compost will have a proportion of lime in it.

So the quality of the product depends very much upon the proportion of casing soil which it contains. The organic matter of spent mushroom compost is generally more decomposed than in strawy farmyard manure and hence it may be less useful for improving heavy soils.

Being fibrous and well-rotted the compost is an ideal material for mixing in with the topsoil of all soils. The nitrogen content of fresh spent horse manure compost including soil is usually lower than farmyard manure and the phosphate and potash content is just slightly lower.

The lime-rich composts are unsuitable for rhododendrons and other lime-haters, and may contain excessive amounts of lime for fruit crops.

Normal rate of application is 5–10 lb per square yard.

Fertilisers and manures must, as a general rule, be bought and must therefore add to the overall cost of your gardening. It is possible to a great extent to make your own by using waste products. Well-made, home-produced compost can be most helpful.

Compost heaps
There are several ways in which compost heaps can be made and various theories exist as to the way in which they should be treated. There are two important points which are essential for successful compost making and these are adequate drainage and aeration and sufficient moisture.

A compost heap is a necessary feature in the average garden. It provides a means of collecting the surprising amount of waste material which is gathered together during regular garden maintenance and it supplies the garden, or rather, the soil, with valuable organic matter. This organic matter fulfils several vital functions. It helps to improve the structure of the soil, especially the heavy clay types and the light sandy kinds. It encourages a vigorous root system and also acts as a sponge to retain moisture. Light, sandy soils tend to dry out rather badly and a high humus content is necessary to overcome this problem. Well-rotted composted vegetable waste can be used as a mulch around plants and between rows of vegetables where it will smother small annual weeds and prevent the surface soil from drying out badly.

It is advisable to give some thought to the siting and layout of a compost heap, particularly where the garden is small. A compost heap can look ugly and untidy if neglected, but fortunately there are several ways in which the material can be contained neatly and efficiently. Although the heap should be placed in an unobtrusive position in the garden, it should not be put in a position which is damp, heavily shaded or closed in. In these conditions the waste material can become offensive and will certainly not rot down into the dark friable mass it should.

The size of the area a compost heap will require will depend naturally on the size of the garden and especially on the number and sizes of the lawns, for the biggest proportion of compost heap ingredients consists of lawn mowings. The usual recommendation is that the heap should not be more than 3 feet wide or 3 feet in height when first built. There will be considerable shrinkage later on due to the decomposition of the waste vegetation in the heap. One of the neatest ways of making a compost heap is to purchase a specially constructed bin or container. Some are made from extra stout gauge wire, stove enamelled dark green, others have a rustic appearance with a strong wooden framework. Most types have either a removable side or one which hinges so that the heap can be filled or emptied easily. Generally these commercial bins hold about 1 cubic yard or 1 ton of material in their 3 feet square area.

It is quite an easy matter to construct a compost bin from the following material: four corner posts 4 feet long (1 foot to be inserted in the ground), and 2–3 inches square. The sides or 'filling' in pieces are made from 3 foot lengths of timber 3 inches wide and at least 1 inch thick. Six will be required for each side making a total of 24 pieces. They are spaced approximately 4 inches apart and screwed into the corner posts. To provide for a removable side, one set of side pieces, 1¼ inches less in length than the others, are screwed to two separate corner rails 2–3 inches wide and 1 inch thick. The complete unit slides into two of the fixed corner posts, in a groove or channel made from two 3 foot pieces of 3×1 inch timber spaced from the two fixed corner posts by two thin strips of wood 1¼ inch thick and 1 inch wide. All timber must be thoroughly treated against rot and Cuprinol, Rentokil or Solignum are suitable. The ends of the corner posts should be well soaked for several hours before they are inserted in the soil.

Where appearance is not important, or where the compost heap is so sited that it can be hidden from view, old sheets of corrugated iron could well be used in the construction.

The successful decomposition of waste material in a heap depends on the action of bacteria and fungi. The bacteria depend on plenty of nitrogen as food and the rate of decay can be increased by supplying some readily available nitrogen. This can be provided by sprinkling the material with a nitrogenous fertilizer such as sulphate of ammonia or Nitrochalk. Another method of adding Nitrogen is by placing layers of good quality, fresh animal manure between the layers of garden waste. The heap is, in fact, built up in sandwich fashion with alternate layers of manure and waste.

To get rid of air pockets, each 6–8 inch layer of material to be rotted down is trodden fairly firmly. It is customary, though not absolutely essential, to cover each trodden layer with a further layer of soil, about an inch thick. The next layer of waste material is put on this and trodden when it is about 6–8 inches thick, sprinkled with fertiliser, then covered with soil, and so on.

There are proprietary preparations on the market which accelerate the decomposition process. Some are specially formulated to deal with tougher ingredients of a heap such as herbaceous trimmings, pea and bean haulms, or top growths. Others are particularly suited to the softer materials such as lawn clippings, lettuce leaves, annual weeds and such. Some proprietary formulae include seaweed which produces a very rapid fermentation of the heap. These accelerators are sprinkled on the layers of waste as the heap is built up, in lieu of the nitrogenous fertilisers mentioned above.

Where the tougher materials are to be rotted down without the use of a proprietary compost maker, it is a good idea to bruise or chop the stems to aid rotting. Plenty of water must be provided also as this type of harder waste is built into a heap. Some gardeners can obtain quantities of straw and this is very useful as an addition to the compost heap. As a successful heap requires plenty of aeration and drainage, it is wise to start a heap with some of this coarser material at the bottom. Some gardeners like to drive in one or two stakes into a heap so that, when they are withdrawn, air holes or passages are provided which pass right into the material.

Although a well-made compost heap should rot down satisfactorily by itself, the contents can be turned after a period of three to four weeks. This is done by transferring the heap to a position close by its original one. Forkfuls of rotting waste are placed in the

1 Leaves are a valuable source of organic material and unless diseased should never be burnt. In autumn the leaves should be raked up and collected into a wire enclosure. 2 Waste organic matter is rotted down in heaps to make compost but the process must ensure the destruction of weed seeds

same area, but as the work is carried out, the outer portions of the heap are placed towards the centre of the new one. It may be necessary to add a little water to areas which may be a little dry.

It is necessary to appreciate the fact that acids are produced as byproducts of even the most favourable decay and that too much acid will spoil compost. This problem can be overcome if some lime is included in the heap. This can be done if some powdered chalk or limestone is sprinkled on alternate layers of waste vegetation. A fertiliser or a dressing containing lime such as Nitrochalk can be used instead. It is important to note that lime and chalk must not be allowed to come into contact with sulphate of ammonia which might be used as an accelerator. If this is done, ammonia will be liberated and nitrogen lost as ammonia gas.

Decay is also hastened in a fairly warm temperature and in a damp atmosphere. The spring and autumn periods, therefore, will be times when rotting down will be at its peak. One would assume that the summer months would be ideal also. This is true to a certain extent, but if a heap is situated where it receives the direct rays of the sun, considerable drying out of the

material will result and decay will not be as rapid.

Much of the value of the compost can be lost if the heap is exposed for long to rain. The nutrients will be lost by being washed away. Where compost has to be stored for any length of time, it is wise to provide some form of shelter for it. An open-sided shed is suitable or a temporary roof can be made. To do this, four strong posts are required about 2 inches square. Two of these should be about 6–10 inches longer than the others. Their total length should be such that they clear the top of the compost heap by 2 feet.

The longest posts are inserted at the front of the compost heap, close by the existing posts or bin sides. The other two posts are placed at the use of the heap. Across each pair of posts a rail should be fastened on which the roofing material will rest. The two rails should be cut from timber approximately $2 \times 1\frac{1}{2}$ inches in section.

Various types of material can be used for the roof. Corrugated metal sheets or cheap PVC sheets are ideal. The sheets are nailed or screwed down on to the cross rails. Where necessary, an overlap of 2–3 inches on the sheets should be provided. The finished roof will have sufficient pitch or slope to shed rainfall. The sheets must be purchased large enough so that they overhang all four sides of the compost heap by at least 4 inches.

There are different opinions as to the length of time compost should be kept before it is ready for use. It must be kept until it has decayed to such an extent that the individual ingredients of which it is composed can no longer be distinguished. Usually the material is in an ideal condition when it has become a dark, friable or crumbly mass. A slimy state is not satisfactory and shows that the heap has been made up incorrectly.

In warm weather, soft refuse will take about four to six weeks to decay but in winter the period will be much longer, and anything up to three or four months will be necessary before thorough decomposition has taken place. Where the refuse is harder or tougher, the period necessary for decomposition will be longer.

But the best of soils in both content and texture is useless unless it is moist. Plants need water to sustain themselves and because all plant foods are absorbed in the form of liquid chemical compounds. The source of nearly all the water that a garden needs is natural rain, and only in comparatively rare periods of drought is artificial watering necessary. This is a relatively simple matter today with the many watering aids available to us, some of them automatic. The main rule when watering is to do it thoroughly, for if only the soil surface is moist the roots of plants will tend to turn upwards in the soil towards this area and expose themselves to drought or to burning by the sun. It is almost impossible, except in low-lying areas or poorly drained soils, to over-water artificially. Overwatering occurs with repeated heavy rains.

Drainage

The soil must have adequate drainage otherwise air may be excluded and the more beneficial micro-organisms may be destroyed. Soils which have poor drainage are often sour and acid. It will be necessary to improve this acidity by applications of hydrated lime. Wet soils are cold ones, and this means that plant growth is severely retarded. The situation is even more critical in the northern, colder parts of the country. Waterlogged soils cause roots to rot and a combination of all these problems can produce complete failures in some gardens.

Soils which are well-drained have sufficient natural coarse, gritty material or sand and many soils have a high proportion of small stones also. A high humus or organic content will also ensure good drainage. It is usually the clay soils which are the most difficult with regard to drainage, although a hard 'pan' or layer beneath the surface of some soils can also present a problem. Such a pan is usually produced by mechanical cultivation which, in some instances, can consolidate the lower soil layers. Setting the plough or cultivators to cultivate to the same depth season after season will also produce this hard, unbroken layer. Varying the cultivating depth occasionally usually overcomes this difficulty.

Clay soils are composed of finer particles and these tend to pack so tightly together that they soon form a solid mass through which excess water cannot pass easily. Improving the drainage here consists in opening up these fine particles. This can be done by liming the soil. The particles of soil cling together in large granules after this treatment. If sharp, gritty material such as coarse sand or well-weathered cinders is worked in, the clay particles will be separated and made more open. Bulky materials such as peat, composted vegetable waste and strawy manure are invaluable as soil conditioners. Gypsum is another preparation which has proved excellent for the breaking up of heavy, waterlogged clay soils.

Where cultural methods are not sufficient to provide a marked improvement in difficult conditions, it will be necessary to improve drainage by a system of drains or drainage trenches. The most efficient method is to use field or pipe drains. These are expensive, especially if drainage on a large scale is necessary. The pipes are sold in several sizes; those 2 inches or 3 inches in diameter are the best for the amateur.

Trenches are dug out to receive these pipes, at least 15 inches deep. All trenches should slope in one direction and this slope need not exceed 1 in 40. The trenches should be arranged in a herringbone fashion and should lead to one main trench which runs from the highest point in the garden to the lowest. The side or intermediate trenches should meet this main trench at an approximate angle of 45°.

The pipes should be laid, for preference, on a 2 inch layer of coarse gravel or cinders. Each pipe should be kept about ½ inch away from its neighbour and the junction covered with a piece of slate, broken tile or a small piece of tough plastic sheeting. More gravel or cinders should be carefully placed around and on top of the pipes as work proceeds. The gaps between the pipes are essential to allow excess water to enter them and drain away inside the pipes. Frequent checks should be made with a little water from a watering can or hose pipe to see that water flows steadily along the pipes.

The main pipe line must be taken to a suitable outlet such as a ditch or soak-away. The latter can be constructed by digging out a large hole as deeply as possible and filling it in with stones, clinker, gravel or ashes. This hole must be at least 2–3 feet square and deep. Under no circumstances must drainage water be allowed to flow on to neighbours' property. Where a stream or ditch is available for the emptying of drainage water, the local Borough Surveyor's Department should be consulted to make quite sure whether it is permissible to discharge the water in this way.

An efficient drainage system can be provided if trenches are lined with rubble and coarse cinders. A similar system of trenches should be taken out and the bottom half filled with rubble. This layer of rubble should be then covered with about 6 inches of coarse cinders. The trench is then filled up with soil. Surplus water will run through the coarser base material and finally into the large drainage sump at the lowest part of the garden.

It is possible to use a third system, although this is not quite so satisfactory as the others. This method employs brushwood which is laid in bundles at the bottom of the trench systems. The brushwood is then covered with soil to the surface of the surrounding ground. The unsatisfactory part of this method is that the brushwood gradually rots away and loses its efficiency. It will be necessary to renew the system every few years, and unless the layout is small, this will involve a great deal of time and labour.

Where a new site is taken over, it is a very good idea to examine it thoroughly to see whether or not the soil requires attention to drainage. If it does it will provide an excellent opportunity to gather all the usual kinds of rubble which can be found on a new or neglected site. Builders often leave behind them a surprising amount of broken bricks, old paint tins, and lumps of concrete.

All this type of waste should be placed in convenient piles in the garden and used in the bottom of drainage trenches. If insufficient is available from the garden, it is quite likely that the local builder will be only too glad to supply some from his building sites.

During the planning of a drainage system for a waterlogged or poorly drained garden, it is a good plan to look ahead and visualise the positions for structures such as sheds, greenhouses or home extensions. All these buildings shed water and it will certainly aggravate the situation if this water is allowed to flow into the garden.

The position of a convenient drainage trench should be marked with a stake so that, later on, excess water from a gutter or down-spout can be directed into this drainage trench. The emptying of a fish pond is also facilitated if the water is directed on to an area of ground which is drained in this way, or if an outlet pipe is built into one of these drainage trenches.

It is possible to improve the soil and to add moisture to it, but in the open garden it is either impractical or impossible to provide some of the other essentials to plant growth—light and warmth. Only by correct planning and planting in the first place is it possible to avoid growing a plant in the shade, or to position another plant to gain shelter from cold north or east winds.

Chapter 2

PLANNING THE GARDEN

Planning the garden

Whether you specialise in any particular plant or not, the general design and layout of your garden must be pleasing and practical. There are some hard and fast rules to bear in mind, but in the main gardening is a subject upon which it is very hard to dogmatise, and the thing to remember is that the success or otherwise of your garden depends on the pleasure and satisfaction which you get from it.

If your garden is a new one, just as the builder has left it, the first thing to be done is to make a rough scale plan of the plot, a useful scale being 8 feet to the inch. By doing this you will find that you will be able to get everything into proper perspective right from the start. Then make a list of all the features you and your family would like, or think they would like. You may be tempted to include far more items than would be practical—but remember that a garden overcrowded with features is probably less satisfying and more difficult to maintain than one of quiet simplicity. Quite often gardeners clutter their gardens with so many features that the result is a great deal of unnecessary work with nothing really on which the eye can settle. But even if some items have to be crossed off later for reasons of expense and or space available, do try to get down on your list:

Flowering trees, shrubs and herbaceous border

Kitchen garden

Sundial, bird bath, or similar feature

An ornamental pool (formal or informal)

Screened, paved terrace and paths (paths accessible enough for children's tricycles)

As large an expanse of lawn as possible

Rose beds

Screened rubbish corner and compost pit

Perhaps a rock garden, and even a garden shelter or summer house

If you have a family perhaps you would like to include a corner for the children, with their own planting plot, a swing and a sandpit, which may be screened and sheltered by a rose-covered trellis fence, a beech hedge, or a shrub borders. Try to get the children interested in the garden and feel that part of it is theirs—at least they can have one corner unhampered by restrictions of where not to walk and what not to pull up. It is important that children where possible are given their own garden corner with its attendant pleasures and responsibilities, so that they can enjoy the pleasures of growing flowers from seed, and sharing in the awakening of spring with the unexpected thrill of finding the first snowdrop flower, as well as learning care and tidiness.

However small your garden, it should

have at least one main feature, or focal point. It may be an ornamental pool, a summer house, or perhaps even a specimen standard flowering tree. A paved terrace can also be a focal point for radiating rose beds. When you have decided on these features, position them carefully on your plan. Do not forget the compass direction of the facing aspect, the wind, soil or other factors which must be taken into consideration. Try to set off the features naturally with contrasting elements. For example, the pool should be set off by a lawn, the lawn by a border of shrubs and herbaceous plants, and if the pool is of an informal shape, back it with a bank of carefully-built rock stones. There are infinite variations and possibilities. Let the main features show up as focal points in the garden, and then let the lawns and borders provide a neat, simple foil for them, always remembering that you want to keep maintenance work in the garden to a minimum. Keep the lawn as large as is practicable. Besides being much less work to keep tidy than borders which are perhaps too wide, a large lawn will make your garden appear much larger than it really is. If you wish to have an undulating lawn, give careful attention to the drainage of the

1 In this small garden full advantage has been taken of the ground which rises away from the house. The formal lines of the pool and steps are relieved by the luxuriant plant growth.
2 Ground sloping away from the house can be treated in various ways. Here the bank sloping down the lawn has been planted with shrubs and rock plants.
3 The pergola with its Roses is a major feature in this garden. The two levels are connected by steps.

depressions, or you may have trouble later.

Let at least one of your features be as far away from the house as possible, so that in attracting the eye to it in the distance you will be making full use of the length of your garden; and do not forget the value of vistas, or framed views, when designing and planting. A white-painted seat or a bed of scarlet floribunda roses are good distant eye-catchers. If the garden overlooks a particularly attractive view between two trees or with a break in a shrub border try to create a framed view just as the painter might do.

Another principle to remember is that the garden design is governed more by the architecture and shape of the house

A typical design for a small garden, showing compactness and a wide variety of plants and shrubs.

1 The plan shown is a suggested design for a normal semi-detached plot. The ground slopes about 3 feet from the end of the back garden down to the front entrance to the drive. This was taken into consideration in designing the rock outcrops, the steps down from the lawn to the rear terrace and the step from the path to the front door down to the lawn.

Below the areas to be paved, put a good foundation of clinker and ashes about 4 inches deep, and consolidate it well with a roller or rammer. See that the front and rear terrace paving slopes down slightly away from the house, so that rainwater will not lie against the brickwork and perhaps soak down to the foundations.

Climbers would be planted to train over the 5 feet high square mesh trellis across the back of the border at the end of the lawn to screen the kitchen garden.

Apart from the fruit trees, the kitchen garden could also be the site for a tool shed with or without a greenhouse depending upon your requirements and space.

The bird bath could be a focal point in the garden, set as it is on a square panel of crazy paving alpines.

The retaining wall holding up the higher level of the rose beds and lawn from the rear terrace is an important feature as it is in full view of the house the whole time. Give plenty of thought to the selection of the material with which you build the wall. Let it be something to blend effectively with the paving and provide a pleasing foil for the plants. Before you start to build, excavate along the line of the wall about 9 inches wide and 4 inches deeper than the paving level, and lay a foundation of concrete.

The selection of the type of rock with which to build the two small rear lawn rock outcrops will be your own, bearing in mind that the cost of it will vary considerably with the distance it has to be transported. The main borders would be planted with flowering and evergreen shrubs, interplanted with groups of hardy herbaceous perennials. The soft fruit and herb beds would all be accessible from the main garden path.

The drive would be excavated to a depth of 6 inches and provided with a foundation of rubble and ashes. After rolling, this could be covered with a layer of $1\frac{1}{2}$ inch tarmacadam and well consolidated. The drive could then be surfaced with a layer of $\frac{1}{4}$ inch bituminous macadam, and rolled to a firm and even surface, leaving a slight camber (as a rough guide, 1 ton of $1\frac{1}{2}$ inch tarmacadam should cover 20 square yards and 1 ton of $\frac{1}{4}$ inch bituminous macadam should cover 30 square yards).

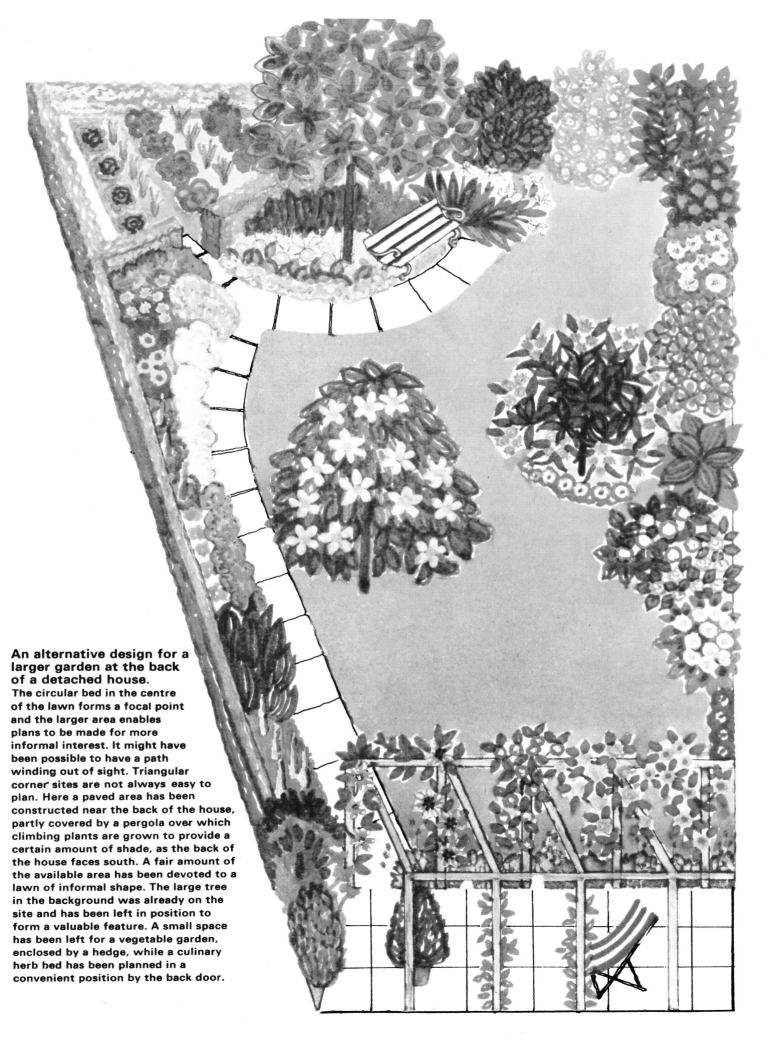

An alternative design for a larger garden at the back of a detached house.
The circular bed in the centre of the lawn forms a focal point and the larger area enables plans to be made for more informal interest. It might have been possible to have a path winding out of sight. Triangular corner sites are not always easy to plan. Here a paved area has been constructed near the back of the house, partly covered by a pergola over which climbing plants are grown to provide a certain amount of shade, as the back of the house faces south. A fair amount of the available area has been devoted to a lawn of informal shape. The large tree in the background was already on the site and has been left in position to form a valuable feature. A small space has been left for a vegetable garden, enclosed by a hedge, while a culinary herb bed has been planned in a convenient position by the back door.

than the shape of your plot. The terrace and formal parts of your garden should be planned in relation to the lines of your house. All straight lines of paving or beds in these areas should be parallel to, or square with, the main house walls. Designing and planting the terrace can be important in creating the look of the back of your house. The terrace, or patio, is a connecting link between house and garden. Bear this in mind when selecting paving for the terrace, so that it will blend with both the house bricks and the garden. Stone is ideal material, but perhaps rather expensive. Nowadays one can obtain good concrete paving in a variety of quiet colours, and often a careful blending of these can give a very pleasing effect. Sometimes a garden may slope down from front to back. This can be turned into an asset by levelling off the paved terrace area, holding up the raised part of it with a stone or brick retaining wall, and building broad steps

down to the lawn (this procedure would be reversed should the garden slope down from back to front). Try always to keep your steps, paths and grassed walks wide enough for at least two people to walk abreast. It is also important that steps are always made easily negotiable. Treads should be at least 1 foot wide and risers (depth of step) never more than 6 inches. Let the treads slope very slightly from back to front so that rainwater will easily run off. Under some circumstances a terrace and garden can be made to appear much wider by building the steps to the full width of the paved area. After all, the terrace is part of the garden, and it seems wrong to screen the garden from the terrace with a heavy planting of shrubs and strong-growing floribunda roses, as used to be the custom. For the sake of privacy the terrace may be carefully but effectively screened with walling, fencing or planting.

In shaping the lawn with graceful curves (remembering that the lawn mower will have to get round them), you may like to allow for a grassed path through a shrub border at the end of the lawn leading to your kitchen garden, which will thus be screened from the house. To some gardeners a kitchen garden is more important than to others, so that the proportion of your garden devoted to fruit and vegetables is something which only you can decide.

It is essential, however, that provision be made for compost and garden rubbish, perhaps in the furthermost corner screened by a hedge.

An essential part of a child's introduction to gardening should be to teach that no part of any plant should ever be put into the mouth without express permission. For there are some 700 species of plants which can cause illness if swallowed and some of these can cause death to children. The greatest dangers are seeds and berries, for some of the most dangerous look both attractive and edible.

Poisonous plants

More than 700 species of plants have been reported to cause illness or death. However, human deaths from eating poisonous plants recorded in Great Britain amount to only a small number each year. Campers and 'mushroom' collectors and others who eat plants they see growing wild are liable to be poisoned. This problem applies particularly in the United States and on the Continent. Children are particularly vulnerable; the United States public health service reports that 12,000 children every year eat potentially poisonous plants. Children are the most susceptible group because of the attractiveness of the fruits of many plants; in particular those with red or black ripe berries. The resemblances of certain fruit pods to pea pods may deceive the unwary.

1 Children can derive endless amusement from a plot of land that is kept for their own use. They also delight in miniature gardens that can be kept indoors during the long winter months. Ferns can be grown in a glass case on a north facing windowledge. Bulbs are easy to handle and produce quick colourful results. Cacti, water plants and sink gardens are other suggestions.

If adults become affected, it is normally due to a plant or part of a plant, such as a root, having been eaten in mistake for the plant or part of a plant of an edible variety.

Most of the poisonous elements in plants are either alkaloidal or glycosidal in form; the remainder being volatile oils or resinous substances, all of which will affect the living cell when consumed. Not all these complex principles are harmful, a few are innocuous and many, consumed in a minute amount, are medicinal in action, only becoming toxic in large quantities.

Many factors influence the degree of poisoning that might occur should a plant be eaten. Factors dependent upon the nature of the plant include the quantity of the active principle present and its distribution within the plant—for example, on whether it is the berry or root. The habitat of the plant in question, the climate, the altitude at which it grows and the season during which it is gathered, may affect the proportion of the toxic principle, or principles, present. An acrid or pungent taste may act as a warning. The factors dependent upon the person eating the plant include his general health, age and any particular susceptibility to the poison; the degree of mastication and the rate of absorption of the poison consumed. Heating, drying or cooking may modify the effect.

Symptoms produced vary and there is generally no antidote. In suspected poisoning, medical or veterinary help should be sought immediately. Bearing in mind that prevention is better than cure, infants and small children should be kept away from colourful berries, mushrooms and house plants and taught that what birds and animals eat are not necessarily harmless to man. Parts of plants, such as seeds, bulbs, and corms should be labelled carefully when storing. These factors having been noted you can still enjoy growing these plants for their beauty and colour and it is not necessary to remove them from the garden altogether.

Many plants, particularly those that grow wild in Britain can be poisonous to a greater or lesser degree, if eaten. Medical or veterinary help should be sought in the event of suspected poisoning from plants. Children ought to be made aware of the dangers of eating plant material, other than that normally served as food.
1 Seed of the Yew, Taxus baccata.
2 Woody Nightshade, or Bitter Sweet, Solanum dulcamara, has red berries.
3 Snowberry, Symphoricarpos albus.
4 The poisonous berries of Arum maculatum, the British native Wild Arum.
5 The Thorn Apple, Datura stramonium.
6 The seeds of Laburnum are poisonous.

Poisonous Plants

Flowering Garden Plants

Scientific Name	Common Name	Poisonous Part(s)	Poisonous Constituent
Aconitum napellus	Monkshood	All, said by some authorities to be the most dangerous of all British plants	Alkaloids, which persist after drying
Colchicum autumnale	Autumn crocus, meadow saffron	All, particularly corms and seeds	Alkaloids, which withstand boiling, drying and storage
Convallaria majalis	Lily-of-the-valley	All	Cardiac glycosides
Delphinium ajacis and other species	Larkspur	Seeds and foliage	Alkaloids
Digitalis purpurea	Foxglove	All	Cardiac glycosides, not affected by drying and storage
Helleborus niger and other species	Christmas rose, black hellebore	All	Glycosides, not destroyed by drying or storage
Iris versicolor and other species	Iris, blue flag	Possibly all	Glycosides not destroyed by drying and storage
Lupinus species	Lupin	All, particularly seeds	Alkaloids, not destroyed by drying or storage
Narcissus species	Narcissus, daffodil, jonquil	Bulb	Toxic alkaloids, still to be identified
Podophyllum peltatum	American mandrake	All, especially green, unripe berries	Crude, resinous material

Vegetable Garden Plants

Scientific Name	Common Name	Poisonous Part(s)	Poisonous Constituent
Rheum rhaponticum	Rhubarb	Leaves (but not stalks, which are edible)	Soluble oxalates
Solanum tuberosum	Potato	Green sprouting tubers, stems and leaves	Glycoalkaloid

Ornamental Shrubs and Trees

Scientific Name	Common Name	Poisonous Part(s)	Poisonous Constituent
Cytisus (Sarothamnus) scoparius	Broom	Seeds	Alkaloids, but only present in small quantity
Daphne mezereum	Mezereon	All, particularly bark and berries	Resin and coumarin glycoside. Toxicity not destroyed by drying and storage
Laburnum anagyroides	Laburnum, golden rain	All, particularly bark and seeds. This tree causes the most cases of poisoning in Britain at the present time	Alkaloid
Prunus laurocerasus	Cherry laurel	All, particularly leaves and kernels of fruit	Cyanogenetic glycosides
Rhododendron species; Azalea and Kalmia species	Rhododendron, azalea, kalmia, American laurel, calico bush, sheep laurel, mountain laurel	Leaves and flowers	Glycoside
Taxus baccata	Yew	Leaves and seeds, the latter are deadly, the aril (red pulpy covering surrounding the seed) is the least harmful	Alkaloid, not destroyed by drying and storage

1 Helleborus foetidus, the Stinking Hellebore, is poisonous in all parts.
2 The seeds of Cytisus scoparius, the native Broom, are poisonous.
3 The Yellow Flag, Iris Pseudacorus, is frequently found in damp places.
4 Aconitum napellus, the Monkshood, is poisonous in all its parts and can be dangerous if there are cuts on the hands when working with the plant.
5 Daphne laureola, a native plant.

Poisonous Plants *continued*

Weeds and Hedgerow Plants

Scientific Name	Common Name	Poisonous Part(s)	Poisonous Constituent
Atropa belladonna	Deadly nightshade	All	Alkaloids, which withstand drying and boiling
Bryonia dioica	White bryony	Roots and berries	Glycoside
Chelidonium majus	Greater celandine	All, particularly roots	Alkaloids
Datura stramonium	Thorn-apple	Leaves, unripe capsules and especially the seeds	Alkaloids, not destroyed by drying or storage
Euonymus europaeus	Spindle	Bark, leaves and fruit	Still to be identified
Euphorbia species	Spurges	All	Volatile oil
Ligustrum vulgaris	Privet	Berries and possibly leaves	Glycoside
Ranunculus species	Buttercups and crowfoots	Sap	Protoanemonin, unstable to drying and storage
Solanum dulcamara	Woody nightshade, bittersweet	All	Glycoalkaloid
Solanum nigrum	Black nightshade, garden nightshade	All	Glycoalkaloid
Tamus communis	Black bryony	Roots and berries	Still to be identified

Woodland Plants

Scientific Name	Common Name	Poisonous Part(s)	Poisonous Constituent
Amanita muscaria	Fly agaric	All	Alkaloid and others
Amanita pantherina	Panther cap	All	Alkaloid and others
Amanita phalloides	Death cap	All	Deadly cyclopolypeptides
Arum maculatum	Cuckoo pint, lords and ladies, wild arum, etc.	All, particularly berries	Still to be identified but destroyed by drying and heating
Daphne laureola	Spurge laurel	All, particularly bark and berries	Resin and coumarin glycoside
Mercurialis species	Dog's mercury	All	Volatile oil which loses toxicity with age and is destroyed by drying and boiling
Quercus species	Oak	Acorns and leaves	Tannic acid and other constituents
Rhus toxicodendron	Poison ivy	All parts	Resinous

Swamp Plants

Scientific Name	Common Name	Poisonous Part(s)	Poisonous Constituent
Caltha palustris	Marsh marigold, kingcup	Sap	Protoanemonin, unstable to drying and storage
Cicuta virosa	Cowbane	Roots, leaves and flowers	Resinous, not destroyed by drying
Conium maculatum	Hemlock	All, especially young leaves or unripe fruits	Alkaloids, destroyed by drying and heating
Oenanthe crocata	Hemlock, water dropwort	All, especially roots	Resinous, not destroyed by drying

House Plants

Scientific Name	Common Name	Poisonous Part(s)	Poisonous Constituent
Dieffenbachia species	Dumb cane	All parts	Toxic protein and oxalate crystals
Euphorbia pulcherrima	Poinsettia	Juice of stem, leaves, flowers or fruit	Various in milky sap
Hyacinthus species and other bulbs	Hyacinth	Bulb	Still to be identified
Ricinus communis	Castor oil plant	Seeds	Phytotoxin
Viscum album	Mistletoe	Berries	Amines

1 The bright red poisonous berries of Black Bryony, Tamus communis, are conspicuous in the autumn.
2 The Winter Aconite, Eranthis hyemalis, is a poisonous plant with yellow flowers.
3 Cowbane, Cicuta virosa.
4 A young Death Cap fungus emerging from the ground. At this stage it should not be confused with the edible Puff Ball fungus.
5 The Death Cap, a poisonous fungus.

Season of use of most vegetables

Month	Fresh from the garden	Fresh from under glass	From store	Blanched	Dried
January and February	Brussels sprouts cabbage, celery coleworts Hamburgh parsley kale, leeks parsnips salsify spinach, tree onions	mustard cress	potatoes artichokes carrots garlic onions pumpkin shallots winter radish	chicory endive seakale	peas haricot beans
March	Brussels tops cabbage, kale leeks, spinach turnip tops tree onions Welsh onions for salads, leeks	lettuce mustard cress	potatoes carrots garlic onions	chicory	peas haricot beans
April	cauliflower-broccoli, leeks kale, spinach sprouting broccoli turnip tops Welsh onions	lettuce mustard cress radish rhubarb	potatoes garlic onions	chicory	peas haricot beans
May	asparagus cauliflower-broccoli, kale spinach, rhubarb spring greens spring cabbages sprouting broccoli turnip tops Welsh onions	lettuce radish rhubarb	potatoes garlic		
June	asparagus potatoes, peas broad beans, lettuce cabbage, rhubarb spring onions	lettuce	potatoes		
July	beetroot, cabbage broad beans, peas carrots, dwarf beans courgettes globe artichokes kohlrabi, potatoes spinach, spring onions radish, turnips vegetable marrow	tomatoes			
August	as for July plus: cucumbers, calabrese self blanching celery runner beans, melons sweet corn, tomatoes	tomatoes cucumbers melons aubergines sweet peppers	garlic		
September	as for August except: dwarf beans, broad beans, globe artichokes but with cauliflowers	as for August	garlic		
October	beetroot, cabbage, cauliflower, cauliflower-broccoli, celery celeriac, kohlrabi turnips, swedes, winter radish	tomatoes lettuce	potatoes, onions carrots garlic tomatoes	endive chicory	
November and December	cabbage cauliflower-broccoli celery, celeriac parsnips, salsify Brussels sprouts spinach artichokes Hamburgh parsley	lettuce mustard and cress corn salad	artichokes garlic pumpkin potatoes swedes onions carrots shallots	endive chicory seakale	peas haricot beans

Note: Savoys are included as cabbages during the winter months

Labour-saving gardening

It is obviously sensible to make a garden as labour-saving as possible; there are always opportunities of carrying out extra work or obtaining more exercise if required, but the reverse is not necessarily true. When planning the garden look to the future.

First you should decide whether the problem is to save time or to reduce physical effort. When you are at the height of your business career, time is probably at a premium. When you retire, you have plenty of time but by then the saving of physical effort becomes of paramount importance. Then, too, there is the question of saving money. On retirement there is usually a drop in income. So that it may be sensible to abandon bedding out schemes and put the area down to long grass or to ground covering plants.

One of the greatest joys of gardening is to produce your own food, and there is no question that vegetables straight from the garden have a flavour and a succulence lost from those which have come from the market and shop. Where space is limited it is generally impossible to devote ground to fruit or vegetables, yet it is possible to sow seed of carrots, lettuce, radish and similar plants in among the flowers in the borders, where they are easily disguised. But if the garden is large enough to accommodate a special place for vegetables it is always worth while to take them seriously from the beginning.

Kitchen garden

It is far easier to plan a kitchen garden where the garden is a new one. The gardener who takes over a garden used by previous occupiers may first have to remove shrubs and trees. Not only do trees, shrubs and hedges rob the vegetable garden of plant foods, but they cast shade over the growing plants. Few of the vegetables we grow tolerate shade and the site for the kitchen garden must, therefore, be quite open and unshaded. Brick walls and wood fences cast shade, too, but a wall or fence at the north side is often advantageous in protecting plants from cold north winds. In the past, many kitchen gardens on large estates were laid out in front of a south facing wall and many sites may be made more suitable for vegetable cultivation if wind-breaks are set up to break the force of strong westerly or easterly winds. This is particularly true of gardens in coastal areas and although chestnut or wire mesh fences are worth consideration, living windbreaks such as blackberries are more decorative and useful if trained to a strong trellis.

Provision must be made for paths, a garden shed, the cold frame, a site for compost heaps and possibly for a greenhouse. Even in the large kitchen garden, the number of permanent paths should be the minimum necessary, but sufficiently wide for the barrow to be wheeled

comfortably without damage to plants nearby. During the season, temporary paths covered with straw, bracken or peat, allow all crops to be reached with ease. The garden shed may be erected in any out-of-the-way corner provided it is linked to a permanent path so that the gardener does not get wet feet when visiting the shed in winter. The site for the compost heap may be somewhat shaded, but not beneath large, spreading trees. Sufficient room must be left for two heaps because when one is fermenting, another will be built alongside it. There must also be sufficient space left for turning and sifting compost. The gardener who uses animal manure will also leave a few square yards where dung may be stacked. Here shade may be of value in preventing the manure from drying out in summer. Both the cold frame and the greenhouse need a south-facing, open site.

Although most vegetable crops are temporary, rhubarb is generally considered as a permanent kitchen garden crop because the clumps remain in the same soil for around ten years. When allocating a plot for rhubarb, the gardener should bear in mind that although the plants tolerate some shade, crops are better from plants grown at some distance from walls, fences and trees or hedges.

Good cultivation is essential if the

A general view of the kitchen garden in the Royal Horticultural Society's Gardens, Wisley, Surrey.

best results are to be obtained. The plot should be dug over with great thoroughness and weeds, both annual and perennial, must be kept down.

Vegetables of one plant species do not extract the same quantities of soil chemicals in the ground as do plants of a different species, but the manuring plan and the cropping plan take this into account. After the soil has been well dug and all weeds and weed roots removed, the garden should be divided (on paper or, at any rate mentally) into three plots. These divisions are made so that what is known as crop rotation may be practised. This practice is also aimed at preventing a build up of soil pests in any one part of the garden. It is understandable that if cabbages and their close relatives, for example, are grown for several years in the same piece of ground, the soil will be impoverished (unless the manuring programme is a very generous one) and that pests, which thrive on the roots of the brassica group of plants, are likely to increase. A three year rotation is generally advised and the following plan suggests how this may be carried out.

The kitchen garden is divided into three plots of approximately equal size— A, B and C.

Cropping plan

First season
Plot A cabbages, brussels sprouts, cauliflower broccoli, turnips
Plot B beans, peas, miscellaneous, small crops
Plot C potatoes, carrots, beetroot, lettuce, onions

Second season The crops shown in Plot C above will be grown on Plot A, crops in Plot A on Plot B and those in Plot B on Plot C
Plot A potatoes etc
Plot B cabbages etc
Plot C beans etc

Third season The position of the crops will be as follows:
Plot A beans etc
Plot B potatoes etc
Plot C cabbages etc

Fourth season In the fourth season, the rotation starts off as in the first year

Until recently the vegetable garden was regularly dressed with animal manures. Those gardeners who are able to obtain farmyard or stable manure (at reasonable prices) are well advised to use them. For all other gardeners, home-made garden compost adequately replaces large quantities of animal manures. Other organic manures such as municipal compost, seaweed, wool shoddy and spent hops are also of great value in maintaining soil fertility and in improving the actual structure of the soil. Manure, compost or other bulky organic materials should not be applied in an unplanned fashion. This is not only because the gardener may have to purchase organic manures but their addition to parts of the garden may lead to poor crops. In the case of parsnips, for instance, the roots are 'fanged' instead of being single, straight and plump, if the crop is grown in soil which had been recently manured. With other crops, there is generally sufficient food left from a previous manuring.

The following plan suggests how manure, compost or other bulky organics should be applied over three years.

Manuring plan

Plot A cabbages, cauliflowers, brussels sprouts broccoli, kale, savoys, turnips. Possibly inter-cropped with radish and lettuce.
Limed in late autumn, if necessary. Manured or composted during winter digging
Plot B potatoes, followed by broccoli, spring cabbage or leeks.
Not limed. Manured or composted during winter digging
Plot C carrots, parsnips, beetroot, peas, beans summer spinach, onions.
No manure or compost except for pea and bean trenches and for onions. Wood ashes (if available) forked in and a complete fertiliser, such as Growmore, may be applied just before sowings are made

Inter-cropping is referred to in the manuring plan. This practice allows two plants to grow in the place of one. Inter-cropping is of great importance in the small kitchen garden. For good results the soil must be very fertile so that neither of the two crops is starved of food. It is also essential that the rows should run from north to south so that shade does not fall throughout the day from the taller on to the shorter plants. Too much shade of this nature is liable to lead to troubles with pests and diseases. Here is an example of inter-cropping. Rows of peas, which make 3 foot high bine, are sown 3 feet apart, leaving 1 yard between which may be used for radish, spinach or lettuce.

Successional cropping is somewhat similar to inter-cropping because many crops, grown for successional crops, may be cultivated between or alongside vegetables needing more time to reach maturity. The aim of successional cropping is to prevent gluts and shortages. The gardener must be able to assess how many lettuces, peas, summer turnips, radishes etc., the family will require from a single sowing. He sows or sets out plants accordingly and he continues to sow every few weeks, providing he has the space for the sowings. He may start with radish, for example, by sowing three short, close rows under cloches in March. A short, double row is sown outdoors in early April, followed by a sowing between the pea rows in mid-April. Further small sowings are made in May, June and July. By sowing in this manner, there will be a supply of fresh, young radishes from mid-May until October. Lettuce seeds should be sown in small batches between March and August. For successional crops of peas, the gardener should bear in mind that there are early, mid-season and late varieties. All three kinds may be sown at around the same time and the plants will come into bearing successionally. There are also varieties of heading broccoli (cauliflower-broccoli) for cutting during the autumn, late winter, spring and early summer. With potatoes, there are kinds which bulk up for lifting in June and July; others mature more slowly for late summer use. Main-crop potatoes are not dug and stored until the autumn.

Catch-cropping, like inter-cropping, is aimed at using every available square inch of the garden. It means no more than making use of any vacant plot for a quick-growing vegetable. Radishes may be sown in April on the site reserved for outdoor tomatoes. The radish crop will have been pulled for use before the tomatoes are set out. The soil banked on either side of leek or celery trenches may be cropped with radish or lettuce.

Even the most experienced gardeners quite often fail to regulate the supply of vegetables throughout the year. In most cases, the weather is to blame. A warm June, for instance, may hasten the summer and autumn cabbage crops but lead to disaster among the lettuces which bolt at once after forming hearts. A severe winter may cripple broccoli and spring cabbages. So very often, too, due to the vagaries of the weather, there are many fine lettuce and radish for use when the family is away on holiday. Arrangements should be made for these crops to be harvested and shared by neighbours while the family is away. Unless friends, relations or neighbours help in this way, the gardener is likely to return from holiday to find his bean plants covered with a useless crop of old, stringy pods.

Some gardeners are reluctant, and bend their efforts to the creation of a garden which is mainly a pleasant place in which to rest and relax. An important part—and in some cases the whole—of a garden of this nature must be paved, and although decorated with plants in containers or in gaps in the paving there should be plenty of space for chairs and tables.

Choice of furniture for the patio is important. Chairs and tables of wood or metal, which will stand being left out in all weathers, should be supplemented by folding chairs for longer and more relaxed sessions. In the latter kind, tubular aluminium and synthetic fabrics are rapidly replacing the wooden frames and canvas of the deckchair. Aluminium garden furniture is light to handle and folds compactly for storage. If it should be left out in a summer downpour, it will come to no harm. Metal garden furniture of the permanent kind can take a number of attractive forms, ranging from wrought iron, painted white and preferably rendered rustproof, to reproductions, in cast aluminium, of old Victorian cast-iron seats and tables of pleasing design. Teak and elm furniture, too, stand up well in all weathers, although they do tend to deteriorate after a few years if they are regularly left out through the winter. Storing bulky furniture of this kind, however, can create problems

A number of creeping and prostrate plants seem to suffer little damage from being trodden underfoot. Crevices left between the stones when the paving is being laid will serve as pockets for this type of plant. Herbs figure largely in this category and all varieties of *Thymus serpyllum*, in particular, stand up well to this harsh treatment. These include 'Annie Hall', with lilac flowers, 'Pink Chintz', *T. s. lanuginosus*, with grey, hairy leaves and *T. s. splendens*, with crimson flowers.

The low-growing mint, *Mentha requienii*, a species that makes dense mats of dark green aromatic foliage, is equally useful, while small alpine plants such as thrift, aubrietas and rock pinks can be used in corners and places that get less wear and tear.

If the patio is of reasonable size, it can also have one or more flower beds. Like the patio pool, these should be geometrical in shape. Circles, rectangles or L-shaped beds will usually be most satisfactory. Such beds are ideal for spring and summer bedding schemes. It is probably a good idea, however, to settle for a major display during summer, bearing in mind that the patio will then get its greatest use. Summer-flowering heaths or floribunda roses provide permanent and trouble-free planting

Paradoxically, although a certain formality is a feature of this modern type

A patio, originally a roofless inner court, has in Britain come to mean an area outside, often covered over

40

of gardening, it was an essential part of garden planning and planting many years ago and in some ways the wheel appears to be turning a full circle.

Formal gardens

In the early days of gardening in the British Isles, garden designs were based on geometric patterns, always emphasising regularity of form. During Elizabethan times topiary and terraces with heraldic beasts as ornaments, and quiet lawns were the order of the day; trees were always planted in a row or regular pattern. Later, avenues became longer, 'walks', square fish ponds, and mazes or labyrinths were constructed and parterres of the most intricate design represented the height of garden beauty and decoration. These parterres were intricately designed, the outline traced in clipped hedges, often very low and usually of box, the interstices filled, either with plants or coloured stones and other minerals, one colour to a space, to form a pattern in the parterre garden as a whole. There were frequent variations on this theme, height being added by clipped trees, often cut into formal shapes, but always the gardener's handiwork imposed formal arrangement upon nature. Frequently great vistas were treated in this way, always executed on level ground and matching the design of the house. Terraces and vantage points were usually constructed so that these large designs could be looked down upon and enjoyed as a whole. Examples still exist at Cliveden, in Buckinghamshire, and at Oxburgh Hall, Norfolk, where from the 80 foot high gatehouse one can look down upon the formal garden.

Thus, up to the eighteenth century, every garden was formal, regularly designed and ornamented with topiary, statues, arbours and fountains. Pope and Addison had in their writings loudly criticised formality and when Lancelot ('Capability') Brown some years later advocated the great sweeping aside of the closely designed plots in favour of landscape effects, such great parks as Longleat, Harewood House and Blenheim were created. Humphry Repton, working in the late eighteenth and early nineteenth centuries, followed in Brown's footsteps, although his schemes were not on as large a scale and he made the transition between house and garden more gradual by introducing terraces and balustraded walks. But the great sweep towards the natural, spacious style, where plants were used to emulate nature in woodland, water gardens and stonework continued; except for a sudden retrogression during

1 Knot beds, at Vannes, using Box edging, coloured earth and plants.
2 Clipped trees are a feature of the formal garden at Blickling Hall, Norfolk, a National Trust property.

The eyes of the potato are in fact buds. When seed potatoes are put in the dark to sprout before planting the shoots grow from these eyes or buds

Bud formations

Buds help to identify trees still barren of foliage. More important, buds are a key to correct pruning and propagation.

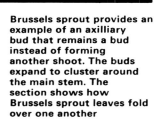

Brussels sprout provides an example of an axilliary bud that remains a bud instead of forming another shoot. The buds expand to cluster around the main stem. The section shows how Brussels sprout leaves fold over one another

An axilliary bud is one that arises in the axil of the leaf or in the angle between the leaf stalk and main stem. Example: the catalpa

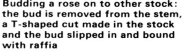

Budding a rose on to other stock: the bud is removed from the stem, a T-shaped cut made in the stock and the bud slipped in and bound with raffia

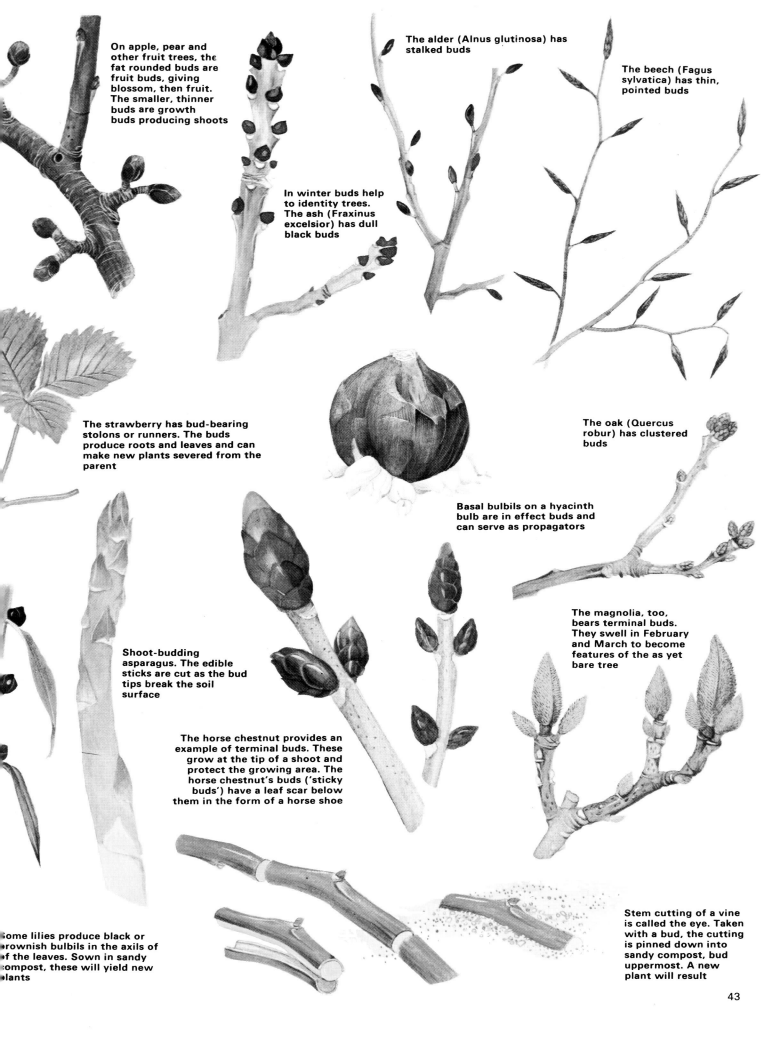

On apple, pear and other fruit trees, the fat rounded buds are fruit buds, giving blossom, then fruit. The smaller, thinner buds are growth buds producing shoots

The alder (Alnus glutinosa) has stalked buds

The beech (Fagus sylvatica) has thin, pointed buds

In winter buds help to identity trees. The ash (Fraxinus excelsior) has dull black buds

The strawberry has bud-bearing stolons or runners. The buds produce roots and leaves and can make new plants severed from the parent

The oak (Quercus robur) has clustered buds

Basal bulbils on a hyacinth bulb are in effect buds and can serve as propagators

Shoot-budding asparagus. The edible sticks are cut as the bud tips break the soil surface

The magnolia, too, bears terminal buds. They swell in February and March to become features of the as yet bare tree

The horse chestnut provides an example of terminal buds. These grow at the tip of a shoot and protect the growing area. The horse chestnut's buds ('sticky buds') have a leaf scar below them in the form of a horse shoe

Some lilies produce black or brownish bulbils in the axils of of the leaves. Sown in sandy compost, these will yield new plants

Stem cutting of a vine is called the eye. Taken with a bud, the cutting is pinned down into sandy compost, bud uppermost. A new plant will result

The Royal Horticultural Society's wild garden at Wisley, Surrey.

Victorian days. Then intricate and elaborate bedding schemes became fashionable. Carpet bedding was used for effect and drawing-board design returned to the flower garden. Since then, chiefly through the work and writing of William Robinson and his followers, natural planting schemes have been very widely used, exploiting plant colour, form and texture in many ways. But formality still had its adherents in such men as Sir Reginald Blomfield, Harold Peto and Sir Edwin Lutyens, all architects. Modern examples of formal gardens are those of several private houses designed by Lutyens, the gardens perfectly integrated into the design by his partner Miss Gertrude Jekyll. Such places as Orchards, Godalming (1896), The Deanery at Sonning, on the Thames (1899) and Tyringham, Buckinghamshire (1924) were designed by this remarkable partnership. Around the turn of the century Major Lawrence Johnston, architect and artist, started to make his famous garden at Hidcote Bartrim, Gloucestershire, one of the finest examples of a formal garden, although it is informally planted. It consists, in fact, of a number of gardens, separated by fine hedges, each one a perfect garden on its own.

Examples of formal gardens open to the public are Belton House, Lincolnshire; Castle Ashby, Northamptonshire; Cliveden, Buckinghamshire; Compton Wynyates, Warwickshire; Easton Neston, Northamptonshire; Hampton Court, Middlesex; Haseley Court, Oxfordshire; Hidcote, Gloucestershire; Holkham Hall, Norfolk; Lanhydrock (rose garden), Cornwall; Oxburgh Hall, Norfolk; Packwood House, Warwickshire; Shrubland Park, Suffolk; Wightwick Manor, Staffordshire.

Wild gardens

The wild garden is best described in reverse: it is not formal in any way, it should not appear to be designed, it should not contain florists' or garden strains of flowers. It may be defined as cultivating hardy species in surroundings which suit them, and enjoying the best effect they can give. It followed as a natural revulsion from the artificiality of Victorian times, when the species of plants grown in shrubberies and flower beds was generally very limited, despite those who tried to catalogue and distribute the many new plants becoming available. In short, the gardeners in Great Britain after having been collectors of 'simples' and popular flowers, having passed through the Dutch formal era, followed by the park-planting era and the monotony of the late nineteenth century, became collectors again.

Types of wild garden The wild garden can be nature unadorned but slightly tidied, as may be found on English commons where heather and gorse are offset by slender birch and rugged pine, the whole creating a satisfying picture by means of a little pruning and shaping of the view; or it may be the chalky upland complete with its scabious and knapweed in the turf, supplemented by wild rose, juniper and whitebeam; or in an oak wood, with a small brook adorned by hazel and woodbine, bluebells and ferns. Such scenes sometimes adjoin country gardens. They lead on to the second type of wild garden produced by embellishing such landscapes with a sympathetic planting of exotics. Chinese birches and pines, tree heaths, and different kinds of broom could be used in the first instance; on the chalk various viburnums, cotoneasters and berberis would blend well with the natives, and Japanese maples, azaleas and rhododendrons seem the obvious choice in the oak woodland.

The embellishment thus added is regarded as 'painting' the landscape. The gardener not only needs new situations for his ever-increasing acquisitions, but feels the desire to add colour to a view. The most usual idea of this sort is the planting of daffodils in grassy meadows and thin woodland; the larger colourful hybrids should be eschewed in favour of the smaller wild species together with the unsophisticated smaller hybrids, both new and old, to achieve a natural effect.

A third type of wild garden is made by taking an unadorned plot and creating a 'natural landscape' of exotic plants and shrubs. It often degenerates into a hotch-potch of trees and shrubs growing in the rough grass—simply the overflow from the designed garden area around the house belonging to a keen plantsman. The influx of species and the creation of innumerable hybrids, coupled with the ease with which they can be grown in the right conditions with little labour has resulted in innumerable woodlands throughout the country being filled with colourful plants such as rhododendrons, rather than the woodland landscape being gently embellished with them.

In size a wild garden can be quite small or run to many acres. A grassy bank with a rough hedge behind can be given bulbs and species of roses, honeysuckles and a tree or two; a ditch or depression can be planted with moisture-loving irises, rodgersias and peltiphyllum if in sunshine, while shady banks will take ferns and hostas. The heath garden is a well-known style of wild gardening, where sheets of erica, calluna, vaccinium, gaultherias, mingle with burnet roses, tree lupins, brooms and gorse. On arid limestone and chalk numerous Chinese species of shrubs and plants will thrive. In general the choice among bulbous plants should be confined to species (double daffodils, big florists' tulips, gross hybrid lilies, fancy-coloured hemerocallis are not suitable). Among herbaceous plants the choice should be confined to those which will make a dense clump, slowly increasing, or a dense mass of stems which may increase quickly by underground roots: examples of the former are hemerocallis and hosta; of the latter, *Senecio tanguticus* and *Macleaya microcarpa;* they should also be plants which will stand erect without staking. Turning to shrubs, here again species are preferable; the choice should avoid gawky awkward growers, and concentrate on those which cover the ground densely, such as *Viburnum tomentosum* and *Cotoneaster conspicua,*

A border of mixed shrubs selected for either their flower or foliage colour makes a decorative feature.

or which grow aloft gracefully, allowing light and air to something growing beneath them, such as *Magnolia wilsonii*. A stalky prickly shrub will prove an awkward plant when a nettle or bellbind settles itself among the roots. In the English landscape, composed of softly rounded wild shrubs and trees in a gently undulating landscape, a fastigiate conifer or poplar can strike a disturbing note; likewise a recurrence of a weeping tree can mar, although one specimen may be an asset. In many ways a rock garden may be considered as a wild garden, when its plants are chosen from among those which will take care of themselves and cascade over well-placed rocks.

Shrub gardening

There can be no other form of gardening that has enjoyed a more rapid growth in popularity since the Second World War than the cultivation of shrubs. This is understandable, since the great majority are easy to grow, tolerant of a wide range of soil conditions—apart from the calcifuges, or lime-haters, such as rhododendrons, camellias and other similar groups of shrubs. Most shrubs are also relatively undemanding as far as maintenance operations are concerned.

In Britain gardeners are fortunate as the climate makes it possible to grow plants from almost every country in the world. Shrubs are no exception and plant hunters such as Robert Fortune, George Forrest and Frank Kingdon-Ward have explored five continents to provide an astonishing wealth of material for gardens. Camellias and rhododendrons from the Himalaya and other parts of Asia can be grown with the striking Chilean firebush, *Embothrium coccineum*. Brooms from Spain, Portugal, Morocco and Madeira grow happily alongside miniature shrubs from the Alps and the Canadian Rockies. South African shrubs grow next to whin and gorse from the Scottish moors.

Ways of using shrubs There are many different ways of making use of shrubs in the garden. Although the 'shrubbery' of Victorian gardens, which was generally an uninteresting collection of dingy laurels and privets, still lingers on in some of our parks and open

Shrubs for specific purposes

For partly shaded situations

Acer japonicum (Japanese maple)
Aucuba japonica (spotted laurel)
Berberis (various) (barberry)
Buxus sempervirens (box)
Camellia
Choisya ternata (Mexican orange)
Cotoneaster simonsii
Daphne mezereum (mezereon)
Garrya elliptica (silk tassel bush)
Genista (various) (broom)
Hedera (various) (ivy)
Hypericum (St John's wort)
Ilex (holly)
Kerria japonica (Jew's mallow)
Viburnum tinus (laurustinus)
Mahonia aquifolium (Oregon grape)
Pernettya
Pyracantha (firethorn)
Ruscus aculeatus (butcher's broom)
Sambucus nigra aurea (golden elder)
Vinca major and Vinca minor (periwinkle)

Foliage effects

Artemisia abrotanum (southernwood, lad's love)
Arundinaria and Phyllostachys (bamboo)
†*Cornus alba sibirica* and *C. alba variegata* (dogwood)
**Cotinus coggygria* (smoke bush)
†*Elaeagnus pungens variegata* (wood olive)
*Euonymus alata
 Hebe (shrubby veronica)

**Hypericum patulum* (St John's wort)
 Laurus nobilis (sweet bay)
 Pachysandra terminalis
 Phlomis fruticosa (Jerusalem sage)
*Ribes americanum (American black currant)
 Romneya coulteri (Californian tree poppy)
 Rosmarinus officinalis (rosemary)
 Ruta graveolens (rue)
 Santolina chamaecyparissus (cotton lavender)
 Senecio maritima
 Sorbaria arborea
 Spiraea arguta (bridal wreath)
 Viburnum davidii
*Vitis coignetiae
†*Weigela florida variegata*
*Good autumn leaf colour
†Variegated foliage

Berried shrubs

 Arbutus unedo (strawberry tree)
 Aronia arbutifolia (red chokeberry)
 Aucuba japonica (spotted laurel)
 Berberis (various, barberry)
***Celastrus orbiculata* (climbing bittersweet)
 Clerodendrum trichotomum
 Gaultheria procumbens (partridge berry)
 Hippophaë rhamnoides (sea buckthorn)
 Ilex (various, holly)
 Pernettya
**Pyracantha (firethorn)
 Skimmia japonica
 Symphoricarpos albus laevigatus (snowberry)
 Vaccinium myrsinites (evergreen blueberry)

Viburnum (various)
**Wall shrubs

Shrubs for chalk

Aesculus parviflora (bottlebrush buckeye)
Azara microphylla
Berberis (all) (barberry)
Buddleia davidii (butterfly bush)
Choisya ternata (Mexican orange)
Cistus (rock rose)
Cotinus (all)
Cotoneaster (all)
Deutzia
Erica carnea, E. x *darleyensis* (heaths)
Escallonia (Chilean gum box)
Forsythia (golden bells)
Hibiscus syriacus (tree hollyhock)
Syringa (all) (lilac)
Philadelphus (mock orange)
Potentilla (shrubby cinquefoil)
Rhus (all)
Spiraea (all)
Symphoricarpos (all) (snowberry)
Viburnum (all)

Waterside planting shrubs

Arundinaria, Phyllostachys (bamboo)
Cornus alba, C. stolonifera (dogwood)
Cortaderia (pampas grass)
Philadelphus (mock orange)
Sambucus (elder)
Viburnum opulus sterile (snowball tree)
Weigela

45

spaces, it has all but disappeared from private gardens.

Today shrubs are used individually, at focal points of interest, as lawn specimens, in borders devoted entirely to them, or in conjunction with herbaceous perennials and bulbous plants in a mixed border (a type of planting that is becoming increasingly popular).

The ancient Japanese adopted a very different attitude and imposed a rigid discipline on their designs. Their three styles of gardening create the "garden of movement", the "garden of contemplation", and the "garden of the borrowed landscape", all self-descriptive terms. They can be lovely, but we generally prefer to use our gardens rather than merely look at them, and the effects are gained largely as a result of constant attention and meticulous grooming.

Seaside gardening
The almost constant enemies of seaside gardening are wind, salt and sand. Frost, however, is neither so prolonged nor so severe on the coast as it is inland, and seaside gardeners have been able to grow many frost-tender plants in the milder climate of their coastal gardens.

Inland gardeners have little idea how powerful is the effect of coastal wind on the growth of plants, and because none or few trees or buildings present a barrier to soften its effect during windy conditions the wind sweeps continuously in from the sea. Wind stunts and it

Shrubs for milder maritime areas

Abelia grandiflora
Abutilon megapotamicum
  A. vitifolium
Artemisia canescens
  A. stelleriana
Azara dentata
  A. microphylla
Berberis thunbergii atropurpurea
  superba
Buddleia auriculata
  B. globosa 'Lemon Ball'
  B. nivea
Calceolaria integrifolia
Callistemon citrinus
Cassia corymbosa
Cassinia fulvida
  C. ledifolius
  C. leptophylla
Ceanothus 'Autumn Blue'
  C. impressus
  C. 'Indigo'
  C. rigidus
  C. veitchianus
Centaurea gymnocarpa
Choisya ternata
Cistus crispus 'Sunset'
  C. 'Paladin Pat'
  C. palhirhaii
  C. purpureus
  C. skanbergii
Clianthus puniceus
Colquhounia vestita

Convolvulus cneorum
Corokia virgata
Crinodendron hookerianum
Daphne mezereum
  D. odora
Desfontainea spinosa
Echium fastuosum
Elaeagnus macrophylla
Embothrium coccineum
Erica australis
  E. alpina
  E. lusitanicus
Escallonia hybrids
Eucalyptus globulus
  E. gunnii
  E. niphophylla
  E. pauciflora
Eupatorium micranthum
Fabiana imbricata
Fatsia japonica
Fremontia californica
Fuchsias (large-flowered)
Halimium alyssoides
  H. ocymoides
Hoheria glabrata
  H. sexstylosa
Hebes (in variety to include *H. hulkeana*)
Helichrysum petiolatum
  H. plicatum
Hypericum moserianum tricolor
  H. 'Rowallane'
Jasminum polyanthum

Shrubs for milder maritime areas (cont.)

Jasminum primulinum
Jovellana violacea
Lavandula stoechas
Lavatera assurgensifolia
Leonotis leonurus
Leptospermum scoparium nichollsii
   L. 'Red Damask'
Lippia citriodora
Muehlenbeckia complexa
Myrtus communis
   M. luma
   M. ugni
Olearia insignis
   O. × *scilloniensis*
   O. semidentata
   O. solandri
Paulownia tomentosa
Phlomis fruticosa
   P. italica
Phormium tenax
Piptanthus laburnifolius
Pittosporum eugenioides

Pittosporum ralphii
   P. tobira
Polygala myrtifolia
Rosmarinus angustifolius
   R. 'Corsican Blue'
   R. lavendulaceus
   R. 'Majorca Pink'
   R. 'Severn Sea'
   R. 'Tuscan Blue'
Salvia grahamii
   S. involucrata bethellii
Sambucus nigra foliis aureus
Senecio cineraria
   S. c. 'White Diamond'
   S. glastifolius
   S. huntii
   S. heritieri
   S. leucostachys
   S. rotundifolius
Solanum crispum
   S. jasminoides
Teucrium fruticans azureum
Yucca gloriosa

Shrubs for colder maritime areas

Amelanchier canadensis
Arbutus unedo
Atriplex canescens
   A. halimus
Aucuba japonica

Baccharis patagonica
Berberis aquifolium
   B. darwinii
   B. stenophylla
   B. thunbergii atropurpurea

deforms—one has only to observe the fantastic shapes of trees close to the sea to realise this.

Salt can kill outright. Salt is carried in the spray and when this is caught up by the wind it is often deposited many hundreds of yards inland. Few plants are able to withstand the continual battering of sea-wind heavily charged with salt, which is heavily scorching to plants.

Sand-blast is often too lightly regarded by newcomers to the coast, though its effect can be quite as damaging as that of salt. Seashore gardens suffer badly from its searing effect when the wind picks up the sand from a nearby beach. Small seedlings are killed and adult foliage is bruised and blackened.

The only answer to the problem of wind, salt and sand is shelter, and it is not possible to create a worthwhile garden in extremely exposed positions on the coast without it, though where a garden has protection a very wide range of plants will thrive which would not succeed in frosty gardens inland. Many plants will grow only when given adequate shelter at the outset, and the planting of newly-made gardens exposed to the full ravages of gales off the sea is

1 Fuchsia 'Pink Galore'.
2 Fatsia japonica, an evergreen shrub.
3 Abelia grandiflora.
4 Yucca gloriosa.
5 Convolvulus cneorum.

Berberis wilsonae
Buddleia davidii (in variety)
  B. globosa
Caragana arborescens
Caryopteris × *clandonensis*
Ceanothus × *burkwoodii*
  C. 'Cascade'
  C. 'Gloire de Versailles'
  C. 'Henri Defosse'
  C. 'Topaz'
  C. thyrsiflorus
Cistus corbariensis
  C. ladaniferus
  C. laurifolius
  C. populifolius
  C. 'Silver Pink'
Clematis flammula
Colutea arborescens
Coronilla glauca
  C. emerus
Cortaderia argentea
Cotoneasters (in variety)
Crataegus (in variety)
Cytisus battandieri
  C. scoparius hybrids
Elaeagnus ebbingei
  E. pungens aureo-variegata
Escallonia 'C. F. Ball'
  E. edinensis
  E. × *langleyensis*
  E. macrantha
Euonymus japonicus
Euphorbia veneta (*E. wulfenii*)
Garrya elliptica
Genista aethnensis
  G. lydia

G. hispanica
Griselinia littoralis
Hebe brachysiphon
  H. dieffenbachii
  H. 'Midsummer Beauty'
  H. salicifolia
Hibiscus in variety
Hippophaë rhamnoides
Hydrangeas (in variety)
Hypericum patulum 'Hidcote'
  H. androsaemum
Lavandulas (in variety)
Lavatera olbia rosea
Leycesteria formosa
Lonicera ledebourii
Lupinus arboreus
Lycium chinense
Medicago arborea
Olearia albida
  O. haastii
  O. macrodonta -
Perovskia atriplicifolia
Phormium tenax
Pittosporum tenuifolium
Potentillas (in variety)
Prunus spinosa
Pyracanthas (in variety)
Ribes alpinum
  R. atrosanguineum
  Romneya × *hybrida*
Rosa rugosa (and its hybrids)
  R. spinosissima (and its hybrids)
Rosmarinus 'Miss Jessup's Upright'
  R. officinalis
Santolina chamaecyparissus
  S. incana

S. neapolitana
S. virens
Senecio laxifolius
  S. monroi
Spartium junceum
Symphoricarpos orbiculata
  S. microphylla
Tamarix pentandra
Teucrium fruticans
Ulex europaeus plenus
Viburnum tinus
Yucca filamentosa

Some plants for seaside gardens (including tender kinds)

Agapanthus (species and hybrids)
Amaryllis belladonna
Aster pappei
Alstroemeria 'Ligtu Hybrids'
Convolvulus mauritanicus
Crambe cordifolia
Crinum (species and hybrids)
Crocosmia masonorum
Dimorphotheca barberiae compacta
  D. ecklonis
Gazanias
Kniphofias such as 'Maid of Orleans'
Mesembryanthemums
Montbretia (hybrids)
Myosotidium nobile
Odontospermum maritimum
Othonnopsis cheirifolia
× *Venidio-arctotis*
Zantesdeschia aethiopica

rarely successful without the aid of some artificial wind-screen.

Plantings of shelter belts of trees on a large scale benefit from an open fence of a two-bar wooden structure interwoven with foliage of gorse or spruce. For small gardens there is nothing better than a fence of wooden laths, one inch wide with spaces between of similar size, set vertically on a stout wooden framework and posts at either end for driving into the ground. Avoid a solid barricade such as a wall, which causes wind-turbulence on the lee side, since the aim is always to filter the wind rather than obstruct it.

Plants which tolerate salt and wind are nowadays very largely selected from those grown in Australia and New Zealand. As a result of long coastlines and varied climatic conditions more successful seaside shrubs have evolved in Australia and New Zealand than in any other part of the world. Shrubs that successfully resist salt-spray are planted facing the sea. These are often equipped with toughened leaves such as are found in the genus *Olearia. O. haastii* and *O. albida* stand any amount of salty wind. Others have shiny leaf surfaces. *Euonymus japonicus* and *Griselinia littoralis* look bright and glossy within a

few yards of the sea. Or the leaves of some may be coated with a gummy secretion as in *Escallonia macrantha,* enabling them to endure a coating of salt. Yet another form of protection is afforded by a multitude of tiny hairs which cover the leaf surfaces of grey-leaved and silver-leaved shrubs. It is a curious fact that most of these are well adapted to withstand the first brunt of a salty blast. Sea buckthorn, *Atriplex halimus, Senecio laxifolius* and *S. monroi* are among the best we have for prominent positions in exposed coastal districts. If sand-blast is a menace, tamarisk will grow with its roots in pure sand and is also useful for adding height to rough banks and walls.

Less violent and more insidious are the obstacles to creating a garden in any major industrial town, for some of the essentials for plant growth—good soil, clean water, clear light—are just not found. But no one needs a garden more than the town dweller, so attempts go on, sometimes with surprisingly effective results.

Town gardening
Town gardens tend to be on the smaller side, and planning a town garden is not always easy. You can call on the advice of a garden designer for a surprisingly

low fee, or plan it yourself, remembering to make simplicity the keynote of your design.

You will have to take into account the need for privacy, often difficult to obtain owing to the nearness of tall, overlooking buildings, and allow for the effect of fumes and smoke. Even in 'smokeless zones' there can still be chemical fumes and deposits harmful to plants (see Pollution).

On the other hand some of the most beautiful small gardens in Britain are to be found in towns, such as the walled and paved gardens of Georgian and Victorian houses in the heart of London, with their fine trees, sun-baked walls and sheltered beds and borders full of plants chosen with an eye to their situation.

Lawns and paving For gardens smaller than ¼ of an acre paving is generally more suitable. In smaller country towns where the atmosphere is freer from pollution a small lawn might be practical, but where the space receives a lot of use paving combined with a sand pit for the younger children would be more suitable to resist the inevitable wear. In general, it is better to keep to neutral grey or natural colours for slabs and let flowers and foliage provide the brighter colour. Borders and geometrically-shaped 'cut-out' beds will provide room for bedding plants and perennials and climbing plants and wall shrubs can be trained against the wall of the house. Small raised ornamental lawns or beds of clipped dwarf box might do much to relieve the effect of uninterrupted expanses of paving.

Soil Unless you can replace the top spit of soil with good, fresh loam, it will be necessary to concentrate on improving the soil by incorporating organic materials, such as peat, hop manure, straw, compost or well-rotted manure

Privacy Artificial screening can be used to supplement the seclusion already provided by a wall or the angle of the building. If the screening is combined with climbing or trailing plants the effect will be more pleasant. For the modern-styled town house slatted or louvred plank fences will harmonise with the restrained lines of present-day architecture.

Formal bedding

Wallflowers and forget-me-nots associate well with spring bulbs but can prove unreliable if there is much winter smog. Wallflowers suffer particularly from industrial pollution of the atmosphere and the exhaust from motor vehicles.

In summer, stocks, antirrhinums, French and African marigolds, petunias, asters, alyssum and lobelia seem to thrive in towns. Salvias, begonias and the exotic-looking gloxinias stand out against an urban background. The protection from autumn frost provided by a sheltered town garden can prolong the display of half-hardy plants, such as the small bedding dahlias 'Coltness Gem' and 'Bishop of Llandaff', which are seen to good advantage in this setting. Fuchsias are a showy and long-lasting feature of town gardens: 'Ballet Girl' cerise and white; 'Constance', purple with a pink fringe; 'Penelope', white with a pink centre; 'Hidcote Beauty', salmon-pink centre with white calyx tipped green; these are all well worth growing. Zonal pelargoniums do well in towns. The bright scarlet 'Paul Crampel', the turkey-red 'Henry Jacoby' and the orange-scarlet 'Gustav Emich' are all popular. Their rather brash colours can be toned down with ornamental-leaved kinds, such as the cool silver 'Caroline Schmidt' or the golden-leaved 'Maréchal McMahon'. Two of the main fungal diseases of roses seldom affect plants growing in towns.

Walls These provide a useful background for roses. Although ramblers do not flower long enough to make them worthwhile, an exception is the lovely 'New Dawn', which first produces its flesh-pink blossoms in June and often continues flowering until December. Spicily fragrant 'New Dawn' grows best against a west wall, 'Mermaid' is a fine perpetual-

A closely planted town garden, full of carefully-placed plants.

climber that is practically evergreen, will flourish in any aspect and even produces its large primrose-yellow saucer-shaped blooms abundantly on a north wall. The fiery orange 'Danse du Feu' and the fragrant, reddish-brown 'Zéphirine Drouhin' both look good against a wall.

Although evergreen shrubs are seldom seen at their best in town gardens, pyracanthas (firethorns) seem to thrive in towns, and will provide a display of scarlet berries on a west, or even a north wall. *Berberis darwinii, B. stenophylla, Cotoneaster franchettii, Euonymus radicans* and some of the less rampant hederas (ivies) make good evergreen wall cover. The ivies are self-clinging and the erect and compact habit of the others makes it unnecessary to provide any support for the plants. The wide choice of deciduous wall shrubs includes the large-flowered clematis hybrids and *C. montana* (they should have a westerly aspect and cool root run). *Chaenomeles japonica*, the Japanese quince, and the forms 'Knap Hill Scarlet' and *C.* x *superba simonii* are good wall plants (see Chaenomeles). For the north wall there are the climbing hydrangea, *H. petiolaris* and the winter jasmine, *Jasminum nudiflorum.*

To cover a wall quickly the Russian vine, *Polygonum bilderdyckia baldschuanicum,* and the less rampant *Vitis coignetiae* are two vigorous climbers. The creepers, *Parthenocissus quinquefolia*, the true Virginian creeper, *P. henryana* and *P. tricuspidata*, should be considered, though the last is rampant and tends to smother everything it covers, so use it with care. Walls can also be used for hanging baskets and plaques and other ornamental devices.

Basements Many shade-loving shrubs and climbers will grow in the cool, shady conditions of a basement area. They will usually have to be grown in tubs or boxes. Lack of room may prevent the planting of any but the slower-growing varieties of ivies. Where a fair amount of wall needs covering you might try the attractive *Hedera colchica*, Persian ivy, sometimes known as elephant ivy on account of the size and shape of its leaves

For the more restricted wall space the slower growing varieties of the common ivy, *H. helix*, would be more appropriate, such as 'Buttercup', *conglomerata* and *tricolor.*

All the Virginian creepers already mentioned will also do well and camellias will flourish in tubs, etc. Although the flowers may be less profusely borne the beauty of their foliage will compensate for this. The tropical-looking, evergreen, palmate leaves of *Fatsia*

1 A tranquil garden in the heart of
a town.
2 The formality of paving and
evergreens blend well in town
gardens; Roses provide colour.
3 A pool and its waterside plants make
a peaceful London garden.

japonica, the false castor-oil plant,
are handsome throughout the year
Other shrubs In addition to the shrubs
recommended above for walls, most
of the barberries, including *B. darwinii,*
cotoneasters, Japanese laurel (plain
and variegated), box, holly and euonymus will thrive in town gardens.
If you do not like privet, remember the
golden form can add lustre to a garden
in winter. Spraying and syringeing
help to reduce the effect of atmospheric
pollution in winter.

Most of the popular deciduous shrubs
seem to thrive in towns, including the
butterfly bush, *Buddleia davidii,* and
all its varieties and newer hybrids,
such as 'Black Knight' and 'Royal
Red'. Brooms and heaths also adapt
well, and a combination of summer and
winter flowering heaths with varieties
of the British native, *Cytisus scoparius,*
will provide continuity of colour. Forsythias often flower several weeks
earlier in towns and mingle well with
flowering currants.

Smaller forms of philadelphus (mock
orange) add beauty to the early summer
display, including 'Belle Etoile',
'Virginal' and 'Manteau d'Hermine',

together with the crimson weigela 'Eva
Rathke' or the pink 'Vanhouttei', the
showy snowball bush, *Viburnum opulus
sterile,* and other summer-flowering
viburnums, as well as the lovely single
and double lilacs.

In winter *Hamamelis mollis,* witch
hazel, and *Viburnum tinus,* laurustinus,
and *Garrya elliptica* do well, followed a

little later by the daphnes and early-
flowering deciduous viburnums, *V.
juddii, V. carlesii* and *V. × carlcephalum.*
Trees Although large trees, such as the
London plane and the full-sized horse
chestnuts and *Sorbus aucuparia,* the
rowan, and *S. aria,* the whitebeam, will
thrive in towns, the average town garden
is more suited to the smaller ornamental

trees. The flowering crabs, such as *Malus floribunda*, seldom exceed 30 feet, and most stop at 15 or 20 feet. Other attractive species include *M. eleyi*, *M. × aldenhamensis* and *M. lemoinii* Among the many ornamental fruits 'Dartmouth Crab', 'Golden Hornet' or 'Toringo' are suitable.

Thorns (crataegus) are good small trees for the town garden. Their flowering coincides with that of the laburnum. *Laburnum × vossii* has foot-long racemes of golden flowers and grows 25–30 feet tall. It looks best as an individual specimen. The more compact *L. alpinum*, Scotch laburnum, would suit a very small garden. The laburnums contrast excellently with *Crataegus oxyacantha coccinea plena* and *C. o. rosea flore pleno*

Magnolia soulangeana grows to perfection in some of the most densely built-up areas, and *M. stellata* also flowers with considerable freedom in town gardens. Almonds, peaches and cherries begin their display in February with the pale pink blossoms of *Prunus communis*, followed by the purple-leaved plum, *P. cerasifera atropurpurea*, and the deeper crimson pink of the double peach 'Clara Meyer', then the whole range of Japanese cherries, many of which provide rich autumn leaf colour.

The false acacia, *Robinia pseudo-acacia*, is very adaptable, and although at 70 feet the type would be generally too big, the small mop-headed *R. p. inermis* seldom exceeds 15–20 feet.

Conifers and miniature trees Miniature conifers associate particularly well with paving. *Juniper chinensis pfitzeriana*, for example, is a low-growing wide-speading variety with branches that are thrust out at an angle of 45 degrees. The foliage is grey-green and the plants attain and ultimate height of 6 feet with a spread of 12 feet. *J. c. kosteriana* has a more ground-hugging habit. 'Grey Owl', a named form of *J. virginiana*, has lighter and more feathery foliage. These two last-named junipers reach about 3 feet tall and their spread extends to about 10 feet.

Several forms of *J. communis* are even more restricted. *J. c. prostata* is a wide-spreading variety with green and silver foliage; *J. c. repandens* is also low growing. Its branches spread all round and are packed with deep-green needles. *J. c. hornibrookii* is similar in habit, with grey-green foliage, making good ground cover. Others with this useful characteristic are 'Bar Harbour', a named form of *J. horizontalis*, *J. procumbens nana*, a bright-green carpeting form, and *J. sabina tamariscifolia*, which has grey, feathery foliage turning green as it approaches maturity.

The dwarf Japanese maples, with their finely-cut lacy foliage contrast with the darker-coloured more solid textured conifers. Elegant and slow growing are

Acer palmatum dissectum atropurpureum and *A. p. d. palmatifidum* (see Acer). These miniature trees, which have the gnarled look and much of the general appearance of Japanese bonsai, do best in partial shade. By planting *Aesculus parviflora*, the dwarf buckeye, it is possible to enjoy the beauty of horse chestnut blossom. Dwarf rhododendrons also retain the charm and flamboyance of their taller hybrid relations. The more compact kinds, such as 'Bluebird', 'Blue Tit', and 'Carmen' and 'Elizabeth' with blood-red and orange-scarlet flowers respectively, given acid soil, will flourish.

Many town or city dwellers have no land which they can cultivate as a garden, but can get on to the roof of their building, and despite the set of double disadvantages with which they are faced it is still possible to create on a town roof a garden which can be a real delight.

Roof gardens

The problems involved in roof gardening are entirely different from those encountered in gardening at ground level. Basically the main difference is in depth of soil. At ground level one plants and grows in soils that have greater depth, even though the productive surface may be only a few inches deep. Even in the dryest weather there exists under the growing plants a reservoir of moisture from which the roots can obtain some sustenance, however slight. In well-drained soils this may not be apparent in the top few inches but it can easily be replaced by a few hours of thorough

The parapet of a roof garden richly clad with a mixture of plants to give both foliage and flowering effect.

watering. On the roof soil must necessarily be so shallow that moisture drains away quickly and can be replaced only by constant watering. There is no underground supply on which to draw.

Shallow soil also means that thick, strong, anchoring tap roots cannot move downwards in the soil without quickly meeting the impervious surface of the roof. So large trees and shrubs cannot normally be grown to maturity, although while young some can be useful as a foil and protection to the mainly low-growing vegetation.

The necessarily swift drainage from the shallow soil on roof gardens means that essential plant foods and minerals are quickly leached by the constant natural or artificial watering. The nutrients lost must be replaced with much greater frequency than is necessary at ground level.

Roof gardens are much more likely to be affected by changes in the weather. The sun is always hotter on the roof, the rain more concentrated, the wind stronger and less predictable. On the other hand a roof garden is probably always slightly warmer in winter, partly because of slight heat from the building below, and partly because the sharp drainage does not allow a base of frozen soil. Frosts also tend naturally to drift down from the roof to the streets

below and find their own level.

As roof gardening is an artificial form of gardening compared with that practised at ground level, design and planning should be equally artificial. You should not, to take just one example, try to make a naturalistic hill on a roof garden. Because the tendency on a roof is for the visitor to cast his eyes outwards to the distant view beyond, you should aim to provide a barrier to the eye in the form of such masses of colour that the overwhelming brightness attracts and holds the eye.

Before planning the creation of a roof garden you should always check first on your roof surface. You should ask yourself (and if in doubt get expert advice) whether the roof structure is strong enough to take the burden of the extra weight involved in possibly large quantities of moist soil. You should ensure that the actual surface material is sufficiently thick and impermeable to withstand both constant contact with moisture and the considerable pressures exerted by the hard edges of weighty containers, particularly when the roof surface may be softened by the heat of

1 In the centre of a large city the only space for a garden may be on the roof. This one is over a large London department store.
2 Paving and stonework make a clean surface for a roof garden.
3 An urban roof garden can be a bright spot in spring.
4 A pleasant screening effect.

52

the sun. You should ascertain that drainage from the roof is both efficient and sufficient. You should also investigate local bye-laws or landlord's agreements to discover whether there exists any ban on roof gardening. The considerable time, effort and expense involved should not be employed until these questions have been satisfactorily answered.

The design, pattern or layout of a roof garden is normally dictated largely by the space available. For most householders this space is comparatively small and rectangular. It will probably be bounded on two or more sides by some sort of wall or parapet. The actual roof surface will probably be of lead, a bitumen compound or of tiles or paving slabs. Whatever the surface it will always be better, though by no means necessary, to cover it with duckboards to protect the feet in wet weather, to allow unimpeded drainage, and to give added protection to the surface material of the roof.

In some instances it is possible to place soil directly on the roof surface, contained on the outer edge by the wall or parapet and on the inner side by timber shuttering, bricks or by a peat brick wall. The last is the most effective, both visually and because peat bricks absorb and hold moisture, releasing it only slowly to the soil which they contain.

The making of a flower bed directly on a roof surface is not always to be recommended because of its permanency and possible damage to roof and to walls.

so it is usually best to contain soil in a series of boxes, troughs or pots, raised sufficiently from the roof to allow good drainage and the passage of a current of air below. If these are to be of timber they should be well coated with one of the non-creosote timber preservatives (based on copper naphthenate) to prolong their lives, and they must have drainage holes in their bases or low in their sides. Some bricks are sufficiently permeable to allow excess moisture to drain away, but others are not, so a test should be made where you are in doubt.

All containers should have in their bases a layer of drainage material between the drainage holes and the soil, otherwise the holes are apt to become blocked with soil particles or fibrous roots.

If John Innes compost is used ask for compost No 3, which is normally for potting mature plants, trees or shrubs. This may initially be too strong a mixture for smaller plants, but so quickly are fertilisers leached from the soil on a roof garden that no harm is likely to be caused.

A more practical alternative to John Innes compost for most gardeners, ordinary garden soil, may cost you nothing but the effort of sterilising it and transporting it to the roof garden. Some garden suppliers offer unsterilised loams. If soils are of a heavy clay they should be lightened by the addition of peat and coarse sand and should be enriched with a good handful of bonemeal to every bucketful. If the soil is not sterilised weeds are certain to germinate and in their early stages they are not always distinguishable. However, a roof garden generally gets much closer inspection and more attention than can be given to the larger gardens crowded with plants at ground level, and weeds are quickly cleared.

It is helpful to be generous with fertiliser applications. Use an all-purpose balanced fertiliser, generally in granular form, but a liquid fertiliser may be used. One reason for giving plenty of fertiliser is that the thin soil will result in considerable wastage, although the thrifty gardener will avoid this by careful attention to watering. Another reason is that if flowers and plants are to be grown at all under such artificial conditions, then it is as well to grow them as lushly and lavishly as possible. Close planting with the intention of creating as much interest and colour as possible will take considerable quantities of plant foods out of the soil and they should be replaced regularly to obtain good results.

Watering is sometimes necessary twice a day under hot and sunny conditions. A standpipe is seldom available on a roof top, but the expense and all the attendant difficulties of having one installed are not really necessary, for it

is a comparatively simple matter to attach a hose to a downstairs tap and lead this through a window to the roof.

As space is usually limited vertical growth must be encouraged, and the roof is one of the best possible places for climbers and trailers. All walls and parapets should have their surfaces decorated and concealed by climbers, some of which can be allowed to grow rampant and spill over the top and down the sides of the building. Even as rampant a grower as the Russian vine, *Polygonum bilderdyckia baldschuanicum,* will grow freely on a roof top. Given sufficient space for its roots and properly supported and trained it will cover large areas in summer with its attractive twining trails and after the first year or so will produce a profusion of creamy, foamy flowers. Passion flowers (passifloras) grow and flower well. The colourful and interesting cup and saucer flower, *Cobaea scandens,* will quickly cover a wall and will produce not only flowers, but fat and interesting fruits. Ivy grows well and will cover walls with an evergreen background, and even acts on occasions as a weed suppressing ground cover.

Pelargoniums should not be despised because they are so popular, for they are obtainable in wonderful colours and, with proper attention, flower lavishly.

The roof is a wonderful place for many alpine plants, preferably grown together in special containers. A sink garden can provide great interest and much subtle beauty.

There are many alpines from which to choose for a special feature such as this, but do not forget to include a proportion of dwarf shrubs and conifers, some of which can be charming, in order to get added interest in shapes, textures, heights and colours.

Other special features particularly successful on roof gardens are hanging baskets and examples of bonsai, or dwarf trees.

Balcony gardening

Gardening on a balcony demands different techniques, presents different hazards and offers different rewards from gardening in a garden. The impact of a balcony must be immediate, striking, powerful for it must compete with the drama of the world beyond. The only way to ensure this is to provide masses of aggressive colour; reds rather than greens, yellows rather than blues; colour that is in urgent contrast to the view above and below.

Colours of this nature, however, are not obtained as easily on a balcony as they are at ground level. All plants must be grown in containers, none of which can be very large. Small containers mean a confined root run, a meagre supply of soil and hence a tendency to dry out quickly causing plants to wilt or die.

The usual balcony breezes hasten the

1 Balcony gardens can be made colourful in summer by using annual plants
Flowering and foliage plants grown in urns, ornamental vases, plant-boxes of many kinds, tubs or large pots, will all help to furnish the balcony garden

drying out process. They scurry round corners, whistle through gaps in buildings and seldom leave flowers and plants with a quiet opportunity for contented growth. Some balconies may be protected by glassing in one end or side.

The wind limits the range of plants available just as much as the lack of space does. Tall growers will bend and break, trailers will become unanchored, top heavy plants in small containers will be blown over. Except for special cases therefore, balcony plants should be low growing, compact, sturdy.

A further and highly practical problem posed by winds concerns garden debris. Just as the balcony gardener must consider his neighbours, particularly those who live on the floor below, when watering his plants, he must also keep control of fallen leaves and flower petals. They should be collected frequently in a windproof container and disposed of. Down pipes etc. must be kept clear of debris which, after a storm, can collect quickly, block openings and cause flooding.

These are real problems and the balcony gardener should consider them seriously before planning. Intelligent purchase of plants and containers can help to solve them.

Containers should be firmly based, squat rather than tall. Troughs are better than pots, although for most purposes the best of all are pots plunged into troughs. Of course, all containers must be secure. There must be no risk that an accidental displacement will lead to any of them falling into the street or garden below.

All containers should have drainage holes in them and should be lifted from the balcony floor sufficiently to allow excess moisture to escape. Where drips or splashes may annoy neighbours or passers-by it is advisable to use drip trays.

We can now come down from the city clouds and have a look at an entirely different form of gardening, one that really needs some expertise if it is to be carried out successfully. The creation of a rock garden is not to be undertaken lightly, for it must be done well to succeed and it can involve considerable cost as well as a great deal of hard physical work in the early stages, described in the following chapter. Rock plants, however, are some of the most exquisite and endearing to be seen in our gardens and it is no wonder that there are so many rock or alpine gardening enthusiasts.

Rock garden plants
The choice of plants which can be grown on a rock garden is very wide indeed, and may bewilder a novice faced with the selection of plants from long lists of

1 Sea Pinks, Armeria maritima.
2 A rock garden display in early spring. No clump of plants is too large for the general effect.
3 The bright purple flowers of Gentiana septemfida.
4 The flowers of Campanula carpatica make large, deep blue drifts on the rock garden in summer.

names in books and catalogues. Although the plants suitable for this purpose are collectively known as 'alpines', it must be admitted that a great many of them are not, in fact, alpine in the truest sense of the word, but they are all plants which enjoy the conditions provided by a rock garden, and look appropriate in such surroundings.

The rock garden is frequently built in the soil excavated during the construc- of a garden pool.

Water gardens and water plants

Since the introduction of fibre glass pools tremendous interest has been shown in medium-sized garden pools.

Paint the pools in dark or natural colours, and try for a general natural effect. The edges may either be disguised with plants, paving or stones, which should slightly overhang the water. Or you may cover the edges with *Myriophyllum proserpinacoides*, a very rampant grower. As it is sometimes destroyed by frost, a pan of young cuttings should be removed to frost-free quarters in autumn.

Deep water aquatics Great care should

be taken in the selection and subsequent planting of nymphaeas (water-lilies). Shallow-water, marginal aquatics require plain loam, and bonemeal should be added only when the soil is poor, as most of these plants are difficult to keep within limits. Most water plants flourish freely if they are planted directly on the base of the pool, but many fibre-glass pools do not retain the soil on the shelves, and the plants may have to be put in containers. The main advantage of planting directly into a soil base is that most of the plants remain undisturbed for four or five years (except for thinning operations), whereas in containers they have to be repotted every third year. On the other hand, it is much simpler to lift and replant containers than resoil the whole pool. Choose large plastic containers, or make them from 1×1-inch timber nailed together with 1-inch spaces between the slats, or you can use old wicker baskets.

Tall marginal aquatics, such as *Scirpus albescens*, should be reduced in height to 9 to 10 inches to prevent them from being blown over before the roots have obtained hold. Underwater or oxygenating aquatics need only be pushed into the soil in the deep parts of the pool or planted in containers beside the water-lilies, etc. Most marginals require slight thinning each year,

especially some of the more vigorous varieties. Most spread readily and small pieces can easily be removed and replanted.

The nymphaeas are by far the most important deep water aquatics, but there are a few other plants in this section worthy of mention. These may be grown in formal pools on their own or informally with the water-lilies. Sometimes they succeed where water-lilies fail because of overhanging trees or insufficient room for the latter to develop. The genera *Aponogeton* and *Nuphar* contain suitable species.

Hardy marginal aquatics The majority like to have their roots covered with 2 or 3 inches of water, although some will grow in more and others are perfectly happy in permanently wet soil. Suitable species will be found in the following genera: *Acorus, Butomus, Caltha, Cotula, Cyperus, Eriophorum, Iris, Juncus, Menyanthes, Mimulus, Orontium, Pontederia, Sagittaria, Scirpus* and *Typha.*

Submerged and floating aquatics These are vital for the well being of the pool to correct balance and obtain clear water. Oxygenating aquatics replace lost oxygen to the water and provide cover and a breeding ground for the fish. Many oxygenators are very rampant and so have to be kept in check. This is not

difficult; the garden rake should be forcefully pulled through the underwater vegetation when it is becoming overcrowded to remove all surplus. It is advisable to introduce four or five different varieties of oxygenating plants at one time. It will be found that some will grow at an alarming rate and others either stand still or die. This will have no adverse effect, as those that are growing well will do the work of the less vigorous varieties.

These are just some of the many different types of gardens and gardening that can be of interest. Yet gardening is basically an art and not a science, which means that you, the gardener, have an opportunity of creating something bearing the stamp of your own taste and your own personality. Remember, in your garden planning and designing, that it is *your* garden and that you can do what you like with it, subject to the comfort and convenience of your neighbours.

Law and the gardener
Your garden is ruled not only by the laws of nature. The laws of the land play a very large part. Here is an outline of the main ways in which the gardener, whether he knows it or not, can fall foul of the law. If the encounter is to be a happy one, the basic rules should be understood.

Traps and trespassers An Englishman's

1 Informal planting of a water garden with Aponogeton distachyus to be seen in the foreground.
2 Caltha palustris plena, the double Marsh Marigold, is excellent for planting at the water's edge.

home is his castle. So is his garden. The occupier of a garden is entitled to decide who may and who may not be there. Subject (as we shall see) to rights of way, you are entitled to give people permission to be on your land and to order those who do not have your permission to leave it.

Visitors may have your express authority to be there. You may have invited them to come. Alternatively, they may have your implied consent. They may have used your property as a short cut or have wandered in to admire your flowers without your raising any objection. But whether the permission was express or implied, you can revoke it at any time. Once the visitor ceases to have your permission, he becomes a trespasser and must leave.

If a trespasser is asked to leave your property and refuses, you are entitled to use 'reasonable force' to eject him. The amount of force which is 'reasonable' depends upon all the circumstances of the case. You must use no force at all until you have asked the visitor to leave and he has refused. At this stage, a firm hand on the shoulder or a determined frog-march should meet the situation. If that fails, you should call the police. You are not entitled to use any dangerous weapon except in self-defence. Even then, the methods used must bear reasonable proportion to the violence offered to you.

If someone trespasses on your land, you are not responsible if he suffers injury, unless you have actually laid a trap for him. Setting spring guns or man traps even for trespassers is definitely unlawful. But note that (except in exceptional circumstances, such as those involving railway property) trespassers cannot be prosecuted. They do not offend against the criminal law. But if you are bothered by persistent trespassers, you can bring a civil action against them. In such cases, a court may grant an injunction restraining the trespassers from repeating their wrongful behaviour in the future. You may also get damages, if you can show that you suffered any financial loss as a result of the trespass.

Trespass by animals In general, the owners of animals are bound to fence them in. If an animal strays and causes damage on neighbouring property, the owner of the animal will be liable to pay compensation. But a special exception is made for dogs and cats. These are regarded as friends of mankind until the contrary is proved against them. If you wish to keep dogs and cats out of your garden, it is up to you to fence them out.

But if it is proved that a particular dog or cat has caused damage, he is then known to have a 'mischievous propensity'. At this stage, his privilege ceases. His owner keeps him at his peril, in the same way as if he were any other sort of animal. A dog is not actually allowed one bite, but until he has once bitten, his owner is unlikely to know that he is liable to bite. Once a dog has misbehaved, his owner is at risk.

If animals stray on to your garden from the highway, however, you will generally have no remedy against their owner. Provided that the owner has not been negligent and that the highway is being used for the ordinary, proper purposes of 'passing and repassing', the owner will not be liable in law.

Rights of way Other people may have a right to cross your land. This right is known as an 'easement'. It is generally called a 'right of way'.

People may aquire a right of way over your garden because you expressly grant it to them. You may allow them to cross your land in return for payment. In

1 Dogs and cats are regarded as friends of mankind until proved otherwise. If you wish to exclude them it is up to you to fence them out.
2 To prevent a right of way arising you should put up a notice like this.

EDGE

PRIVATE ROAD
NO PUBLIC RIGHT OF WAY
TO VEHICLES

that case, you are bound by your agreement to let them pass. But equally, if people use your land openly, freely and as of right for a period of twenty years or more, a right is said to arise by 'prescription'. If, then, you are willing to allow people to cross your garden but you do not wish a right of way to arise, you should make this clear. Put up a notice to that effect. Close off the garden at least one day a year. And then it can never be said that anyone used the path 'as of right'.

Squatters' titles It is essential, if you wish to preserve a legal right, that you should exercise it. So called 'squatters' titles' arise because people do not exercise their rights over their own land.

Suppose that you have a patch of land at the bottom of your garden which is derelict. You wish to use it for yourself. First you should attempt to trace the owner. Try the Town Hall. Ask the neighbours. But if all else fails, fence the land off so as to form part of your garden; alternatively, put a fence around it and put in a gate to which you alone have the key. If the owner fails to take any step whatsoever to indicate his intention to retain his ownership and inaction continues for twelve years or more, he will lose his rights; you will acquire a squatter's title; and you should register your title at once.

Neighbours' rights If your neighbour builds in his garden so as to rob your windows of their light, your plants of their sunshine and your house of its view, what can you do about it?

If windows of a house have enjoyed uninterrupted light for twenty years or more, an easement is said to arise known as 'ancient lights'. This is a right to have as much light as is reasonably necessary for the enjoyment of life in the room in question. But in fact, very little light is regarded as 'reasonably necessary'. Very few legal actions founded on 'ancient lights' actually succeed.

As for gardens and plants, they have no right to light or to sunshine. There is no such easement known to the law. Even if a flower-bed has been drenched in sun for centuries, you cannot prevent your neighbour from interfering with the sunlight. Nor can he prevent you from doing so, if you wish.

Equally, there is no 'right to a view'. If your neighbour blocks your view or you block his, the sufferer acquires no legal remedy.

Weeds Conscientious gardeners often

1 Large trees may block out light from your garden or house, or block the view. Unfortunately, you have no remedy in law. 2 Children visiting your garden may be less careful than adults. So you should take extra care for the safety of child visitors, or children who come to play with your children in your garden.

complain about the unsightliness of an unkempt garden next door. Unfortunately, just as you cannot complain about a view which is taken from you, so the law gives you no remedy if the view is unpleasant. If weeds spread from next door, you might be able to establish that a 'nuisance' has been created (see below). Alternatively, you might be able to get your local council to take action under the Weeds Act (if the weeds are particularly noxious and the council particularly active). But the odds are, in practice, that you can do precious little about it.

Nuisance Each of us must use our property in such a way as not to cause unreasonable disturbance to our neighbour's enjoyment of his property. In other words, you are not allowed by law to do anything in your garden which would unreasonably disturb your neighbour's enjoyment of his garden. Each one of us has to put up with a certain amount of disturbance as 'part of the give and take of neighbourly life'. But if the disturbance goes beyond reasonable bounds, the law will intervene and force the offender to stop his unneighbourly behaviour.

Smoke and fires You may burn bonfires, incinerate your rubbish and create smoke at any time of the day or night. There is no law which places any restriction on garden fires, provided that they are safe. Neighbours have to put up with a reasonable amount of smoke. But if smoke is unreasonable in volume, or fires are habitually lit in such a place and at such times that the next door house is made well-nigh uninhabitable, there is a 'nuisance' in law, as well as in fact.

Noises and smells Voices from the next door garden can be a real aggravation to the gardener, particularly if he is resting. But noise must be expected, especially from children. Only if the reasonable, healthy, normal person would regard the noise as thoroughly unreasonable would the law say that there has been a 'nuisance'.

Similarly, we all have to put up with a certain amount of smell. Fertilisers in gardens may produce unpleasant odours. So may compost heaps. But if the smells are unreasonably severe, those who suffer from them will have a legal remedy. But note that whether or not a particular unpleasantness constitutes a nuisance will depend, among other factors, upon the situation of the garden in question. That which is a 'nuisance' in a high class, residential district may be part of the ordinary hazards of living in a heavily populated, industrial neighbourhood or, for that matter, in farming country.

Children—and occupier's liability Under the Occupier's Liability Act, 1957, occupiers owe a 'common duty of care' to all lawful visitors. This is a duty 'to take such care as in all the circumstances of the case is reasonable to see that the visitors will be reasonably safe in using the premises for purposes for which he is invited or permitted by the occupier to be there'. So you owe exactly the same duty to the visitor who is welcome as you do to the visitors (other than trespassers) who are unwelcome.

If someone is hurt in your garden, the court would have to look at all the circumstances of the case to see if you were liable. 'The circumstances relevant for this purpose', says the Act, 'include the degree of care and want of care which would ordinarily be looked for in such a visitor'. It follows that 'an occupier must be prepared for children to be less careful than adults; and an occupier may expect that a person, in the exercise of his calling, will appreciate and guard against any special risks ordinarily incident to it, so far as the occupier leaves him free to do so'.

So you must take extra care for the safety of children who visit you—or who play with your children in your garden. But if you employ a gardener, you may reasonably expect him to guard against such risks as he ought to realise existed.

Garden buildings What you do in your own garden is, to a large extent, your own affair. Subject to the laws on nuisance, your garden is for your own enjoyment. But before you build a garden shed, a greenhouse or any other substantial building, there are a few points to check.

First, if you are a leaseholder, make certain that you are entitled to build. Many leases (particularly long leases at low rents) lay down that nothing shall be built without the landlord's consent. If you need his consent, get it. Fail to get it and you may be forced to pull down the building you have just spent money putting up. Next, check that there are no local bye-laws or regulations which you are about to contravene. A phone call to your town hall should put you in the picture. Finally, if the building is of any size, check with your local planning authority that planning permission is not necessary. If there is any 'material change' in the use of the land, there is

said to be a 'development'. And, with certain rather complicated exceptions, when you 'develop', you need planning permission.

Boundary lines Provided that you keep it on your own soil, you can put up any sort of fence, hedge or wall that you see fit. If your neighbour does not like the look of it, that is his misfortune. If he objects to the fence posts being on his side of the fence, he can build another fence on his own soil to improve his own view. If you wish a high fence, to preserve your privacy, that is your business. You are master on your own land.

But what if the fence, wall or hedge is on the boundary? To whom does it belong?

The general rule is that the law runs a notional line along the full length of a boundary, wall, fence or hedge. That portion of it which is on your side is yours. The portion on your neighbour's side is his. Neither can force the other to rebuild it or replace it or even to contribute half the cost of doing so. Wise neighbours share costs. But the law cannot possibly force them to do so.

If the buttresses of a wall or the posts of a fence are on one side only, the wall or fence will usually belong to the person on whose side the buttresses or posts

1 A fence usually belongs to the person on whose side the posts are. A finer point arises when the posts are centred. **2** Roots and branches of trees may trespass on your neighbour's soil or air space.

come. But even then, he cannot be forced to keep it in good condition. Nor can he force his neighbour to contribute towards its upkeep.

Boundary disputes If you and your neighbour cannot agree on where the boundary line comes between your gardens, you will be wise to call in a surveyor, give him the plans of your property, and let him measure up. Boundary disputes not only cause trouble between neighbouring countries —they are a constant source of discord between neighbours.

Trees that trespass Just as you must keep your buildings on your own soil, so if your trees thrust their roots into your neighbour's soil or their branches into his air space, you commit a 'nuisance' and probably a trespass as well. The neighbour is entitled to cut off the roots or the branches at the point where they enter his soil. They do not belong to him and he must throw them over the fence into your garden. He may not even keep the fruit or the flowers off the branches. But he is fully within his rights in demanding that you keep your plant life in, under and above your own property. Moreover, if the roots thrust themselves far into your neighbour's property (as is common with poplar roots) and damage is done to your neighbour's paths or, worse, to the foundations of his home, you will be liable in damages.

If your trees overhang the highway, you are, technically at least, just as much at fault as if they were over-hanging your neighbour's garden. But most important, if an overhanging tree should fall and cause injury, loss or damage, you can be held responsible if it can be shown that you knew or ought to have known that the tree was defective and you did not take steps to cut it back or chop it down.

That which adheres to the freehold Trees, plants and flowers 'adhere to the soil'. They form part of the freehold. And they belong to the freeholder. So if you are a tenant and you have created a glorious garden, do not think that you can take it away with you at the end of your tenancy. In the absence of some special agreement to the contrary, everything growing in the garden belongs to the landlord.

The same rule applies if you are selling your home and garden. You may remove your favourite plants, if you obtain the purchaser's permission (this, in practice, is often given if asked for), or if in the contract certain plants are expressly excluded from the deal (which is very rare). But otherwise you have no right to remove garden produce. You have sold it. But, of course, the converse applies. If you buy a garden, you are just as entitled to insist that the trees, shrubs and plants be left, as you are to prevent the seller from tearing out

1 Overhanging branches may fall and cause injury, loss or damage and the owner of the tree may be held responsible. 2 Paths may be damaged by tree roots.

radiators, fireplaces or fitted cupboards from the house itself.

Buying When you purchase garden produce or garden equipment, whether you know it or not, you are entering into a contract. In consideration of your paying the agreed price, the supplier is providing for you the agreed items.

Section 14 of the Sale of Goods Act, 1893, lays down that, in the absence of agreement to the contrary, you are normally entitled to goods which are 'of merchantable quality' and, usually, reasonably suitable for the purpose supplied. If it turns out that the goods are faulty or that they do not do the job for which they were sold, you are entitled to your money back or, if you wish, to keep the goods and to have them put into proper order at the seller's expense.

It follows that when you buy trees, plants or shrubs, there is an implied term in the agreement that they will be healthy when they are supplied to you. If as a result of faulty planting or careless siting they die or fail to flower or fruit, that is not the fault of the seller. He has kept to his bargain by providing the goods. But if, on the other hand, you can show that the goods were faulty in the first place, you are entitled to your money back. And most reputable suppliers will give it to you (or at least give you credit) without demur.

Similarly, if you buy garden equipment, then, whether the purchase is by mail order or in person, you are entitled to goods which are in good order. If your new garden shed leaks, your greenhouse subsides, your lawn-mower proves useless or your hammock collapses, the odds are that you have a good claim against the seller—even though he has given you no guarantee'.

Guarantees and warranties The gardener who buys equipment is protected by Parliament. But this protection only applies 'in the absence of agreement to the contrary'. So called 'guarantees' and 'warranties' often take away the protection which Parliament has provided. Before you buy goods under 'guarantee', read the document very carefully. If it takes away your Sale of Goods Act rights, tear it up. If the seller insists upon giving you a 'guarantee', take your custom elsewhere.

On the other hand, if you choose to buy a 'bargain' on the basis that you are getting the items cheaply and the seller specifically tells you that he cannot accept responsibility if they are defective, that is a matter for you. You have made your bargain and you will be bound by it.

Repair costs Garden equipment and garden buildings need repair and maintenance. Gardeners who employ contractors to do repair or maintenance work often complain of the prices they are charged and of the poor standard of workmanship.

The law says that you must pay the agreed price for a job. If, for instance, a firm of landscape gardeners agree to do a particular job in your garden for a set price and you accept that price, you cannot cry off simply because you find another firm who could do the job much cheaper. In the same way, the contractors will have to do the job at the agreed price, even if they find that they have underestimated.

But what if no price has been agreed? What of the extras which always crop up, for example?

Where the parties have not agreed upon a price, the law implies a term into their contract that the contractor will be entitled to make a 'reasonable charge'. As usual, to find out what charge is or is not 'reasonable', all the circumstances of the case have to be

Trees, plants and flowers 'adhere to the soil' and are part of the freehold. Therefore, everything growing in the garden belongs to the landlord.

considered, including the nature and standard of the work, the amount of time taken, the price of any materials used, the wages of the men concerned and so on.

Faulty workmanship There is another implied term in every contract for work and services that the work will be done in a proper and workmanlike manner and with suitable materials. If the job is bungled or the materials are defective, the contractor has broken his contract. You are entitled to deduct from his bill a reasonable cost of putting his job into proper order.

Stealing and borrowing 'Scrumping' may be a popular pastime amongst the young, but it is quite illegal. A person steals who takes and carries away property capable of being stolen, without the owner's consent or other lawful excuse, intending at the time of taking per-

manently to deprive the owner thereof.

Growing crops are capable of being stolen. A person who steals your fruit or flowers is a thief.

On the other hand, the man who borrows your gardening equipment, even without your permission, commits no criminal offence whatsoever. He has no intention 'permanently to deprive you thereof': however immoral it may be to help yourself to your neighbour's ladder, mower, sprinkler or drill without his consent, no law is broken. The only exception to this rule is in the case of motor vehicles. It is a crime to take and drive away someone else's motor vehicle without his consent or other lawful excuse.

Lawyers and law suits Litigation is a luxury. Law suits are very expensive. But legal advice is obtainable at a very low fee under the Legal Advice Act and under The Law Society's scheme. If your gardening activities bring you into conflict with neighbours, contractors, visitors or anyone else, consult your solicitor as early as you can. Do not leave it too late.

Chapter 3

GARDEN CARE AND CONSTRUCTION

Cultivation

Our soil, which is the home and the anchor of all we grow, may be in the best of condition, well drained, well fed, balanced, rich and crumbly, but it still needs cultivating before it can be made wholly suitable for the seeds, the seedlings or the plants that we are to put into it.

Cultivation is the practice of working the soil to produce and maintain conditions favourable to healthy plant growth. It has to be carried on continuously, and has short lasting effects and varies according to the soil.

Destruction of weeds Before any land can be cultivated weeds have to be destroyed or got rid of, either by weed-killers or by mechanical means. Perennial weeds are always the most difficult to eradicate and there is no short cut to getting land really clear of them. Much can be learned from the kinds of weeds that a soil supports. Sorrel, spurrey, bracken and foxglove tolerate high acidity in the soil, whereas wild clematis (old man's beard), campion, chicory and toadflax usually abound on the chalky, alkaline soils. Silverweed, plantains, dandelions and horsetails thrive on clay soils.

Once the surface is clear, and the land is fallowed for a few weeks, it is easy to ascertain if it is badly drained because surface water will not drain away. Apart from introducing mechanical drains underground, the improvement of the texture of the soil will often relieve the drainage problem.

When to cultivate Only coarse textured or very sandy soils can be cultivated soon after wet weather, the medium textured soils tend to make clods if worked too soon and the clay or fine textured soils simply turn slimy and their structure is spoiled for many months. It is general, therefore, to carry out deep or main cultivation operations in the autumn or during the winter in open weather, not only because the soils are drier at this time but to harness the help of frost in breaking up the particles to fine tilth and improving the texture of the soil.

Winter operations Digging is the major soil operation carried out with a spade, and designed to aerate, level, and turn the earth. Soils left rough during the winter are broken down in the spring, using the fork or where heavy clods are concerned, the Canterbury hoe

Forking is carried out in both autumn and spring and on heavier soils a flat-tined fork may be found easier to manage for autumn or winter work. The object of the operation is to break up and aerate the top 6 inches of the soil, hand clearing weeds as work progresses. Forking is less laborious than digging and can be carried out among established plants in the border, the shrub garden, and among soft fruit bushes. One always works backwards when forking to avoid walking on the land already forked.

When a vacant piece of land is to be forked, begin by working right across one end of it. It is useful to put a line across the plot and work over an area about 2 feet wide before moving the line back another 2 feet. The fork is plunged into the soil at an angle of about 50°, the soil lifted, slightly turned and dropped back. Work progresses across the plot, working strips of 2 feet at a time until the whole plot has been forked.

Dressings of lime, manure, compost and such slow acting fertilisers as bonemeal are added to the soil in autumn and winter and it is often convenient to spread them at the same time as the forking is being done.

Spring and summer operations Forking is the quickest way of grooming the garden in spring. Annual weeds which make an early appearance, such as groundsel can be cleared at the same time and the winter surface of the soil just pricked over to aerate it and break down any clods.

Treading Once spring forking is done on ground that is destined for seed sowing or vegetable planting it can be lightly rolled or trodden to prevent it from being too puffy. Treading is especially useful (and easy to do) on sandy soils that might dry out too quickly otherwise.

Walk sideways across the land, keeping the feet almost together and shuffle across the soil. The surface is tidied afterwards by raking.

Raking The rake is used not only to collect up the surface rubbish, but to level the surface and break down the top inch of soil into a really fine tilth, like grains of rice, in preparation for seed sowing.

Digging

The various operations carried out on the soil by the use of a spade are all known as digging. The general purpose is to break up the soil to improve its physical nature, rendering it more suitable for supporting plant life.

Digging is generally carried out in the autumn and winter, when a solidly compact soil can be broken up and left rough throughout the winter. The more surface that can be exposed to the weather the better, and the action of frosts, drying winds and rain break up the surface into small crumbs or tilth, generally increase aeration, and render the soil more open in texture. Rain and snow drain from the surface more quickly, leaving the surface dry and, therefore, the soil absorbs warmth from the spring sunshine more easily. Drainage is improved and the air that exists between the soil particles supports the beneficial bacteria.

The term digging means turning over

the top soil one spit deep or the depth of the spade's blade, i.e. 10 inches. Surface weeds are buried, the level of the land remains the same and the clods of earth are left unbroken.

It is important that the spade is thrust into the soil to its full depth and in a vertical position. If this is not done, the land is dug quicker but cultivation is not deep enough or thorough enough and the weeds will not be properly buried.

Single digging To dig over a plot of land, a trench a spade's width and a spade's depth is dug out across one end and the soil removed and taken in a wheelbarrow to the other end of the plot and left in a heap so that when the plot has been dug there will be soil ready to put into the last trench. Alongside the first trench mark out with a line another strip and by standing facing the open trench and working along the line soil can be dug out and thrown well forward into the open trench, at the same time making a new trench. The importance of throwing

Cultivations should vary according to requirements. For seed sowing: 1 any accumulation of rubbish is removed. 2 The soil is lightly forked to break up clods and create a tilth. 3 The seed bed is made firm by treading. 4 Large stones and clods are removed with a wooden rake. 5 A fine tilth is obtained. 6 Borders are forked over to remove perennial weeds in the spring

each spadeful of soil well forward cannot be emphasised too much because a slight discrepancy will after several trenches result in there not being sufficient space in which to work properly. Repeat the method of filling the last trench while making a new one and when the last strip is dug at the other end of the plot the soil heaped there from the first trench is ready to fill the last one.

Manure or compost can be put on the land at the same time and is scattered along the trench and the soil is thrown on to it.

No-digging

A system of organic surface cultivation. In an English method of no-digging heavy dressings of garden compost are spread on top of undug soil. Seeds are sown on the compost and are covered with more of it. To prevent weed growth and to conserve soil moisture the seed rows may be mulched with an inch or more of sawdust or the seedlings mulched similarly. Neither the spade nor the garden fork are used except where bushes, trees and potato tubers are being planted. No-diggers claim that the system conforms with nature's own practice of not burying seeds and that the results justify the method.

An American variant omits garden compost and uses spoilt hay as a mulch. All growing crops are mulched quite thickly with hay each season. The hay rots down adding organic matter to the soil surface. The hay mulch method has an advantage, it is claimed, for gardeners situated in areas of very low rainfall and where conservation of water supplies is most necessary.

Spade

Whether one digs or not a spade is still a necessary implement, probably the most important tool in the gardener's armoury; other vital tools in the cultivation of the soil are forks, rakes and hoes.

Spades are of several types ranging from those made for garden work to special ones which have long, narrow blades for digging out drains and trenches. Spades for gardeners are made in various blade sizes. The larger types have blades 12½ inches × 8 inches. Medium digging spades are manufactured with blades of 10 inches × 6½ inches and the lighter border models have blades which are only 9 inches × 5½ inches. There is also a 'junior' model with a 7 inch × 5 inch blade.

Handle design also varies. The most popular are those which are shaped in the form of a 'D'. However, many spades used in northern England have a handle in the form of a 'T'

Some handles and shafts are covered with a PVC sleeve, which adds considerably to the comfort of handling and which gives greater durability and better appearance.

The more expensive spades have stainless steel blades. The highly polished

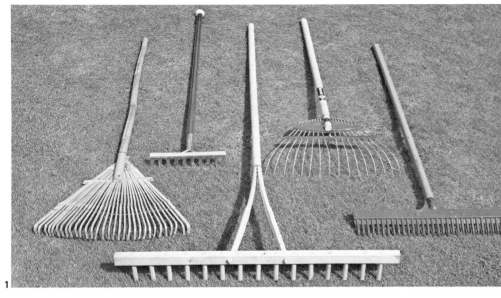

1 Different types of rakes, left to right: bamboo, iron, wooden, Springbok and rubber.
2 The Tudor multi-purpose lawn rake for scarifying and raking up grass.
3 The rake has many uses in the garden, not least in the drawing of drills and the covering in of seeds.
4 *R to L*: Border fork, digging fork, flat-tined fork and, in front, a hand fork.

surfaces enable the blades to slip easily through the soil—especially the heavy sticky types.

There is a specially designed spade for those gardeners who have to deal with these stubborn, heavy soils. It has four pointed cutting teeth on its blade edge. The blade itself is $11\frac{1}{2}$ inches $\times$ $7\frac{1}{2}$ inches. Also suitable for heavy soil is a spade with a polished steel blade which has a double-tapered self-sharpening edge.

Many gardeners prefer a tread above the blade, as there is less wear on boots. Spades with such treads are sometimes referred to as 'London-treaded' types.

A spade is made using a lever and spring system, which turns over the soil much faster than can be done with the conventional spade. This is the Wolf 'Terrex' automatic spade. The spade head can be changed for a special fork head.

Forks

The garden fork is one of the important basic tools and can be used for many jobs. It is an ideal tool for soil cultivation and is especially useful where the soil is on the heavy side, as the thin, strong tines penetrate the soil more easily than does the blade of a spade. It is also invaluable for the preliminary operation of breaking the soil down after the autumn or winter digging. The large clumps of soil can be broken down into smaller particles with the back of the fork.

The fork can be used as an aerator for the lawn if the tines are thrust into the turf as deeply as possible all over the lawn at spacings. For lifting plants or roots and for raking up rubbish, the fork is especially useful. An important operation is the maintenance of a good surface tilth or cultivation. Some soils pan or harden badly on the surface, and for good growth it is essential to keep it broken or open. The fork is ideal for this purpose as it can be inserted lightly into the top few inches in between plants, in the operation known as 'forking over'.

There are many different types or designs of fork, although some of these are of little importance to the amateur gardener. For the lady gardener and for work in confined areas, the smaller, lighter border fork is ideal. Some of the more expensive designs are manufactured from stainless steel or chrome-armoured metals.

Prongs vary in size and in number; in length they range from as little as 5 inches to as much as 15 inches. Some prongs are flat and these are useful for lifting potatoes and other root crops. Prong numbers vary from 2–10. The larger types are for the professional gardener and are designed for potato and beetroot harvesting.

One other type of fork must be included; this is the small hand fork which usually has 3 prongs, although some have 2 and others 4. This is usually a companion to the hand trowel and is extremely useful for planting small plants. Handle lengths range from about 5 inches to as much as 3–4 feet. Those with longer handles are used for cultivating the soil especially towards the back of deep borders, but are also useful light tools for those who wish to avoid too much stooping

Rakes

One of the most useful and versatile tools in the garden is the rake, which usually has from 10 to 14 teeth (or up to 34 in the 'Springbok' type of lawn rake). The more teeth there are the easier it is to obtain a really fine soil surface (tilth). The handles usually measure 5 feet, but one firm also makes handles 6 inches longer or shorter. The head may measure from 6 to 16 inches wide, largely depending on the number of teeth. It is usually slightly curved to improve balance.

Although they are more expensive the best rakes are those which have teeth cut out of one piece of steel, which may be plain, stainless or chromium-plated. The head is welded to a tapering tube which is fastened to the handle (ash or tubular steel). Cheap rakes or rake heads may survive a season or two, but these rakes will last a life-time.

The rake is used extensively during the busy sowing and planting season in spring. It is ideal for breaking down the soil to the required tilth immediately before sowing or planting. After the prior stage of breaking down the heavier lumps of soil with the back of a fork, if the soil is in the right condition the smaller remaining lumps should crumble quickly as the rake head is drawn over them.

Turned on one corner, the edge of the rake can be used to make shallow, V-shaped seed drills, and for covering seeds after sowing it is returned to its normal position. Held vertically the rake head is useful for light firming with a gentle tapping movement. A special type of rake is made for the lawn surface. Specially light lawn rakes are also made from plastic, flexible rubber or split bamboo. They cannot harm even the finest turf.

For raking up mowings left behind by rough grass cutters or after you have cut down weeds or grass with a scythe or bagging hook, the wooden hay rake is best. It has about 12 teeth (when broken easily replaceable by anyone handy with tools), and the handle is longer than those of other rakes. It is not expensive and may also be used for making the final tilth on seed beds, particularly on lighter soils.

Raking

Apart from raking to remove autumn leaves from lawns and flower beds, this gardening term more generally refers to the final stage in the levelling of soil for sowing or planting. It should never be done when the soil is wet, and is more effective when the surface is drying out but not quite dry. The soil will have been dug and may have been left rough over winter. The latter is a common procedure when the soil is heavy, to enable the frost to break down the lumps.

The teeth of the rake should never be pushed into the soil. The rake is best applied with a light backward movement so that there is no danger of stepping forward on to the raked soil. In pulling the rake towards the body unwanted clods, stones and other debris are drawn away from the area being prepared. After raking the debris should not be left piled up, as it is not only unsightly but a potential hiding place for slugs, etc.

Using the rake to prepare a seed bed demands skill, which is usually gained through experience. The top inch or so of soil must be quite fine so that small seeds are in close contact with the soil particles around them and the particles can help them to germinate. When raking a bed to level off recently dug soil for planting, less skill is needed as the tilth does not have to be so fine as for a seed bed.

When preparing ground for broadcast sowing as in making lawns, the surface is first raked in one direction only. This results in many shallow furrows into which the seed falls. By raking after sowing in a cross-wise direction, these furrows are broken down and the seed is automatically covered with fine soil.

Hoes and hoeing

Hoes are essential tools for surface cultivation of the soil, used to break it up, thus facilitating the entry of air and moisture and also destroying weeds. Numerous patterns are made and from time to time new 'improved' models appear for which various claims are made. Basically, however, there are two main types, the draw hoe and the dutch hoe.

Draw hoes In these the blade is set nearly at right angles to the handle. This type is used with a chopping action, the operator moving forward over the hoed soil. For working close to plants, hoeing hard-packed soil or for clearing very weedy patches this is a more useful and powerful tool than the dutch hoe. It is also used to draw seed-drills. Variations of pattern and width of blade occur. The traditional patterns have either half-moon-shaped or rectangular blades, the cutting edges varying in width from 1–8 inches. The former pattern which has a curved shaft, is usually known as a swan-necked hoe. One type has a triangular head, the three sides each having a blade-edge. Handle-lengths vary from $4\frac{1}{2}$–5 feet and handles are usually of ash, a durable wood.

Another type of draw hoe has a short handle and is often known as an onion hoe. This is a useful tool for thinning rows of seedlings and weeding between them, but also makes a useful little hand-tool for weeding in other places in the garden.

A much heavier tool, which may be classified as a draw hoe, is the round-eyed hoe. This is virtually a mattock, but without the pick which forms part of that tool. It is of strong construction with a heavy, pick-type handle and is used not so much for weeding or hoeing in the normal sense as for clearing rough ground, as it may be used to chop through the smaller roots of trees, to uproot such things as brambles and saplings and to break up heavy clods of clay. But a better tool for the latter purpose is the Canterbury hoe, which is very similar but has three stout fork-like prongs. This, too, has its uses in clearing rough ground, dragging up weeds, roots and garden debris generally.

Dutch hoes In this type the blade is more or less in the same plane as the handle and socket, instead of being set at right-angles. It is pushed forward, practically flat, to cut through the soil just below the surface, severing weed roots and breaking up any surface pan. For this reason it is sometimes known as a push-hoe. The operator works backwards and does not tread on the ground he has hoed. Again, there are different blade widths and different patterns. In one pattern the solid blade is replaced by a thin wire.

Hoe blades in general become dulled through use in the soil and need to be sharpened with a file occasionally. A sharp hoe is a much more effective tool, easier to use, than a dull one. This does not apply to the modern stainless-steel types, which are so much easier to keep clean. To avoid blistering the hands with prolonged use, the handles should always be kept smooth. Refinements include rubber grips and plastic sheathings.

Hoeing to keep down weeds is not merely a matter of tidiness. Weeds allowed to develop will compete for the available light, air, moisture and plant food, and may be the host-plants of various pests. Weeds are dealt with properly only if they are cut off just below the soil surface. If they are dragged out of the soil with a blunt hoe they may root again, particularly in warm, moist weather. In sunny weather it is usually sufficient to leave the weeds on the surface to be withered by the sun, although they should eventually be collected for adding to the compost heap.

There are various types of mechanical cultivators which are designed to fulfil the functions of the tools mentioned above, and to a greater or lesser degree they succeed. As a very general rule they are larger, heavier, noisier, smellier, more expensive and less effective than the owner of the average small garden prefers or requires and they are therefore not examined here. Unless a considerable area is being cultivated a machine is not a labour saver, for some require considerable

effort to handle. There are also problems of storage and of transport of the machine to the site where it is to be used, over garden paths generally unsuited to such traffic.

Garden Paths

The actual layout of a path should take into consideration the time and amount of money which is available. The garden may be a new one, where paths are to be laid down for the first time, or an existing garden which is to be re-designed. If an old-world, or cottage garden effect is required, it is unlikely that a formal pattern will be suitable.

If the site is very undulating it may be necessary to match paths with steps and terraces. In the smaller gardens the boldness of a length of path can be reduced or avoided if stepping stones are used, or if the monotony of the path is broken up by means of patterns or by the use of different materials.

Before any planning is contemplated, it is as well to have a good idea what is available in the way of materials.

Concrete The most popular material is concrete. Many gardeners mix this themselves by purchasing the basic ingredients, which are bags of cement, a load of sand and shingle or a load of mixed ballast. Some firms supply bags which contain all the necessary ingredients ready mixed and all you need to do is to tip the contents out, add water carefully and mix thoroughly. This is an expensive way of using concrete for large amounts of work, but ideal for small jobs and for patching

Crazy paving Another popular paving material is crazy paving. This is available as York stone or broken paving stone. The best type of stone to use for its hard-wearing qualities is the former. There are two thicknesses which are generally available, 1½ inches and 2 inches. The irregular outline of crazy paving breaks up the monotony of a plain surface to a path, and it is particularly suitable for the old-world or cottage type of garden.

Precast slabs Paths can be made from precast slabs which are available in a

wide range of sizes and colours. This enables you to plan and lay paths of outstanding design and appearance. You do not need a great deal of skill to produce these effects, provided you make quite sure that the foundations are secure. So versatile are these slabs that they can be used for any situation.

Mixtures of materials By mixing materials it is possible to provide endless variations of path design. Old bricks can be used very effectively, especially if they are laid in herringbone fashion or in other unusual patterns. Cobble stones are available as a path-making material and are ideal for mixing with other materials. For example, a square of these pebbles can be framed by old bricks or paving slabs. With a little ingenuity and some artistic skill it is possible to use more than two materials. Various sizes of slab can be patterned or interset with pebbles or old bricks. It is important in this type of design to work it out carefully beforehand, either on paper or on the actual site itself by marking out the pattern with a pointed stick. Careful measurements must be made to make sure that all the designs fit accurately together.

Cold asphalt compound This provides yet another method of making paths in the garden. The process is extremely simple and as a long-term investment, compares very favourably in price with other ways of path making. The special material is available in 1 hundredweight sacks, together with special granite chippings which are used on the surface for decorative purposes. Two colours of compound are available, black and brown and a bag covers approximately 20 square feet.

Granite chippings Paths can be made from granite chippings but the big drawback with these is that they pick up

1 Several patterns of hoe are obtainable, although there are only two basic types —the Dutch hoe (as shown second from the left) and the draw hoe (the remaining tools).
2 A small hand hoe used for weeding.

badly on the feet. They are also liable to drift towards the lower parts of the path if it is on a slope. This type of material is best used for a path or sweep under a bay window, for example, where little treading will be necessary.

Laying the pathway Once the type of material has been decided upon, the preparations for laying should be carried out carefully and thoroughly. The route the path is to take must be marked out with pegs and line. If a curved or winding path is required, make sure that the curves are not acute or that the path weaves unduly. It is best to aim for gentle curves.

The amount of foundation preparation necessary will depend on several factors. The first is the type of soil in the garden. Light sandy ones need much more consolidation than the heavy clay types. Where there is any doubt about the firmness of the soil, plenty of small rubble must be rammed well into the foundation. Usually a depth of at least 6 to 9 inches should be taken out and the bottom 5 to 8 inches filled with rubble and rammed in well. Allowance must be made for the thickness of the paving material itself, also any bedding cement or mortar which may be required. In all calculations the finished level of the paving material should be just above soil level. This will do much to keep the path dry and will prevent the splash back of dirt or soil during periods of very heavy rain.

The width of a path should be considered and should not be under 2 feet for comfortable walking. It is as well to consider the wheelbase of trucks and wheelbarrows so that sufficient path width is allowed for them. Wider paths should be allocated for main routes to the busy parts of the garden where the wheelbarrow will be required a great deal. Areas around the greenhouse and frames are good examples.

There are several ways in which the paving materials can be laid. One is to place them on a 1-inch layer of sifted soil, sand or ashes. Make sure that the bedding material is as level as possible

and as each slab or brick is placed in position it should be tapped firm. It will be necessary to add or take away the bedding material to provide as level a surface as possible. Slight gaps can be left between slabs and filled in with the same material afterwards.

A slightly more secure way of bedding is to lay paving on the soil, sand or ashes and add under the centre of each a trowel full of mortar which is made up of 1 part of cement to 5 parts of sand. It is a good idea to apply a little more mortar for the larger slabs of paving and this can be done by adding extra amounts of mortar to the four corners.

The best method is to apply about $\frac{3}{4}$ inch of mortar evenly over the soil, sand or ashes, spreading the mortar over the area one slab will occupy. Work should proceed in this way slab by slab until the site has been completely prepared. Afterwards, a drier mortar mix should be brushed into the joints, taking great care that any excess is removed from the surface of slabs to prevent discoloration.

Particular care is necessary when smaller paving material is laid, such as old bricks or pebbles. The latter can be set in the mortar mix so that approximately $\frac{1}{4}$ of the base of each pebble is inserted and held in the concrete. The pebbles should be graded for size so that an even pattern is produced. It is advisable to have a 'dummy run' beforehand so that the pebbles can be arranged neatly and to size.

All paving set in mortar should be allowed to set thoroughly for 2 to 3 days before it is used. Work should not be carried out in very cold or frosty weather, but protection can be afforded from wet weather after work has been completed if large sheets of plastic material are placed over the paving.

The use of cold asphalt has revolutionised the art of path making for the garden. All that is required is the provision of a solid level foundation over which the preparation is raked to an even depth of about $\frac{1}{2}$ inch. A light rolling is given and then the granite chippings which are usually provided, are scattered carefully over the surface and lightly rolled in. The path is ready for immediate use and becomes firmer the more it is walked on. For the first few days after laying it is wise to avoid the use of heavily laden wheelbarrows as their wheels tend to make a slight impression until the path has been made firmer by walking on it.

It is most useful, if not essential, to know how far materials will go when trying to estimate for layouts. The tables in this article provide a guide to the approximate quantities of most of the popular paving materials for given areas or lengths of path. Most materials can be obtained from local horticultural sundries shops, garden centres or

1 On a gentle gradient a pathway consisting of a series of stepping stones looks attractive.
2 At Sissinghurst Castle, Kent, slabs and random stone are used together.

Making a path—length 10 feet

Material	Width of Path		
	2 feet	2½ feet	3 feet
Bricks laid flat	71	89	107
Bricks laid on edge	107	134	160
Crazy paving ¾–1½ inches thick	3 cwt	3¾ cwt	4½ cwt
Crazy paving 1½–2½ inches thick	5¼ cwt	6½ cwt	8 cwt
Paving slabs	4 cwt	5 cwt	6 cwt
Gravel 2 inches thick	3¼ cwt	4 cwt	5 cwt

	Amount used	Area covered
Pebbles	2 cwt	1 square yard
Cold Asphalt	1 cwt ½ inch thick	22–25 square feet
Slabs (pre-cast)		
9 inches × 9 inches	16	1 square yard
12 inches × 12 inches	9	1 square yard
18 inches × 9 inches	8	1 square yard
18 inches × 18 inches	4	1 square yard

Quantities for making paths (per square yard)

Path	Using shingle			Using mixed ballast	
Thickness in inches	Cement	Damp Sand	Shingle	Cement	Mixed Ballast
	lb	cu ft	cu ft	lb	cu ft
1½	16.6	0.36	0.55	16.9	0.75
2	24.8	0.54	0.83	25.3	1.12
3	33.2	0.72	1.11	33.7	1.50
4	49.7	1.08	1.66	50.6	2.25

builder's merchants. A big advantage with the garden centre is that many materials are on view and in some cases actually laid. This enables you to see the paths as they would be when completed. For making a path 10 feet long see the table 'Making a Path'.

As far as concrete paths are concerned, for the best possible results a suitable mixture of materials would be 1 part of cement, 2 parts of sand, 3 parts of shingle. If mixed ballast is preferred, the proportions should be 1 part of cement, 4 parts of mixed ballast. The aggregate size of the ballast should be graded from ¾ inch to 3/16 inch. The dry materials should be mixed together thoroughly on a clean, smooth, hard surface before water is added. Water should be added in small amounts as mixing proceeds until the final mix has the consistency of thick, smooth porridge.

It is necessary to be able to calculate material quantities with reasonable accuracy for paths of various lengths, widths, thicknesses and for difficult mixes. Based on the mix formulae already given, the quantities per square yard are shown in the table 'Quantities for Making Paths'.

Example of calculations to find the material quantities required for a path measuring 30 × 1 yard, using concrete 3 inches thick, with shingle as coarse aggregate:

Quantities per square yard 3-inches thick (as table);

Cement	33·2 lb.
Sand	0·72 cubic feet
Shingle	1·11 cubic feet

Area of proposed path, 30 × 1 yard = 30 square yards, therefore,

Cement	33·2 × 30 = 996 lb.
Sand	0·72 × 30 = 21·6 cubic feet
Shingle	1·11 × 30 = 33·3 cubic feet

It is best to order to the next hundredweight for cement and the next half cubic yard for the aggregate. Therefore, the following materials should be ordered:

Cement	9 cwt
Sand	1 cubic yard (27 cubic feet)
Shingle	1½ cubic yard (40½ cubic feet)

The appearance of a plain concrete path can be enhanced considerably if the surface is provided with a design while the material is still 'green' or wet. One simple method is to trace or score the surface lightly with a pointed stick or point of the trowel. The outline or false joins of paving slabs can be represented in this way, or crazy paving can be reproduced. Circles of different sizes can be lightly scored if round, empty tins or lids are pressed into the moist surface. A very pleasing rough cast finish can be provided if a stiff brush, such as an engineer's wire brush or stiff yard broom, is carefully used on the concrete when it is practically dry.

Paving flags used singly run down the centre of a grass path between flower borders making a neat effect in this fine example of an English cottage garden.

A little sharp sand lightly scattered on the surface and worked in with the brush will produce the same effect.

Colouring can play an important part in path construction and special colouring powders can be added to the cement as it is mixed. The only difficulty with this method is where several mixes of cement have to be made up during the work. It is difficult to ensure that every batch is of the same shade. Very thorough mixing is also required so that an even colouring is produced.

Once the concrete work has been completed it should be covered with damp sacking, hessian or plastic sheeting if it has been undertaken during hot weather. This will permit the concrete to dry or mature slowly and set thoroughly hard. Concrete should not be laid during very cold or frosty weather but in late autumn or spring the work can be carried out safely, provided some protection in the way of covering, is handy should there be light frosts.

Levelling

All paths in a garden must be made at a gradient which is comfortable and convenient not only for walking unencumbered, but for pushing a wheelbarrow or transporting a mower from one part of the garden to another. Where the garden is on a slope it may be necessary to make steps to change the levels.

There are very few gardens where the operation of levelling is not required in some form or other. Perhaps most of the work is required in new gardens, especially where the ground is very uneven. Old-established ones often require some reorganisation in places. There is a limit to the amount of levelling which should be carried out and before any work is started, it is most important that the site is carefully examined. This will enable you to plan your work so that the minimum amount of soil has to be moved during levelling operations.

If the garden has considerable differences in level, you would be wiser to work with the contours. This might involve the construction of sunken gardens, terraces, walling, pools, waterfalls and streams. It is surprising how very effective this type of design looks when incorporated in a difficult site. The most dramatic type of feature would be the construction of a series of waterfalls which finally empty into a pool at the lowest part of the garden.

The actual method of levelling is quite simple and there are several ways in which it can be undertaken. Sites which will need particular attention to levelling are those which are intended for the lawn and patio. To reduce work to the minimum, a place should be selected on the site for the required level which will not entail too much soil removal or addition to bring up the rest of the site level to this mark.

Once this has been decided upon, a peg should be driven in. From this master level peg, others are then inserted in the site and spaced apart according to the length of the level-board which is being used. This board should be a straight piece of plank, about 1 inch thick and 6–8 feet long. The level of these other pegs must be the same as that of the master one and this is checked at the start as each is inserted by placing one end of the board on the master peg and the other end on the peg which is being inserted. If a spirit-level is placed at the centre and on the edge of the board, the peg can be driven into the ground until a perfect level is registered on the spirit-level.

Work proceeds by placing one end of the board on this newly inserted peg and a third peg is levelled in the same way. The whole site is dealt with in this fashion peg by peg. The work is completed by either adding to or excavating the soil on the site until the soil is brought to the top of the pegs. In some cases it may be necessary to add a few barrow-loads of soil. A rake should be used to provide a good level finish.

Another method of levelling is by the use of boning rods. These are usually made of wood, 3 feet in length, with a cross piece 15 inches long at one end forming a 'T'. There are three to a set. Boning rods are used in the following manner: insert a peg ($1 \times 1 \times 9$ inches) into the ground, leaving about 2 inches protruding. This is the master peg, and should be driven in on the high or average high point of the plot. A second peg is knocked in, not more than 2 feet away, in the general direction to be sighted along. Check the level of these pegs by placing a spirit-level on the top bridging the two. A straight-edge board will be required if a short spirit-level is the only one available. Using the two pegs, place a rod upright on each, and sight across the tops of these to the third one into the distance, held by a second person. By this means you are able to see by how much the third peg requires to be adjusted. Other sight lines may be set out from the master peg, by inserting another peg not more than 2 feet away, and in the direction of a third in the distance. This method can be used for most levelling purposes, but it is invaluable where the site is very rough and undulating, because sightings can be made over heaps of soil and debris, whereas some difficulty can be experienced using a straight-edge board and spirit level. After all pegs have been inserted it is time to review the whole levelling operation, for an inch taken off the general level all round at this stage will save money in material, soils etc., and of course labour. Whether the pegs are knocked further into the ground or marked with brightly coloured paint, matters not, provided they are firm in the ground.

This type of levelling should be used where the site is very undulating, and will provide a rough first levelling of the soil. To produce a more accurate or even level, it will be necessary to use pegs, level-board and spirit-level as described in the first part of this section.

No matter what type of levelling is used, it is very important that the good top soil should be kept to the top of the site. It is too easy a matter to bury good soil and finish up with a newly levelled site filled with infertile soil. Where necessary therefore, quantities of the good top soil must be carefully removed as deeply as is necessary and placed in convenient positions around the site for re-use later on. Where it is necessary to fill in with quantities of new soil this should be consolidated every 6 inches in depth, by treading, or time should be allowed for it to settle down or consolidate before the site is made use of. Lighter types of soil can be trodden or given a light rolling for this purpose but

1 To establish a level at the height of the path, a peg is driven in and
2 checked with a spirit level.
3 The level is extended in this way.

only when they are in a dry, friable condition.

Lawn construction and maintenance

Most gardeners regard a lawn as an important, if not essential, feature of the garden. The lawn may in fact be the major feature, being a big expanse suitable for garden parties and surrounded by sufficient flower beds to set it off. Alternatively, the lawn may be a minor feature designed to set off flower beds. In either case the requirement is usually a good lawn, i.e. one which has a uniform cover of good grass and which is free of weeds and blemishes caused by disease, earthworm casts and the like. A lawn which is mainly for children's play or for use as a drying ground does not demand the same high standard as does the real ornamental lawn but should, at any rate, be capable of being regarded without horror!

Layout The general shape and contours required should be decided at an early stage, always bearing in mind that about 6 inches of top-soil should remain overall on completion with gradients designed to allow easy mowing in more than one direction and to allow surface water to escape, without collecting into hollows. The nature of the site—its contours, shape and features such as the levels of the paths, doors, existing trees or rock outcrops determines the form of the new lawn. Generally, simple contours and shapes with no awkward corners or mounds are most satisfactory and these can often be produced with little movement of earth. More ambitious programmes require stripping the top-soil before carrying out the necessary grading in the sub-soil. It is not necessary to think exclusively in terms of a square or oblong patch of lawn surrounded by borders. Some measure of landscaping should be introduced and an irregular shape can be planned with borders of varying width. The site can also be broken up by minor undulations, by terracing, by a shrub break or it can be combined with a crazy path, a rock garden or other features. The effect should nevertheless be bold rather than petty and frivolous.

Clearing the site The first step is to remove as thoroughly as possible any builder's debris or old ironwork, tree roots, etc. There may even be the odd load of gravel which can be used elsewhere. Small bushes and long grass can be cut and burnt.

Grading On a great many sites, a new lawn can be made without major alterations in the levels and, in fact, few of us have the energy required to embark on extensive work of this kind. There is no need for the lawn to be absolutely level but it should, of course, be smooth to whatever gradient is accomplished. A gentle slope, say 1 in 80

A two-year-old lawn, grown from seed.

is, in fact, quite a good thing to help shed surface moisture during rain. Minor adjustments in levels can be achieved by moving top-soil, always subject to the limitation that at least 6 inches (or at any rate a minimum of 4 inches) of good top-soil must obtain everywhere on completion. Sometimes it is convenient to buy in a few loads of top-soil to improve levels.

Where considerable grading is required, the really hard work of stripping the top-soil so as to allow grading in the sub-soil is necessary. Such work may have to be accomplished in sections because of space limitations. The top-soil is piled up on one side and the sub-soil gradients altered (usually by cut and fill) before returning the top-soil. There will be few sites where it is necessary to become very technical and use various devices to achieve satisfactory levels; most people will be able to manage satisfactorily by the use of pegs, string and possibly a straight edge.

It is important to remember that soil handled in wet conditions is adversely affected and particularly so where machinery is brought in to help out. Care should be taken to work under dry conditions if at all possible.

Drainage On many sites, particularly where grading has been carried out by machinery, the sub-soil as well as the top-soil is heavily consolidated and, unless this consolidation is removed, the moisture penetration is severely impeded. On relatively small areas,

double digging may be needed in order to break up both the sub-soil and the top-soil. On larger areas the sub-soil cultivation can be achieved by means of a tractor-drawn sub-soiler which is usually best used in two directions after replacement of the top-soil.

Whether or not tile drainage or any other form of drainage is required depends on individual site peculiarities. From experience it would seem that most people are able to manage without drainage for their lawns but certainly the possible need for drain-pipes ought to be given some consideration. Clearly, it is not possible to have healthy grass and a good lawn if the soil is waterlogged. On wet land a simple line of clayware land tiles will often suffice provided that some form of outlet can be provided. It is best if the drains can be connected to a main drain somewhere since soakaways, while not without merit, are seldom entirely satisfactory. On large lawns on wet land a proper herring-bone system of drainage may be wanted and whenever land tiles are used it is a good plan to cover them with coarse gravel or clinker ash to within about 6 inches of the final surface of the lawn this being covered finally with 6 inches of top-soil (i.e. no sub-soil)

Preparing the top-soil All debris such as large stones, big plant roots etc., should be removed and all steps taken to prevent contamination with sub-soil or any deleterious material. Digging is the first operation and any old turf which exists should be buried. If this digging is done in autumn or winter the soil may be allowed to weather during frost. The land can then be worked down by Dutch hoes, rakes etc., in the drier spring weather. During the preparation of the soil it is a good idea to improve it by digging in various materials. Thus, on really heavy soil up to 1 cwt of gritty lime-free sand per square yard can be worked in with advantage and also on such sites, to keep the soil open after the lawn has been made, up to 7 lb of granulated peat per square yard may be advantageous. Light, sandy land benefits from organic materials designed to improve moisture-holding capacity. Well-rotted stable manure at say 14–28 lb per square yard is an excellent thing but this is in short supply and may have to be substituted by such things as leafmould or granulated peat (up to 7 lb per square yard).

The next thing is to try and ensure that the prepared land is free from roots and seeds of undesirable plants which may establish themselves and compete with the new grass. The best way of accomplishing this is to give a complete summer's fallowing, i.e. allowing the weeds to germinate and then raking or hoeing them out. To take some exasperation out of all this it is a good plan to grow a potato crop or similar which gives some encouragement and return for the work involved. Chemical cleaners have some merit but they are not the complete answer to the problem.

Whether the lawn is to be established from seed or turf, the final preparations are fairly similar in that in either case we need a firm, fine soil bed. Repeated cultivations and consolidation are needed. The site may be broken down by means of a Canterbury hoe or mechanically as seems most appropriate and then rough raking follows with the removal of the larger stones. To try to eliminate air pockets in the body of the soil it is wise to 'heel' the surface, an operation which involves close treading with the weight of the body thrown on the heels so that the soil is pressed down into the soft spots. For this operation the soil should be dry enough not to adhere too much to the boots.

Further raking and heeling at right angles to the first set of operations should follow. Final working should aim at achieving a smooth surface from which small bumps and depressions have been entirely eliminated while the soil is sufficiently firm (though not over compacted) to minimise the risks of sinkage later producing an uneven surface. A rather better tilth is required for seeding than for turfing.

Turfing This is popularly accepted as being the best way to produce a satisfactory lawn. This is not strictly true, but undoubtedly the use of turf does simplify matters for the amateur and does make possible the use of less perfect soil conditions. Unfortunately good turf is both rare and expensive so that many people become disappointed with the lawns they have obtained by this method. Frequently the supplier is blamed for the unsatisfactory results despite the original acceptance of the turf as satisfactory, there possibly having been some mistaken idea that the turf would improve after laying. There is now a

British Standard Specification for turf so that purchasers buying to the standard have some control over what they receive, though they may in fact require a higher standard than that covered. The major gain from turfing is that of time, since the turf can be laid in the autumn when it is too late for seeding and with good management can appear as a really good lawn, capable of being used, the following summer. Turf laid in spring and summer runs the risk of drying out and not establishing satisfactorily.

Great care should be taken when buying turf, which should preferably be established in soil of a sandy loam nature and free from stones. The delivered turf should be in mown condition, of close texture and good uniform density and colour. There should be sufficient fibre to hold the turf together for handling but excess leads to unsatisfactory results. The quality of grasses in the turf which is bought depends on the requirement but for a first-class lawn there should be little in the turf except fine bent and/or fescue grasses and, even for second-class lawns, weeds and diseases should be absent.

The delivered turf is best in 1 foot squares (or possibly 2 feet × 1 foot) and cut to a uniform thickness of say 1¼ inches. If the turf which arrives is uneven in thickness it may be desirable to box the turf, i.e. to lay the turf, roots up, in a shallow tray of suitable depth and then draw a stout knife across the top edge of the box, thus bringing the turf to the standard thickness.

Before laying the turf the soil should receive such chemical treatment as is required. Acid soils may need lime and this is best decided as the result of a soil test. Usually it is wise, whatever

the nature of the soil, to give a fertiliser on the following lines:
6 lb of fine hoof and horn meal
6 lb of fine bone meal
6 lb of powdered superphosphate
3 lb of sulphate of potash
per 100 square yards
The fertiliser should be raked in, preferably a few days before laying the turf.

When the actual turfing operation starts it is wise to choose weather conditions when the soil is reasonably dry to avoid damage to the prepared site. On many sites it is convenient to start by laying a single turf round the perimeter of the site. After that, laying turf across the body of the site should be done in a forward direction, working to face the unturfed part which should be maintained in its prepared condition. Traffic should be on planks laid across the turf as required. The turf should be laid with broken joints, rather like bricks in a wall. Each turf should be laid flat and tight up to its neighbours. Where a turf seems to be either high or low adjustment should be made in the soil below rather than by beating down etc. When the whole of the turf has been laid it should be carefully rolled with a light roller and then a sandy compost material applied at 4 or 5 lb per square yard and carefully brushed in.

Seeding The best time for sowing grass seed on a new lawn is about the end of August. Spring sowings are not ruled out entirely but they do run a greater risk from drought since May is often very dry and in the spring, weed competition tends to be greater than in the late summer. Seeding is the cheapest and probably the best way of getting a good lawn but the best results are only achieved if sufficient skilled work is put into the work of seeding and of looking after the lawn in the first year or so.

In the final stage of preparations and a few days before sowing a suitable

1 The grass on a newly-sown lawn should be only lightly clipped over.
2 Young perennial weeds which appear in the sward should be removed by hand.

complete fertiliser should be given and this might well take the form of:

3 lb of sulphate of ammonia
3 lb of fine hoof and horn meal
3 lb of dried blood
6 lb of powdered superphosphate
6 lb of fine bone meal
3 lb of sulphate of potash
per 100 square yards

This should be carefully raked into the soil a few days before sowing. Soils of an acid character should have been limed appropriately a week or two earlier.

The kind of grass seed to use depends on the kind of lawn required and on the amount you are prepared to pay. For a first-class lawn a really fine mixture such as 8 parts of Chewings' fescue (preferably a good variety such as 'Highlight') and 2 parts of browntop bent (American origin) is suitable and the rate of sowing is about 1 ounce per square yard. Less fine mixtures may be used for hard-wearing, second-quality lawns and, for children's playground type of lawns, even coarser mixtures containing perennial ryegrass may be used. For all these grass seeds a rate of application of 1 ounce per square yard is satisfactory. There are, of course, good proprietary mixtures available from reputable lawn seed suppliers and generally speaking one can go on price. The more expensive the mixture the better the quality, with prices varying from 25p to 50p per pound of seed.

Sowing is best done on a dry, raked surface and it is wise to divide the seed into two lots for sowing in transverse directions. For really careful work it is best to divide the lawn into sections and weigh out the amount of seed for each section and then again split this into two halves for transverse sowing. The seed should be lightly raked in and there has to be emphasis on the lightness of this operation, particularly for the very fine mixtures, since the grass seeds should not be deeply covered. It is not usually necessary or desirable to roll after raking but rolling will be needed when the grass is showing through in order to tighten up the soil round the grass roots preparatory to mowing.

The question of bird damage often arises in suburban areas and certain preparations are sold for treating the grass seed. These are of limited benefit

A new lawn should not be cut too high at first but gradually worked down to the height of cut that is required. It is a mistake to cut very short since no grass really thrives on such severe defoliation. The really fine grasses of a first-class

1 Putting piles of top dressing on the lawn ready for working it in.
2 Working in the top dressing, using the back of a rake.
3 The lute is another tool which may be used to work top dressing into the lawn by drawing it backwards and forwards.
4 Brushing off surplus top dressing.

lawn stand the closest cutting but even they should not be cut closer than $\frac{1}{4}$–$\frac{1}{2}$ inch. For medium lawns $\frac{1}{2}$–1 inch is suitable, while for ryegrass lawns 1 inch is more satisfactory since ryegrass (even the best varieties) does not like mowing any shorter. For lawns which are not required to be very fine many people use the so-called rotary mowers. Infrequent mowing damages the grass and during the vigorous growing season a good fine lawn needs mowing as much as three times a week while even a second-class lawn should be mown not less than once a week. It is an advantage if the lawn can be mown in different directions each time it is cut.

Less frequent mowing is necessary when growth is not vigorous but at no time should the grass get very much longer than its accepted height. Even during the winter months careful topping in the right weather conditions may be desirable. At whatever time of the year the lawn is being mown, the best results are produced if the operation is carried out when the grass is dry.

Although allowing the cuttings to fly means the return of plant foods, it is nevertheless considered wise to remove cuttings since they encourage disease, weeds, earthworm castings, coarse grasses and a soft surface.

Edging No matter how good a lawn is produced it looks second rate if the edges are not kept trimmed. Most owners of small lawns use ordinary hand

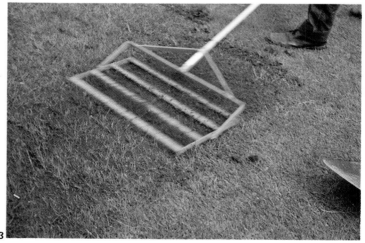

shears for cutting the grass at the edges but long-handled shears or special lawn edge trimmers are more favoured if the lawn is large. Even when given regular attention, edges tend to become uneven and attention with a straight spade or turf cutter is required about once a year. Permanent edges of metal, wood or concrete have decided advantages in keeping clean lines round the lawn.

Top dressing For a really good finish from mowing it is necessary that the surface of the lawn be smooth, otherwise in that frequently most damage is done by birds not so much eating the seed as spoiling the seed bed by having dust baths! The best protection is usually the very elementary one of having black cotton across the lawn supported by sticks. Some people lay polythene over the newly-sown lawn area but if this expedient is used it is important to get the cover away as soon as the grass shows through or disease attack may well undo all the good work and certainly do more damage than the birds.

After-care Lawns which have been established by turfing need occasional top dressing with bulky material such as sandy compost, or of an artificial compost made up from soil, sand and peat. The purpose of this dressing is to smooth out the surface and fill in any cracks, so it needs careful working in by a suitable drag brush or other piece of equipment. Occasional rolling may be required but this should not be overdone. During the first year the grass will need mowing regularly but over-close mowing should be avoided, particularly if it shows signs of skimming any prominent piece of turf. In the spring following turfing a good general fertiliser should be given as for an existing lawn.

New-sown lawns should not be mown until the grass is about 2 inches high and then it should be carefully topped, preferably using a side-wheel machine which is sharp and in good condition. Before mowing, stones should be picked off the surface and the area carefully rolled. Mowing should then be done when the grass has regained its upright condition. Any coarse grass or weeds which appear in the new sward should be removed by hand at intervals but mowing will dispense of annual weeds satisfactorily. On no account should the grass be allowed to get too long and regular mowing is essential with the height of cut being gradually lowered to the chosen final height. A lawn which has been sown at the end of the summer or early autumn will not need any further fertiliser treatment until the following spring. It should then receive a dressing of general fertiliser such as for an existing lawn.

The surface levels on a seeded lawn are unlikely to be as good as those of a turfed lawn and occasional top dressing with sandy compost at about monthly intervals during the first full year's growth will help to produce the smooth surface which is such an attractive feature of a good lawn. A few weeks after sowing, bare patches which have been missed despite the best endeavours may become visible and at this stage it is useful to have reserved a small quantity of seed so that over-sowing can be carried out straight away with the result that the patches soon catch up.

On new-sown turf the disease called 'damping-off' sometimes attacks, more particularly when heavy rates of seeding have been used or when a normal rate has been washed by heavy rain into concentrated collections in heel marks or similar depressions. Sometimes recovery occurs by natural means but if the disease is serious it is necessary to treat the grass with a suitable fungicide such as Cheshunt compound, which is applied by means of a watering-can, or more conveniently with an inorganic mercury fungicide applied as a dry dust.

Maintenance The essence of a good lawn is that it is uniform in texture, colour and surface smoothness with freedom from patches caused by weeds, disease, earthworms, or bad mowing. The lawn needs to be sufficiently hard-wearing to stand what is required of it and it should maintain a good colour both in summer and in winter. This colour at the various seasons is in part a reflection of the grass variety, in part of the feeding and in part of moisture control. The earth should hold sufficient moisture to keep the grass growing in dry weather but should not be waterlogged in winter.

Mowing Regular, not too keen mowing, is essential if the lawn is to be attractive and satisfactory. The first requirement is a good mower in good condition and, of course, buying mowers has much in common with buying cars. Personal choice comes into the matter as well as the engineering performance and the price. For best results the most expensive conventional mower (roller type) of a given size may well be the best and, of course, an important factor as far as grass is concerned is the number of cuts to a linear yard. A motor mower has advantages in reducing muscular effort particularly on large lawns but it is wise to buy as light a machine as possible since regular use of a heavy machine results in considerable compression of the top soil

you will find long grass in the hollows and skimmed turf (and later, moss) on any high patches in the lawn. Obviously the smoothness of the surface owes something to the original preparation of the lawn and rolling will help to push down some of the higher areas. Unfortunately rolling accomplishes this smoothing out at the expense of producing consolidation and this is not good for root development or for moisture penetration. Rolling must, therefore, be kept to a minimum.

The best way of achieving a really smooth surface is to follow the practice of professional groundsmen or greenkeepers, i.e. top dressing the surface with bulky material of suitable texture. What is best for most lawns is a sandy compost material which might be made up for example by mixing sand, soil and peat to make a product of a consistency something similar to good potting compost but, of course, without any added fertilisers. This material is spread over the lawn by hand or shovel fairly evenly and then worked into the surface by means of a drag mat or drag brush. On small areas the back of a wooden rake can be used to work the material backwards and forwards so that it disappears into the base of the sward, obviously going preferentially into hollow areas. Care must be taken to avoid smothering. Amazing benefits in the appearance of the lawn can be achieved by this often neglected practice.

Fertiliser treatment Requirements for fertiliser on existing lawns vary considerably: on rich soils fertilisers may not be needed more than once in five or ten years while on poor soils where wear on the lawn is heavy two good fertiliser dressings a year may be advisable. On average, once a year is at least enough and a reputable brand of lawn fertiliser can be given each spring. If you wish to know what you are putting on, you may care to make up a mixture yourself on the following lines:
3 lb of sulphate of ammonia
1 lb of fine hoof and horn meal
1 lb of dried blood
4 lb of powdered superphosphate
1 lb of fine bone-meal
1 lb of sulphate of potash
per 100 square yards.
Such fertilisers must be well mixed with sandy soil or similar material to the extent of about 28 lb of this per 100 square yards in order to give more bulk to help uniform distribution and also to minimise scorch risk. The addition of 1 lb of calcined sulphate of iron per 100 square yards to the above mixture helps to improve grass colour and to check weeds and disease. Careful, even, spreading of fertiliser is best carried out during showery weather but if no rain falls within one or two days of the application the fertiliser should be watered in to avoid damage to the grasses.

An experienced professional groundsman obtains the best distribution by hand spreading and the amateur gardener should not despise this method though it needs to be done carefully. Small distributors are available but difficulty is always experienced in matching up adjacent 'breadths' to avoid missing strips or overlapping, while the turns also worry many people.

Liming A good gardener has to use lime

occasionally in many parts of the country but he should not transfer this wise practice to the lawn since liming encourages weeds, worms and disease in the lawn. The soil sometimes does, in fact, become too acid and require liming but the disadvantages of liming are such that it pays to try to make sure that liming is really necessary before starting. The soil test, of course, is the ideal way. When liming a lawn a light dressing only, of a material such as ground limestone (ground chalk) is needed at a rate of 2–4 ounces per square yard. Excess of lime encourages worms, weeds etc. and reduces the proportion of fine grasses.

Mechanical operations While a great deal of mechanical work is necessary on bowling greens, golf greens, tennis courts etc., it is possible to over-emphasise the amount of work required of this kind on the average lawn.

Nevertheless, regular brushing or light raking of the lawn keeps the grass in good condition, prevents the formation of excess fibre and keeps the grass growing vertically to give the appearance of a nice, new carpet with the pile standing upright. Light raking also brings up the runners of weeds such as clover and thus prevents them from spreading. On old lawns which have become over-fibrous, vigorous scarification with a wire rake to get out some of the fibre is a good idea. Such vigorous work is best carried out at the end of the summer while there is still sufficient growth to heal up any disfigurement which might be caused, or to a less severe extent in the spring when growth is beginning. If you have a large lawn you may be able to use a mechanical scarifier.

Rolling is useful in the spring to firm up the ground after any upheaval caused by the winter frosts, but after that its use should be kept to a minimum if, in fact, it is done at all following the first spring rolling. This, of course, is because of the consolidation which rolling creates.

To compensate for over-compaction some kind of aeration of the soil is occasionally desirable, but on the average lawn it should not be necessary to do this heavy work annually. Much depends on how much compression is produced by the amount of wear given, by the weight of the mower etc., but probably on the average lawn some kind of forking every three or four years would be sufficient. There are so-called hand forks which can be used. They are pressed into the ground by the foot and make holes which allow water and air to penetrate and also encourage rooting. If there is severe compaction it is wise to use forks which have hollow tines which remove a core of soil, thus allowing the surrounding soil to expand and thus, of course, in turn relieving the pressure.

The grass roots very well down these holes and it will be appreciated that a good deep root system helps the resistance of the grass to drought and indeed to wear and tear. Some of the special forks for aerating the lawn have solid tines which may be cylindrical or flat in shape. These do not make such a complete job as the hollow-tine forks, but on the other hand they do not leave holes which are easily invaded by weeds. There is no doubt at all that hollow tine forking can be overdone. Various types of machine, ranging from hand pushed to complex motorised models, are available for carrying out forking work and in view of the labour involved, if you have a large lawn, you will no doubt consider purchasing or hiring such a machine

Watering Grass cannot grow without sufficient moisture, so that in dry weather a really good lawn needs artificial watering occasionally to keep it at its best. Watering should start early on in the dry weather, i.e. before the grass starts turning brown and the watering should be done quite copiously when it is done at all, so that the moisture penetrates deeply down to the roots. Light damping of the surface from time to time may do more harm than good by encouraging surface rooting and thus making the grass more liable to damage by drought. Many gardeners apply water to their lawns by means of the hosepipe with some kind of spraying device at the end, but a simple kind of sprinkler, of which there are many now available, is extremely useful and, in fact, may be so used as to water the lawn and the adjacent flower beds at the same time. Where difficulty is experienced in getting the water to penetrate, shallow spiking is useful to start the moisture penetrating the surface.

Artificial watering is not an unmixed blessing in that it tends to encourage annual meadow grass and weeds such as pearlwort, especially if the water is hard.

Weed control If management practices are satisfactory, weed invasion is kept to a minimum but some weeds will always manage to invade even the best kept lawns. The problem is fairly easy to deal with these days since the new selective weedkillers are so effective. Generally speaking, it is best to use one based on a mixture of the chemicals 2, 4-D and CMPP of which there are a number of proprietary compounds available. Repeated applications may sometimes be necessary for resistant weeds. The best conditions for using the weedkillers are when growth is active, when the weather is warm and the soil

**2 Aerating a compacted lawn, using a fork and thrusting the tines into the turf.
1 An oscillating sprinkler may be used to water both the lawn and the border.**

moist, though there is little prospect of rain, which reduces effectiveness. It is important to ensure that the chemical does not get anywhere but on the lawn since obviously all broad-leaved garden plants and greenhouse plants are susceptible. Any containers used should be carefully and thoroughly washed out before they are used for other purpose. Weedkiller applications are normally best carried out by means of a sprayer but, particularly in small gardens, sprayers are not recommended for lawn use since risk of spray drift on to plants in the flower beds is considerable. It is better to use a watering can fitted with a fine rose or with a dribble bar attachment. Uniform distribution is, of course, essential since missing strips means that some weeds will be untouched, while overlapping or excessively generous treatment to a given weed patch may cause severe damage to the grass.

Moss causes a great deal of anxiety to lawn owners—sometimes out of all proportion to the amount of moss. Usually moss in a lawn is a sign that there is something wrong somewhere in the management; either the lawn is starved, or is mown too severely, or has bad drainage, or is suffering too much from the shade of trees and buildings. Even low shrubs slightly overhanging the lawn can result in moss invading the shaded area and then spreading. The first essential, if moss is to be eliminated, is to find out the cause and to remove it or ameliorate it as far as possible. If this is done, then good results against moss can be obtained by using proprietary preparations containing mercury compounds such as a mercurised turf sand.

Pests The most important pest on a lawn is the earthworm. Generally the earthworm may be the gardener's friend but on the lawn the detrimental effects of the casts are considerable. They make the surface dirty, while their tunnels make the surface soft and the whole effect is that the lawn is wet and muddy. In addition, the casts smother grasses and act as first-class seed beds for weed seeds which may be brought up from below with the casted soil or which may be blown in from elsewhere. The use of lime or excessive amounts of organic fertiliser, or the retention of cuttings on the lawn, all of which encourage earthworms, should be avoided. It is better (and cheaper) if worms can be kept out rather than that they should have to be treated with chemicals. If it becomes necessary to control the earthworms by chemical treatment, mild conditions in autumn (or, rather less satisfactorily, in spring) when the worms are actually working near the surface, provide the best conditions. The two materials most usually used by professionals are lead arsenate and chlordane both of which are poisonous so that many lawn owners would prefer not to use them, especially where there are children and pets. Probably the best material to use in such circumstances would be one of the proprietary derris preparations sold for the purpose. The powder preparation can be applied dry and either watered in or may be left to be watered in during the next rain storm. Most of the earthworms die below ground with this treatment but a few will come to the surface and should be removed. Even derris products cannot be used if there is a fish pond adjacent, since derris is very poisonous to fish.

There are few other pests of lawns (other than the neighbours' pets) but leather-jackets are occasionally troublesome, particularly near the seaside and these can be dealt with by BHC or like powders sold for the purpose, or by lead arsenate if this is more convenient.

Diseases The most common disease of lawns is that known as fusarium patch disease (or snow mould) and this is most frequently met on over-fed lawns, particularly in damp, shaded situations sometimes occurring. Another fairly common but less damaging disease is corticium which shows as brownish discoloration, generally over quite large areas. This fungus disease is usually associated with insufficient feeding and quite often a dressing of fertiliser is the best remedy, but fungicidal treatment may be necessary to cure bad attacks.

Renovation From time to time patches of lawn become bare as the result of burning with fertiliser or wear and it is necessary to make these good. Sometimes it is convenient to bring a patch of turf from a less important part of the lawn but often it is necessary to prepare the earth and sow a little grass seed, and protect it from the birds. If the edges of the lawn become bare the best procedure is to strip the outside band of turf carefully, say 1 foot wide, to replace with turf cut from the next foot of the lawn, and then put the worn turf in place of this. The thin turf can then be overseeded

We can renew or increase many of the plants we have put out in our gardens by various means of propagation. The simplest method is aptly described by the name "division". It applies to plants which grow in the form of a clump, such as Michaelmas daisies. The roots are dug up in spring or autumn, divided, and the best and youngest sections replanted and the older and worn out pieces discarded. Many bulbs can also be divided.

Seed

Seeds are produced by plants following the fertilisation of the flower, as a means of reproducing the plant. Each seed is a plant embryo, which consists of a minute shoot and root and a store of food. The food reserve enables the embryo to grow before its root is devel-

1 A self-propelled cylinder type of lawn-mower powered by a petrol engine.
2 A self-propelled rotary grass-cutter.

oped to absorb nutrients from the soil and before the leaves emerge above the ground and make sugars by photosynthesis, a complex process. In some seeds, such as those of sunflowers or peas, the food reserve is starch but in others it may be oils or fats. The food reserve occupies the bulk of the volume of a seed. The seed is enclosed in a protective coat called the *testa,* which frequently has a small hole through which water can enter before germination.

Many seeds undergo a dormant period for some time before germination. This dormant period is useful in that it prevents the seed from germinating in the mild autumn only to be killed off when the frosts arrive. In many seeds the dormant period occurs because germination is delayed by reason of the very hard testa which has to be cracked open by the expansion and shrinkage that occurs during the cold weather. In other types of seeds growth-inhibiting chemicals have to be washed out by the rain before germination will occur. These growth-inhibiting chemicals can prevent the germination of the seeds of other species of plants. The rain washes them into the soil and germination of neighbouring seeds is prevented. Some seeds such as those of lettuce and mistletoe, require light before they will germinate, others not only will germinate in the dark but actually are prevented from germination by light.

When the seed is ready to germinate, water enters and the food reserve provides energy for the growth of root.

Treatment to ensure the germination of seeds is generally applied before they are sold commercially. Lack of knowledge of the treatment a particular seed needs often accounts for the failures gardeners may encounter when trying to harvest and germinate their own seeds.

Seed bed
This is a specially prepared site where seeds are to be sown. It may be in a frame or in the open garden but seldom in a greenhouse. Seed beds made in the open garden during early spring are often given cloche protection. There are two types of seed bed. In the first seeds are propagated to provide seedlings for transplanting elsewhere at a later date. In the second plants are permitted to develop where the seeds were sown. Excess seedlings in this type of bed are thinned when quite small. The term is more usually applied to the first type of bed which may be prepared between early spring and autumn. For most gardeners this form of seed bed is more likely to be made during the main sowing season from February to April.

A good tilth is necessary and where the soil has a high clay content it is advisable to dig the site fairly deeply in late autumn or winter. The dug soil should be left quite rough and no

1 A seed drill is drawn with the edge of a hoe along a garden line.

attempt be made to break it down. Disintegration of the surface soil will occur through the weathering action of frost and snow.

Where a light soil has been dug in autumn or winter it can become consolidated by heavy rains, and before a seed bed may be prepared in spring forking to a depth of 2–3 inches may be needed (see also Nursery bed; Raking;

Seed drills
These are the shallow trenches in which seeds of many garden plants are sown. Drills made in the open ground are generally made with the garden draw hoe (see Hoes and Hoeing). The onion hoe or even a sharp-pointed stick are more suitable for sowings in the cold frame or where the short rows are to be cloched. To ensure that the rows are straight, use the garden line. For frame rows, a straight piece of wood is more useful.

Care must be taken to make the drills of even depth. The depth should vary according to the size of the seeds being sown. Generally, the smaller the seeds, the more shallow should be the drill. As a rough guide consider the smallest seeds as needing a soil cover of ¼ inch. Larger seeds may be sown more deeply up to a maximum of 2 inches. The average depth for flower and vegetable seeds is between ½ and 1 inch. The width of a seed drill depends on what is being sown. Seeds of most garden plants are sown in a single straight row in V-shaped drills. Flat-bottomed, rather wide drills are best for some vegetable sowings, such as those of peas, where double or even treble rows of plants are to be grown close together.

Should the soil be on the dry side—as it so often is during late spring and summer, the drill should be flooded with water before sowings are made. Sow when the water has drained away. After sowing refill the drills by drawing the soil into them with the back of a rake. On light, sandy soils it is sometimes an

advantage to tread lightly along the rows after sowing (see also Seed bed).

Seed sowing
Many garden plants are propagated from seed and good germination is encouraged by providing the seeds with the best conditions. Moisture and air must be present in the propagating medium (whether soil or a special compost) and the temperatures must be suitable. Very high temperatures are seldom necessary. Most garden and greenhouse sown seeds need temperatures of 50–60°F (10–16°C) in which to germinate. Some seeds, notably those of tomatoes, cucumbers, melons and tropical plants need much higher temperatures.

In early spring and in autumn the garden soil is normally damp. Later in spring and in summer insufficient moisture can lead to poor germination. This condition may be remedied by watering seed drills before sowing, the seeds being sown on the wet surface. Straight seed rows are obtained by the use of a garden line or a length of straight wood.

Planting
Of all the operations that contribute to successful gardening, correct planting procedure is one of the most important. Digging a hole, pushing in the plant and hoping is not enough. Any gardener who does just this is doomed to constant disappointments.

Before the actual planting is carried out, careful preparation of the site is necessary, whether the project involved is an extensive border, the planting of a bedding scheme, or the tiniest pocket for an alpine plant. Beds, borders or planting holes should be deeply dug before planting. As far as beds and borders are concerned, full-scale trenching is best although nowadays, most busy gardeners settle for double-digging, or bastard trenching as it is sometimes called.

The surface soil must be broken down to a tilth of a fineness appropriate to the size of the specimens which are to be planted. Obviously, the ground for trees and shrubs will not require such careful preparation as it will for annual bedding plants or alpines.

As well as being thoroughly broken down, the soil should be in good heart. This means that it must contain enough humus and plant foods for the initial requirements of whatever is being planted. This can be achieved by digging in adequate quantities of humus-rich materials such as peat, leafmould, well-rotted garden compost, or animal manures.

These can be supplemented by a dressing of a slow-acting organic fertiliser such as bonemeal or steamed bone flour, forked into the topsoil a week or two in advance of planting or, where individual plantings are concerned, sprinkled into the holes.

Different kinds of plants will obviously

need different planting procedures. The smaller they are, the more carefully should the operation be carried out. Appearances, however, can sometimes be deceptive. Nothing could look more delicate and vulnerable than a seedling that has just made its first pair of true leaves. And yet, at this stage—the best stage for planting out most seedlings—they can be surprisingly tough, perhaps because transplanting causes less damage to their rudimentary root system provided that they are transferred, without undue delay, from seed pans into boxes or nursery beds.

Seedlings should be handled gently, yet firmly, easing them carefully out of the seed compost and grasping them firmly by the leaves between thumb and forefinger as you plant them out in their new soil.

After this operation, particular attention should be paid to watering. Little and often is the rule to follow. Over-watering can cause damping-off, but seedlings should never be allowed to dry out completely; this can prove equally disastrous.

Planting trees and shrubs When planting trees and shrubs strict adherence to right procedure becomes a matter of the greatest importance. If an annual plant, or even a perennial, is incorrectly planted, a year's growth only is lost, but trees and shrubs are long-term garden investments and any that get away to a bad start seldom attain full health and vigour. Careless planting, in fact, is probably responsible for more failures than pests, diseases and adverse weather conditions.

Planting holes should be both deep and extensive enough to contain the roots with room to spare. In heavy clay soils, it may be advisable to replace all or part of the earth taken from the planting hole with a mixture similar to the one already advocated for alpines. Alternatively, well-made and well-rotted garden compost can be used as replacement soil. Newly-planted trees and shrubs always seem to get away particularly well when good garden compost is made use of in this manner. They seem to develop an extremely high resistance to disease.

1 When seed is sown in pots the surface can be firmed with another pot.
2 River sand provides a seed compost for alpines.
3 Annuals sown in irregular areas will make a colourful border of flowers.
4 A broad flat drill for Peas.
5 Seed sown in drills in a seed box.
6 Seed sown broadcast in a seed box.

With the exception of dwarf shrubs and small subjects such as heaths and lavender, which are easily planted with a trowel, planting trees and shrubs is essentially a two-man operation—one to hold the plant in position in the hole and jiggle it gently up and down, while the other carefully fills in the soil round its roots and firms it in. The nursery soil mark gives a clear indication of the correct planting depths and if an inch or two of soil is allowed above this mark for subsequent settling, this will be satisfactory.

When plants arrive, as they often do, during or after periods of unsuitable planting weather, it may be several weeks before the soil returns to a suitable consistency for planting. Heavy clay soils, in fact, often remain in a sticky, unworkable condition for most of the winter.

Although the packing of plants for despatch has been revolutionised, so that they come to little or no harm if they remain in the packing material for several weeks, it is always better to get them into the ground immediately on arrival, unless a really hard frost or a heavy snowfall makes planting impossible. An ordinary winter frost that forms only a thin crust on the soil surface need not prevent the planting of

trees or shrubs, unless they happen to be partially tender. It is possible to plant, however sticky the soil may be, if a reserve of good garden soil, fibrous loam or compost, or a mixture of old potting soil, compost and peat, is kept under cover for the purpose. It is only necessary to keep off the worst of the weather; if the reserve supply is slightly moist, so much the better. The wet, sticky soil is removed from the planting holes and the reserve mixture is used in its place.

Normally, newly-planted shrubs will not require staking unless they are in very exposed situations where high winds can cause root disturbance. Heavy frosts, however, often lift the plants in their first winter and severe gales may rock them, causing holes round the base of the stems where moisture can stagnate. It is important, therefore, to make the rounds of newly-planted specimens at regular intervals and firm back any that show signs of displacement.

Certain shrubs, such as rhododendrons and azaleas and most conifers come from the nursery with their roots 'balled', i.e., surrounded with a ball of soil and tightly wrapped in hessian or polythene. After removing this covering, care must be taken not to disturb this root ball

Planting a Magnolia is a simple job.
1 The hole has been prepared with a good dressing of moist peat. The bush with its root-ball intact is lowered carefully into the hole. The stick laid across the hole is used as a guide to the correct planting depth.
2 Soil and peat are returned round and over the root-ball.
3 Firming the soil round the shrub.
4 Applying a final dressing of peat completes the job.

when planting. Rhododendrons and azaleas, incidentally, scarcely need 'planting' as such. They do best resting in holes filled almost to the top with peat or leafmould, and surrounded with more of the same material or with a lime-free compost.

With trees, stakes are essential. They must be stout enough to support the tree during its first few seasons. Ideally, they should be driven into the ground before the trees are planted, so that the fibrous roots can be spread round them. This, however, is not always practicable and the risk of root damage when stakes go in after planting is not great, provided a sharp-pointed stake is used. An alternative method uses two shorter

stakes, one driven in vertically 2 feet away from the main stem, with another meeting it at an angle of 45 degrees. The main stem is secured to the diagonal cross-piece. This is a particularly effective way of staking half-standards, or of staking any tree in a windy situation.

When the tree is being secured to the stake, a tie of sufficient width must be used to avoid cutting into the stem. Narrow ties of string or twine are both useless and dangerous. They invariably get overlooked until it is too late and they have bitten into the cambium layer, with disastrous results. The best things to use are adjustable plastic or rubber ties. Failing these, strips of sacking or hessian make an effective substitute.

Developments in container-grown plants and garden-centre marketing have made it possible to plant trees and shrubs at almost any time of year. Large tins are favourite containers for plants grown in this manner. It will be necessary to slit the tins down on both sides, in order to simplify the removal of the contents without disturbance to the root ball.

Paper pots can be stripped away when the plant is actually in position and the contents of clay pots can usually be removed by upending the pot and gently tapping the edge on a wooden surface. If necessary break the pot rather than damage the root ball.

Some plants send up new shoots from roots which may have travelled some way from the parent plant. These shoots, known as suckers, can be removed with a spade or knife, together with a portion of root, and replanted.

The most common means of propagating the greatest number of plants is by taking cuttings. These cuttings can consist of young, green stem-growths, semi-ripe wood, single leaves, buds and roots. Most cuttings are rooted in a greenhouse and are therefore discussed in detail in the chapter on that subject, but hardwood cuttings of many trees, shrubs, fruits and hedging materials can be taken in the open. The best time is in the early winter and the cuttings should be made from pieces of the current year's growth, about 9–12 inches in length, pencil thick, with a clean cut just below a bud eye. Remove all the leaves except a few at the top and insert the cuttings in sandy soil to a depth of about 4–6 inches, firming the soil around the cuttings. By the following spring most of these cuttings will have pushed out roots and they can then be planted out or potted up to be grown on for a while.

Root cuttings These consist of pieces of root about 2 inches in length taken from plants with fleshy roots, such as anchusas, oriental poppies, gypsophilas, verbascums, romneyas, seakale and horse-radish. This is an autumn or winter job, the roots being lifted and then cut into pieces of the required length. The cuttings are usually made from roots which are about the thickness of a pencil, though where seakale and horse-radish are concerned they are made from side-roots and may be thicker than this. When making the cuttings make a clean, flat cut across the top and make the base wedge-shaped, then there will be no problem as to which way up the cuttings are to be placed when they are rooted in deep boxes of sandy soil. The top of the cuttings should only be just below the surface and the pieces of root can be placed side-by-side, horizontally or vertically (wedge-shaped end downwards), and made firm in the soil. The boxes should be stood in a cold frame or cold greenhouse for the winter months, and may be stood in the open in the spring. When top growth is evident, which is usually by the spring, the cuttings should be planted or potted up separately. With plants, such as herbaceous phlox, *Primula denticulata*, or the little alpine *Morisia monantha*, which have much thinner, thread-like roots, these may be treated in the same manner except they are merely placed lying on the soil in boxes, or pots, and then lightly covered with sandy soil. The greenhouse, evergreen, flowering bouvardias may also be increased in this manner, but with these it is best to take the cuttings in spring and bring them along in gentle warmth.

Pipings The rooting of pipings is a method of propagation used primarily for members of the dianthus family, particularly carnations and pinks. Pipings are in effect a type of cutting, but instead of using a knife to make the cutting, the shoot is pulled out from the main stem. The tip of the leading shoot is held gently between the thumb and forefinger, just above the first node, and pulled until it slides out of the node where the first pair of leaves has formed. The main part of the stem should be held with the other hand. There is no need to prepare it in any further way, and the piping can be inserted in a sandy compost to root in the usual way. Pipings are usually taken in early summer from young non-flowering shoots.

Layering Numerous shrubs, such as rhododendrons, magnolias, syringas (lilacs), hardy heathers, as well as figs, loganberries and cultivated forms of blackberries, are readily increased by this means. With these plants the work is done in the autumn or during the dormant season, as with clematis, jasmine and honeysuckle. Border carnations and pinks, however, are layered in July, after they have flowered, and the layers will root in a matter of weeks in the warm soil. The more permanent shrubs may take six months or longer to develop sufficient roots for the layer to be severed from the parent plant. A layer should consist of a long, healthy shoot that can be bent down to the ground where it is pegged down into

3

1 Root cuttings are made of Horse Radish during the winter, taking side roots and cutting them into short lengths. The pieces are trimmed with a flat cut across the top and a slanting cut at the base.
2 The cuttings are dibbled into open ground, a few inches apart.
3 Pulling the shoot out of a carnation stem to make a piping.

moist soil to which peat and sharp sand have been added either in the open ground or into a pot filled with a similar compost. Before the layer is pegged down, or kept in place with a stone or brick, a cut should be made with a sharp knife on the underside of the stem, so that the stem is severed horizontally for about 1–2 inches, the cut being made so that it passes through a node or joint. This is the part which should be pegged into the soil. The object of making the cut is to check the flow of sap and the cut will then callus and roots develop at this point. The same object may be achieved with many shrubs by merely twisting the shoot, or bending it until it is partially broken, at the point where it is to be pegged into the soil. With such vigorous plants as the blackberry and loganberry all that is necessary is to peg down the tip of a stem and this will quickly make roots in moist soil. This is known as tip layering. With strawberries, the runners are pegged down in June and July. Roots are made quickly and the rooted layers can be severed from the parent plant in August and September and transplanted or potted.

Layers of clematis should not be made from the current year's growth, but from parts of the stem that are 18 months old or more. This also is done in the dormant season and the same method applies to the climbing honeysuckles (loniceras).

Every good gardener wishes not only to propagate new plants from his existing stock but also to keep it in good health and as beautiful and productive as possible. This means pruning, a much misunderstood subject. The basic rule should always be: if you are not sure about pruning a particular tree, shrub or climber, don't do it at all.

Pruning ornamentals

Ornamental shrubs and trees by no means all require pruning; certainly not regularly. A number profit from it, however, even though they may survive without it. Pruning ornamentals is simply a matter of assisting them to appear at their best.

Whether to prune or not to prune depends to a great extent on the nature, performance and growth characteristics of individual species and specimens. The subject is not difficult to understand.

Pruning before flowering Many shrubs flower during the second half of summer and after. These should be pruned early to allow time enough for the production of the maximum amount of new growth which should bear flowers of the best quality. However, not all shrubs which flower late need pruning—hibiscus, for example.

Among those shrubs that flower in late summer are *Buddleia davidii*, hypericums, deciduous ceanothus, *Spiraea × bumalda*, perovskias, *Ceratostigma willmottianum*, *Leycesteria formosa*, *Hydrangea paniculata grandiflora*, hardy fuchsias, and *Potentilla fruticosa* in its many varieties.

The buddleia, perovskia and ceratostigma should be cut hard back in spring, to encourage as much new growth as possible (in any case, buddleias will become large and ungainly if left alone, even though they will survive). Treat deciduous ceanothus and the taller hypericums in this way, too, if necessary though they do not demand it. Leycesteria may be required to grow very tall; if it is cut back in spring, it will do so. *Hydrangea paniculata grandiflora* will grow particularly vigorously and flower profusely if cut hard back in spring.

Spiraea × bumalda will soon make a probably undesirable thicket if it is not relieved of some of its older wood and its young growths shortened in March. And, while *Potentilla fruticosa* rarely requires much attention, March is also the time for any pruning that may be needed. Hardy fuchsias—*F. magellanica riccartonii*, for example—when cut back

1 Strawberry runners can sometimes be pushed into the ground.
2 Alternatively, they can be trimmed of excess leaves first.
3 Then pegged down into the soil so that roots will grow behind the bud.

in spring, thrust up strong new growth to bear fine flowers in late summer. The old stems, tied together at their tops, as the year wanes, will give some protection to the crowns against winter weather. Left unpruned, fuchsias flower a little sooner, but in time can attain somewhat unmanageable proportions.

Pruning after flowering Early-flowering shrubs on the whole require to be pruned after they have flowered. This allows new flowering wood a chance to arise and mature in readiness for another year's display. It also allows existing unflowered wood scope for full development, so that it may also flower, probably the following year. The point is that many shrubs flower on one-year-old and older wood. Sufficient of this must be promoted and encouraged to ensure regular and worth-while crops of flowers.

The growths to cut away are, conveniently enough, those that have just flowered. This, basically, makes much of the pruning of this kind of shrub self-explanatory.

Forsythia is a good example of an early-flowering shrub calling for pruning after it has bloomed. If the job is done before the leaves have fully developed, flowered wood is more easily seen and removed and the risk of severing the growths that will flower the following year is reduced. Forsythia is a shrub which is better for minimal pruning, otherwise it may well throw up much non-flowering, leafy growth. Removal of spent growth, only, therefore suits it very well as a general rule.

Kerria japonica flowers on the early side and the flowered growth is best cut away when the blooms have faded. *Spiraea arguta* and *S. thunbergii* repay similar attention. Philadelphus, or mock orange, flowers in early summer, so does weigela or diervilla. These shrubs also need pruning after they have finished flowering. They soon make unproductive thickets if the older growths are not cut away. Kept clear of spent wood, they will remain in good form, producing ample new growth which will flower

when it ripens.

Syringas (lilacs) require the removal of spent flowerheads when at last the petals have all browned and shrivelled. The buds below the flowerheads should not be damaged; new flowering growth will be produced from these. Thin, twiggy growth, can be cut away at the same time. Brooms (cytisus), too, respond by producing new growth if they have their old shoots with developing seed-pods removed. This pruning helps to ensure that there need be little or no cutting back into old wood as the plants mature, because brooms respond poorly to this.

It should also be remembered that there are plenty of shrubs which do not require any pruning at all, even though they flower in the spring and summer period. The viburnums, which flower in spring and summer are examples. The winter-flowering species and hybrids also need little attention.

A number of evergreens flower during the first half of the year. *Berberis stenophylla* is one, well-known for its sprays of golden-orange flowers and as an excellent hedging shrub. *Berberis darwinii,* with miniature holly-like leaves, produces its orange flowers in April and May. This, too, makes a good specimen shrub and hedging plant. Both these evergreens may be pruned after they have flowered, though when they are grown as individual specimens, such attention is not essential. Indeed, left unpruned, full pleasure can be taken from their annual crop of handsome dark fruits. When they are used for hedging

1 Perovskia atriplicifolia is one of the shrubby plants that benefit from being cut hard back before flowering.
2 Perovskia atriplicifolia 'Blue Spire' having been pruned will throw up good flowering shoots in the summer.

purposes, however, the need for control does arise.

No pruning needed *Mahonia aquifolium* and *Mahonia japonica* are two very showy, early-flowering evergreens which need no pruning at all. Nor does the evergreen *Garrya elliptica,* whose silver catkins are so handsome during February, although it is better for removal of its dead catkins. If necessary, light trimming is permissible in May. However, those familiar with garrya's excellence for indoor decoration may have trimmed away some of the growth while its catkins were at their best.

Deciduous, winter-flowering shrubs such as daphne, chimonanthus and hamamelis, call for no pruning, though chimonanthus when grown against a wall will. Laterals will require to be shortened after flowering is over.

Pruning for bark effects A number of shrubs and trees bear particularly brilliant bark if they are encouraged to throw up plenty of new wood. Examples are certain dogwoods such as *Cornus alba sibirica*—vividly red—and willows such as *Salix vitellina britzensis*—glowing orange. Hard spring pruning is necessary to induce these to produce the maximum amount of young wood with the brightest bark. *Rubus giraldianus* is one of the showiest of the brambles with

'whitewashed' stems. The strongest and most spectacular canes arise from healthy plants which have been cut back annually after flowering.

Wall shrubs and climbers Many shrubs lend themselves to being trained against walls, as well as making good free-standing specimens. Examples include *Cotoneaster lactea* and pyracanthas, both evergreen, grown for their colourful autumn and winter fruits. Prune these lightly during summer, in order to encourage them to grow as required.

Chaenomeles (cydonia, japonica or flowering quince) is a deciduous shrub which responds well to wall culture. It needs to be spurred back when grown in this way. Cut away laterals after flowering, and then pinch out the tips of resultant young growths during summer. Alternatively, leave the plant unpruned until early autumn, then shorten the lateral shoots well back. Keep forward-pointing growths (breastwood) cut back or pinched back as they develop.

Wisteria is a climber which requires to be spurred back, not only to encourage flowering, but to curtail the long whippy growths which are characteristic and freely produced at the expense of flowering growth. The end of July is the time when, if practicable, all side growths made during the current year should be reduced to about 6 inches in length. A further shortening to an inch or two may take place in November.

Hydrangea petiolaris, an excellent climber for north walls, conveniently requires no pruning at all. The hederas, or ivies, also self-clinging, can strictly

speaking, be left alone too. But clipping them over in spring will keep them tidy and encourage the production of fresh young growth. The summer-flowering fragrant white *Jasminum officinale,* needs no pruning either, though it may be thinned in spring, if necessary. Old, neglected plants may need more drastic treatment. Thin the growths of winter jasmine after flowering, if necessary. Honeysuckle can be left alone, but thin in spring, if necessary, too.

Clematis pruning is straightforward enough if given a little thought and if basic facts about the genus are noted.

The small-flowered species can be left alone, though if the late flowering kinds among them grow too vigorously, hard pruning in February will correct matters. After flowering is the time to attend to the early flowering kinds, should they become a little out of hand.

Splitting the large-flowered varieties into their groups: varieties belonging to the *jackmanii* and *viticella* groups require hard cutting back to the lowest pair of healthy buds on each stem, every February, just as the buds begin to show green. Flowers are prolific on their new growth of the current year. Clematis in the *florida, lanuginosa* and *patens* groups need no pruning at all to all intents and purposes, after the initial cutting back in February after planting. They may, however, need a little pruning in February, where growth definitely appears dead. And should growth ever become beyond control, then they should be cut back hard in February.

Tools for the job Light to medium pruning may be done easily enough with secateurs. There are many different makes. It may be wise to have two pairs, one for lighter work and the other for heavier tasks. It is important to choose a pair which you can use comfortably. There are different styles, sizes and weights, and if work is to be done skilfully and easily, secateurs must fit the hand properly and be used without tedium and strain.

Cuts should always be made in the same plane as the secateur blades. Twisting will result in mangling cuts and straining the tool. Making sloping cuts for the purpose of shedding rain is wise, but cuts must still be made in the same plane as the secateur blades. Cuts should not, of course, be so sloping as to

1 Forsythia is an example of an early-flowering shrub that is pruned after it has flowered in early spring.
2 The stems that have flowered of Forsythia suspensa are cut hard back.
3 The branches of the shrub after the pruning has been completed.
4 Ribes sanguineum, the Flowering Currant, is pruned after flowering.
5 Old flowered wood is cut hard back.
6 The shrub, when pruning has been completed, looks like this.

slice wood away from behind a bud or growing point, thus allowing it to dry out.

Secateurs as opposed to shears, should be used for pruning or shaping certain hedges, where practicable. Examples include the larger-foliaged chamaecyparis varieties and the thujas. Cherry laurels and other large-leaved evergreens should be pruned rather than clipped, otherwise the cut leaves will turn brown and die, and look unsightly.

There are several powered trimmers, driven from the electric mains, portable generators, petrol engines, batteries, by flexible drive, and by power take-off units from motor mowers or cultivators.

Loppers, both short-arm and long, are useful. Short-arm loppers or pruners enable tougher cuts to be made with efficiency and speed where it is impracticable to use secateurs. Both anvil-cut and scissor-action kinds are available. Blades are short and very strong. Long-arm loppers, their blades operated by long arms, a form of remote control, enable distant and more inaccessible cuts to be made.

There is a fair range of pruning saws, both single-sided and double-sided. Especially useful is the Grecian pruning saw, short-handled or long. It is curved and pointed and cuts on the backstroke, making awkward cuts very easy.

Pruning knives were once widely used, but have largely been superseded by secateurs for general pruning. Some craftsmen, however, still use them, particularly in nurseries. They are still useful to have on hand for general purposes, and are still the best instrument for the all-important job of paring smooth the edges of large pruning cuts, especially those made by the saw. They should be used carefully; cuts are best made away from the user.

For the sake of efficiency and safety all pruning tools should be kept in good working order, sharp, clean and well-oiled.

White lead paint, bitumastic paint and proprietary tree-healing compounds should be used for sealing large cuts, to ensure that they heal rapidly and to prevent the entry of disease spores.

1 Treat large pruning cuts with a lead-based paint or a proprietary compound.
2 Use sharp secateurs and cut just above the buds to avoid damage.
3 A thin-bladed pad saw is useful for thinning overcrowded basal shoots.
4 A hand saw cuts awkward shoots.
5 A long-handled pruner can be used for shaping taller trees.

Normally little or no pruning is required for plants growing in beds or borders unless these consist entirely of shrubs.

Borders

There is no strict definition of the somewhat loose gardening feature known as a border, and there may, on occasions, be some confusion between beds and borders. However, for the sake of convenience, a border may be looked upon as a bed which is considerably longer than it is wide. True beds are normally round, oval, square or rectangular, or of some other geometric shape in which the length is not much more than, perhaps, two or three times greater than the width, although even this cannot be considered to be an exact definition since a bed, say, 2 feet wide and 6–8 feet long would be better described as a bed rather than a border; longer than this it may be considered as a narrow border,

sometimes described as a 'ribbon' border.

Borders may be of several different kinds. The most popular is the herbaceous border, in which are grown hardy herbaceous perennials in variety (see Herbaceous borders). A development of this which is seen more often nowadays, is the mixed border in which may be grown hardy herbaceous perennials, bulbs, flowering and foliage shrubs and even hardy and half-hardy annuals. Such a border needs careful planning and annual maintenance tends to be more complicated where bulbs are planted as there is always the danger of damaging these when the border is forked over in the late autumn or winter unless their positions are carefully marked. Again, the complete overhaul of the mixed border which is necessary occasionally and which necessitates digging up and dividing many of the herbaceous perennials, digging over the ground and incorporating bulky fertilisers such as manure or compost, is not a simple matter since the shrubs grown there are permanent features of the border and so do not need digging up; a mulch round them each year is usually sufficient.

Despite these reservations the mixed border can be an attractive feature in the garden for the shrubs, particularly the evergreens, provide an air of permanence and a certain amount of form and colour during the winter when there is normally little of interest in the traditional herbaceous border. It is also possible to plant shrubs which provide a certain amount of autumn colour in their foliage or fruit

Spring-flowering bulbs will provide much early colour and it may also be worth planting such early-flowering hardy perennials as the hellebores and bergenias, and such winter-flowering heathers as the *Erica carnea* varieties, thus extending the season of interest throughout much of the year. By comparison, the normal herbaceous border is usually looked upon as a summer and autumn feature.

The planting of young shrub specimens and small plants of hardy perennials tends to make the mixed border look a little sparse in its early years, but this may be overcome to some extent by interplanting with hardy or half-hardy annuals, or by sowing seeds of annuals where they are to flower.

Another way of filling bare patches during the summer particularly, is to plunge pots of plants in flower into the ground, to their rims. Such plants as dahlias and early-flowering chrysanthemums may also be used to provide extra colour. The imaginative gardener will find still more variations of planting up

In late June the perennial borders are most effective. This border edged with catmint is planted with Achillea, Lupins, Monarda, Delphinium and Kniphofia.

the mixed border to provide a satisfactory and colourful feature. As with any feature of this kind, it is best to plan it on paper first, taking into account such factors as height, colour and flowering period.

Two kinds of border which are occasionally seen, more often in large gardens than in small ones, are those devoted to one kind of plant and to plants of one colour. These can make pleasant features, but the drawback to a border devoted to one kind of plant is that its season is a short one. Thus a border planted up entirely with, say, lupins, paeonies, or delphiniums will be effective for not much more than three to four weeks. This may be tolerated in the large garden but is wasteful of space in smaller gardens. The one-colour border can be planned to have a much longer life, probably throughout much of the summer, but it is not easy to design to give continuity without awkward gaps appearing as plants go out of flower.

Another kind of border is the annual border, consisting entirely of hardy and half-hardy annuals. It is not too easy to plan a successful annual border, but properly planned and looked after it can be one of the most colourful features for many weeks during the summer and early autumn. In the process of preparing the plan, which should be done on paper first, it is essential to take into consideration the differing heights of the plants to obtain a satisfactory overall effect, and their colours to avoid colour clashes, particularly as many of the more popular annuals tend to have bright colours, not all of which associate well together. The unfortunate visual effect which can be produced by grouping orange and the brighter reds together, can usually be avoided by separating these colours with patches of white-flowered plants or with grey-leaved annuals.

To prolong the flowering period as much as possible it is essential to dead-head the plants as soon as the flowers fade, otherwise they will run to seed and cease to flower. Regular feeding with weak liquid fertiliser will also help to make the plants flower longer.

The range of plants which may be grown is wide, with great variation in height and colour. It includes a fair number of plants grown for their colourful foliage. A pleasant effect, especially in a long, narrow border, may be obtained by using dwarf annuals only, those up to about 9 inches tall.

Like the herbaceous border and the annual border, the shrub border is devoted to the cultivation of one group of plants, the shrubs, grown for their foliage or flowers or fruit, or sometimes a combination of two of these attributes, or all three. The same careful planning should be devoted to a shrub border as to any other type of border. Perhaps even more attention should be paid to the ultimate height and spread of the plants to avoid over-crowding and the subsequent need for drastic pruning which should be unnecessary in a properly planned shrub border

Garden pools

Siting the pool Before constructing any pool careful thought should be given to the siting. To create a successful bog garden or water garden, it must be situated right out in the open, in full sun. Although not essential it is advantageous to give protection from the north, if possible, as this will extend the flowering period both in autumn and spring. A belt of trees, a hedge or buildings on the north are all suitable. Overhanging trees are a disadvantage, both because of the amount of shade they cast and on account of their leaves which will undoubtedly fall in the water during the autumn. Weeping trees, although aesthetically pleasing in their early stages can mar a pool in a few years, as without sunlight you will get leaves on aquatic plants, but no flowers.

Give consideration also to the water supply, whether this is natural or artificial. Generally speaking large quantities of water are not required after the initial filling. Even in a discoloured pond you should not continuously run in fresh water or make frequent changes as this tends only to keep the water murky. Provided the pool can be reached with a garden hose a normal domestic supply is quite adequate. Drainage should be considered but is not very important, provided there is lower ground nearby or a drain on a lower level, into which water can be siphoned or baled during emptying

All the advantages of the border—concentration of colour and interest, labour saving effect, long life—are also to be found in a garden pool, for with reasonable care once the pool has been installed and planted it will require only minimal attention between the clearances and replantings that may be necessary every three or four years.

Concrete was at one time the only material suitable for the construction of a permanent garden pool, which meant that because of the very heavy work and considerable time involved comparatively few small gardens were able to enjoy the very special pleasures of water in the garden.

Pool liners Constructing a pool with a polythene or PVC liner is much less arduous but not nearly as permanent. It has some advantages in that it is relatively cheap, easy to install and can be removed when it is no longer required. On the other hand, if the pond is not kept permanently full of water the sun will cause the sheeting to become brittle above the water-line, and it may then become easily broken or porous. Remember, also, that if at any time any sharp object is dropped into the pool it will pierce the fabric.

Having decided on the site, excavate it to the exact depth and shape, allowing about 20 inches to 24 inches in the deep part and 10 inches to 12 inches in the shallow areas. Examine the excavated site carefully and remove any sharp or large stones and then cover the whole area with approximately 1 inch of sand This will cover any small sharp stones which may not have been noticed. Next lay the sheeting in place and if unreinforced polythene is used, use 1000 gauge or two layers of 500 gauge. Hold the film in place with bricks or stones at the edges and then put an inch or so of water in to prevent it from blowing about and this will push the sheeting into the shape of the excavation. When putting the planting compost in it must be finely sifted to remove any sharp objects, or use planting containers which should be stood on surplus pieces of film to prevent any sharp edges from puncturing the pool.

Never stand in the pool; if any part cannot be reached from the edge use a scaffold board or ladder laid over the pond and climb across for easier access.

With fibre-glass or other prefabricated pools, the area should be excavated in the same manner as for a polythene sheet pool, except that it is not necessary to line the site with sand. In a small garden, fibre-glass pools are probably the most satisfactory, as they require the least amount of work on installation especially where there is limited space to mix concrete. Unfortunately, they are not as easy to disguise as concrete and frequently are manufactured in unpleasantly bright colours. If possible, purchase dull colours such as stone or black, as these are easier to disguise and

A formal treatment of a circular pool where paving and formal bedding has been introduced into the scheme. This effect can be achieved quite quickly in a new garden.

1 Westmorland water-worn limestone
is of a cool grey colour.
2 Forest of Dean weathered sandstone
has a soft grey-pink hue.
3 A sandstone rock garden forms a small
outcrop on a lawn.
4 Large flat slabs of stone are used for
a stratified rock garden.

look much more natural. Before purchasing examine the pool carefully to see that there is adequate space on the marginal shelves to place planting containers or compost—without this sliding into the deeper parts of the pool.

Rock gardens

Having made his pool the gardener is faced with the decision of what to do with the considerable quantity of excavated soil. Frequently the decision is to leave it where it is, incorporate some stone and make a rock garden. Water and rocks go well together and it may be possible to merge the two into one integrated feature.

Design and construction Where design is concerned it is obviously desirable that a rock garden should fit as harmoniously as possible into its surroundings. Sometimes this is not possible, especially within the confines of a small town garden lacking any natural landscape features, in which case the rock garden must be regarded as an arbitrary, functional feature. If it is well constructed it will not offend the eye. If there are to be paths, they should always divide a smaller from the greater part of

the whole, and not be exact divisions between equal areas. Paths should also be wide enough to permit easy and comfortable passage, even if one is reluctant to spare what may be already limited space.

Building on a slope lends itself to a system of outcrops, each composed of a number of closely joined rocks. The object in building an outcrop is to make it look as much as possible like one rock, seamed, if you like, with crevices and fissures, all of which will accommodate the smaller, cushion-forming plants so admirably.

A flat site calls for more adventurous treatment to create the illusion of heights and valleys. On a small area it can be done by a gradually ascending gradient instead of in outcrops. An abrupt stop when the maximum desired height is reached will create a shady cliff face, most useful for such plants as ramondas and haberleas, which delight in horizontal or vertical crevices with a cool aspect.

It is important that the line of slope of all the rocks should be in the same

direction and to approximately the same angle. Rocks falling this way and that may look like the result of a volcanic eruption and will not, unlike more orderly stratification, be restful to the eye. Of equal importance is the placing of the stones in close association. Isolated stones do not make a rock garden, they only preserve the traditional appearance of a 'dog's grave' so rightly condemned by Reginald Farrer, in his day the doyen of alpine gardeners. Outcrops may stand alone, but not single stones except in a few places where a well-placed rock serves to link two or more separate masses.

Without training or experience in rock garden building it can be a frightening thing to be faced with a great pile of stones, a heap of compost and an empty site. Time should be taken to study the situation, creating as far as possible a picture in one's mind of what is desired. The first stone is the most difficult one to place and it is fatal to make too hasty a beginning.

When a very great gardener was once reproached for doing everything so slowly, he took little heed, for he was a taciturn, though not unkindly man, but at last, goaded into speech by repeated requests for advice, he said that the best way to garden was to 'make haste slowly'. How right he was, and many mistakes can be avoided by unhurried work and thorough preparation. The novice will do well to experiment with a few smaller stones before the actual construction begins, discovering how to arrange them so that they seem to have grown together naturally.

The precise form of construction must obviously differ according to the kind of rock which is being used. If it is possible to see the rock either in the quarry, or where it outcrops naturally, or is exposed by erosion, it will be found very helpful. If this is not possible, spare a little time to visit a few good rock gardens and study carefully the arrangement of the stones.

It is difficult to learn from the written word how to build a rock garden, although some help in the basic principles may arise from book work. An excellent volume to digest before attempting to build a rock garden is *Natural Rock Gardening* by the late Captain Symons Jeune.

Paths which traverse a rock garden made on sloping ground will have to have steps here and there to adjust the different levels. Such steps, whenever possible, should be composed of the same stone that is used for the rock garden. If sandstone is being used there is little difficulty in splitting large stones to a thickness appropriate for steps. Stones which do not cleave readily have to be used whole and this may involve burying a considerable proportion below ground. This is no bad thing since it ensures stability.

On a flat site the paths should have flat stepping stones let into the ground until they are almost flush with the surface and placed at intervals convenient for a comfortable stride. The area between the stepping stones can be filled with good compost and surfaced with a suitable stone chipping, in which many plants will grow very comfortably and which will often prove fruitful seed beds.

To enjoy the rock garden and the pool, in fact to appreciate in general the amenities of the garden, it is well to have a place from which it can be seen, a comfortable and convenient place, a place very much like an outdoor room.

Patio gardens
The patio, as a feature of our gardens, is a comparative newcomer to Britain although it has, for many years, been popular on the other side of the Atlantic. Its introduction here dates approximately from the end of World War II, when contemporary architects became more greatly concerned with the fusion of house and garden into a unified concept. The word patio, in fact, is something of a misnomer; its original Spanish meaning referred to an *inner* court or enclosed space open to the sky, a feature commonly encountered in Spanish and South American houses.

Today, the description is applied to almost any kind of outdoor paved space adjacent to the house. On a small scale, in similar manner to the terraces of larger houses, the patio has become very popular as a sitting-out place. Even brief spells of fine weather can be enjoyed there when lawns are soggy under foot or cold winds make sitting in the open garden too chilly for comfort.

A patio, too, can provide an effective link between the formality of the house itself and the informality of the garden proper. It should always be in proportion to the actual size of the house and garden of which it forms a feature. The materials of which it is constructed are important, since they must be in harmony with those used for the house as well as with its individual architectural style.

Period cottages seem to demand mellow brick or random paving. Note, however, not 'crazy' paving, which is all too often a mixture of broken concrete slabs and builders' leftovers. What is wanted is natural stone paving broken up into pieces of reasonable size and varying shapes. They should be laid in a random fashion, with or without cemented joints. Where the joints are left uncemented many attractive creeping plants, of the type that are able to recover after being trodden underfoot, may be grown in the crevices between the stones.

Cobbled or gravelled surrounds formed the normal features of Victorian and Edwardian houses. Although these can be made quite attractive by using plants in tubs or terrace pots, they are hardly conducive to relaxation and are better replaced with paving, drier underfoot and a more suitable setting for the garden furniture and other accoutrements of the present-day patio.

Contemporary houses, often with stark lines, call for complementary treatment. Rectangular York paving looks magnificent, but it is not only expensive but also difficult to lay owing to considerable variations in thickness. Synthetic stone slabs, on the other hand, as well as being a good deal cheaper, are of uniform thickness, which makes them easy to lay in a bed of sand or on a concrete foundation. These slabs are obtainable in a variety of shapes, colours and sizes, useful for blending into interesting patterns and designs to suit all tastes and surroundings.

With many new houses, the patio becomes an integral part of the design, having been planned that way by the architect. This is a particularly satisfactory procedure, since it can be correctly sited to take full advantage of sun and shelter. At the planning stage, too, it is possible to arrange for an outdoor hearth with its flue connecting to those of the indoor fireplaces. This would be ideal for those who want to enjoy the evening air without the chill that so often comes at twilight in our climate.

A fireplace of this nature is also useful for al fresco meals. Patios and barbecues go together and, judging by the number of appliances and recipes that one sees nowadays, it would seem that the barbecue, as a form of entertainment, is here to stay. If the patio is to be used for

this purpose, it will be necessary to provide some form of lighting. This should always be in keeping with the surroundings and, as with all outdoor electrical work, installation should be carried out by an experienced electrical contractor.

Plants on the patio will consist mainly of climbing and wall shrubs and any other plants suitable for growing in tubs, urns and other containers. Decorative tubs and jardinières are obtainable in terracotta and natural or artificial stone. Antique pots and figures are costly and increasingly hard to come by, but there are plenty of effective substitutes in artificial stone and other similar materials. Lead urns and cisterns, too, now sell for very high prices. It is possible, however, to obtain reproductions of old ones that are authentic in every detail, down to the grey-green patina that lead acquires with age and exposure to weather. Even these are not exactly cheap, but their cost is only a fraction of that of the genuine article. These fibreglass containers have the added advantage of being extremely light and easy to handle. One that, in lead, would take several strong men to lift it, can be easily moved by one person.

Plants grown on the walls adjacent to the patio are best grown in beds. This, however, may not always be practicable because of damp courses, drains or other constructional hazards. But many climbers will do quite well in tubs or boxes. Although their rate of growth may be slowed down considerably, this is not necessarily a disadvantage, as it enables a greater variety of plants to be grown.

Most people require privacy in their gardens. There are various ways of screening a patio to provide this, together with protection from cold winds and draughts. To perform the latter function screens, such as walls or

Round units are used to pave this patio. Plants in pots and in beds surrounded by a low wall provide colour.

Screens and Windbreak trees

Name	Deciduous	Evergreen	Chalk Soils	Damp Soils	Dry and Sand Soils	Seaside	Autumn Colour	Remarks
Acer platanoides (Norway maple)	X		X	X	X	X	X	ideal for exposed sites
A. platanoides 'Crimson King'	X		X	X	X	X	X	purple on under surfaces of leaves
A. pseudoplatanus (sycamore)	X		X	X	X	X	X	ideal for exposed sites
A. pseudoplatanus purpureum	X		X	X	X	X	X	purple on under surfaces of the leaves
Alnus glutinosa (alder)	X		X	X				fast growing—attractive catkins in autumn and spring
Betula pendula (silver birch)	X		X		X	X	X	fast growing—attractive white bark
Carpinus betulus (hornbeam)	X		X	X			X	attractive catkins
Castanea sativa (sweet or Spanish chestnut)	X			X				fairly fast growing
Crataegus (hawthorn, quickthorn or May)								
C. oxyacantha	X		X	X	X	X	X	very wind hardy, often holds its red berries right through the winter
C. prunifolia	X		X	X	X	X	X	large red fruits and crimson foliage
Cupressus macrocarpa (Monterey cypress)		X	X		X	X		ideal as separate screen trees, fast growing
C. macrocarpa lutea		X	X		X	X		golden-yellow foliage, not so fast growing as the species
Chamaecyparis lawsoniana (Lawson's Cypress)	X	X	X					fairly fast growing, requires protection against winds when young
C. lawsoniana allumii		X	X	X				glaucous-blue foliage
C. lawsoniana fraseri		X	X	X				grey-green foliage
C. lawsoniana lutea		X	X	X				golden-yellow foliage
C. lawsoniana stewartii		X	X	X				golden-yellow foliage
× *Cupressocyparis leylandii*		X	X			X		fast growing, reaches 30–40 ft.
Eucalyptus gunnii		X	X		X	X		fast growing, hardiest of the eucalyptus, requires firm staking when young
Fagus sylvatica (common beech)	X		X				X	brown foliage in autumn
F. sylvatica purpurea (copper beech)	X		X				X	copper coloured foliage in autumn
Ilex aquifolium (holly)		X	X		X			slow growing, very tough
Larix decidua (larch)	X		X		X		X	
Metasequoia glyptostroboides	X		X				X	fast growing, prefers moist soil
Olearia macrodonta		X	X		X	X		dark, glossy green holly-like foliage
Picea abies (Norway spruce)		X	X					fine for planting mixed screens
P. omorika (Serbian spruce)		X	X					both are excellent as screen trees well spaced out
P. sitchensis (Sitka spruce)		X	X					
Pinus laricio (Corsican pine)		X		X				bad transplanter, therefore plant very small plants
P. laricio nigricans (Austrian pine)		X	X					very wind hardy
P. radiata (Monterey pine)		X	X			X		fast growing, needs a mild maritime area
P. sylvestris (Scots pine)		X	X		X			very wind-hardy
Populus (Poplar)								
P. alba (white poplar)	X		X			X		fast growing, very hardy and resistant to salt winds
P. nigra italica (Lombardy poplar)	X		X					upright habit, very hardy also fast growing
Quercus ilex (evergreen oak)		X	X		X	X		very hardy and flourishes in coastal districts
Q. robur (common oak)	X							does best on stiff loams, but will tolerate light-sandy soils
Rhododendron ponticum		X				X		dislikes chalk soils, fairly fast growing
Sorbus intermedia (Swedish whitebeam)	X							good for street planting and industrial areas
Thuja occidentalis (American arbor-vitae)		X	X	X			X	useful where a colourful permanent conifer screen is needed
T. plicata		X	X					attractive dark green foliage
Tsuga albertiana		X	X		X			fast growing

1

2

fences, need not be solid or close-boarded. Trellis, wattle, or interlap fencing will filter most of the sting out of any but the fiercest gales, but perhaps the most suitable screen of all for a patio is one constructed of pierced concrete walling blocks. These are obtainable in a number of pleasing openwork designs, and provide a permanent screen that encloses without producing a shut-in feeling. Living screens, too, can be effective and most of the less rampant hedging plants such as box, yew, holly or cypress are suitable.

Boundaries and Shelterbelts

Where a boundary hedge is planned merely to provide privacy during the summer months, then a deciduous hedge will be suitable: flowering currant (ribes), forsythia, hawthorn or beech are among the possibilities.

If a permanent peep-proof hedge is required, any evergreen, such as holly, yew or one of the many other conifers or even privet is suitable, though the last can sometimes drop its leaves, especially in very hard winters.

Screens or shelterbelts must also be considered from the point of view of their ultimate use. If it is desirable to block out some eyesore such as a factory, a railway line, or to give shelter in the garden so that other plants can be grown successfully, then screening is more than ever necessary, particularly in coastal gardens. If, however, the screen is to add interest to the skyline, then a mixture of deciduous and ever-green trees, and conifers is the answer. Farm hedges, screens and shelterbelts are usually designed to break the pre-vailing wind or to keep in animals and shelter them from wind and rain.

Preparation of site Preparation of the ground for a hedge, screen or shelterbelt must be thorough. Once the shrubs or trees are planted they will remain there for a long time; therefore, see that they get off to a good start.

In light soil, humus must be added: a heavy soil will need to be lightened by digging in peat, leafsoil, rotted farmyard manure or garden compost. In heavy clay soils drainage is important, and path or road sweepings or weathered ashes will help to improve it. When marking out the site, dig a strip 4 feet wide; this will leave 18 inches on either side of the hedge. Bastard trench the ground, i.e. double dig it. This entails digging out a trench 2 feet wide, removing the top spit of soil and tho-roughly breaking up the second spit, i.e. the sub-soil. Then place the top spit of the next trench on top of the broken up sub-soil; continuing this process until the strip of ground is

1 Formal hedges at Hidcote Manor, Gloucestershire.
2 An archway has been formed in this mixed Beech hedge.

completely dug. If humus is available this can be incorporated in the top spit at the time of digging. And, of course, if well-rotted farmyard manure can be obtained so much the better. When leaf-soil or garden compost is used, the addition of National Growmore or bonemeal at a rate of 4 oz per square yard will be beneficial. Prepare the ground some weeks before planting time, to allow the soil to settle. Never dig out the trench for the hedge before the day of planting arrives.

If many yards are to be planted, do not attempt to do it all in one day. Therefore, when the plants arrive from the nursery, lay them in or heel them in on a spare piece of ground. By laying the plants in, their roots will be kept plump and moist and they will make new root action more quickly when they are finally planted. If the roots are dry on delivery, give them a thorough soaking before they are laid in.

When all is ready for planting dig out a trench 1 to 1½ feet wide and about 1 foot deep. Throw the soil each side of the trench. If you are planting beside a lawn lay down some old sacks or plastic sheeting to protect the grass. As planting proceeds, cover the roots of each plant, first with fine soil, followed by the coarser soil, firming the ground by treading, until normal soil level is reached. If the day is frosty or sunny or there is a drying wind, see that the roots of the plants are covered until each plant is actually placed in the trench.

Times to plant Deciduous hedges are planted from October or November (according to season) until March. Evergreen hedges are planted from September to October or March to April.

Staking It is not usually necessary to stake hedges, but where large bushes are planted, such as yews or hollies, then posts and one or two strands of strong string or plastic-covered wire will prevent movement at the base of the stem at soil level. Trees planted as screens or shelterbelts are best staked until they are sufficiently established and rigid to stand up to gales.

Pleached screens These are useful for adding height to a wall or fence where privacy is required. A pleached screen entails planting young trees, with good straight stems, 8 to 12 feet apart. All shoots below the top of the wall or fence are removed, while those above are trained out horizontally to long bamboo canes or poles, such as runner bean poles, and wires to which the shoots are tied. Any shoots which grow out at right angles to the wall or fence, back or front, are removed. The result is a living trellis.

Watering This must not be overlooked either at the time of planting or after-wards. If the roots are at all dry at

planting time, soak them in a bath or bucket of water. After they have been set out, the hedging plants must have sufficient moisture at the roots. See that they are given several gallons of water if the soil is very dry. The foliage of evergreens should be kept moist by spraying the foliage after sunset.

Trimming hedges The time to clip or trim a hedge depends on the type, deciduous or evergreen, whether it is newly planted or established and whether it is to be clipped to form a formal hedge or an informal one. Newly planted deciduous hedges are best cut hard back to within 9 to 12 inches of ground level in March or April. Some evergreens such as privet and *Lonicera nitida* may be treated in the same way. On the other hand Lawson's cypress, yew, holly, etc., are best not trimmed, except for a few of the tips of shoots being nipped back. Beech and hornbeam should not be pruned for two years after planting.

To encourage good bushy growth, train the hedge in a wedge shape, wider at the base than at the top. With big-leaved evergreens, such as laurel or holly it is better to trim with secateurs rather than shears, as then there is less likelihood of the larger leaves being cut in half. With established hedges this is not quite so serious. Allow hedges to reach their required height before they are stopped, i.e. before their leading shoots are cut off.

Overgrown deciduous hedges such as blackthorn, hornbeam, myrobalan plum and quickthorn can usually be re-juvenated by hard pruning during the winter months. Evergreens such as box, laurel, privet and yew are hard pruned in late March or early April.

Farm hedges are frequently rejuven-ated by laying them. To do this all unwanted growths are cut out to ground level, while the rest, except thick growths, are partly severed near the base. These growths are then bent over at an angle of 45° to the ground and intertwined with dead stakes driven into the ground, 6 to 8 inches from the centre and behind the cut down growths. Suitable stakes can be made of hazel, thorn, beech or sweet chestnut.

General cultivation Once a hedge is planted continual cultivation is neces-sary. The soil on either side of the hedge should be kept free of weeds and lightly forked over from time to time. An annual mulch given in late spring will help to keep the soil moist and will also feed the hedge. If well-rotted farmyard manure can be obtained, so much the better. If not, leaf-mould or well-rotted garden compost can be used.

Weeds can be kept under control by spraying with Dalapon, in accordance with makers' instructions. The weed killer should be dewed over the young

Hedges

Name	Deciduous	Evergreen	Flowering	Fruiting	Chalk Soils	Damp Soils	Dry and Sand Soils	Fragrant	Seaside	Autumn Colour	Remarks
Acer campestre (field maple)	X			X	X	X	X			X	
Atriplex halimus		sX			X		X		X		silver-grey foliage
Aucuba japonica		X		X	X						must plant male and female forms for fruit. Good for industrial areas
Aucuba japonica variegata		X		X	X						
Bamboo	X	X				X					soil must not be water-logged, in a frost pocket
Berberis (barberry)											
B. darwinii		X	X	X	X		X				
B. stenophylla		X	X	X	X		X	X			B. stenophylla is quick growing.
B. thunbergii	X		X	X	X						All make decorative
B. thunbergii atropurpurea	X		X	X	X		X			X	garden hedges
B. verruculosa		X	X		X		X				
Buxus (box)											
B. sempervirens		X	X		X				X		X
B. suffruticosa		X			X						X used as edging to paths and borders
Calluna vulgaris (ling) and its varieties		X	X								best on peat or acid soils
Carpinus betulus (hornbeam)	X				X					X	foliage retained well into the winter
Chaenomeles (Japanese Quince)	X		X	X	X		X				fruit makes good jelly
Corylus avellana (hazel)	X						X			X	for farm or garden
Cotoneaster											
C. simonsii		sX	X	X	X		X				
C. watereri		X	X	X	X		X				
Erica (heather)											
E. carnea		X	X								both will grow in soils
E. mediterranea		X	X		X						containing chalk or lime
Escallonia (many varieties)		X	X			X	X		X		
Euonymus japonicus		X			X				X		good for industrial areas
Fagus sylvatica (beech)	X				X		X			X	foliage retained well into the winter
Fagus sylvatica purpurea (copper beech)	X				X		X			X	
Fuchsia magellanica	X		X		X		X		X		plant base of shoots 4 inches below soil
Griselinia littoralis		X			X		X		X		will grow in towns
Hebe speciosa		X	X		X		X		X		H. speciosa subject to frost damage
H. brachysiphon (syn. H. traversii)		X	X		X		X		X		
Hippophae rhamnoides (sea buckthorn)	X			X	X		X		X		must plant male and female forms for fruit
Ilex aquifolium (holly) and varieties		X		X	X				X		thrives in towns and industrial areas
Lavandula (lavender)		X	X		X			X	X		
Ligustrum (privet)		X		X		X					good in towns and industrial areas. Quick growing

sX = semi-evergreen

Hedges

Name	Deciduous	Evergreen	Flowering	Fruiting	Chalk Soils	Damp Soils	Dry and Sand Soils	Fragrant	Seaside	Autumn Colour	Remarks
Lonicera nitida (Chinese honeysuckle)		X			X		X		X		grows well in towns
Mahonia aquifolium (Oregon grape)		X	X	X	X		X	X		X	good in towns and industrial areas
Olearia (daisy bush)		X	X		X		X		X		does well in towns
Osmarea burkwoodii		X	X		X		X	X			good in industrial areas
Pittosporum		X			X		X		X		subject to frost damage
Prunus											
P. cerasifera (myrobalan plum)	X				X				X		
P. × cistena	X		X							X	
P. laurocerasus (cherry laurel)		X					X				good in industrial areas
P. lusitanica (Portugal laurel)		X					X				
Pyracantha (firethorn)		X	X	X	X		X				good for industrial areas
Rhododendron ponticum		X	X			X				X	needs an acid or neutral soil
Ribes sanguineum (flowering currant)	X		X		X	X	X				Quick growing
Rosa (rose)											
'Zephirine Drouhin'	X		X					X			thornless
'Kathleen Harrop'	X		X					X			thornless
'Cecile Brunner'	X		X					X			ideal for a dwarf hedge
'Nathalie Nypels'	X		X					X			
'Old Blush'	X		X					X			
R. eglanteria (sweet briar or eglantine)	X		X					X			
'Penzance Hybrids'	X		X					X			
Hybrid musk, several varieties	X		X	X				X			
R. rugosa, several varieties	X		X	X				X			
Floribunda roses	X		X								
Rosmarinus officinalis (rosemary)		X	X		X			X	X		has fragrant foliage
Ruta graveolens 'Jackman's Blue' (rue)		X	X		X				X		glaucous-grey aromatic foliage
Santolina chamaecyparissus (lavender cotton or cotton lavender)		X	X		X				X		grey, aromatic foliage makes a good dwarf hedge or edging plant
Senecio laxifolius		X	X		X		X		X		attractive silver-grey foliage
Spiraea, several species and varieties	X		X		X	X	X				S. thunbergii has coloured foliage in autumn
Syringa vulgaris (lilac) many varieties and species	X		X		X			X		X	
Tamarix (tamarisk) several species	X		X		X		X		X		
Viburnum lantana (wayfaring tree)	X		X	X	X					X	
V. opulus (guelder rose)	X		X	X	X	X	X			X	
V. tinus (laurustinus)		X	X		X				X		
Weigela florida variegata	X		X								
W. hybrida and its varieties	X		X								

growth, but do not soak the ground.

More expensive but longer lasting and labour saving is the construction of a wall as a boundary or as the provider of privacy.

Wall construction

The site for any type of wall must be levelled very carefully and consolidated to provide secure foundations. If necessary, rubble should be rammed into a trench before the concrete foundation is applied. Walling stone is *very* heavy; for example—220 walling stones 12 inches × 4 inches × 2½ inches can weigh up to 1 ton, and 36 such stones are required to the square yard.

The foundation concrete should be several inches wider than the maximum width of the walling in order to spread the load as wide as possible. The mortar courses must be kept constant at about ⅜ inch thick. Mix the mortar with 1 part cement and 3 parts of sand (by volume). Constantly check vertical and horizontal levels with a spirit level. Tap each stone in place well and use plenty of mortar. Clean off the joints as work proceeds and where rougher faced walls are concerned use a rounded stick to slightly score out the mortar before it sets, to emphasise the textured finish and 'natural' look of the wall. Do not work in frosty weather; if the weather is very hot and dry, cover the work with plastic sheeting to prevent too rapid mortar setting.

For low walling, rough-faced walling stone in many different sizes is most attractive and popular. Lengths are from 9 inches to about 18 inches, widths

4, 4½ and 6 inches, and thicknesses from 2 inches to 8½ inches. Random-sized stone walling is very attractive. Colours include attractive shades of pink, light grey, dark grey, York stone, slate blue, sandstone, red, Cotswold, lilac and lavender.

Dry stone walling is less rigid and formal but suits only dwellings in comparatively rural areas. It has the charming advantage that a number of plants can actually be grown in its surface to decorate and soften the otherwise somewhat austere feature. Also informal and suited to more urban areas is the pierced screen walling now available so widely, and suitable even for do-it-yourself construction. It is much easier to erect a fence than to build a wall.

Fences

Two things are very important in the garden. They are privacy and shelter. The latter is often a problem in gardens which are exposed to cold prevailing winds. Both these points are important not only for the gardener himself, but also for the plants in his garden. Young growth can be severely damaged by cold winds and frequent buffeting will cause a great deal of root disturbance. Although privacy and shelter can be provided by trees and shrubs, fences also have an important part to play.

The choice of fencing must never be undertaken lightly, for serious consideration must be given to its appearance and construction. Strength is very important, especially in exposed, windy localities. A fence is only as strong as its supports, and particular care must be taken to see that these are not only substantial but inserted securely. Most fences are supplied with strong posts, usually 4–6 inches square, depending on the type of fence that has to be supported. Sometimes concrete posts are supplied; these are extremely strong, although a little more cumbersome to install. It is very important to see that concrete posts are inserted deeply and firmly. Strength of timber also depends on the prevention of rot, and unless cedar wood is used (except for posts), all timber should be treated with a suitable preservative. Creosote can be used, although it should be allowed to soak into the timber for several weeks before plants are trained against it. Unless this is done, there is the danger of stem and leaf scorch and its use is not generally recommended where plants are to be grown against or near a fence. A safer treatment consists of the use of copper naphthenate preservatives such as the green, horticultural grades of Cuprinol or Solignum.

Types of fence The most popular types are purchased as units or panels. Usually they are from 5–6 feet in length with heights varying from about 3–6 feet. A solid or close-boarded fence is, as its name implies, a design which consists of upright or horizontal strips of wood, some

6 inches wide and ¾–1 inch thick. The strips are nailed to two or more supporting rails at the rear of the panel. These provide complete privacy and wind protection, but are rather uninteresting in appearance.

Weatherboard fencing provides a little more interest in its appearance as it consists of wedge-shaped strips of wood, ¾ inch in thickness at one edge, tapering to ¼ inch at the other. Each strip overlaps the next by about ¾ inch. The advantage of this design is that it is virtually peep proof.

Interwoven fencing is very attractive but inclined to open up a little, especially in the cheaper units. Thin strips of wood, approximately 4 inches wide and ¼ inch thick, are interwoven one with another. It is a strong fence if it is supported well. Trellis fencing is very cheap and more suited as a support for climbing and trailing plants. It is not a strong design but can be used to good effect for covering unsightly walls or as an additional part of a fence design. Sections 18 inches to 2 feet deep look most attractive if attached to the top of, say, a close-boarded fence. Used in this manner it helps to lighten an otherwise heavy, solid design.

Trellis fencing usually consists of laths of wood 1 inch by ½ inch thick, fastened across each other vertically and horizontally to form 6–8 inch squares. The laths are attached to a more substantial framing of 1 inch or 1½ inch square timber.

Two other cheap types of fencing are wattle and cleft chestnut. The former is useful where a rural or rustic effect is desired. The woven, basket-like construction produces a very sturdy fencing panel. The panels are usually attached to lengths of oak stakes driven securely into the ground. The latter fence can be purchased with the individual pieces of cleft chestnut spaced out at different intervals. It is possible to purchase rolls of this fencing with the paling nearly touching. The rolls are usually attached to strong oak posts by galvanised wire.

A wooden fence remains neat if repaired and painted regularly.

In their construction, individual cleft chestnut palings are wired top and bottom to strong horizontal wires.

One of the latest advances in fence production is the sale of kits which are so accurately machined and complete that even an unskilled person can erect panels without any trouble. With these kits have come new ideas in design, and many can be made up into contemporary designs. This is especially useful where bold effects are required in the construction of patios. Many ultra-modern properties are being built and this advance in fence appearance will be welcomed by their owners.

Fencing can also be provided in the form of chain link or mesh netting. The best quality is heavily galvanised to withstand the rigours of the weather. Chain link is sold in 25-yard rolls in 2 inch mesh in the following heights: 36, 42, 48, 60 and 72 inches.

A more recent innovation is the plastic coating of chain link over the galvanised wire. Standard colours of dark green, black, white, yellow and light green can be obtained. Rolls of 25 yards are available in heights of 36, 42 and 48 inches.

Wire netting is another cheaper and

Rough-faced walling stone in varying sizes looks effective.

useful fencing material. It is available in 50-yard rolls in mesh sizes of $\frac{1}{2}$, $\frac{3}{4}$, 1, $1\frac{1}{2}$ and 2 inches and in heights of 12, 18, 24, 30, 36, 42, 48, 60 and 72 inches. Gauges or thicknesses of wire range from the thinnest, of 22 gauge to the heavier 19 gauge. Wire netting is easy and quick to erect as it requires only moderately substantial supporting posts of timber or angle iron spaced approximately every 6–8 feet apart according to the height and length of the fence being erected.

Another type of fencing is known as rustic. This is constructed from larch or pine wood of circular section. The main uprights are usually quite substantial and are cut from 3–4 inch diameter timber while the design work between them is of thinner section, usually about $1\frac{1}{2}$–2 inch diameter. The most popular design consists of a diamond pattern approximately 18 inches in area. It is sold by the square foot either with the bark on or removed, stained and varnished. The result is a most natural fence or screen which blends in very well with the surroundings.

Very often older, neglected property may have trees and shrubs of enviable maturity, but boundary walls or fences that have not been repaired for so long that they are falling down.

Derelict gardens and their renovation

At a first glance, a derelict garden seems a most depressing problem and one which would appear to be insurmountable. Certainly its renovation and reclamation will require a great deal of hard work but it is a task which can be made much easier and pleasanter if a plan of campaign is worked out beforehand.

There are, of course, degrees of neglect. Some gardens may have been unoccupied for a few months only, a few will have been neglected for years. Whatever the condition, the work of reclamation should be tackled in easy, logical stages. A garden is as good as its initial soil preparation and any hurried or glossed over soil cultivation will repay in poor growth and even more vigorous weeds later on.

Examining the site The first thing which will have to be done will be to examine the site carefully to see where original beds and borders are and to identify these with long stakes. In extreme instances, it may even be difficult to trace paths, but these must be given priority as, if they are in reasonable condition, they will be most useful when the wheelbarrow is required.

The extent of the site examination must depend on the time of the year the garden is taken over. The work will be difficult at the height of the season when most of the garden's occupants are in full growth, but it will prove to be a most useful time as it will be possible to assess the quality of these plants. Those which are obviously weak and of very poor quality should be suitably marked or noted so that they can be removed. It might be possible to salvage some if they are cut back hard at the end of the season to encourage sturdier growth the following year.

If the garden is occupied in the autumn or winter, most of the plants will have died down and may be rather difficult to find and examine. It will, however, be an easier time to tackle the clearance problem, as much of the growth, including that of the weeds will have died down.

In the spring the weeds will begin to grow and it will then be necessary to make the difficult choice of which weedkillers to use to help in the task of clearance.

Weeds and weed control

The most obvious way in which weeds do harm is to overgrow and shade cultivated plants, depriving them of sunlight. Less evident is the way in which weeds rob garden plants of water and minerals. The mere presence of the weed root in the soil can in some cases prevent germination and growth of cultivated plants. It has been shown that the roots of many weed species release growth-inhibiting chemicals. Weeds can also be injurious by acting as an alternative host for some diseases of cultivated plants. A few British weeds, e.g., dodder, are actually parasitic on the crop plants.

There are three principal groups of weeds: annuals, biennials and perennials. The summer annuals germinate in the spring and die in the autumn, the seed lying dormant in the winter. Herb Robert, goosegrass and many other common hedgerow species fall into this group. Winter annuals germinate in the autumn and winter, the seed lying dormant through the summer months. Both types of annuals are usually rather shallow rooters and owe their nuisance value to the abundance of their seed. Shepherd's purse produces about 4,000 seeds per plant, corn poppy 14,000 to 20,000. They are usually controlled easily by either hoeing or digging. Once the growing plants are buried most annual weeds will be killed.

Biennial weeds usually develop a swollen root or stem below ground which stores food for growth in the second year. Few troublesome weeds fall into this group. Wild carrot and burdock do, however. They are easily eradicated by removing them during the first year before they store food.

Most perennial weeds reproduce by seed and many are able to spread by vegetative reproduction. Simple perennials spread only by seed though if broken up can produce new plants, as can dandelion or dock roots. The creeping perennials also produce seed but mainly spread by means of runners or stolons, if above ground, e.g., ground ivy and creeping buttercup; or by root-like rhizomes below ground, e.g., convolvulus, couch grass, common nettle and ground elder, all of which if unchecked, spread rapidly. Digging and hoeing are usually unsuccessful in removing them. Digging out the food-storing tap roots of dock or dandelion frequently results in breakage and therefore removal of a large portion but not all of the rooting system, the remainder growing into new plants. Roots of convolvulus and equisetum are brittle and small portions left in the soil during weeding will produce new shoots. Rhizomes of equisetum often grow to a depth of 2 feet. If the shoot is cut at ground level two or more shoots arise from the buds located on that portion of the stem just below the soil surface. Regular mowing sometimes helps to control perennials, removing the shoots. Though more develop, they do so at the expense of the reserve food stored in their rhizomes, which after a time results in death of the plant.

Annual weeds may also be eradicated by cutting before they have the opportunity of producing seeds. In lawns, the more successful weeds are those with a rosette of leaves flattened against the ground. Mowing actually favours their growth since it removes competition. Dandelion, plantains and daisies are often, therefore, common lawn weeds.

Herbicides Sodium chlorate is a popular herbicide for clearing areas of all weeds. Complete eradication of such perennial weeds as coltsfoot, couch grass, ground elder and even bracken has been achieved by applications of sodium chlorate at the rate of about 2 ounces to the square yard. Great care must be taken not to get it on to clothing. On drying out friction may cause it to ignite.

Many herbicides tend to be rather drastic, rendering the soil sterile for some time. Sodium chlorate for example can render soil sterile for up to a year. This can be an advantage in places in the garden where it is not intended to cultivate.

Selective chemicals New effective herbicides which were relatively expensive to produce but much more effective in minute doses came on to the market in greater amounts after World War II. Naphthylacetic acid was shown to kill charlock and sugar beet but leave grasses unharmed Even more effective is the now famous 2, 4-D herbicide and the other phenoxy acetic acids such as MCPA.

The development for agriculture of selective herbicides effective against most broad-leaved plants, but ineffective against cereals, has also proved useful to the gardener. With these newer herbicides the time of application may largely determine their usefulness. A 'pre-emergence herbicide' is one which is applied before the weed or crop appears above the ground. A 'post-

emergence herbicide' is one applied as a spray after the crop has developed above the soil. Most have cumbersome chemical names and are commonly known by abbreviations.

All herbicides in large enough quantities may be harmful to man, so caution is necessary. Herbicides are thoroughly safety-tested for use on vegetables before sale to the public and if a herbicide is unsuitable for such use the manufacturer's label should clearly say so. Carefully follow the manufacturer's instructions. Excessive use can often produce spectacular results in terms of the dying down of the aerial portion of the plant but because this is so rapid the herbicide does not get translocated to the deeper rhizomes and roots. Lower concentrations take longer to produce their effects, but all parts of even perennial plants will be killed.

Many manufacturers combine lawn herbicides with fertilisers, adjusting the proportions to produce combined nourishment as well as removal of the broad-leaved weeds. British manufacturers mix herbicides 2, 4-D and 2, 4, 5-T with fertilisers; 2, 4-D being easily absorbed by the plant leaves or roots and at its most effective during a dry spell. It kills the growing points by being 'translocated' throughout the plant after being absorbed by leaves or roots. Some plants, such as cleavers or chick weed are resistant to 2, 4-D and 2, 4, 5-T, consequently other herbicides must be used. Mecoprop is effective against both these plants. Some manufactures mix two or more herbicides such as 2, 4-D and mecoprop and 2, 4-D and fenoprop to provide an effective control of a wide range of plants.

Not all herbicides are 'translocated'. The so-called contact herbicides produce their effect at the point of application. It is important with this type of herbicide to ensure more or less complete wetting of the leaves by the spray. Other 'translocated' herbicides include simazine, atrazine and monuron. Unlike 2, 4-D these do not attack the growing points directly but interfere with photosynthesis, a vital activity. Amitrole (aminotriazole) acts by inhibiting the formation of the green pigment chlorophyll which is necessary for photosynthesis.

Paraquat and diquat are activated by light and oxygen and very rapidly affect the photosynthesis of the plant. They are widely used for removing weeds in rose beds, etc. As they are taken up by the leaves but not via the stem, spraying between rose bushes will not harm the

roses. Both paraquat and diquat are readily inactivated in the soil so will not be absorbed by the roots of the bushes. grasses. Once weed free, an annual application of simazine and paraquat can keep them clear.

Flower borders Paraquat can be used especially for the annual weeds but care must be taken to avoid spraying the leaves of the border plants.

Fruit tree areas Paraquat can be used between bushes. Simazine, which controls many of the broad-leaved weeds, is also effective, since most bush and fruit trees are reasonably tolerant of simazine. Avoid over-dosing, however. If some weeds persist in patches, use a paraquat herbicide to remove them.

Vegetable plots For peas and beans use dinoseb. In carrot patches linuron, if Broad-leaved weeds such as dandelion and daisies can be removed adequately using MCPA or 2, 4-D. Mecoprop controls white clover, pearlwort, mouse ear chickweed 2, 4-D does not. A mixture of 2, 4-D or MCPA with either mecoprop or fenoprop is best used. Lawn sand can be used for more resistant plants. It should be noted that it is best to apply these herbicides to lawns in 2 to 3 applications at intervals of 3 to 4 weeks. The final treatment should not be later than September. Coarse grass weeds are probably best removed by hand.

Paths Most of the broad-leaved weeds are cleared by 2, 4-D and mecoprop or fenoprop. Dalapon can be used for many

Plants may resist the effects of herbicides. For example, waxy leaves usually absorb herbicides much more slowly than leaves which have little wax. The red currant is resistant to 2, 4-D because it oxidises the herbicide to a harmless chemical very rapidly whereas the sensitive black currant does not.

A few weeds such as equisetum (horsetail) still defy chemical efforts at eradication. The aerial shoots can be destroyed using 2, 4-D or MCPA but once the plant is established the deeply situated rhizome system cannot be effectively removed.

Recommended methods *Lawns* Moss can be eradicated by the use of calomel. applied as a pre-emergence killer, will control annual weeds and at higher doses can be used as a post-emergence killer. If the weeds are small prometryne may be used provided the young carrot plants have 1 to 2 leaves. Prometryne can also be used as a post-emergence spray with celery provided the celery has 2 or more true leaves. Propachlor may be used as a pre-emergence spray in cauliflower beds and as a post-emergence spray if the young plants are out of the cotyledon stage. Chlorpropham is suitable for use with lettuce and onions as a pre-emergence spray, linuron as a pre-emergence spray with parsnips and chlorpropham as a post-emergence spray. Apply EPTC to the soil before planting.

1 The root-like rhizomes of the Greater Bindweed or Convolvulus.
2 A seedling growth of annual weeds:
3 Fat Hen (Chenopodium album).
4 Applying a weedkiller, using a spray bar.

Weeds

Most weeds are common wild flowers, more welcome in hedgerow than garden. They are tough but can be removed by the right weedkiller ·

Sun Splurge, Euphorbia helioscopia, is an annual that flowers the whole season and is commonly found in both cultivated and waste places

Common Speedwell, Veronica officinalis, is a weed found in dryish places. It flowers all summer

Shepherd's Purse, Capsella bursa-pastoris, has distinctive seed pods. The roots can plunge deep. It flowers all year round. Probably the world's commonest weed

Groundsel, Senecio vulgaris, found abundantly all over Britain and Europe as a weed of cultivated places. The fluffy seeds blow away easily and germinate if the plant is not pulled up

Charlock, Brassica sinapis, is sometimes called Wild Mustard. A common weed of cultivation easily recognised by its bright yellow flowers and long seed pods

Mouse-eared Chickweed, Cerastium vulgatum, one of the commonest of weeds in the garden. Soft in growth and easily torn from the ground

Black Nightshade, Solanum nigrum, flowers in summer and autumn and produces black berries later. Sometimes the berries are green or a dingy red-brown

Lesser Bindweed, Convolvulus arvensis, has underground creeping stems and twines round flowering plants in the border and shrubs. It is hard to get rid of. Tearing out may spoil the 'host' plant itself

Dandelion, Taraxacum officinale, with bold yellow flowers, forms a rosette of leaves. Root plunges deep into the soil. Unsightly on lawns and grassy banks

Stinging Nettle, Urtica dioica, is a coarse-growing weed of waste places. It has a creeping rootstock and rough leaves that 'sting'

...wort, Senecio ...baea, a ...rse-growing ...d of ...ivated and ...te land. It ...vers through-... the season, ...etimes until ... late in the ...

Creeping Thistle, Carduus arvensis, a weed with very prickly leaves. The commonest of all the Thistles found in Britain

Ground Elder, Aegopodium podagraria, is particularly persistent on heavy soils. Forking out small pieces of root repeatedly is the only way to eliminate it

Horsetail, Equisetum arvense, a weed that is difficult to eradicate, usually indicates waterlogged or starved soil. Best banished by improved cultivation

Curled Dock, Rumex cripsus, is a tough growing weed of waste land and cultivated places which has a tenacious root that often snaps off when pulled

95

Chapter 4

GROWING PLANTS AND BULBS

One so often sees specific names used for different plants (e.g. *Primula vulgaris*, the common primrose, and *Ligustrum vulgaris*, common privet) that it is useful to know the meaning of those most commonly used. Many others, of course, refer to countries of origin, or are named after the person who discovered the plant or a person commemorated for some other reason. The following list is found helpful by most gardeners.

Plant names

It is important that each different plant should have an unambiguous name, internationally accepted and understood. If plants were classified by their vernacular, or common, names, there would be great confusion, because the same common name may refer to one flower in one region and another flower somewhere else. Regional names, or names which are used for different plants in different areas, can be particularly confusing. One of the best examples of regional names is bachelor's buttons, which refers to no less than 16 distinct species distributed in 13 genera and 7 families.

There would also be language difficulties. As the common names of flowers and plants vary from country to country it would be necessary to know the names of flowers in other languages in order to communicate about plants with people in other countries. The solution to the problem was found by having a classified system of plant names in a language universally accepted in all countries. Latin was the language adopted. It had predominated in Europe as the language of science and culture throughout the Middle Ages, and although its use declined it was found convenient to apply it to the scientific naming of all forms of plant and animal life. The Latin used for scientific names is a bastardised one in which a large number of Greek names were mixed up. This bastardised language is popularly known as 'Dog Latin', as distinct from Classical Latin. About the only exhaustive text-book on this subject is *Botanical Latin*, by Dr W. T. Stearn.

For convenience, the plant kingdom is divided into easily recognisable sections known as species. Groupings of a more general kind than species are known as genus, tribe, family, order and class—each with subdivisions. Categories more particular than species are subspecies, variety, forma and cultivar, the latter term referring to the fact that the plant has been evolved as a result of deliberate cultivation. In general, each plant is referred to by two names—generic and specific—sometimes referred to as its surname and Christian name.

Both generic and specific names may refer to a plant's real or supposed virtues—medical or culinary. They may also refer to a distinctive characteristic —including resemblance to earlier or better-known plants; or to country of origin. They may commemorate the finder or honour a well-known person not necessarily associated with the plant, and whose name is not even connected with horticulture or botany. Generic names, in particular, may be derived from the names of, or honour, Some names are coined by Latinising the common names used in the plant's country of origin.

In accordance with Latin grammar, a plant name may have a masculine, feminine or neuter ending. The gender of generic and specific names of the same plant must agree. A knowledge of certain types of species name endings usually enables the gender to be easily ascertained even by one who is ignorant of Latin. Descriptive masculine epithets usually end in *–us*, *–is*, or *–er;* feminine in *–a*, or *–ra*, but sometimes *–is*, or *–ris;* and neuter in *–um*, *–e*, or *–re*. Typical examples are the Latin for black, variously spelled *niger* (masculine), *nigra* (feminine) and *nigrum* (neuter); and 'of, or pertaining to marshes', *paluster* (masculine), *palustris* (feminine) old Greek names for the genus Daphne.

Cultivated plants present certain problems not always resolvable from a strictly botanical point of view. This was discussed at the first Botanical Congress in 1866, and there is evidence the problems were known about at least 19 years previously. However, it was not until September, 1952, that an acceptable and separate code was drawn up for the naming of cultivated plants, at the thirteenth International Horticultural Congress. The *International Code of Nomenclature for Cultivated Plants* was first published the following year. Since 1955, a commission representing botanical, gardening, farming and forestry interests has been responsible for amendments to this code.

The main changes incorporated in the code concern the classification of hybrids, clones, strains and mutants (sports) that have arisen in cultivation or are maintained there. Most important has been the adoption of the controversial word 'cultivar' for varieties of plants that have either arisen in cultivation or are wild mutants that only persist when cultivated. These include albino and double flowers, which occur as not infrequent sports in the wild, but soon die out if not brought into cultiva-

Gerard's Herbal 1597 shows the long Latin names used for garden plants at that time. *Bottom right* **The rules of the modern naming of wild and cultivated plants can be found in the codes, and** *upper right* **for etymology and general understanding see the books.**

tion. There are exceptions where a plant is propagated in the wild by vegetative means, and persists there. For example bouncing Bet, or soapwort, *Saponaria officinalis*, is a naturalised plant in this country and is frequently met with only in the double form. The criterion here is that any variant of a wild species brought into cultivation should be given a fancy cultivar name, unless it is known to form a true breeding population in the wild. The saponaria would not come into the cultivar category, as it appears to be an extra vigorous clone that has originally escaped from cultivation.

The code recommends that cultivar names should be placed between single quotation marks, and should also start with a capital letter. Also they should not be names of Latin form, as was hitherto the practice. However, the names of old cultivars should not be changed, but like the fancy names placed between single quotation marks and given a capital initial letter. Like the fancy names they should also be in Roman typescript (this sentence is in Roman typescript), if the preceding botanical name is set in italic typescript. Ideally, the full botanical name should precede the cultivar name, for instance, *Clarkia elegans* 'Salmon Queen', or *Iris pseudacorus* 'Variegatus' (the latter cultivar name being of Latin form because it is an old cultivar). When giving

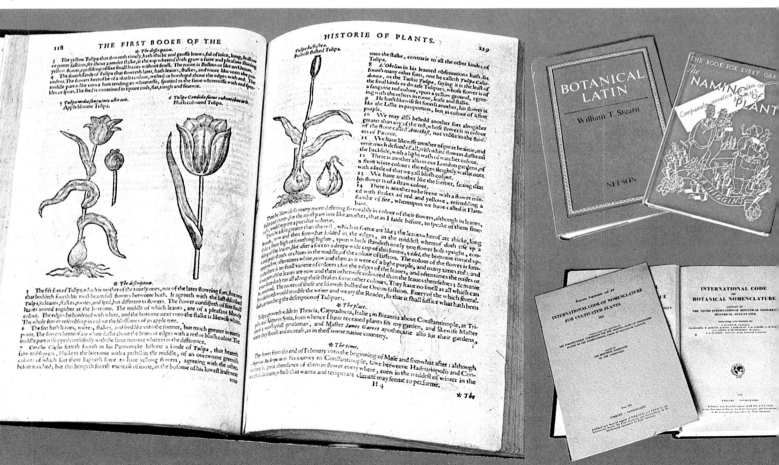

the cultivar name it is permissible to use the generic name only, or even the common name, for the genus or group, as in, for example, sweet pea 'Noel Sutton'.

Specific names

The debt we owe to Carl von Linné (Linnaeus) for his use of the binomial system is immense. In this all plants and animals are given a scientific name consisting basically of two words, the generic and specific terms. The latter may be commemorative, but is usually descriptive, replacing the old practise of using a short phrase or sentence for each plant. In pre-Linnaean times, for example, one would have had to learn: '*Veronica flosculis oblongis pediculis insidentibus, Chamaedryos folio, major*', 'The greater speedwell with little oblong flowers on short stalks and leaves like *Chamaedryos*', for the pretty little weed now known as *Veronica persica* (*V. buxbaumii*), Buxbaum's speedwell. This is an extreme example quoted in the book *Companion to Flowers*, by David McClintock. The advantages of having one word only for the specific name can, therefore, clearly be seen, however obscure, inapt or unpronounceable it may appear.

The glossary that follows includes most of the commonly used specific names and some of the more interesting less common ones, each with a free English translation. In most instances the feminine gender endings are given, as, in general, these are more commonly used. It does not include those specific names which refer to places or persons.

Specific name glossary

abbreviata	Shortened, particularly by comparison with allied plants
acaulis	Stemless, or seemingly so
acetosa	Somewhat acid
acicularis	Needle-shaped or pointed
aciphylla	With leaves like needles
acris	Acrid, sharp
acuminata	Long-pointed, tapering
acutifolia	With leaves narrowed to a point
adenocarpa	With glandular fruits
adpressa	Pressed flat against
adscendens, ascendens	Turning or rising upwards
adsurgens, assurgens	Erect or rising upwards
adunca	Hooked or bent backwards
aemula	Similar to
aeruginea	The colour of verdigris
aestivalis	Of the summer (usually flowering)
affinis	Related to (another species)
aggregata	Bunched together in a cluster
agrestis	Growing in arable land
aizoon	Everliving or evergreen
alata	With wings (usually the stem)
albescens, albida	Whitish, turning or shading white

alba	Dead white, without lustre
alcicornis	Shaped like antlers
alpestris, alpigena	Found in the lower Alps
alpina	From the Alps or other high-mountain regions

Aster alpinus.

alterniflorus, alternifolia	Respectively, with flowers or leaves arranged alternately
amabilis	Lovely, usually the flowers
amarella	Slightly bitter, from *amara*, bitter
ambigua	Doubtful or uncertain (identity)
amentacea	Catkin bearing
amethystina	The colour of amethyst
amoena	Pleasing or lovely
amphibia	Living in water or in land equally well
amplexicaulis	Stem clasping; the dilated leaf base clasping the stem
anceps	Two-edged, flattened (often of stems)
androgyna	Male and female flowers on the same plant
anemophila	Wind-loving, as applied to wind-pollinated flowers
angustifolius	With narrow leaves

Pulmonaria angustifolia.

annularis, anularis	Ring-shaped, referring to organs arranged in a circle (usually of flowers)
anomala	Unusual or irregular; in relation to allied plants
anserina	Meadow loving (liked by geese)
aparine	Clinging on to
aperta	Opened or exposed
apetala	Without petals
aphyllus	Without leaves
apiculata	Tipped with a point (usually the leaves)
appendiculata	Possessing appendages
applanata	Face to face, usually of leaves in the bud
appressa	Lying flat or pressed together
aquatica, aquatilis	Living or floating in water
aquifolius	With spine-pointed leaves
arachnoidea	Covered with spider's web, cobwebby
arborescens	Tree-like growth

Crassula arborescens.

arbuscula	Like a small tree
arcticus	Native to northern polar regions
arenarius	Sand loving
argentea	With a silvery coat or lustre
arguta	Sharp toothed
arietina	Shaped like a ram's horn
aristatus	Bearded
armata	Armed with thorns or other defence
articulata	Distinctly jointed
arundinacea	Resembling a reed or rush
asper	Rough with minute points
asterias	Shaped like a star-fish
atrata	Darkened or blackened
atropurpureus	Dark or black-purple
atrorubens	Very dark red
attenuata	Thinning out or tapered
aucuparia	A decoy for birds
aurantiaca	Orange or orange-yellow
aurea	Golden-yellow
auricoma	Golden-haired
auriculata	Ear-shaped, referring usually to leaves or leaf bases
aurita	With long ears
australis	Of the southern hemisphere

Erica australis.

autumnalis	Of the autumn (flowering)
avellana	A filbert; or drab, the colour of a filbert nut
avicularis	Sought by birds
axillaris	Growing in an axil (the angle between stem and leaf)
azurea	Sky blue
baccata	Berry-like (fruits)
baccifera	Bearing berries
balsamea, balsamica	Having the qualities of balm
barbata	Bearded; bearing tufts of long hair
bella	Beautiful
bicolor	Two coloured

Fascicularia bicolor.

bicornis, bicornuta	With two horns
biennis	Biennial; flowering in the second year from seeds
bifida	Cleft or divided in two
biflora	Flowers in pairs
bifolia	Leaves in pairs
biserrata	Doubly toothed or serrate
biternata	In two clusters of three, usually of leaflets in a compound leaf
blanda	Agreeable, charming or pleasant

borealis	Of the northern regions
brachybotrys	With a short raceme
brachypus	With a short foot or base (usually the rootstock or stem)
bracteata	Bearing bracts (usually at the base of a flowering pedicel or peduncle)
brevicaulis	With a short stem
bryoides	Resembling moss
bulbifera	Having a bulbous rootstock
bulbosa	Bulbous or swollen like an onion
bullata	With a puckered appearance (leaf)
caerulea, coerulea	Sky or true blue
caesius	Milky or grey blue
caespititius	Growing in carpet-like patches
caespitosa, cespitosa	Growing in tufts
calcarata	Having a spur
calcarea	Lime-loving or chalk-white

Sempervivum tectorum calcareum.

calciphila	Chalk loving
calliantha	With beautiful flowers
callizona	With a ring-like swelling
callosa	Bearing hard skin or callosities
calvescens	Almost hairless
campestris	Growing in fields
campylocarpa	Bearing bent fruit
canaliculata	Having grooved or fluted stems
cancellata	With a surface resembling a lattice or network
candicans	Shining white
candidissima	Brilliant white
candida	Pure white
canescens	Hoary or greyish white
canina	Common, in the sense of as common as dogs. Also, armed with spines or sharp teeth
capillaris	Fine as hair
capitata	A head (e.g. flowerhead of a daisy)
capreolata	Having tendrils
cardinalis	Cardinal red
carnea	Flesh coloured

cathartica	Having a purging effect
caudata	Bearing a tail
caulescens	Producing stems
cernua	Nodding or drooping
chrysantha	Golden yellow
chrysocarpa	With yellow fruits
ciliaris	Fringed with hairs (like an eyelash)
cinerea	Ashen grey
circinalis	Curled in a spiral
clandestina	Bearing hidden flowers
clavata	Club shaped
coarctata	Crowded together
cochlearis	Spoon shaped
cochleata	Shaped like a shell
colorata	Coloured
comata	Tufted
communis	Growing in a community, gregarious, common
commutata	Changed or altered
comosa	With tufts of hair
conferta, congesta	Compact or crowded together
conglomerata	Densely pressed together
conspicua	Easily seen or remarkable
cordata	Heart-shaped, usually of leaves
coriacea	Leathery textured (leaves)
corniculata	Bearing small horns
cornuta	Bearing horns or spurs
coronaria, coronata	Crowned or wreathed
corticata	Bark-like
costata	Ribbed or fluted
crassifolia	With thick leaves
crenata	Having a scalloped or notched margin; usually leaves or petals
crinita	Long haired or mane-like
crispa	Closely curled or crested
cristata	Crested or comb-like
crocata, crocea	Saffron-yellow
cruciata	Cross-shaped
cruenta	Blood-red
cuneata	Wedge-shaped
cuprea	Copper-coloured
cuspidata	Tipped with a firm point
cyanea	Azure or cornflower-blue
cylindrica	Cylindrical (of stems)
cymosa	Flowers borne centrifugally (in a cyme)
cystocarpa	With bladder-like fruits
dasyantha	With woolly flowers
dasyphylla	With thick or woolly leaves
dealbata	Whitened, as with powder
debilis	Weak, frail or small
decapetala	Having ten petals
decidua	Soon falling off
decipiens	Deceptive or misleading
declinata	Turned aside or bent downwards
decorata	Decorated or beautiful
decora	Pretty or ornamental
decumbens	Bearing prostrate stems with ascending tips
decurrens	Running down; the leaf blade extends as a winged ridge down the stem
decussata	Cross-shaped, as when leaves are borne in alternate opposite pairs
defoliata	Appearing leafless

delicata	Usually meaning delicate, dainty, tender, charming
deliciosa	A delicious; of good flavour
demissa	Hanging down
dendroidea	Tree or shrub-like
densiflora, densifolia	Respectively with dense flowers or leaves
dentata	Toothed like a saw
denticulata	Minutely toothed
denudata	Bare or naked, as when flowers are borne before the leaves
dependens	Hanging down
depressa	As if pressed down flat
descendens	Flowering downwards
diacantha	With thorns in pairs
diandra	With two stamens only
dictyophylla	With net-veined leaves
difformis	Of irregular shape or formation
diffusa	Loosely spreading
digyna	Having two styles or one deeply cleft
dilatata	Widened or expanded; of leaves
dioica	Having separate male and female flowers on different plants
dipetala	With two petals
diphylla	With two leaves or leaflets
discolor	Having different or contrasting colours
dissecta	Cut-up, as when a leaf is divided into many segments
distans	Well separated or straggly
disticha	Arranged in two rows
divaricata	Spreading apart
divergens	Spreading in different directions
diversiflora	With flowers of different forms
diversifolia	With different shaped leaves
domestica	Used in the home
draco	Dragon
dracunculus	Dragon plant
dubia	Of doubtful or uncertain origin
dulcis	Sweet
dumetorum	Growing into a thicket
dumosa	Bushy or shrubby
dysenterica	Used against dysentery
ebulus	Dwarf
ecalcarata	Without spurs
echinata, echinacea	Prickly like a hedgehog
edulis	Edible, palatable
effusa	Loosely spreading
elastica	Yielding a rubber latex
elatior	Taller (in relation to allied species)
elegans	Elegant, graceful or neat
elegantissima	Exquisitely elegant
elephantipes	Elephant footed (thick stemmed)
elodes	Bog loving or dwelling
emarginata	Having the leaf notched at the apex
enneaphylla	With nine leaves or leaflets
ensata ensifolia, ensiformis	Sword shaped
epigyna	Above the ovary (other floral organs)

epiphytica	Growing above the soil on trees and rocks (e.g. certain orchids)
erecta	Upright
eriantha	With woolly flowers
erinacea	Prickly
eriocarpa	With woolly fruits
erubescens	Pale red or turning red
erythraea	Tinged with red
euchlora	Dark green
exaltata	Erect, tall or commanding
excelsior excelsa	Lofty, eminent
exigua	Narrow, small or insignificant
eximia	Exceptional, distinguished, uncommon
exotica	Of foreign origin

Sisyrinchium filifolium.

falcata	Sickle-shaped (leaves)
fallax	Spurious or not genuine
fascicularis	In tight clusters or bundles
fastigiata	With erect clustered twigs or branches
fastuosa	Proud, stately or bountiful
fecunda	Fruitful or fertile
femina	Female
fenestralis	With windows; having pellucid patches on leaves or petals
ferox	Set with strong spines
ferruginea	Red-brown or rust coloured
fertilis	Abundantly fruitful
ficaria	Fig-like in shape
filifolia, filiformis	Fine, thread-like
filipendula	Jointed by threads (e.g. the tuberous root system of meadow sweet)
filipes	With thread-like stems
fistulosa	Hollow, tubular (e.g. like an onion leaf)
flabellata	Fan or wedge-shaped
flammea, flammula	Flame coloured
flavida	Pale yellow
flava	Pure yellow
flexilis	Flexible or whip-like
flexuosa	Bent to left and right, zig-zag (of stems)
floccosa	Woolly-haired
flore-pleno	With double flowers
floribunda	Flowering profusely

Oxalis floribunda rosea.

florida	Rich in flowers
florulenta	Small flowered
fluitans	Floating in water
fluminalis	Growing in running water
foetens	Unpleasant or evil smelling
foetidissima	Extremely unpleasant odour
foliosa	With abundant foliage
fontana	Growing in or near springs
formosa	Beautiful
formosissima	Superbly lovely
fragilis, frangula	Brittle or fragile
fragrans	Fragrant
fragrantissima	Extra sweetly fragrant
frigida	Erect or frigid

Cotoneaster frigidus.

frondosa	Covered with ample leafage
frutescens, fruticans, fruticosa	Shrubby or shrub-like
fulgens	Glowing or shining
fulva	Reddish-brown, tawny
furcata	Forked, or with pronged lobes
fuscata	Tan-coloured
galacifolia	With attractive or showy leaves
gemmata	Having buds, or bud-like
geniculata	With knee-like nodes or joints

gibbosa, gibberosa, gibba	With a prominent hump	hyperborea	Northern	lepidota	Set with small scurfy scales
gigantea	Huge or gigantic	hypogaea	Growing beneath the soil	lepida	Neat or pretty
glaber, glabrata, glabella	Smooth or hairless	hystrix	Porcupine or hedgehog-like	leucocephala	With white flowerheads
		imbricata	Covered with overlapping scales	lilacina	The colour of lilac
glacialis	Growing in icy regions			liliputana	Very small or minute
glandulifera, glandulosa	Bearing glands	imperialis	Majestic or imperial	linearifolia	With narrow flax-like leaves
		impressa	Marked with small depressions	linearis	With narrow parallel-sided leaves
glauca, glaucescens	Grey-blue	inaequalis	Asymmetrical or irregular in shape or outline (usually of leaves)	lingua	Tongued, or tongue-shaped
globosa	Rounded or ball-shaped			litoralis, littoralis	Growing on the sea shore
glomerata	Clustered into a head	incana, incanescens	Greyish or hoary	livida	Of leaden hue
glumacea	Having chaffy bracts			lobata	Divided into lobes (usually leaves)
gracilis	Graceful or slender	incisa	Deeply cut into irregular lobes		
graminea, graminifolia	Grass-like	indivisa	Entire or undivided leaves	longiflora, longifolia	With long flowers and leaves respectively
grandiflora, grandifolia	With large flowers or leaves respectively	inermis	Unarmed or without thorns		
		inflata	Inflated or distended		
grandis	Great or large	inflexa	Abruptly bent over or incurved		
gratissima	Very pleasant or agreeable				
griseus	Greyish or hoary	infundibuliformis	Funnel-shaped		
guttata	Spotted or dotted	innominata	Nameless		
gyrans	Moving in a circle	insignis	Remarkable or distinguished		
haemantha	With blood-red flowers	integerrima, integrifolia	With a smooth edge		
haematodes	Blood-coloured				
halophila	Growing in salt marshes	intermedia	Intermediate between two species or forms		
hamata	Hook-shaped				
hastata	Spear head shaped				
hederacea	Ivy-like in habit				
helioscopia	Turning towards the sun				
hemisphaerica	Shaped like half a globe				
heterantha	Bearing flowers of different form				
heterophylla	With leaves of differing shape				
hexapetala	Having six petals				
hiberna, hiemalis, hyemalis	Of winter-time				
hirsuta	Roughly hairy				
hirtella	Minutely haired				
hispidula, hispida	Rough with bristly hairs				
horizontalis	Prostrate or horizontal				

Aucuba japonica longifolia.

Hydrangea serrata intermedia.

Cotoneaster horizontalis.

horrida	Offensive or bristly
hortensis	Originating in gardens
humifusa	Creeping flat on the ground
humilis	Of lowly growth
hybrida	Of hybrid origin or appearing so
hymenodes	Bearing membranes

jubata	Bearing a name
jucunda	Lovely
juvenalis	Youthful or juvenile
kermesinus	Deep carmine, the colour of the dye extracted from the kermes bug
laciniata	Fringed or slit into narrow lobes
lactea, lactiflora	Milky white
laeta	Joyful, pleasing or of gay appearance
laevigata	Smooth or slippery
lanata, lanuginosa	Covered with long woolly hair
lanceolata, lancifolia	With lance-shaped leaves
lasiantha	With woolly or shaggy flowers
lasiocarpa	Woolly fruited
latifolia	With broad leaves
laxiflora	With flowers in loose clusters
leiophylla	With smooth leaves

lunata	Shaped like the crescent moon
lurida	Brownish-yellow
luteola, lutescens	Yellowish
lutea	Yellow
luxurians	Of exuberant or excessive growth
lycoctonum	Wolf-killing
lyrata	The shape of a lyre
macrantha	With large or long flowers
macrobotrys	With long flower spikes
macrocarpa	With large fruits
maculata	Spotted or blotched

Rosa macrantha.

maculosa	Thickly spotted
magnifica	Imposing or splendid
majalis	Flowering in May
majus	Greater or larger
mammillaris	Teat or nipple-shaped
manicata	Long-sleeved
maritima	Confined to sea coast areas
marmorata	Veined like marble
mas	Male
maxima	The greatest or largest
medius	Intermediate between two types
megacarpa	Bearing large fruits
mellita	Sweet
micrantha	With minute flowers
microcarpa	With small fruits
micropetala	With small petals
microphylla	Small leaved
millefolia	With many leaves or leaf segments
miniata	The colour of red lead or cinnabar

Clivia miniata.

minima	Very small
minor, minus	Lesser or smaller
minutiflora	Bearing tiny flowers
mirabilis	Wonderful or astonishing
mitis	Without spines or defenceless
modesta	Modest or unpretentious
mollis	With soft velvety hair
monophylla	One-leaved
monstrosa	Of abnormal development
montana	Growing in the mountains
monticola	Growing in the hills
moschata	With a musky scent
multicolor	Of many colours
multiceps	Many-headed
multiflora	Many-flowered
multiplex	Many-fold (e.g. extra petals)
muralis, murorum	Growing on walls
muricata	Rough with short, sharp points
mutabilis	Changing in form or colour
nana	Of dwarf stature
neglecta	Overlooked or insignificant
nemophila, nemoralis, nemorum	Growing in woods
nervosa	Having distinct veins or nerves
niger, nigra	Black or very dark
nigrescens, nigricans	Turning black
nitida, nitens	Lustrous, shining or smooth
nivalis	Growing near the snow-line
nivea	Snow white
nivosa	As if snowed upon
nobilis	Stately or noble appearance
nodosa	Knotty, or with prominent nodes
nonscripta	Not described
nudicaulis	Having leafless stems
nudiflora	Having naked flowers
nummularia	Shaped like a coin
nutans	Nodding or drooping
obcordata	Inversely heart-shaped (leaves)
obesa	Swollen, fat
obovata	Egg-shaped in outline, attached at the smaller end (leaves)
obtusa	With a blunt apex
ochroleuca	Pale ochre-yellow
occidentalis,	Western
odora	Sweet smelling
officinalis	Of use or service to man
oleraceus	Aromatic (of herbs)
oppositifolia	With leaves in pairs opposite each other
opulus	Snowball (the flowerhead)
orbicularis	Disk or ball-shaped
orientalis, orientale	Eastern
ornata	Ornamental or beautiful
ovalifolia	With oval leaves
ovata	Elliptic but broader in the lower half
ovina	Sought by sheep
oxyacantha	With sharp spines
oxypetala	With pointed petals
pachyphylla	Thick-leaved
pallidiflora	With pale coloured flowers
pallida	Almost colourless, pallid
palmata	Of leaves lobed like a hand
palustris	Marsh loving
panduriformis	Fiddle (violin) shaped
paniculata	Flowers borne in panicles
pannosa	Ragged like ravelled cloth
paradoxa	Contrary or paradoxical
parasitica	Living as a parasite
pardalina	Spotted like a panther
parviflora, parvifolia	Small flowers or leaves respectively
patens	Spreading
patula	Somewhat spreading
pectinata	Comb-like
pedata	Shaped like a bird's foot (fancifully)
peduncularis	With a distinct stalk
peltatus, peltate	Shield-shaped
pendula	Hanging down, pendulous
pennata	Feather-like or veined
pentandra	With five stamens
perennis	Of perennial duration
perfoliata	The leaf blade completely surrounding the stem
persicaria	Peach-like (usually leaves)
pescaprea	Like a goat's foot (leaves)
petraea	Growing in stony places
phaeus	Reddish-brown
physocarpa	With bladder-like fruits
picturata	Pretty as a picture
picta,	Coloured as if painted
pilosa	Thinly covered with soft hair
pinetorum	Growing under pines
pinnata	Feathered; a compound leaf with leaflets in parallel pairs
pisifera	Pea bearing
planus	Flat, plane
platycarpa	With broad fruits
platypetala	With broad flat petals
plena	Double-flowered

Paeonia officinalis rubra plena.

plicata	Folded, e.g. leaf margins (folded back)
plumosa	Feathery or plumed
podophylla	With stalked leaves
poeticus	Appertaining to poets
polaris	From the polar regions
polyandrus	Bearing many stamens
polycarpa	Bearing many fruits
polychroma	Many-coloured or hued
polygonata	With many nodes or knots
polypetala	With many separate petals
polyphylla	Many leaves or leaflets
polystachya	With many flower spikes
pomifera	Bearing apple-like fruits
populnea	Poplar-like in habit
praecox	Developing early or prematurely

Stachyurus praecox.

Polystichum setiferum proliferum.

praestans	Outstanding or excellent
pratensis	Growing in meadows
princeps	Foremost or most distinguished, princely
proboscidea	Having a terminal snout or horn
procera	Tall or slender
procumbens	With trailing prostrate stems
prolifera	Bearing prolific progeny
prostratus	Lying flat, prostrate

Rosmarinus lavandulaceus (syn. R. officinalis prostratus).

pruinosa	Covered with a white waxy film
ptarmica	Causing sneezing
pterocarpa	With winged fruits
pubescens	With soft downy hair
pulchella	Beautiful
pulcherrima	Most beautiful
pulla	Almost black (dark purple)
pulvinalis, pulvinata	Cushion-shaped
pulverulenta	Powdered
pumila	Dwarf stature
punctata	As if marked with dots
pungens	Pungent, piercing, sharply pointed
punicea	Scarlet
purpurascens	Purplish or turning purple

purpurea	True purple
pusilla	Small, weak, puny or insignificant
pycnocephala	With flowers in dense heads
pycnostachya	With densely clustered flower spikes
pygmaea	Of dwarf stature
pyriformis	Pear-shaped
quadrangularis	With four angles (stems)
quadrifolia	With four leaves or leaflets
quinquefoliata	With five leaflets
quinquelocularis	The fruit having five divisions
racemosa	Flowers borne in racemes (branched clusters of varying forms)
radiata	Spreading out like rays; usually petals or florets
radicans	Rooting from stems
radicata	With a tap-root
ramosa	Much branched
ramosissima	Very much branched
rectiflora	With upright flowers
recurva	Bent over and downwards
rediviva	Revived or renewed to life
reducta	Reduced in size
reflexa	Bent back on itself
refulgens	Reflecting
regalis	Royal or kingly
reginae	Queenly
remotiflora	Few flowers spaced far apart
reniformis, renifolia	With kidney-shaped leaves
repanda	With a wavy or bent back margin
repens, reptans	Creeping and rooting (stems)
reticulata	Netted; usually leaf venation
retusa	With a rounded or notched apex
revoluta	Rolled back from margin or apex
rhodocyanea	Rose and blue
rhomboidea, rhombifolia	Diamond-shaped
rhytidophylla	With grooved leaves
rigida, rigescens	Rigid, inflexible
ringens	Gaping open (flowers)
riparia, rivularis	Growing by rivers and streams
robusta	Big, strong, robust
rosea	Rose-coloured
rostrata	Having a beak (usually fruit)
rosularis	Leaves borne in a rosette
rotundifolius	Round-leaved
rubella	Shining red
rubens	Blush-red
rubescens	Turning red
rubiginosa	Rust-coloured
rubrifolia	With red leaves
rufescens	Reddish-brown
rugosa	With wrinkled leaves
rupestris	Growing among rocks
rupicola	Growing on ledges or cliffs
rutilum	Glowing (used of red, orange and yellow flowers, but usually red)
saccharata, saccharum	Sweet; yielding sugar

sagittalis, sagittata, sagittifolia	With arrow-shaped leaves
sambucina	Smelling of or resembling elder
sanguinea	Blood-red
sapida	Having a pleasant taste
sarmentosa	With long slender runners
sativa	A crop plant (usually for food)
saxatilis, saxosa	Growing among rocks
scaber, scabrum	Rough to the touch
scalaris	Ladder-shaped (leaf form or markings)
scandens	Climbing
schizocarpa	A fruit which splits when ripe
schizopetala	With split petals
sclarea	Clear, alluding to its use in eye lotions
scoparia	Brush or broom-like

Cytisus scoparius.

scutellata	Shaped like a small shield
secundiflora	Having all the flowers turned or bent over in the same direction
segetalis, segetum	Of the cornfields
semperflorens	Ever flowering
sempervirens	Ever green
senescens	Grey, as from old age
senilis	Appearing to be old
sensitiva	Responding immediately to touch
septemloba	With seven-lobed leaves
serpens	Snake-like or undulating (stems)
serratifolia	Leaves with a saw-edge
sessiliflora	Bearing stalkless flowers
sessilis	Stemless
setacea, setosa, setigera	Bearing bristle-like hairs
sicula	From Sicily
siliquastrum	From *siliqua*, a pod
silvestris, sylvestris	Growing wild
simplex	Of one piece (see next item)
simplicifolia	With entire leaves; not divided into leaflets
sinuata	Having a deep wavy margin

103

solida	Solid or firm; enduring; or genuine
sparsiflora, sparsifolia	With scattered flowers or leaves respectively
spathacea	Bearing spathes (modified leaves) around the flower clusters
speciosa	Showy, splendid, handsome
spectabilis	Remarkable, worthy of note
sphaerocephala	With round flowerheads or fruits; or of rounded form
spicata	Arranged in spikes (flowers)
spinosa	Bearing spines
splendens, splendida	Bright, shining
squalida	Dull yellow
squamata	Scaly
squarrosa	Rough or scurfy
stagnalis	Growing in still water
stellaris	Star spangled
stellata	Star-shaped

Tulipa stellata chrysantha.

stenocarpa	With narrow fruits
stenopetala	With narrow petals
stenophylla	Narrow leaved
sterilis	Infertile, sterile
stolonifera	Bearing stolons or runners
succisa	Appearing bitten or broken off (e.g. the root in sheep's-bit)
suffrutescens	Shrubby or shrub-like
sulcata	Furrowed or fluted (usually stems)
sulphurea	Sulphur-yellow
superbus	Superb, proud
supina	Prostrate, but facing upwards
suspensa	Weeping or hanging down
sylvatica, silvatica	Growing among trees
syphilitica	A supposed cure for syphilis
tabuliformis	Flat topped like a table
tardiflora	Late flowering
tectorum	Growing on roofs
temulenta	Nodding top-heavily, drunken
tenax	Tough, strong (the fibres)
tenella	Delicate or soft
tenuicaulis	Slender-stemmed
tenuifolius	With slender or fine leaves

Phormium tenax veitchii.

terminalis	Arising at the apex (flowers)
ternata	With organs in threes (usually leaves or leaflets)
terrestris	Of the soil (as distinct from epiphytic)
tetralix	A whorl of four leaves arranged cross-wise
tetrandra	With four stamens
textilis	Bearing fibres used for weaving
tigrina	Marked like a tiger
tinctoria	Used for dyeing
tomentosa	With a covering of dense short hair
tomentella	Finely covered with felt-like hair
torminalis	Supposedly a cure for colic
tortuosus	Much twisted
trachycarpa	With rough fruits
trachyphylla	With rough hard leaves
triandra	Having three stamens
tridentata	Three toothed or pronged
trifida	Divided into threes
triflora	With the flowers in threes
trimestris	Maturing in three months
tripetala	With three petals
triquetra	Three angled (stems)
tristis	Sad or weeping, or of a dull colour
triumphans	Exultant, victorious
trivialis	Common or ordinary
truncata	Ending abruptly
tuberosa	Bearing or resembling tubers
typhina	Antler-shaped (leaves or branches)
uliginosa	Growing in wet places
umbellata	With the flower cluster shaped like an umbrella
umbrosa	Growing in shady places
undulata	With a wavy margin
unguicularis	Narrow-clawed (the base of a petal)
uniflora	One flowered
unifolia	One leaved, or appearing so
urbanica, urbica	Growing in or near towns
urens	Bearing stinging hairs

urnigera	With urn-shaped organs (often flowers)
utilis	Useful (to man)
vagans	Wandering or widespread
vallicola	Growing in valleys
variabilis	Not constant in appearance
varians	Changeable in colour or form
variegata	Marked with another colour, (usually white, cream or yellow)
velutina	Covered with velvety hairs
ventricosa	Inflated (usually flowers)
venusta	Charming, lovely, graceful
vernalis, verna	Of the spring (flowering)
verrucosa	Warted or covered with raised glands
versicolor	Changing, or of more than one colour
verticillata	With leaves in whorls
vesicaria	Inflated
victorialis	Victorious

Vinca major variegata.

villosa	With shaggy hairs
viminalis	Bearing long flexible stems
violacea	Violet coloured
virens, viridis	Green
virescens	Turning green
virginalis	Maidenly; purest white
viridiflora	With green flowers
viscaria, viscosa	Sticky to the touch
vitalba	White vine; the Virgin's bower
vivipara	Producing plantlets or bulbils vegetatively (without seeds)
volubilis	Twining round, climbing
vulgaris	Common or ordinary
vulgata	Well-known
vulneraria	Said to heal wounds
vulpina	Fox-like (smell)
xanthina	Golden-yellow
xanthocarpa	With golden fruits
xerocarpa	With dry fruits
xerophila	Inhabiting dry regions
xiphoides	Sword-shaped
zebrina	Striped like a zebra
zonata, zonalis	Marked with a ring or zone of another colour (usually leaves)

Most of us would prefer to call a sweet pea a sweet pea rather than *Lathyrus odoratus*, and where there can be no confusion there is every reason for doing this. Again, in the cause of simplicity one of the easiest, and certainly one of the cheapest, means of growing plants for the garden is to raise them from seed. But to grow some of our larger and longer-lived plants such as trees and shrubs by this means would take so long that we generally leave this task to the nurseryman and buy from him semi-mature specimens. The seeds we buy and sow are of quick growing, quick germinating plants such as the sweet pea just mentioned.

Some seeds require either protection or warmth if they are to germinate satisfactorily and the techniques of seed sowing in a frame, under cloches or in a greenhouse or propagator are discussed in a later chapter.

Similar to seeds in many respects but frequently even easier to grow are bulbs.

Bulb cultivation

Botanically, bulbs are buds, commonly subterranean, producing roots from their undersides, and consisting of layers of fleshy rudimentary leaves, called scales, attached to abbreviated stems. There is considerable uncertainty in the minds of many gardeners as to the difference between bulbs, corms, rhizomes and tubers, for their function is the same—to tide the plant over a period of adverse conditions, such as summer droughts and winter cold. All have common factors: food storage; rapid growth under suitable conditions; and the same life-cycle, in that during growth and flowering, next year's flower is formed in miniature, the foliage soon reaching maturity and dying away, as do the roots in most cases when the whole plant enters a period of rest.

A true bulb, such as that of a tulip, hyacinth or narcissus, is a bud surrounded by fleshy or scaly leaves, arising from a flat disc of 'basal plate'. In 'tunicated' bulbs the fleshy leaves are rolled close together, as in the tulip. In 'imbricated' bulbs the bulb leaves are thick and overlapping, as in the lily.

The determination of whether or not a particular plant is a bulb depends upon the structure of the storage organ. If the botanical definition of the bulb is strictly accepted, many plants that gardeners ordinarily consider bulbs, such as crocuses, calla lilies, cannas and dahlias, must be eliminated. These and many other plants not technically true bulbs have bulb-like organs that function in the same way as bulbs but are not structurally scaly buds. They include rounded or flattish, solid, swollen stem bases called corms as in gladioli, crocuses; elongated thickened stems called rhizomes as in cannas, calla lilies, lily-of-the-valley; thickened terminal portions of stems called tubers as in anemones, begonias, caladiums; and swollen tuber-

like roots as in dahlias (see Corm, Pseudobulb, Rhizome and Tuber).

Propagation This article will use the word 'bulb' like the ordinary gardener does and include all organs obviously bulb-like as well as true bulbs. Nearly all bulbs produce offsets sooner or later, and these, except for rarities, give sufficient stock for the ordinary gardener. All that needs to be done is to dig up the clumps, separate the bulbs, sort out the small ones and replant them, treating them like mature bulbs until they reach the flowering stage. Rhizomes and tuberous roots may be treated in the same way, so each eye will produce another plant if care is taken of it. The exceptions are erythroniums, which rarely produce offsets, and cyclamen, which never do, and therefore can only be increased from seeds.

This leads to a consideration of raising bulbs from seed. Except for the most enthusiastic of amateurs, this should be left to the specialist. Where seed is produced, it is easy to obtain a supply, but the seed of many bulbs does not come true. That is the seedlings raised have characteristics which differ from their parents. There is also the question of cross fertilization to take into account, and, of course, raising bulbs from seed is a lengthy undertaking, often a risky one as well. However, with these provisos it may be said that raising lilies from seed is an interesting process

Corms replace themselves annually. After having thrown up their leaves and flowers, each corm shrivels away and a new corm, sometimes several, forms while the leaves and flowers of the old one are growing.

Without bulbs all gardens would be the poorer the whole year round, but particularly in autumn, spring and summer. Bulbs are so popular because they yield such big rewards for so little in terms of money and care. Bulbs make it possible to have a continuous succession of colour outdoors and indoors throughout the year. Bulbs will flourish in virtually any kind of well-drained soil. Bulbs will thrive in almost every conceivable position or situation in the garden, in sun or partial shade. Bulbs offer infinite variety in colour, form and texture. When in bloom they vary from an inch or two in height to several feet and the characteristics of their foliage are as diverse as their flowers. The flowers of most bulbs last well when cut and are ideal for flower arrangements. Gardening with bulbs requires a minimum of work. Bulbs are easy to cultivate, giving a high percentage of successful results even for the beginner. Bulbs are not only inexpensive but are easily obtainable.

Planting Always purchase good-size, healthy bulbs from a reputable dealer. Early ordering is vital to ensure the best selection. Plant immediately the bulbs

arrive and if this is inconvenient open the bags for ventilation and keep the bulbs in a cool, dry place until you are ready to plant them. Plant in well-drained soil. The vast majority of bulbs will do well in any soil provided it is well drained. It is advisable, however, to treat heavy soils with applications of peat or well-rotted leafmould.

The planting period for bulbs will depend upon their flowering season. The planting period for spring-flowering bulbs extends from September 1 to December 15 in Britain, but daffodils should be planted before the end of October. Autumn-flowering bulbs (crocus and colchicum) should be planted in August. Most summer-flowering bulbs should be planted in March and April, although some, such as lilies, should be planted in November and December. Stem-rooting lilies can also be successfully set out in early spring.

Plant bulbs at the right depth. Although there are exceptions, bulbs are generally set with their tops about three times the diameter of the bulb below ground; small bulbs deeper proportionately. Usually it is the pointed end of the bulb which should be uppermost, but some tubers are planted horizontally. Some bulbs, such as anemones, give no indication which end is up, but there are usually signs of previous stem or root sources. Spring-flowering bulbs such as hyacinths, daffodils and tulips are planted 6 inches deep and most spring-flowering small or miscellaneous bulbs are planted 3–4 inches deep. Variation in depth depends upon the height of the stem and on the type of soil—the longer the stem and the lighter the soil, the deeper the planting.

No general guidance can be given on spacing of bulbs, for this may range from 1 inch to 2 feet apart, depending upon the size of the plant, its flower and foliage. Bulbs planted in groups or clusters produce the best effects, and if flowers are wanted for indoor decoration extra bulbs should be planted in the vegetable garden or special cutting garden.

Bulbs can be grown virtually anywhere in the garden. There is a place in every garden for some kinds of bulbs in beds, borders, edges, shrubberies, rock gardens, orchards, woodlands, lawns, on walls, between paving stones, in tubs or window-boxes. Many bulbs can be naturalised, that is, planted in informal groups or drifts and left to increase naturally. This is often done in rough grass or woodland. The grass should be left uncut until the bulb foliage has died down naturally, usually in June.

Most bulbs do not require full sun but can be planted in partial shade. Indeed, partial shade makes for longer lasting blooms. Flowers should be removed when petals fade and the foliage should not be cut off, but should be allowed to die down naturally, permitting the bulb to replace energy and flower the following season. Most spring-flowering bulbs (the exceptions are lilies, anemones and ranunculuses which require winter protection) should be lifted. Lift bulbs carefully only after the foliage has died down and store them in a cool, frost-free and well-ventilated place until it is time to replant them again. Generally, if bulbs are doing well, natural increase will make lifting of the clumps and separation of the bulbs necessary every few years. Be careful when separating clumps of bulbs not to damage them. Bulbs should always be handled carefully to avoid physical injury.

The most commonly grown bulb flowers in our gardens are narcissi, tulips and hyacinths, with lilies, snowdrops, grape hyacinths and several others also represented in the list.

Daffodil is merely the common name for narcissus, of which there are more than 10,000 named varieties, with some 500 in normal commercial cultivation.

With the exception of one or two kinds, such as tazettas, narcissi are hardy, tolerant and adaptable plants. They will grow in almost any situation except heavy shade or in badly-drained soil. In open ground they flower from February to the end of May. Normally most varieties remain in flower for three to four weeks and if they are picked in bud for cut flowers they will last in water for ten days or more.

Narcissi will flourish in beds and borders, naturalised in meadows, open woodlands, lawns, orchards or under scattered trees, among shrubs, in tubs and window boxes. The smaller kinds do well in rock gardens and many varieties are suitable for forcing.

Out of doors daffodils will flourish in any well-drained soil although *N. bulbo-codium* prefers sandy soil and *N. cyclamineus* peaty soil. The best sites are in sun or light shade with shelter from sweeping winds. Plant the bulbs as early in the autumn as they can be obtained. Robust kinds that have large bulbs should be planted 5–6 inches deep, less vigorous kinds with smaller bulbs 3–4 inches deep, and tiny species 3 inches deep. Space vigorous growers 6–9 inches apart, moderately vigorous growers 4–5 inches apart, and small species 2–4 inches apart. In naturalised plantings these distances are varied considerably and it is best to scatter the bulbs at random, in groups or drifts, planting them exactly where they fall.

For planting bulbs out of doors, especially in turf, special planting tools are available. Some of these are long-handled tools, shod with a circular metal cutter which is forced into the soil. When the tool is lifted a core of turf and soil is removed intact. A bulb is then placed in the hole and the core of turf replaced over it and firmed with the foot. To enable the cutter to be driven easily into hard turf the tool is fitted with a foot bar. There are versions of this tool with short handles, without the foot bar. Otherwise, when planting in soil or in the rock garden it is always advisable to do so with a trowel, never with a dibber. If a dibber is used an air pocket may be left below the bulb, into which the roots will not grow, thus preventing proper development. If the soil is dry, water thoroughly after planting.

Where winters are severe, protect bulbs which are not planted in grass with a covering of leaves or other suitable material. Feed established plantings in early autumn and early spring, using a complete fertiliser in spring and a slower-acting organic fertiliser in the autumn. Water copiously during dry spells when the foliage is above ground. Never remove the foliage until it has died down naturally. When plantings become crowded so that the bloom deteriorates in quantity and quality, lift, separate and replant the bulbs as soon as the foliage has died down.

Tulips are equally numerous, with several thousand named varieties and some 800 in commercial cultivation. They differ more than narcissi and are divided into 23 main groups or classes, of interest mainly to the specialist.

Some tulips flower early (in mid-April, some in mid-season (late April), and others bloom late, in May. The colour range is from white to almost black, from softest pink to deepest purple; there are broken colours, self-colours, striped, streaked, shaded and tinged. Some have oval flowers, some are shaped like turbans, and others are square at the base. Some tulips resemble paeonies, others have lily-like flowers. There are tulips with fringed or curled petals and others with pointed petals. A number produce several flowers on a stem. Some have tiny flowers, while others produce blooms up to 15 inches in diameter. Heights range from a few inches to nearly 3 feet.

Cultivation Bulbs can be planted out of doors between mid-September and mid-December. Species or botanical tulips should be planted 4 inches deep and about 5 inches apart with the exception of *T. fosteriana*, which should be planted 5–6 inches deep and some 6 inches apart, like all divisions of

Narcissus 'February Gold' is an early-flowering, long-lasting plant with bold trumpets of a fine golden-yellow.

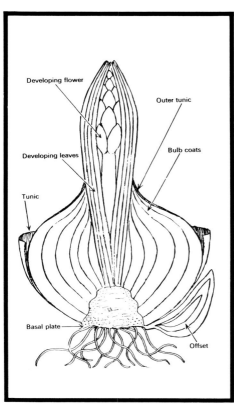

1 Bulbs and corms are storage organs that enable onions, tulips, and gladioli to over-winter in or out of the ground.
2 A longitudinal section through a hyacinth bulb showing it at an early stage of growth

1 Lilium 'Green Dragon' is one of the beautiful modern lilies known as Olympic Hybrids, bred in Oregon, USA. It is not a difficult bulb to grow, provided the soil is well-drained.

2 Crocuses are favourites for spring colour, but though listed by bulb merchants they are not bulbs, but grow from corms which are thickened stem bases, renewed annually.

3 Fritillaria imperialis is a spring-flowering bulb, usually known as Crown Imperial. It grows from a large, rounded bulb and sends up a stem about 3-4 feet tall. The nodding flowers are borne in May. There are various colour forms.

1

2

3

garden tulips. Good drainage is essential; they will thrive in virtually any well-drained soil, but in light sandy soils the bulbs should be planted an inch or two deeper than normal. Tulips can be interplanted with roses or with annuals or with other bulbs flowering at the same time, taking into account the differing heights of other plants when interplanting. Species tulips do best in sunny positions, but garden tulips can be planted in sun or in partial shade. Early-flowering garden tulips planted in sheltered sunny spots will come into flower sooner, or if late-flowering tulips are planted in partial shade, they will last longer.

Apart from *kaufmanniana* tulips which are naturalised, all tulips should be lifted every year when the foliage has turned completely yellow and begun to die off. The old flower stems should be cut off an inch or so above the newly formed bulbs at the end of June or early July. They should, under no circumstances, be left on the bulb in storage trays. If the bulbs must be cleared from the ground before the foliage begins to die, to make way for other bedding plants, they may be lifted and heeled into a shallow trench in a spare corner until the leaves yellow. The lifted bulbs should be kept out of sunlight, cleaned and stored in a cool, airy, frost-free place until planting time comes round again. Indoor cultivation is the same procedure as narcissus, but forced tulip bulbs are not really worth keeping for later outdoor planting.

There are far fewer hyacinths than tulips or daffodils, but because of their beauty and their perfume they continue to be firm favourites for the garden.

Cultivation Bedding hyacinths are best planted in late October about 4 inches deep in well-drained soil and in a sunny position. Space the bulbs about 8 inches apart for maximum colour effect. Bone meal forked into the soil before planting at the rate of 4 oz to the square yard will ensure good heads of flower in April.

Watering, feeding, mulching It is essential for all bulbs to have plenty of moisture when growing actively, but excess water during the dormant period is harmful. Like all plants, bulbs respond to fertile soil, but manures and fertilisers must be used carefully. Well-rotted manure improves soil structure and provides nutrients for all plants and may be used to advantage with bulbs as long as there is a protective layer of soil between the bulbs and the manure. Fresh manure should never be used. Slow-acting fertilisers other than manure are particularly recommended for feeding bulbs. Bonemeal is one of the best and five or six pounds to a hundred square feet is not too heavy an annual application.

Mulches are useful in the summer to

A Recommended List of Bulbs

Early Spring (February–March)

Botanical Name	Common Name	Botanical Name	Common Name	Botanical Name	Common Name
Camassia	Quamash	*Iris reticulata*	Iris	Tulipa (Species tulips)	Tulip
Chionodoxa	Glory of the Snow	*Iris danfordiae*		T. kaufmanniana	
Crocus	Crocus	Leucojum vernum	Spring Snowflake	T. fosteriana	
Eranthis	Winter Aconite	Narcissus cyclamineus		T. greigii	
Galanthus	Snowdrop				
Ipheion uniflorum		Scilla sibirica	Siberian Squill		

Mid-season (March–April)

Hyacinthus	Hyacinths	Narcissus Medium Cupped	Daffodil	Tulipa Double Early	Tulip
Muscari	Grape Hyacinth	Tulipa Single Early	Tulip	Triumph	
Narcissus Trumpet	Daffodil			Mendel	

Late (April–May)

Iris (Dutch)	Iris	Tulipa Lily-flowered	Tulip	Tulipa Darwin Hybrid	Tulip
Narcissus Short Cupped	Daffodil	Double Late		Parrot	
Scilla campanulata	Spanish Squill	Paeony-flowered		Cottage	
				Darwin	

Summer (June–September)

Acidanthera	Abyssinian Wildflower	Galtonia	Spire Lily	*Ornithogalum thyrsoides*	Chincherinchee
		Gladiolus	Gladiolus	Ranunculus	
Anemone	Windflower	Iris	Iris	Sparaxis	African Harlequin Flower
Begonia	Begonia	English Spanish			
Brodiaea				Tigridia	Shell Flower
Crinum	Cape Lily	Ismene		*Vallota speciosa*	Scarborough Lily
Crocosmia		*Leucojum aestivum*	Summer Snowflake	Zantedeschia	Arum Lily
Dahlia	Dahlia	Lilium	Lily		
Freesia	Freesia	Montbretia	Montbretia		

Autumn (September–November)

Crocus (some)	Crocus	Sternbergia	Winter Daffodil	*Zephyranthes candida*	Flower of the West Wind
Colchicum	Autumn Crocus				

Rock Garden

Chionodoxa	Glory of the Snow	Galanthus	Snowdrop	Narcissus Dwarf Species	Daffodil
Crocus	Crocus	*Ipheion uniflorum*			
Erythronium dens-canis	Dog's Tooth Violet	Iris Dwarf Species	Iris	*Scilla sibirica*	Siberian Squill
Fritillaria Dwarf Species		Muscari	Grape Hyacinth	*Sternbergia lutea*	Winter Daffodil
				Tulipa Species	Tulip

Naturalising

Anemone blanda		*Endymion nonscriptus*	Bluebell	Leujocum	Snowflake
Camassia	Quamash			Muscari	Grape Hyacinth
Colchicum	Autumn Crocus	Eranthis	Winter Aconite	Narcissus	Daffodil
Crocus spring and autumn-flowering	Crocus	*Erythronium dens-canis*	Dog's Tooth Violet	*Ornithogalum umbellatum*	Star of Bethlehem
		Fritillaria meleagris	Chequered Lily	*Puschkinia libanotica*	Striped Squill
		Galanthus	Snowdrop	*Scilla sibirica*	Siberian Squill

Cut Flowers

Alstroemeria	Peruvian Lily	Iris	Iris	*Ornithogalum umbellatum arabicum pyramidale*	Star of Bethlehem
Anemone De Caen St. Brigid, etc.	Windflower	Spanish English			
		Lilium	Lily	Ranunculus	
Convallaria majalis	Lily-of-the Valley	Montbretia	Montbretia	Scilla	Squill
		Muscari	Grape Hyacinth	Tulipa Taller Species all tall-stemmed garden tulips	Tulip
Crocus chrysanthus	Crocus	*Narcissus triandrus* N. cyclamineus			
Dahlia	Dahlia	N. jonquilla Doubles			
Freesia	Freesia	Trumpet		Tritonia	
Gladiolus	Gladiolus	Small Cupped			
Iris Dutch	Iris	N. poeticus		Ixia	African Corn Lily

help the soil to retain moisture and peat is excellent for this purpose. Mulches intended for protective winter covering should be applied to the surface of the ground after the ground has frozen and should be removed after bulb growth is under way in the spring.

Weeds, pests, diseases Areas planted with bulbs should be kept as free of weeds as possible and the surface soil should be loosened from time to time. Injured or infected foliage should be removed and burned. Diseases can be avoided by buying only healthy, top quality bulbs, and few gardeners who do this are troubled by diseases.

Lilium szovitzianum is a fine June-flowering lily.

The major pests are slugs and snails and fortunately these can be controlled by modern slug killers. In dealing with any diseases or pests, proper diagnosis is important before resorting to drastic measures. Should a disease appear among a planting, lift the healthy bulbs, disinfect them, and move them to an area not previously used for growing bulbs of the same kind. This will usually save them from infection.

Annuals

Hardy annuals are easy to grow and will give a quick and brilliant display provided they are grown in an open, sunny position in any good garden soil. Many annuals are tender and easily killed by frost, so these kinds are sown under glass in the spring and planted out when all danger of frost is over. Some hardy and half-hardy kinds make excellent pot plants for the greenhouse and there are others that need greenhouse cultivation entirely.

Some, such as the nasturtium, flower better if grown on rather poor soil. Most annuals will make too much leaf growth if grown in soil that is too rich or in shady places. Their rapid growth makes them invaluable for the new garden when flowers are wanted the first year, or for filling in gaps in newly-planted herbaceous borders. Some, such as trailing lobelias, dwarf nasturtiums and petunias are useful plants for hanging baskets. Many are useful for providing colour in urns, terrace pots, window boxes, tubs and other plant containers. Certain low-growing annuals find a place in carpet bedding schemes such as are still found in public parks. Although the purist may frown upon their use in this way, a few annuals are suitable for the rock garden.

A number of annuals have very fragrant flowers, as well as rich colour. Some have flowers or seed heads which may be dried for winter decoration indoors.

Some annuals, including a number of those used for carpet bedding, are grown for the sake of their colourful foliage.

Apart from removing faded flowers, keeping them weeded and staking the taller kinds they need little attention.

Growing hardy annuals The soil should be broken down to a fine tilth and well firmed before the seeds are sown. Sow in shallow drills or scatter the seed broadcast after previously marking out the position for each group of annuals selected. Cover the seeds in the drills by drawing the soil over them, or rake in the seeds sown broadcast. It may be necessary to protect the seeds and seedlings from birds and cats by placing wire netting or brushwood over the seed bed.

Some hardy annuals may be sown in August or September to flower early the following summer. See Table page 51. As soon as the seedlings are large enough to handle they should be thinned. With autumn-sown annuals leave the final thinning until the following spring. Distances apart vary considerably, depending on the ultimate height of the annual, but as a general guide dwarf-growing annuals should be thinned to 4–6 inches apart. Those that grow to 15–18 inches tall should be thinned to

A Selection of Hardy Annuals

Botanical Name	Common Name	Height inches	Colour
Althaea	Annual Hollyhock	48–60	various
Anagallis linifolia	Pimpernel	6	blue, red
Argemone	Prickly Poppy	24	yellow, orange, white
Calendula officinalis	Pot Marigold	24	orange, yellow
Centaurea cyanus	Cornflower	12–30	various
Centaurea moschata	Sweet Sultan	18–24	various
Chrysanthemum carinatum	Tricoloured Chrysanthemum	24	various
Chrysanthemum coronarium	Crown Daisy	12–24	various
Clarkia elegans	Clarkia	18–24	various
Collinsia	—	12–15	various
Convolvulus tricolor	Annual Convolvulus	12–18	various
Delphinium ajacis	Larkspur	24–36	pink, red, blue, white
Dianthus sinensis	Indian Pink	6–9	various
Eschscholzia	Californian Poppy	12	various
Gilia × hybrids	—	3–6	various
Godetia	Godetia	6–30	pink, crimson, white
Gypsophila elegans	Annual Gypsophila	18	white, pink, carmine
Helianthus annuus	Sunflower	36–96	yellow, bronze, brown
Helipterum	Everlasting	12	white, pink, yellow
Lathyrus odoratus	Sweet Pea	cl	various
Laverata trimestris	Mallow	24–36	white, pink
Leptosyne stillmanii	—	18	golden-yellow
Limnanthes douglasii	Butter and Eggs	6	white and yellow
Linaria maroccana	Annual Toadflax	9–15	various
Linum grandiflorum	Annual Flax	15–18	red, blue, pink, white
Lobularia	Sweet Alison	3–12	white, pink, lilac
Lupinus hartwegii	Annual Lupine	12–36	various
Malcolmia maritima	Virginia Stock	6–12	various
Malope grandiflorum	Mallow	24–36	pink, crimson, white
Matthiola bicornis	Night-scented Stock	12	lilac
Mentzelia lindleyi	Blazing Star	18	yellow
Nemophila menziesii	Baby Blue-eyes	tr	blue
Nigella damascena	Love-in-a-mist	18	blue, pink, white
Papaver rhoeas	Shirley Poppy	18–24	various
Papaver somniferum	Opium Poppy	18–36	various

A Selection of Hardy Annuals

Botanical Name	Common Name	inches	Colour
Phacelia campanularia	—	9	blue
Reseda odorata	Mignonette	12–18	red, yellow, white
Rhodanthe manglesii	Everlasting	12	rose and white
Salvia horminum	—	18	blue
Saponaria vaccaria	Annual Soapwort	30	pink, white
Scabiosa atropurpurea	Sweet Scabious	18–36	various
Silene pendula	Annual Catchfly	6	various
Thelesperma burridgeanum	—	18	yellow, red-brown
Tropaeolum majus	Nasturtium	6 & tr	oranges, yellow, red
Tropaeolum peregrinum	Canary Creeper	cl	yellow
Viscaria oculata	Catchfly	6–12	various

Hardy Annuals to Sow in the Autumn

Botanical Name	Common Name	inches	Colour
Calendula officinalis	Pot Marigold	24	orange yellow
Centaurea cyanus	Cornflower	12–30	various
Cladanthus arabicus	—	30	yellow
Clarkia elegans	Clarkia	18–24	various
Delphinium ajacis	Larkspur	24–36	pink, red, blue, white
Eschscholzia	Californian Poppy	12	various
Godetia	Godetia	6–30	pink, crimson, white
Gypsophila elegans	Annual Gypsophila	18	white, pink, carmine
Iberis	Candytuft	6–15	various
Lathyrus odoratus	Sweet Pea	cl	various
Limnanthes douglasii	Butter and Eggs	6	white and yellow
Lobularia maritima	Sweet Alison	12	white, pink, lilac
Lychnis githago (syn. Agrostemma githago)	Corn-cockle	24–36	pale lilac
Malcolmia maritima	Virginia Stock	6–12	various
Nigella damascena	Love-in-a-mist	18	blue, pink, white
Oenthera biennis	Evening Primrose	30	yellow
Papaver rhoeas	Shirley Poppy	18–24	various
Saponaria vaccaria	Annual Soap-wort	30	pink, white
Scabiosa atropurpurea	Sweet Scabious	18–36	various
Specularia speculum-veneris	Venus's Looking Glass	9	blue
Viscaria	Catchfly	6–12	various

cl=climbing   tr=trailing.

1 Lychnis githago, the Corn-Cockle, is one
of many easily-grown hardy annuals
2 Linum grandiflorum, a hardy annual
Flax has flowers in scarlet, red or rose
3 and 4 Two forms of the Californian
Poppy, Eschscholzia california, a hardy
annual now available in a wide colour
range with single or semi-double flowers
5 'Yellow Pygmy' with double flowers is
a useful variety of the tall annual
sunflower, Helianthus annuus
6 Papaver somniferum, the opium poppy,
a hardy annual with single or fully
double flowers in shades of pink and red

9–12 inches and taller kinds should be
thinned to 1–2 feet apart.

If seed is wanted for sowing again next
year it is best to mark a few good plants
early in the summer. The seed-heads
should not be gathered until they are
fully ripe.

Biennials

This is a valuable division of garden
plants for by the biennial habit of storing
up in the first season a reserve which is
expended wholly in the second season, a
much greater quantity of blossom is possible than with either the annual or perennial habit of growth.

Most Verbascums are biennials; 'Pink
Domino' and 'Cotswold Queen' may be
treated as biennials or short-lived perennials

It is also notable that many of our important vegetable crops are in this category; though where these are concerned (e.g. cabbage, beet, turnip, etc.) the plant is not permitted to flower and seed but the food stored up for these functions is taken for culinary use.

Where a new garden is being made annual and biennial plants will be of great service for it generally takes from three to five years to achieve a garden furnished satisfactorily with perennials and shrubs; and even then biennials will still be needed.

The chief drawback to the cultivation of biennials is the space which must be given to them in the reserve garden or frame, since they are not moved into their final stations until they are large healthy plants.

The term biennial is not used too strictly by the gardener and some short-lived perennials, some monocarpic plants, and certain annuals also are sometimes given biennial treatment.

As with annuals, biennial plants are sub-divided into hardy and half-hardy biennials

Cultivation Biennials may be sown in spring in a frame or cold greenhouse or outdoors from May onwards in beds of fine weed-free soil.

If seeds are sown in drills instead of broadcast it will be easier to keep them free from weeds by running the hoe between the rows from time to time.

After a severe thinning seedlings should be pushed on with adequate feeding until by October they will be large

Dianthus barbatus, the well-known Sweet William 1 and Lunaria biennis, the Honesty 2 are two of the plants known as biennials, seeds of which are sown one year to flower the following year

leafy plants, which may then be put into their final stations in the flower border. If the weather is dry when the time comes to transplant give the bed a thorough watering. Careful lifting, using a trowel, will minimise root disturbance, and subsequent checks to growth.

If it is intended to treat hardy annuals as biennials (excellent results in mild areas) the only way in which the operation differs from that described above is in the time of the seed sowing, which should be at the end of the summer or even in early autumn, but do not sow too early or the plants will flower in their first year. Given this biennial treatment annuals will make much larger plants than when grown in the normal way and this must be allowed for when they are planted out in their final positions.

Half-hardy biennials will need overwintering in frost-free conditions in a frame or a cold greenhouse. They are not an important section and one may well do without them, devoting precious greenhouse space to other things.

The following are biennials, or are often treated as biennial: adlumia, althaea (hollyhock), antirrhinum (snapdragon), *Campanula medium* (Canterbury bell), cheiranthus (wallflower), cnicus (fishbone thistle), *Dianthus barbatus*

(Sweet William), *Digitalis purpurea* (foxglove), *Erysimum arkansanum*, *Hedysarum coronarium* (French honeysuckle), *Humea elegans* (half-hardy), hunnemannia, lunaria (honesty), matthiola (Brompton, Nice and Intermediate stock), some meconopsis, myosotis, *Oenothera biennis* (evening primrose), onopordon (cotton thistle), *Papaver nudicaule* (Iceland poppy), verbascum (mullein).

Perennial

This term is used to describe a plant which does not die after flowering, but persists for a number of years, in contrast with an annual which flowers once and then dies after setting seed, and a biennial which completes its life-cycle in two years. The term 'perennial' may properly be applied to shrubs and trees but is more often used in conjunction with the term 'hardy herbaceous' to describe the plants which form the mainstay of herbaceous borders, though they are often grown in other parts of the garden, either in company with other plants or as isolated specimens. Though the term is applied to plants which live for more than 2 years, many perennials live for many years and such plants as herbaceous paeonias and the oriental poppy *(Papaver orientale)* are particularly long lived. By contrast some perennial plants, for instance lupins, may have a life-span of five or six years only

The plants we grow from seeds or bulbs are usually planted in a bed or border, for they make a much greater decorative impact if they stand together.

Herbaceous borders

The herbaceous border, which is a comparative newcomer to the garden scene, is still one of its most popular features. Introduced at the turn of the century by Gertrude Jekyll as a protest against the monotonous formality of Victorian garden design, its popularity has steadily increased until today there are few gardens without some kind of perennial border to enhance their beauty throughout the months of summer and autumn.

Restricted originally to plants of purely perennial habit—in the main, those whose growth begins afresh from ground level each year—the terms of reference have gradually been extended so that today we find included not only spring and summer bulbs and corms but also small shrubby plants and those curious in-betweens whose woody top growth persists throughout the winter, but which otherwise display most of the characteristics of true perennials. These are the sub-shrubs, of which plants such as the plumbago-flowered *Ceratostigma willmottianum, Caryopteris clandonensis,* and the Russian sage, *Perovskia atriplicifolia* are typical examples.

Preparing the site Preliminary preparation of the site for an herbaceous border is of paramount importance. Much of its subsequent success or failure will depend on the thoroughness with which it is carried out. Some soils, of course, are a good deal more difficult to prepare, than others but whether you garden on heavy, back-breaking clay or easily managed well-drained sandy loam there must be sufficient supplies of humus in the soil if the plants are to give of their best.

Deep digging and thorough cultivation are two further essentials. Most of the occupants of the border will remain in the same positions for at least three years, while other more permanent specimens such as paeonies, hellebores, romneyas and hemerocallis can stay put almost indefinitely, without the necessity for division or replanting.

To make sure that such conditions are fulfilled it may be necessary to double dig the whole of the projected plot. This will result in a thorough breaking up of both the surface and second spits of soil. As far as medium to light well-drained loams are concerned, bastard trenching, which leaves the lower spit *in situ* but broken up with a fork, is probably just as effective, but it is better to give wet, heavy soils the full treatment.

Humus Thorough digging, however, is not sufficient to create the soil conditions in which perennials thrive best. To provide them, plentiful supplies of humus or humus-forming material must

be present in the soil, enough, in fact, to satisfy much of the plants' needs for several seasons, as normally the border will be due for a complete overhaul only once in every three to four years.

Humus can be provided by a variety of materials, the best of which, of course, is the almost impossible to obtain stable or farmyard manure. Most of us, however, will have to settle for alternatives. Compost, properly made and well rotted down, heads the list of these but supplies of this are quickly exhausted unless we supplement our garden and domestic waste with straw, sawdust, or other similar materials brought in from outside.

Leafmould is excellent, but expensive unless you are lucky enough to have access to natural sources of supply. Oak and beech leaves are the richest in plant foods, while bracken rots down to a material of peat-like consistency, good for stepping up the humus content of the soil but otherwise lacking in plant foods. Young bracken shoots, on the other hand, are rich in plant foods and minerals and make a valuable contribution to the compost heap.

For the town gardener and for those who cannot readily obtain the materials mentioned above, peat is the best soil conditioner. It is clean both to store and

handle, and can hold many times its own bulk of moisture.

Spent hops are another first-rate humus forming material. If you can obtain supplies in bulk from a local brewery, they will be relatively cheap. The so-called hop manures with added organic fertilisers are a convenient but expensive method of supplying humus to the border.

These, or any other similar materials, are best worked into the upper spit as digging progresses. Alternatively they can be forked into the soil a few weeks before the plants are put in.

Fortunately, the vast majority of the more widely-grown herbaceous perennials are very accommodating. They will thrive in most types of soil although characteristics such as height, vigour and rate of increase will vary considerably between, for example, light, sandy loams and heavy, sticky clays. It is a good rule never to coddle temperamental plants. There is neither time nor room for them in the herbaceous border, where plants are grown more for their effect in the mass than as individuals.

Weeds The best time of the year to prepare the site for planting is late summer or early autumn. This will give the winter frosts a chance to break up heavy clods to a fine planting tilth.

An established and carefully planned herbaceous border adds an air of permanence to a garden.

A hedge provides an ideal background for a herbaceous border.

This, of course, is not so important with light sandy soils which can be cultivated at almost any season of the year. As digging progresses, it is imperative to remove every possible vestige of perennial weeds; the aim should be to start with a site that is completely weed-free, although when fresh ground is being taken over this can be no more than a counsel of perfection.

Watch particularly for the roots of bindweed, ground elder and couch grass. Any of these can soon stage a rapid comeback even if only a few pieces remain in the soil.

Couch grass, or 'twitch' as it is sometimes called, is easily recognisable; the narrow leaf blades are coarse, with serrated edges; leaves and underground runners are sectional, like miniature bamboo shoots, with nodules at the joints. Ground elder has leaves similar to those of its shrub namesake and quite attractive flowers. It is easily identified by the pungent aroma of its bruised leaves and stems. Bindweed, also known as bellbind in some parts of the country, has attractive white trumpet-shaped flowers and a twining habit that can strangle any plant that

is the object of its attentions.

Any of these weeds are anathema in the border and once established will prove well-nigh impossible to eradicate without a complete overhaul. Other perennial weeds—not quite as difficult but still a nuisance—include docks, thistles, clover and creeping buttercup. In acid soils sorrel, too, can be troublesome.

If annual weeds multiply alarmingly, and they will, in very wet summers, there is no need for undue despondency. Regular sessions with a hand fork or a lady's border fork will keep them in check. Vigorous low-growing perennials will act as their own ground cover.

In autumn, and in early spring if possible, the border should have a thorough forking over, removing and burning all perennial weeds. Any clumps of plants that show signs of weed infestation should be dug up. After shaking or washing their roots free of soil, offending weed roots or runners that have penetrated the latter should be carefully teased out and removed. The clumps can then be replanted in situ, or if their size warrants it, be split up and re-grouped. If the replanting is carried out without delay the plants will not suffer any check. In fact, very vigorous growers such as Michaelmas

daisies, *Campanula lactiflora* and *Chrysanthemum maximum* will benefit from this procedure.

It follows from the foregoing that new stocks received from the nursery or from generous fellow-gardeners should have their roots carefully examined for invading weeds before they are put in. We may not be able to suppress entirely the weeds that are present in the soil, but there is no point in deliberately planting trouble.

Supplementary dressings Unless farmyard manure has been available in generous quantities it will be advisable to give a booster of some kind of fertiliser a few weeks before the border is planted up. Bonemeal and fish manure, which are both organic and slow acting, will give good results, applied at a rate of 2–3 oz to the square yard. As an alternative, a good general fertiliser, such as 'Growmore' can be used at the rate recommended by the makers.

A good way of distributing this supplementary plant food is to rake it into the soil when the final preparations for planting are being made. Alternatively, it can be pricked lightly into the surface with a fork. An established border will benefit from a similar dressing when growth starts in spring.

Siting Most of the more widely-grown perennials are sun-lovers, so that a position facing south or west will be the most suitable for the border. But since this feature is seen as its best when viewed lengthwise, it may be necessary, if we plan to enjoy its beauty from some fixed vantage point such as a terrace or the living room windows, to effect some sort of compromise where aspect is concerned.

Generally speaking, any position except a sunless north-facing one, or one where the plants suffer shade and drip from overhanging trees, will be quite satisfactory.

Background Just as a fine picture deserves an appropriate frame, so the herbaceous border needs a proper setting for its beauty. In the past this has usually been supplied by a background wall or hedge, but nowadays doublesided and island borders are becoming popular, where the only background is provided by the adjacent grass or paving. Nothing, however, makes a more suitable backcloth than a wellkept evergreen hedge—yew, holly, cypress, beech, or hornbeam. Mellowed brick or stone wall, too, can act as a pleasing accompaniment, and even wattle hurdles or a wooden fence, when discreetly covered by climbing plants, can provide an attractive setting.

Plants grown against walls or fences will require additional attention where staking and tying are concerned. In rough weather strong gusts and eddies develop at their base which can have disastrous results unless the plants are

1 Herbaceous plants are divided by levering them apart with two forks plunged back to back through the clump.
2 The small divisions can be replanted.
3 Twiggy stakes are pushed in around each plant to provide support.
4 Taller plants need to be tied around individually to stouter stakes.

strongly secured.

Hedges, beautiful though they may be as backgrounds, also have their disadvantages. Most, if not all, hedging plants are notorious soil robbers. Some, such as privet, are much worse than others and should be avoided if a new planting is to be made. The roots of an established hedge can be kept in check by taking out a trench a foot or so away from the base of the plants and chopping back all the fibrous roots with a sharp spade. This operation, which should be carried out while the hedge is dormant, could very well coincide with the periodic overhaul and replanting of the border.

If space permits, it is a good plan to leave a gap of 2–3 feet between the foot of the hedge and the rear rank border plants. This, incidentally, will also provide useful access to the back of the border for maintenance work.

Yew, of course, is the best plant for a background hedge. Slow and compact in growth, it requires a minimum of attention—one 'short back and sides' trim annually will suffice, and its foliage of sombre green is the perfect foil for the bright colours of the border plants.

Planning Planning the border can be fun. With squared paper and a sheaf of nursery catalogues there could be few pleasanter ways of spending a winter's evening by the fire. Ready-made collections complete with planting plans are useful for the complete novice and can form the nucleus of a wider collection, but it is a good deal more interesting to work out your own colour schemes and to see the plans coming to fruition in the garden.

There is such a wide choice of herbaceous plants that the permutations and combinations of colour, form and texture are infinite in number. Individual tastes vary and so do fashions in flower colours. The pastel shades, popular for so many years, are giving place to the stronger reds, yellows and blues of the Victorian era.

A border composed entirely of any one of these primary colours would be striking in its effect, but the planning would need very careful handling and a thorough knowledge of plant characteristics. If you lack experience, you would be well advised to use a mixture of colours, grouped according to your individual taste.

As a general rule, in a border of mixed colours the paler shades should be at each end, with the brighter, more vivid

1 and 2 Well planned borders where varying height, colour and texture all play a part in the successful effect.
3 Campanula glomerata has clustered heads of deep violet flowers in June.
4 The silver-grey foliage of Artemisia gnaphalodes gives a light effect.
5 The papery silver-lilac bracts of Salvia × superba are attractive.

ones grouped mainly at the centre. For example, the pure whites of *Phlox paniculata alba, Achillea ptarmica* 'The Pearl', and *Gypsophila* 'Bristol Fairy', could melt almost imperceptibly into the cool primrose yellows of *Achillea taygetea* and *Verbascum bombyciferum* (syn. *broussa*), flanked by the deeper yellows of *Hemerocallis* 'Hyperion', one of the best of the free-flowering day lilies, and *Lysimachia punctata,* the yellow loosestrife.

The middle of the border could explode into brilliant colour with scarlet *Lychnis chalcedonica, Lobelia fulgens, Potentilla* 'Gibson's Scarlet', and the garnet-red *Astilbe* 'Fanal'. Once past its climax, the border could progress to white once more through the blues of delphiniums, sea holly, *(Eryngium maritimum)* whose leaves, as well as the flowers are metallic blue, and the stately *Echinops ritro*, with thistle-like dark green foliage and drumstick flower heads of steely blue. Other suitable blue

perennials include the attractive indigo-blue monkshood, *Aconitum* 'Bressingham Spire' and the curious balloon flower, *Platycodon grandiflorum*.

These could be followed by the soft pinks of *Geranium endressii*, *Sidalcea* 'Sussex Beauty', the long flowering *Veronica spicata*—'Pavane' and 'Minuet' are both good varieties—and the later-blooming ice plant, *Sedum spectabile* 'Brilliant'.

And so back to white again, this time represented by Japanese anemones, *Anemone hupehensis* 'Honorine Jobert', *Lysimachia clethroides*, *Potentilla alba* and a good garden form of the sweetly scented meadow sweet, *Filipendula ulmaria plena*.

This, of course, would not constitute a complete planting plan, but is merely suggestion that could form the framework of an attractive herbaceous border. Colour, though it may take pride of place in the overall display, is not everything where the successful herbaceous border is concerned. The form and leaf texture of the plants, as well as the manner in which they are grouped, all play a part that is vitally important to the ultimate effect.

It is important to plant in relatively large groups, each restricted to one kind or variety, the size depending on the overall dimensions of the border. Blocks of three plants should, as a general rule, be the minimum, while, for smaller edging and carpeting plants, six would be a reasonable number if spottiness is to be avoided.

Although the general trend should be towards 'shortest in the front, tallest in the rear', this is a rule that should not be too rigidly adhered to. Some of the taller plants should be allowed to wander to the middle or even, at certain points, to the front of the border while the lower marginal plants can be permitted to flow unobtrusively inwards to make small pools and rivulets of contrasting height and colour among their taller neighbours.

A number of perennials are grown as much for the beauty of their foliage as for the decorative quality of their flowers. Outstanding among these are the hostas, or plantain lilies with their outsize ribbed leaves, acanthus, whose sculptured foliage formed the classic model for the Corinthian capitals of Ancient Greek architecture, hemerocallis, *Iris sibirica* and kniphofias for the contrasting effect of their sword-like leaves, the variety of rue known as *Ruta graveolens* 'Jackman's Blue' and others whose names have been indicated in the list below.

Other plants are cultivated for their attractive seed heads. These include the fascinating but invasive Chinese lanterns *(physalis)*, the silvery tasselled *Pulsatilla vulgaris* or Pasque flower, *Baptisia australis* with its soot-black seed pods and the magnificent *Heracleum mantegazzianum*, a garden plant resembling a giant cow parsley whose outsize flat seed heads are borne on stems, 10 feet or more tall.

Planting The great majority of perennial border plants can be planted with safety between the end of September and the last week of March. In fact, the planting of late-flowering specimens such as Michaelmas daisies and border chrysanthemums could very well be delayed until April.

Planting holes should be of sufficient depth and breadth to accommodate the roots of the plants without bunching or overcrowding. Small plants can be firmed in by hand, but for large clumps the heel of the boot will be required. Although firm planting is desirable, this should not entail embedding the roots in a pocket of sticky 'goo'. In heavy clay soils, planting will have to be delayed until the soil condition improves or, better still, the holes can be filled with sifted compost or a mixture of dry soil and peat that has been kept under cover for this purpose.

With the more vigorous perennials such as golden rod, Shasta daisies,

117

achilleas and campanulas. it is not necessary, if time presses, to be too fussy over planting procedure, provided that the soil has been properly prepared and is in good heart. Others, however, such as paeonies, alstroemerias and hellebores will need more careful attention. Paeonies, for example, should never be planted with their dormant growth buds more than approximately 2 inches below the surface; planting too deeply is one of the commonest causes of failure to bloom satisfactorily. The planting or division of catmint is better delayed until spring. Autumn-planted specimens frequently fail to survive. This is a rule that might well be applied to all grey-leaved border plants. Once established they can tolerate severe weather conditions but in their first winter they often succumb to severe frosts if they are planted in autumn.

For the newcomer to gardening, the importance of dealing only with reputable nurseries cannot be overstressed. Their catalogues, in addition to lists and descriptions of plants, will often contain a wealth of information regarding their likes and dislikes. Plants, too, will be delivered at the most appropriate time of year for planting out.

Choice of plants Anyone starting an herbaceous border from scratch would be well advised to take advantage of the many new plants and modern varieties of older favourites that require little or no staking and tying. By this means, one of the major summer chores in the border can be considerably reduced.

Many of these new-style border plants are entirely self-supporting; others need only a few twiggy sticks pushed in among them to keep them in order.

Plants such as tall delphiniums will, of course, have to have each individual flower secured to a stake or stout cane. If space permits, it is better to segregate these and other similar top-heavy plants; they do better where they are more easy to get at for maintenance.

Not all the taller border plants suffer from this shortcoming; *Artemisia lactiflora*, for example, is a plant whose 6 foot stems of feathery milk-white flowers, smelling like meadowsweet, will stand up to a howling gale without turning a hair, while others, for example the moon daisies and taller perennial asters, will collapse and sprawl at the first hint of rough weather, if they are not securely staked.

Careful and judicious selection at the planning stage, therefore, can make the border practically trouble-free where staking and tying are concerned.

Double-sided or 'island' borders achieve similar results in a different way. Plants grown in an open situation are sturdier and more compact than those grown against a wall or hedge which tends to cause them to be drawn both upwards and outwards. This sturdier

habit makes them less liable to damage by heavy winds and rough weather, and, in addition, access at both sides of the border makes routine maintenance a good deal easier. The idea of a double-sided border is not new. Formerly, in large gardens, they were commonly used as a decorative edging in the kitchen garden where they served the dual purpose of screening the vegetable crops and providing flowers for cutting.

Island borders, however, are a more recent innovation, for whose introduction we have largely to thank Mr Alan Bloom, whose borders at Bressingham, Norfolk attract a host of admirers. One of their attractions, in addition to ease of maintenance, lies in the fact that they can be viewed from above as well as along their length and from the front. For this reason, the height of the plants should not exceed 3 or 4 feet in order that the kaleidoscopic colour effects of the plant groupings

can be seen to their best advantage.

Prolonging the display One of the main disadvantages of the herbaceous border as a garden feature is the comparatively short period during which it makes a major contribution to the garden display. Normally, it is only in early or mid-June that it really starts to make its colour impact, with lupins, oriental poppies, irises, anchusa, aquilegias and other June-flowering perennials.

Reaching its peak in July and August, it continues to delight in early autumn and retires in a blaze of Michaelmas daisies, red hot pokers, perennial sunflowers and border chrysanthemums, which carry it through, in most districts, until mid October.

For the other seven months of the year, however, the border can lack colour and interest, unless steps are taken to extend its scope by supplementing the orthodox planting materials with others that flower both early and

late.

Spring bulbs, such as daffodils, tulips, hyacinths, chionodoxas, scillas and grape hyacinths, all make first-class curtain raisers and will fill the spaces between perennials with bright spring colour. A little later wallflowers, polyanthus, forget-me-nots and other spring bedding plants can be used as gap-fillers.

There are quite a few herbaceous plants proper, beginning in January with the hellebores, that will considerably extend the border's period of interest and relieve the monotony of bare brown earth and dead stems. *Helleborus niger*, the Christmas rose, seldom fulfils the promise of its name, unless it has the protection of cloches or a cold greenhouse, but it can be relied on to open its pure white chalices by the middle or end of January, although even then it will still appreciate a little protection to save its immaculate petals from damage by wind and rain.

Following close on its heels comes the Lenten rose, *Helleborus orientalis* and other delightful species that include the stately *H. argutifolius* (syn. *H. corsicus*) and our native *H. foetidus*, whose green flower clusters are a good deal smaller than those of the Corsican species.

In February and March, too, there will be the pink and carmine flower trusses of the bergenias, among the finest of flowering perennials. These useful plants, that used to be called megaseas, are outsize members of the saxifrage family and most species are evergreen so that their handsome fleshy leaves, bronze or reddish in winter, as well as their striking flowers, make a valuable contribution to the winter border. 'Ballawley Hybrid', a relatively new introduction from Ireland, is one of the most outstanding examples of the group. Other good forms and species include *B. cordifolia* with rounded

crinkly leaves, *B. crassifolia*, probably the most commonly-seen, whose leaves are more spoon-shaped than round and *B. schmidtii*, an unusual species the leaves of which have hairy margins and whose loose sprays of clear pink flowers are the earliest to appear.

Blue flowers are always attractive and there are several perennials to provide them once winter is over. The so-called giant forget-me-not, *Brunnera macrophylla* (syn. *Anchusa myosotidiflora*) is one of these, as are the lungworts or pulmonarias. Both of these have foliage that stays attractive throughout the remainder of the season.

There are several species of pulmonaria, the most striking, of which is *P. angustifolia azurea*, with clear gentian-blue flowers. It looks superb in conjunction with the yellow daisy flowers of the leopard's bane, *Doronicum Harpur Crewe'. P. angustifolia rubra* has coral-red blossoms, those of *P. saccharata* are pinkish-purple turning to blue; the multi-coloured appearance is responsible for its nickname of soldiers and sailors, while its strikingly-mottled leaves have earned it the popular title of spotted dog. Incidentally, the foliage of all the lungworts, which remains tidy throughout the summer, acts as an excellent weed-cover

In the shadier parts of the border *Hepatica triloba* with its leathery, ivy-like leaves and true-blue flowers, together with primulas and polyanthus will all make pools of colour in April and May. The golden flowers of *Alyssum saxatile flore pleno* will shine even more brightly in association with the white flowers of the perennial candytuft *Iberis sempervirens* 'Snowflake', in the sunny spots at the edge of the border.

Heucheras and heucherellas will enliven the early summer scene with their spikes of brilliant coral and clear pink miniature bells. The latter is an interesting hybrid between heuchera and tiarella, the foam flower, which is useful both for its decorative value at this time and as an evergreen carpeting plant later in the season. All these will do well in partial shade.

A complete contrast both in flowers and its ferny foliage is *Dicentra spectabilis*, the lyre flower, better known to cottagers as bleeding heart, lady's locket or Dutchman's breeches. This plant prefers partial shade and blooms

1 Monarda didyma, the Oswego Tea Plant, has aromatic leaves with a slightly pungent scent when crushed.
2 Geranium pratense, a floriferous plant which quickly makes good clumps.
3 Papaver orientale, the Oriental Poppy, with stout stems but frail flowers, has cultivars in various colours.
4 The thick woolly foliage of Verbascum has earned it the name of Blanketweed.
5 The purple spikes of Lythrum 'Robert'.

in late spring, at the same time as the graceful Solomon's seal, *Polygonatum multiflorum*, with its hanging bells of greenish white.

To provide colour continuity from late summer onwards there are, in addition to the indispensable Michaelmas daisies, various other perennial and bulbous plants. The grey-leaved *Anaphalis triplinervis* is one of these. Its papery 'everlasting' white star-like flowers, which appear first in July, will still be immaculate in October. The Japanese anemone, *Anemone hupehensis*, of which there are now many lovely named varieties, will start to throw up clusters of chalice-like blossoms from early August until the first heavy frosts arrive. The single forms, both pink and white are still firm favourites, but if you are looking for something out-of-the-ordinary you might like to try 'Margarete', a double pink, with rows of ruff-like petals. 'Prince Henry', sometimes listed as 'Profusion', is one

1 Pyrethrum 'Eileen May Robinson', a good herbaceous plant, flowers in May.
2 For a moist spot, or the back of the border, Ligularia is a dramatic plant, with large rather floppy leaves.
3 Island borders, an up-to-date idea, can be looked at from all sides.

of the most striking singles, its colour much richer than those of the other pinks.

In sheltered bays in the border from August onwards, two closely-allied South African bulbous plants will make a welcome splash of colour. The blue African lily, agapanthus—the species *A. campanulatus* is perfectly hardy in the south of England—has drumstick heads of powder-blue flowers, while those of *Nerine bowdenii* are similar, but less tightly packed with pink florets. 'Fenwick's Variety', an attractive pink, is the best form for out-of-doors.

And so the year goes by in the herbaceous border, with the first Christmas roses plumping up their buds as the last lingering flowers of the border chrysanthemums shrivel and fade. In the well-planned perennial border there need never be a dull moment.

Winter work Apart from the periodic division, replanting and occasional re-planning of the border, winter maintenance will consist mainly of tidying-up and light forking between the plants. There are two schools of thought where the former operation is concerned. Some gardeners prefer to leave the tidying of the border until spring—the dead leaves and stems, they claim, protect the crowns of the plants in really severe weather. Others, who cannot stand the sight of so much dead untidy vegetation cut down the dead stems at the earliest opportunity.

There is a lot to be said for the former point of view, but a lot will depend on how the border is sited. If it is in full view of the house windows, the sooner it is made ship-shape the better. Only a very small number of popular herbaceous perennials are delicate enough to suffer irreparable damage, even in the severest winter. Plants, such as eremurus and *Lobelia fulgens*, which may be damaged by frosts, can be protected by covering their crowns with weathered ashes or bracken.

Where the border is more remotely situated, clearing up operations can take their place in the queue of urgent garden tasks that make their heaviest demands on us during the winter months.

Other uses of herbaceous plants Perennials have become so closely associated in our minds with the herbaceous border that we tend to overlook their many other uses in the garden. For example, bedding schemes employing perennials can be just as attractive as those in which the more orthodox hardy and half-hardy annuals are used. What is more important, management and upkeep will be simplified and costs will be less where these versatile plants are utilised.

Perennials as bedding plants For bedding purposes, it will be necessary to choose perennials with a relatively long flower-

ing season and/or attractive foliage, plus a solid and compact habit of growth. Among those fulfilling such requirements are *Brunnera macrophylla* (syn. *Anchusa myosotidiflora*), the so-called giant forget-me-not, *Anemone hupehensis*, the Japanese anemone, *Armeria maritima*, thrift, the medium and dwarf Michaelmas daisies and dwarf delphiniums, for example *D. ruysii* or *D. chinensis*. The two last-named, in common with a number of other perennials, have the added advantage of being easy to grow from seed.

Segregation of Groups and species
Another good way of making the best use of certain groups and species is to grow them in beds restricted to the one type of perennial. By growing them in this way, it is easy to make satisfactory provision for their special requirements in the way of feeding, staking, tying and general cultivation.

This works well for herbaceous plants such as lupins, flag irises, paeonies, oriental poppies and the taller delphiniums. A further point in favour of this method is that it avoids the bare patches that tend to appear in the border when such early-flowering perennials form part of the general scheme.

Other herbaceous perennials that will benefit from this method of culture are the Michaelmas daisies. Where sufficient space is available, a representative collection, grown in a bed or border devoted to them alone, will make a far greater impact than they would dotted about in groups in the mixed border.

Waterside planting Although the great majority of perennials will thrive in a wide range of garden soils and situations, there are some that prefer shade and moisture, conditions that cannot always be easily provided in the herbaceous border. These make excellent plants for the waterside—by the banks of streams or artificial watercourses or at the edge of the garden pool.

Primulas, astilbes, *Iris sibirica* and *Iris kaempferi*, kingcups (*Caltha palustris*) and the globe flower (*Trollius* species) are just a few that will grow better in damp, shady positions.

Cut flowers Satisfying the demands for flowers for the house in summer, when they fade so quickly, sometimes results in the display in the border being spoiled by too lavish cutting. A satisfactory way of avoiding this is to grow perennials specially for the purpose, either in rows in the kitchen garden, or bordering the vegetable plot. For this, it is only commonsense to choose those that will not only cut and last well, but will also need minimum attention where staking and tying are concerned. A representative, but not exhaustive list of these appears below.

It should be obvious, from the foregoing, that the uses of perennials are many and varied.

A selection of herbaceous plants

Name	Height in feet	Colour	Season
Acanthus	4–5	lilac-pink	July–Aug
Achillea spp & vars	1–4	white, yellow	June–Aug
Alchemilla	1–1½	yellow-green	June–July
Anaphalis	1–2	white	July–Sept
Aquilegia hybs	1–3	various	May–June
Armeria	1	pinks	June–July
Artemisia	3–5	grey foliage	Aug–Sept
Aster spp & vars	1–5	various	Aug–Oct
Astrantia	2–3	green-pink	June
Bergenia	1–1½	pinks, white	March–April
Campanula	1–4	blues, white	June–Aug
Centaurea	2–5	blues, yellow	June–Oct
Cimicifuga	2–4	creamy-white	July–Sept
Coreopsis	2–3	golden-yellow	June–Sept
Corydalis	1	yellow	May–Oct
Delphinium	3–8	blues, mauves	June–July
Dianthus	½–1½	various	May–June
Dicentra	1–2	pink	April–May
Doronicum	1–2½	yellow	March–April
Echinacea	2–3	purple-red	Aug–Sept
Echinops	2–5	steely blue	July–Aug
Erigeron hybs	1–2	blue, pink	June–Sept
Eryngium	2–4	glaucous blue	July–Aug
Euphorbia	1–3	yellow	April–June
Gaillardia hybs	2	yellow, orange	July–Aug
Galega	2–4	mauve	June–July
Gentiana	1–2	blues	July–Aug
Geranium	1–2½	pinks, mauves	June–Aug
Helenium	3–5	yellows, copper	July–Sept
Hemerocallis	2–3	yellow, orange	July–Sept
Heuchera hybs	1–2½	pinks, reds	May–Aug
Iris	1–5	various	May–June
Kniphofia	1½–4	yellow, orange	July–Sept
Lupin hybs	2–4	various	June
Lythrum	2–4	purple-red	June–Sept
Lysimachia	2–4	yellow, white	July–Sept
Macleaya	5–8	apricot pink	July–Sept
Malva	2–4	mauves, pinks	July
Monarda	2–4	various	June–Aug
Nepeta	1–2	blue	May–Sept
Paeonia spp & hybs	2–4	pink, red, white	May–June
Phlox	2–4	various	July–Sept
Pyrethrum	1–3	various	May–June
Salvia spp	2–5	mauves	June–Sept
Sidalcea hybs	2½–5	pinks	June–Aug
Verbascum	3–8	yellow, pink	July–Oct
Veronica spp & vars	1–3	blues, mauves	July–Oct

Perennials for cutting

Name	Height in feet	Colour	Season
Acanthus mollis	4–5	lilac-pink	July–Aug
Achillea 'Moonshine'	2	sulphur-yellow	June–July
Alchemilla mollis	1–1½	yellowish-green	June–July
Anaphalis triplinervis	¾	white 'everlasting'	July–Aug
Aquilegia hybrids	up to 3	various	May–June
Aster (perennial)	up to 5	white, pinks, purples	Aug–Oct
Astrantia	2–3	greenish-white, pink	June
Coreopsis grandiflora	2–3	golden-yellow	June–Sep
Dianthus	½–1	various	May–June
Heuchera spp & varieties	2	pinks, reds	June–July
Iris germanica	up to 3	various	May–June
Phlox decussata	up to 3	various	July–Sep
Pyrethrum varieties	2	various	May–June
Trollius	2	yellow, gold	May–June

It is perfectly possible to grow trees and shrubs from seed, and under certain circumstances this can be an interesting project. Seeds are obtainable from specialist seedsmen and their price is, as one might expect, considerably less than that of semi-mature trees. The reason why we normally buy our trees and shrubs, our climbers and roses, rather than grow them ourselves is because of the time it takes to bring them to maturity, and the training, pruning, staking, feeding and general care necessary to produce strong and healthy specimens.

Chapter 5

DECORATIVE TREES, SHRUBS AND PLANTS

Tree
A tree can be defined as a woody plant, normally with one stem and at least 12–15 feet tall in maturity. Trees have two kinds of foliage: deciduous, when the leaf cycle from flushing (breaking of the leaves out of the buds) to their fall occurs within one year; and evergreen, when this cycle takes several years—the tree always bearing a series of active leaves. Trees are divided into conifers and broad-leaved types.

Conifers The leaves are generally scale-like, needle-like or linear. The fruit consists of a cone of tough scales which enclose the seed, though in some kinds the scales coalesce and become fleshy. The structure of the wood is distinctive, giving rise to the name 'softwoods' which is, however, not always literally applicable.

Broad-leaved trees The leaves have a network of veins, and most broad-leaved trees are deciduous. The seed-production is by pollen being carried in the anther and transferred to the stigma and through the stigma to the ovule. In conifers the pollen falls directly on to the ovule. The timber of broad-leaved trees, though not invariably harder than that of conifers, is structurally different and gives rise to the name 'hardwoods'.

Trees in the garden
Trees are the most long-lived growing features in any garden. Once they are well established, it is very difficult to move them; pruning them if they become too big is difficult, needing skilled workmanship, and is never a permanent solution to the problems of excessive roots and over-extensive shading that arise.

Since Victorian times the gardener's problems in tree-planting have been made much easier by the introduction from western China in particular, as well as Japan, and also by hybridisation and selection, of a wide new range of trees which are of moderate size. These include excellent maples, whitebeams, rowans, cherries and ornamental apples (crabs), as well as birches. Many of these also provide what is wanted in a small area, a tree that has more than one season of interest, such as decorative bark in mid-winter, attractive unfolding foliage in spring followed by a period of flowering, then brightly coloured fruit and finally gay colouring of the leaves before they fall. Trees often have at least two if not three seasons of interest.

Evergreen broad-leaved trees are of particular interest in winter, and many have variegated or coloured-leaved forms, and the number available is now greatly increased. All are least satisfactory in towns where air pollution takes away the shine of their foliage.

The same applies to conifers, a number of which are of too great a size and too slow growing for gardens, and are seen at their best in forests and pineta.

For road planting and use in smaller gardens narrow (fastigiate) forms of many trees have been selected and are propagated as cultivars. They are also useful in planting on a large scale on account of their beautiful shape. This applies, also to the numerous weeping trees available.

Soil Hardy trees are surprisingly tolerant of soil conditions provided drainage is good. Many come from mountains where soil is not deep, except in the river valleys.

Where the soil is well drained, the limiting factor for a number of species is the amount of lime present. Many trees growing naturally on acid or neutral soils will grow equally well on soils with a moderate lime content, particularly if the soil is deep and fertile. But a certain number are, like rhododendrons among shrubs, strongly calcifuge (lime-hating) plants, particularly on rather shallow, chalky soils as are found in many fine gardens in such areas as the Chilterns, Cotswolds and South Downs.

Apart from the degree of soil alkalinity (see *p*H), depth and soil structure affect the kind of trees that can be grown. In general, with certain notable exceptions, conifers prefer acid or neutral soils. The *Rosaceae,* however, has many genera that are often associated in nature with alkaline soils such as *Malus* (apples), *Prunus* (cherries, plums, peaches, almonds, etc.), *Pyrus* (pears), *Crataegus* (thorns) and *Sorbus* (rowans and service trees).

It is curious that though many calcifuge plants will not live in calcareous soils (containing lime), most of those that are calcipholous (lime-loving) will grow well in neutral and acid soils.

The following list indicates the preferences of some commonly cultivated genera, particularly those that will, or will not, grow on soils with a moderate lime content, and those that on no account thrive on shallow, chalk soils.

1 **Cut branches right to the trunk.**
2 **A transplanted tree is formly staked.**
3 **Wire netting protects the bark.**
4 **Pruning roots prior to transplanting.**
5 **Trees give shelter and background for** smaller, more delicate plants.

Broad-leaved trees

ACER Most maples thrive on lime and chalk, including British natives and those commonly planted. The Chinese species, such as *AA. capillipes, davidii, ginnala, griseum* and *rufinerve*, make a splendid display in chalk gardens. *A. palmatum* and its cultivars need more fertile soil. The American *A. rubrum* will not grow on chalk.

AILANTHUS Tolerates lime.

ALNUS All alders will grow well on lime but must have moisture, with the exception of *A. cordata* and *A. incana*, which will stand drier situations. The former is good on chalk.

AESCULUS The horse-chestnuts and buckeyes do well on lime and chalk, though preferring fertile soils.

AMELANCHIER Though naturally growing on light acid soils, these will tolerate some lime.

ARBUTUS One of the few *Ericaceae* that grows well on lime.

BETULA The birches do well on lime.

BUXUS Good on lime, the common box grows naturally on chalk.

CARPINUS All the hornbeams are successful on either heavy alkaline soils or light chalk.

CARYA Will tolerate some lime in deep fertile soils.

CASTANEA The sweet chestnuts do not like lime, but will tolerate it in small quantities on well-drained fertile soils.

CATALPA Lime tolerant.

CELTIS Will tolerate some lime in deep, fertile soils.

CERCIDIPHYLLUM Lime tolerant.

CERCIS The Judas trees do well on lime and chalk.

CORYLUS Hazels do well on lime, including chalk.

COTONEASTER Most kinds do well on lime, including chalk.

CRATAEGUS All thorns will grow on lime and chalk.

1 Liriodendron tulipifera, the Tulip Tree, will grow on limy soil.
2 Ulmus stricta, the Cornish Elm.
3 Acer pseudoplatanus leopoldii has silvery-yellow leaves.

DAVIDIA The dove tree does well on lime and chalk.

EUCALYPTUS There is still some doubt as to which species will grow well on lime.

EUONYMUS The tree-like species thrive on lime and chalk.

EVODIA Does well in shallow chalk soil.

FAGUS The beeches have a shallow root system and thrive on well-drained soils with high lime content and on chalk.

FICUS The fig-tree grows well on lime and chalk.

FRAXINUS The ashes thrive on soils with high lime content as long as they are fertile.

GLEDITSCHIA Will tolerate a little lime in fertile soils.

GYMNOCLADUS The Kentucky coffee needs a rich, loamy soil and will tolerate some lime.

HALESIA The snowdrop trees will not tolerate lime.

IDESIA This rare tree is good on chalk.

ILEX Hollies are good on lime and chalk.

JUGLANS Walnuts will thrive on lime soils and chalk if it is not too thin.

KOELREUTERIA The golden rain tree will grow in any well-drained soil.

LABURNUM Will grow anywhere.

LIQUIDAMBAR Dislikes more than a trace of lime and will not grow on chalk.

LIRIODENDRON The tulip trees will grow on fertile soils with high lime content but are not happy on chalk.

MAGNOLIA Magnolias are not happy on limy soils, the exceptions among the tree-sized species being *MM. delavayi,* x *highdownensis, kobus, sinensis* and *wilsonii.*

MALUS In varying degrees the ornamental species and hybrids of apples are satisfactory on lime, and the majority do well on chalk.

NOTHOFAGUS The southern beeches so far in cultivation in Britain will, on fertile soils, stand a little lime in the soil but cannot be grown on chalk.

NYSSA A lime hater.

OSTRYA The hop-hornbeams will grow on lime.

OXYDENDRUM A lime hater.

PARROTIA Is not successful where there is more than a trace of lime.

PAULOWNIA Good on lime and chalk.

PHELLODENDRON Good on lime and chalk.

PLATANUS The planes do well on lime.

POPULUS Poplars in general need fertile moist soil and will not object if there is a lime content, but, except for *PP. alba, canescens* and *lasiocarpa*, they will not grow on chalk.

PRUNUS Almonds, apricots, bird cherries, cherries (including the Japanese cultivars), laurels (common cherry and Portugal) and peaches, all grow on soils with a lime content and, in varying degrees, are also successful on chalk.

PTEROCARYA The wing-nuts will stand lime if the soil is fertile and moist.

PYRUS The pears will all grow on soil with a high lime content, including chalk.

QUERCUS Most oaks do well on soils with a high lime content, including chalk, if there is sufficient depth for their tap-roots. Particularly good are *QQ. canariensis, cerris, frainetto, hispanica* 'Lucombeana', *ilex, macranthera, robur* and *petraea*. Willow oaks, *Q. phellos*, and cork oaks, *Q. suber*, are not good on lime.

RHUS The tree-like species will grow on lime, including chalk.

ROBINIA The false acacias will grow on lime soils and chalk, but are not at their best on them.

SALIX The tree-sized willows tolerate lime, but all need abundant moisture, and will not thrive on dry, chalk soils.

SAMBUCUS The common elder will reach tree size on lime and chalk.

SASSAFRAS Requires lime-free soil.

SOPHORA Tolerates lime on well-drained fertile soils.

SORBUS The rowans and service trees are all good on lime, including chalk.

STYRAX The snowbell trees will not grow on lime.

TETRACENTRON This rare Chinese tree does well on lime and chalk.

TILIA The commonly cultivated lime trees grow naturally on limestone formations, but need moderately fertile soils.

ULMUS All elms will grow well on lime and in varying degrees on chalk.

UMBELLULARIA The Californian laurel will tolerate some lime but will not thrive on shallow chalk.

ZELKOVA The ironwoods will tolerate lime but must have deep fertile soils.

Coniferous trees

ABIES Most silver firs need deep, moist soil and in such will tolerate lime. *AA. amabilis, bracteata, forrestii, grandis, magnifica, procera* and *Veitchii* are not good on soils with much lime. *AA. cephalonica* and *pinsapo*, however, will grow on chalk.

ARAUCARIA The monkey puzzle given fertile soil will tolerate lime.

CEDRUS All the cedars, especially *C. atlantica*, will tolerate lime on fertile soils.

CEPHALOTAXUS These small trees grow well on lime.

CHAMAECYPARIS *CC. lawsoniana* and *nootkatensis* and their cultivars do well on soils with high lime content. *CC. obtusa, pisifera* and *thyoides* are not good on lime and will not thrive on shallow chalk.

CRYPTOMERIA The Japanese cedar will tolerate lime if grown in deep, moist soil.

CUNNINGHAMIA The Chinese fir is not happy on lime soils.

1 A narrow form of Spruce, Picea

2 Tsuga mertensiana, the Mountain Hemlock.

3 The Monkey Puzzle, Araucaria araucana.

x CUPRESSOCYPARIS The Leyland cypress grows well on lime and chalk.

CUPRESSUS The hardy cypresses will tolerate lime, and *C. macrocarpa* does well on chalk.

GINKGO The maidenhair tree grows well on fertile soils containg lime.

JUNIPERUS The numerous species and their cultivars grow well on lime.

LARIX Larches grow well on lime.

LIBOCEDRUS The incense cedar needs deep moist loam and will tolerate some lime.

METASEQUOIA The dawn redwood does best on fertile soils, with or without some lime, and will grow slowly and healthily on chalk.

PICEA The spruces are not happy on shallow. dry soils, though most will tolerate some lime, including the much cultivated common spruce, *P. abies*. An exception is the striking Serbian spruce, *P. omorika*, which grows on limestone rocks.

PINUS Though many of the pines grow naturally on light, mountain soils and many will tolerate a little lime, the majority dislike it. Even the Scots pine, *P. sylvestris*, is not at its best on lime. *PP. armandii, contorta, pinaster, radiata*, and *strobus* are unsatisfactory on lime. The handsome stone pine, *P. pinea*, will stand a little. The Austrian pine, *P. nigra austriaca* is good on chalk, as to a slightly lesser extent is the Corsican pine, *P. nigra maritima. P. mugo*, often no more than a spreading shrub, will also grow on chalk, as will the rare *P. bungeana*.

PSEUDOTSUGA The Douglas firs thrive on fertile, moist, well-drained soils, on which they will stand some lime but not chalk.

SCIADOPITYS The umbrella pine will not grow on chalk.

SEQUOIA The giant redwood will tolerate lime if there is a good depth of fertile soil but will not grow on chalk.

SEQUOIADENDRON The wellingtonia also will grow well in deep fertile soils but will not grow on chalk.

TAXODIUM The swamp cypress will not tolerate lime.

TAXUS The yews grow naturally on limestone formations and chalk, and are equally good on acid soils.

THUJA The western red cedar will grow on soils containing lime, as will the Chinese and American arbor-vitae and their cultivars.

THUJOPSIS This needs fertile, moist soils and thrives better on neutral or acid sites than on limestone.

TORREYA These yew-like trees do well on limestone and chalk.

TSUGA The western hemlock will not thrive on shallow soils containing lime or on chalk, nor will the other species occasionally planted. The eastern hemlock, *T. canadensis*, will, however, grow under these conditions.

Permanently wet soils The other soil factor that must be taken into consideration is continuous moisture, that is, soils that are continuously saturated. The majority of trees will not grow in these conditions, but those that will include the numerous kinds of willow (*Salix*), large and small, as well as the alders (*Alnus*), which are mostly trees of moderate size. The handsome and uncommon swamp cypress, *Taxodium distichum*, is also good, though very wet conditions are not necessary for its success.

Planting A tree will normally outlive its planter. However, if it is given a good start the planter will be rewarded all

125

the earlier by vigorous growth. Do not attempt to plant a tree in unsuitable soil. The choice having been made, you should assure yourself that you are buying stock of good quality. You can, if you wish, ask for stock complying with the *British Standard Specification for Nursery Stock, Part 1, Trees and Shrubs*.

Broad-leaved trees (deciduous or evergreen) These may be purchased as standards, in which the clear stem is from about 5 feet 6 inches to 7 feet. The smaller size is more satisfactory as a rule, and will soon catch up a larger one, which may well have an undesirably spindly stem. In some instances, when, as in a Japanese cherry, low branching will look attractive, a half-standard can be used branching at from 3 feet 6 inches to 4 feet 6 inches.

Have ready a sound, pointed stake long enough when driven firmly into the ground to reach to the point on the stem where the branching starts, also one of the several types of tree ties now available.

Dig or fork around where the tree is to be planted for about an area of a yard square. Particularly if the ground is poor or heavy, work in some well-rotted compost or peat.

Remove the wrappings of the roots and cut off any that are broken. Dig a hole which will take the root system, as nearly as possible so that when the tree is stood in it, the soil mark on the stem is level with, or just below, the surrounding soil. It is, except where willows are concerned, very bad practice to plant too deeply. When you have ensured that the planting hole has been dug to the correct depth, lift the tree out and drive the stake well in at about the centre of the hole.

Replace the tree, working the roots round the stake so that the stake is as close as possible to the stem. This is easily done if someone else holds the tree in place. If you are working single-handed, loosely tie the tree to the stake.

Work soil carefully among the roots, the fine soil among the fine roots, firming it carefully with the fingers. Then almost fill the hole, frequently firming it by gentle treading. Next water the tree well; when the water has sunk in, lightly fill the hole up. Finally, attach the tie at the top of the stem.

Conifers Conifers supplied are usually of a much shorter length than broad-leaved trees and seldom need staking. It is most important to disturb the root ball as little as possible. The sacking which binds the ball may be left on until the tree is in the hole. The knot or lacing that holds it is then cut and gently teased loose and left in the hole. If the tree is not absolutely firm, a stout garden cane and strong string should be sufficient to secure it.

Planting of deciduous trees should be done as soon after leaf fall as possible,

1 Planting a conifer—until the plants are established their hardiness is often in some doubt.
2 Incorporating compost in the soil prior to planting.
3 Working soil around the roots.

but may continue until early spring before the buds begin to break.

Conifers are best planted in autumn, when they will make root at once, and be established by spring. It is less desirable to plant in winter when the roots are for long quite inactive. Early spring is the next best time, for root growth will soon be active. But watering during a spring drought with an east wind is then essential. A mulch is also helpful.

Maintenance and pruning The area round the base of the tree should be kept weeded until it is well established. Watch the tie regularly and keep it from becoming too tight, i.e., allow a little play. Strangulation may cause great damage. Remove the stake only when the tree is absolutely firm—this will take at least three years.

To keep the tree shapely, preferably with a single leading shoot, the following rules should always be followed in pruning trees young or old.

Always cut a shoot or branch back to the point where it arises, making the cut as clean and flush and as close to the main branch as possible. If a 'snag' is left, it will not grow and will eventually rot and cause damage.

If the shoot or branch is of any weight, carry out the operation in two stages, the first taking off the weight and leaving a short snag that can then be removed without its bark tearing away back into the main stem. If the scar is large, paint it with one of the proprietary sealing paints.

Ornamental trees are in general best pruned from mid-to-late summer. The wounds then heal quickly and attacks by fungi or bacteria are held at bay. This applies particularly to most species

of *Prunus*, especially cherries. It also applies to maples, birches and walnuts which 'bleed' sap during the winter and spring.

Never attempt to carry out pruning on a large tree; always obtain the services of a qualified tree surgeon. Unless properly done, it will probably result in damage and disfigurement of the tree, and in addition is often a highly dangerous undertaking for the unskilled operator.

Pests and diseases Those affecting ornamental trees can be divided into three main classes: disease due to bacterial or fungal action, damage caused by insects and damage caused by animals (including birds). Of the first, the most seriously affected trees are members of the rose family *(Rosaceae)*. See Roses and their cultivation, later in this chapter, for both pests and diseases of roses.

Bacterial canker attacks cherries and plums. It is associated with the oozing and dripping of gum from branches or the trunks. Some control can be obtained by pruning out branches affected.

Silver-leaf also affects plums, cherries

and apples in particular and occasionally thorns and laurels. The leaves take on a silvery appearance and on a branch that dies a purplish-mauve fungus arises. This should be cut out and burned without delay.

Fire blight may attack pears, hawthorns, rowans, whitebeams and pyracanthus. Whole shoots in leaf go brown, as if burned, and die. If this is found, the Ministry of Agriculture, Fisheries and Food must be notified at once. The most serious 'killer' fungus is the honey-fungus. It occurs generally on ground that has been woodland which has been cleared with the stumps or many large roots left in the ground. Root-like growths, resembling boot-laces spread through the soil and infect a healthy tree, which is eventually killed and should be removed. From the ground around it, toadstools may, but do not always, arise. They are pale yellow, the gills on the underside running a little way down the stalk, which carries a collar-like ring around it. There is no known cure. It generally attacks conifers.

A selection of garden trees

Trees decorative throughout the year

Decorative bark and good foliage colour

Broad-leaved

ACER CAPILLIPES Young bark striated with white; young growths coral red, leaves turning crimson in autumn. *A. davidii,* young bark shiny green, striated with white; leaves usually turn yellow and purple in autumn. Long chains of keys striking. *A. griseum,* paper bark maple, the outer bark peeling in papery flakes to show the copper-coloured inner bark; opening leaves bronze coloured, turning red or orange in autumn. *A. grosseri, A. g. hersii,* young bark green or yellowish striated with white, leaves orange and crimson in autumn. *A. pennsylvanicum,* moosewood, young bark green striped and patterned with white, the large leaves· pinkish on opening turning clear in autumn. *A. rufinerve,* bark green, with an elaborate pattern of greyish markings, persisting on old trunks; leaves red when young and usually crimson in autumn, when the long chains of keys are attractive.

BETULA PAPYRIFERA Paper-bark birch, shining white bark, the large leaves turning pale gold early autumn, making it more effective than other birches with coloured stems.

LIQUIDAMBAR STYRACIFLUA The American sweet gum has interesting corky bark in winter, the leaves usually turning purple and crimson in autumn.

PARROTIA PERSICA Particularly good if trained to standard form, the grey bark flaking away in a pattern resembling the London plane, while the leaves turn brilliant golds and crimsons (see also Early flowering trees).

PHELLODENDRON AMURENSE The grey, corky trunk is of picturesque form, and the handsome yellow leaves turn yellow in autumn.

SORBUS AUCUPARIA BEISSNERI This handsome cultivar of the mountain ash has red branchlets and a copper-coloured trunk, the large leaves with deeply cut leaflets turning

1 The papery, grey bark of Betula ermanii.
2 Quercus ruber, the Cork Oak, has thick, ridged bark.
3 The shining purple-red bark of Prunus serrula from which the thin outer skin peels.

old gold in autumn.

Conifers Many conifers with yellow, silver or variegated foliage (listed under those headings) give interest of form and foliage colour at all seasons. Some pines, when their lower branches are removed, also have interesting bark. *P. bungeana,* the lacebark pine, has bark which peels off to show white patches; *P. nigra maritima,* the Corsican pine, develops a striking erect trunk with pale scales between fissures in the dark bark. The Scots pine, *P. sylvestris,* with its smooth pink or red bark in the upper part of the tree, is singularly picturesque. The bark of the well-named redwood, *Sequoia sempervirens,* never loses its astonishing colour. Except *P. bungeana,* which is rare and slow-growing, these trees are only suitable for large gardens or parks.

On account of decorative bark in winter

In addition to the foregoing, the principal decorative distinction of the following is their bark, the colouring of their foliage not being exceptional.

ARBUTUS x ARACHNOIDES Hybrid strawberry tree. Trunk and branches cinnamon red.

BETULA Several birches have singularly beautifully coloured bark, though this does not always show on young trees. Among the best are *B. albo-sinensis septentrionalis,* orange-brown with a grey bloom; *B. ermanii,* trunk cream-coloured, the bark peeling off, the branches orange-brown; *B. jacquemontiana,* the whitest bark of all—the white can be rubbed off like chalk; *B. lutea,* the peeling, paper-like bark being yellowish; *B. mandschurica,* vars. *japonica* and *szechuanica,* have very white stems and branches; *B. maximowicziana,* the largest-leaved birch, the trunk at first orange-brown becoming white; *B. pendula,* the native British birch, varies greatly in the colour of its stem and good white-barked seedlings must be selected.

CORNUS MAS Old trees of cornelian cherry have interesting trunks with attractive shaggy bark.

CORYLUS COLURNA The pale, corky, scaling bark on the Turkish hazel is attractive.

EUCALYPTUS Several species have interesting grey, peeling bark.

JUGLANS NIGRA The grey bark of this black walnut, deeply furrowed into a network pattern, is most striking.

PLATANUS x HYBRIDA The peeling of patches of bark showing the greenish grey inner bark of the London plane is well known.

POPULUS ALBA The bark of the white poplar is smooth and grey, with black markings, except at the base of the trunk; *P. canescens,* the grey poplar, has bark of a distinctive yellowish-grey colour.

PRUNUS MAACKII The Manchurian bird cherry has smooth bark, brownish-yellow in colour, and peeling like that of a birch; *P. serrula,* the bark is shiny, mahogany coloured, from which the thin outer skin peels, the trunk of a mature tree having white circular scars around it.

QUERCUS SUBER The thick, ridged bark of the cork oak, not hardy in cold situations, makes it a distinctive tree.

SALIX DAPHNOIDES The violet willow owes its name to the purple shoots covered with a bloom giving them in places a violet colour; *S. purpurea*, the purple osier, has reddish-purple slender branches.

ZELKOVA SINICA This remarkable tree has smooth grey bark which peels away in scales to reveal a rusty-coloured under bark.

Trees with outstanding inflorescenses

AESCULUS CARNEA The red hybrid horse chestnut is very variable, the cultivar *briotii* should always be chosen. *A. hippocastanum*, the common horse-chestnut, growing into a very large tree, is well known. The double-flowered *baumannii* is smaller and does not produce conkers. *A. indica*, the Indian horse chestnut, has the largest flower spikes of all, pink-flushed, in June and July; *A. octandra*, the sweet buckeye, a smaller tree, has flowers that are pale yellow; *A. pavia* var. *atrosanguinea* is a small tree with crimson flowers in June.

CATALPA BIGNONIOIDES The Indian bean has many foxglove-like flowers in a pyramidal, erect spike in July and August. The individual flowers are white marked with yellow and purple. Does well in the heart of London.

CLADRASTIS TINCTORIA The yellow wood has pendent clusters of scented pea-like white flowers with a yellow blotch on the standard in June up to 14 inches long. Does not always flower but has handsome foliage.

CRATAEGUS The many-flowered inflorescences of the numerous thorns, mostly with white but sometimes red or pink flowers, are well known and very similar. A choice should be made from those that also bear showy fruits.

DAVIDIA INVOLUCRATA The pocket-handkerchief, or dove, tree has its small flowers surrounded by two large white bracts, making it a remarkable sight in May.

FRAXINUS ORNUS In May the manna or flowering ash is usually densely covered with clusters of small, white flowers.

KOELREUTERIA PANICULATA The golden-rain tree or pride of India carries in August erect pyramidal spikes of many small yellow flowers each with a red spot at the centre. The foliage also is attractive.

LABURNUM By far the best, with the longest chains of flowers and the sweetest scent, is the hybrid *L. x watereri*.

MAGNOLIA Of the large tree magnolias, the following have large and magnificent flowers: *M. campbellii* (pink), *M. delavayi* (creamy-white), *M. denudata* (pure white), *M. grandiflora* (white), *M. mollicomata* (rose-purple), *M. obovata* (creamy-white), *M. sargentiana* (rose-pink), *M. tripetala*, umbrella tree (cream-coloured).

MALUS There are very many floriferous crab-apples, both with white, pink and rose-coloured flowers. It is best to choose those which also produce interesting fruit or have coloured foliage.

PAULOWNIA *P. fargesii* and *P. tomentosa* (syn. *P. imperialis*) have broad spikes of heliotrope foxglove-shaped flowers up to 1 foot long which are not produced every year, because of winter frost damage to the flower buds.

PRUNUS A selection from this very floriferous genus is best made when a second attribute, such as early flowering, decorative fruit, autumnal leaf colour or decorative bark is present. The Japanese cherries, with flowers ranging from white to shades of pink and even yellow, must be chosen on beauty of flower alone.

PYRUS The ornamental pears are with few exceptions not commonly planted other than for their foliage, as neither their flowers nor fruits are significant.

SORBUS The rowans and service trees have decorative clusters, in some kinds large, of white or rarely pink flowers, but they are best selected by giving attention to the merits of their foliage and berries.

STYRAX *S. japonica* flowers freely in June, the bell-shaped flowers hanging from short shoots; *S. obassa* has similar flowers, fragrant, on spikes at the same season and in addition has large, almost round leaves that turn yellow in autumn.

TILIA The very many small clusters of pale yellow flowers that are carried by all species of limes in June and early July must be mentioned if only on account of their scent. *T. cordata* is the best for a small space, as it is slow growing.

Some deciduous trees with exceptionally handsome foliage

AILANTHUS ALTISSIMA The tree of heaven has pinnate leaves sometimes 2 feet long.

CATALPA The Indian bean-trees have heart-shaped leaves up to 10 inches long.

GYMNOCLADUS DIOICUS The Kentucky coffee-tree has compound pinnate leaves which may reach 3 feet long and 2 feet wide.

JUGLANS SIEBOLDIANA The walnuts all have handsome pinnate foliage, but in this species the leaves may reach 3 feet long.

MAGNOLIA DELAVAYI This evergreen tree has exceptionally handsome leaves a foot or more long. *M. tripetala*, the umbrella tree (so called because of the arrangement of its foliage) has very large leaves up to 20 inches long.

PHELLODENDRON All cultivated species of the cork tree have pinnate leaves 1 foot or more long.

POPULUS LASIOCARPA This has typical poplar-shaped leaves up to 1 foot long.

PTEROCARYA The species of wing nut in cultivation all have pinnate leaves from 1 to 2 feet long, those on *P. fraxinifolia* being the largest.

RHUS TYPHINA The pinnate leaves on the stag's horn sumach may reach 3 feet long.

SORBUS HARROWIANA This tender species has the largest leaves of any mountain ash, a foot or more long. *S. sargentiana*, is a mountain ash which has leaves up to 1 foot long.

1 Aesculus carnea is the red hybrid Horse Chestnut and can be variable.
2 Laburnum x vossii is one of the best Laburnums.
3 The leaves and seed pods of Ailanthus altissima, the Tree of Heaven, a fast-growing tree once established.

Some trees with good autumn colour

It should be noted that autumn colour may vary from year to year in every respect, and even from tree to tree of the same species. This list is by no means complete.

ACER CAMPESTRE The native field maple turns a good yellow; *A. capillipes*, deep crimson; *A. cappadocicum*, yellow; *A. circinatum*, orange and crimson; *A. davidii*, variable, yellow and purple; *A. ginnala*, brilliant flaming scarlet; *A. griseum*, orange, bronze and fiery red; *A. grosseri*, also *A. g. hersii*, red and gold; *A. japonicum*, crimson and pink; *A. negundo*, clear yellow, early; *A. nikoense*, orange and red; *A. pennsylvanicum*, clear yellow; *A. platanoides*, clear yellow; *A. rubrum*, scarlet and yellow; *A. rufinerve*, crimson.

AMELANCHIER All cultivated species turn shades of red or russet.

BETULA Most birches turn shades of greenish yellow, but *B. papyrifera* is a good bright yellow.

CARYA Species usually cultivated turn a good yellow.

CERCIDIPHYLLUM JAPONICUM Variable, but can be brilliant in yellow and reds.

CYDONIA OBLONGA The leaves of the common quince turn a good yellow.

EUONYMUS SACHALINENSIS Yellow and red, early, with crimson fruits.

FAGUS The copper colour of the British native beechwoods is glorious in autumn.

FRAXINUS Most ashes turn shades of yellow before their leaves fall early in the season. *F. oxycarpa* 'Raywood', however, turns a distinctive purple.

GINKGO BILOBA The maidenhair tree turns a rich yellow.

1 Autumn colouring of Nyssa sylvatica.
2 Cercidiphyllum japonicum in autumn.
3 Chamaecyparis lawsoniana stewartii has golden-tipped foliage.

GYMNOCLADUS DIOICUS The large leaves turn clear yellow.

LIQUIDAMBAR STYRACIFLUA Variable, but in good specimens can be brilliant, purple to scarlet.

LIRIODENDRON TULIPIFERA Leaves turn a good yellow.

MALUS Apples give little autumn leaf colour, an exception being *M. tschonoskii*, on which the leaves turn yellow and scarlet.

MESPILUS GERMANICA The large leaves of the medlar turn russet colour.

NYSSA SYLVATICA The tupelo turns vivid scarlet.

PARROTIA PERSICA Colouring reliable, yellow through gold to crimson.

PHELLODENDRON Species usually cultivated turn clear yellow.

PRUNUS This genus provides a few only species that colour well, though the Japanese cultivars mostly turn good shades of yellow; *P. avium*, the gean, most years turns a flaming red; *P. sargentii*, infallibly turns a brilliant red early in autumn.

QUERCUS BOREALIS The red oak is rather a

misnomer as the colour is nearer to brown, but it can be effective. *Q. coccinea*, the well-named scarlet oak, retains its brilliant leaves far into the winter, the best form being the cultivar *splendens*. *Q. palustris*, leaves may turn scarlet, but not reliable; *Q. phellos*, yellow and orange; *Q. velutina*, var. *rubrifolia* is a good red.

RHUS TYPHINA Turns orange, red and purple.

SORBUS CASHMERIANA Pale gold, falling early. *S. discolor*, brilliant red; *S. 'Joseph Rock',* leaves turn a rich variety of colours; *S. sargentiana*, striking reds and golds; *S. torminalis*, the native wild service, colours in well in yellows and golds and sometimes scarlets.

STYRAX OBASSIA The large leaves turn a rich yellow.

Trees with decorative fruits

The following list is of trees whose brightly-coloured fruits are usually decorative for some time after the leaves have fallen. Birds soon attack and strip the berries on a number of kinds almost as soon as they are ripe, but the following are less severely attacked. With some trees, berries are only borne on female trees; in many instances nurserymen can select these.

CERCIS SILIQUASTRUM The Judas tree carries red and purple pods from late summer far into the winter.

COTONEASTER FRIGIDUS Heavy crops of clusters of rich bright red are borne in autumn and early winter.

CRATAEGUS All the thorns carry crops of haws, the more striking including *C. durobrivensis* with large red fruit lasting well into winter; *C. lavallei* has large orange-red berries that hang into the new year; *C. mollis*, the red haw, has very large red fruits which drop rather early to make a spectacular carpet under the tree; *C. orientalis* has large oval or yellowish-red fruits; *C. prunifolia* has large, red fruits, combined with crimson autumn foliage; *C. punctata* has large, slightly pear shaped dull crimson fruits; *C. wattiana*, the Altai Mountain thorn, has large, translucent, yellow fruit.

CYDONIA OBLONGA The common quince, has golden fruit which combine effectively with the yellow autumnal leaves.

EVODIA HUPEHENSIS Female trees bear clusters of scarlet berries.

IDESIA POLYCARPA Female trees carry bunches of bright red berries in autumn.

ILEX x ALTACLARENSIS *I. aquifolium*, the hollies, are among Britain's most beautiful berrying trees, though fruiting only on female trees. *I. a. bacciflava (fructu-luteo)* has yellow berries.

MALUS The crab-apples, mostly carry fruit. The best include the following: *M. x aldenhamensis*, fruit numerous small, deep purple; *M. eleyi*, bright crimson; *M. 'Gibb's Golden Gage'*, waxy yellow fruit; *M. 'Golden Hornet'*, bright yellow fruit—hanging late; *M. 'John Downie'*, large, narrow fruits, yellow with red flush, flavour good; *M. prunifolia* and its cultivars, 'Cheal's Crimson', *fastigiata*, *pendula* and 'Rinki' have red fruits hanging long on the tree; *M. purpurea* has light crimson fruit; *M. robusta*, the cherry apple or Siberian crab,

Tree Portraits

This guide presents 10 principal tree forms and shapes. They include the bush form and the "artificial" fan and cordon

FASTIGATE
The Lombardy Poplar,
Populus nigra italica.
Widely grown because
of its form and quick
growth. Other examples:
Prunus 'Amanogawa',
Carpinus pyramidalis,
Taxus baccata fastigata

BUSH Berberis vulgaris. Berberis species
in general and many flowering
shrubs are of true bush form – i.e. growth
springs from the base. Other examples:
Hydrangea macrophylla,
Syringa vulgaris,
Spiraea thunbergi

FAN-SHAPED
The Fig,
Ficus carica.
Often grown
against a wall and
fan-trained to
utilise reflected
heat from the wall.
This helps to ripen
the fruit and give
protection against
Spring frosts. Other
examples: apricots,
peaches, nectarines

CONE-SHAPED
(sometimes called
bush-shaped)
Picea omorika.
An evergreen conifer,
quick-growing in
early stages.
Other examples:
Taxodium distichum,
Abies normanniana

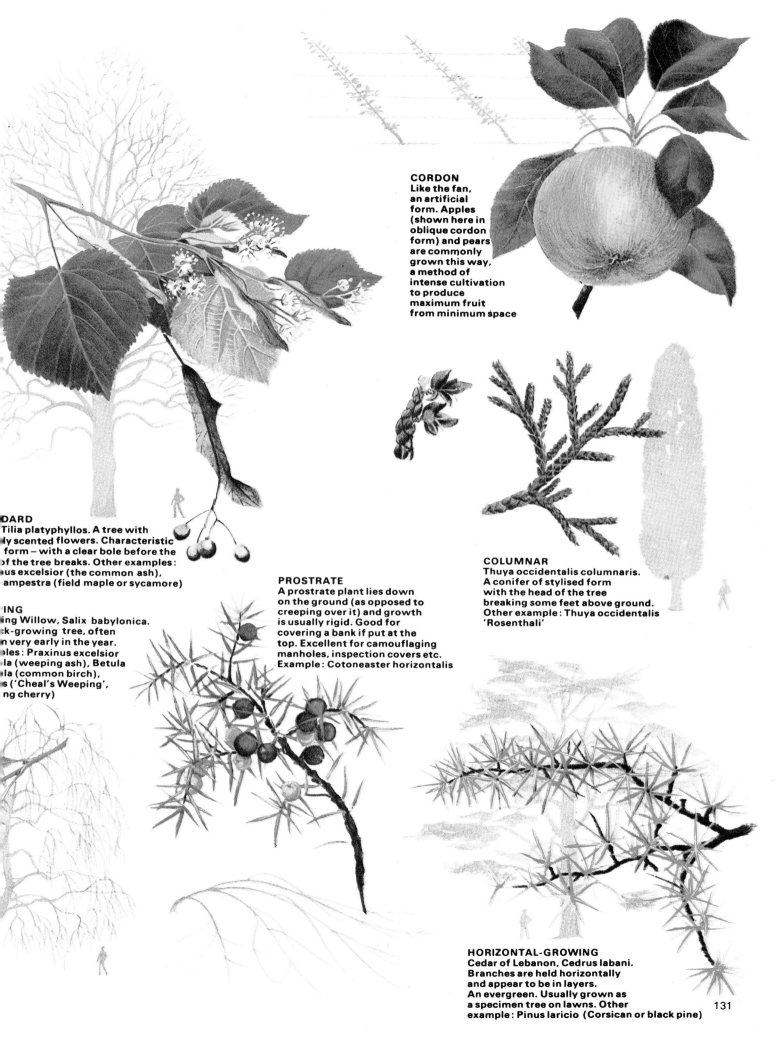

CORDON
Like the fan,
an artificial
form. Apples
(shown here in
oblique cordon
form) and pears
are commonly
grown this way,
a method of
intense cultivation
to produce
maximum fruit
from minimum space

DARD
Tilia platyphyllos. A tree with
ly scented flowers. Characteristic
form – with a clear bole before the
of the tree breaks. Other examples:
us excelsior (the common ash),
ampestra (field maple or sycamore)

ING
ing Willow, Salix babylonica.
k-growing tree, often
n very early in the year.
les: Praxinus excelsior
la (weeping ash), Betula
la (common birch),
s ('Cheal's Weeping',
ng cherry)

PROSTRATE
A prostrate plant lies down
on the ground (as opposed to
creeping over it) and growth
is usually rigid. Good for
covering a bank if put at the
top. Excellent for camouflaging
manholes, inspection covers etc.
Example: Cotoneaster horizontalis

COLUMNAR
Thuya occidentalis columnaris.
A conifer of stylised form
with the head of the tree
breaking some feet above ground.
Other example: Thuya occidentalis
'Rosenthali'

HORIZONTAL-GROWING
Cedar of Lebanon, Cedrus labani.
Branches are held horizontally
and appear to be in layers.
An evergreen. Usually grown as
a specimen tree on lawns. Other
example: Pinus laricio (Corsican or black pine)

131

has heavy crops of long-lasting small fruits, the two cultivars being 'Red Siberian' and 'Yellow Siberian', *M.* 'Wisley Crab' has large, deep-red fruit.

PRUNUS though some of this genus, e.g., cherries, carry attractive fruit, they are eaten by birds even before ripening.

SORBUS The mountain ashes and whitebeams often have decorative berries, but on most species they are eaten at an early stage by birds. The following are usually exceptions: *S. cashmeriana*, large, glistening white, hanging late; *S. esserteauiana*, very large clusters of small scarlet, or in *flava*, yellow fruit, hanging late; *S. hupehensis*, large clusters of small white fruit, turning pink, and hanging late; *S.* 'Joseph Rock' has amber-coloured, long-lasting berries; *S. sargentiana* has great clusters of small, orange-red berries; *S. scalaris* has bright red, small fruits.

Trees with yellow or golden leaves

Included here are some trees which do not retain their exceptional colour throughout the entire season, but are attractive during the early part of the summer. All are cultivars that must be propagated vegetatively since they rarely come true from seed. When suckers arise from ground level they should be watched, and, if they are not true, removed.

Broad-leaved trees

ACER CAPPADOCICUM AUREA Deep yellow leaves on opening and again in autumn. *A. negundo auratum*, golden-yellow foliage; *A. pseudoplatanus corstorphinense*, the golden sycamore, has leaves changing from pale through rich yellow to green in late summer, makes a large tree, *worlei* has soft yellow leaves until late summer.

ALNUS GLUTINOSA AUREA A golden-leaved form of the common alder. *A. incana aurea*, yellow leaves and young shoots with red catkins; it is a beautiful form of the grey alder.

CATALPA BIGNONIOIDES AUREA A small growing cultivar of the Indian bean tree with large golden leaves.

FAGUS SYLVATICA ZLATIA A yellow-leaved beech.

FRAXINUS EXCELSIOR AUREA A large tree with yellow shoots and yellow leaves in autumn.

GLEDITSCHIA TRIACANTHOS 'Sunburst' This has bright yellow unfolding leaves.

LABURNUM ANAGYROIDES AUREUM The yellow-leaved laburnum.

PTELEA TRIFOLIATA AUREA A yellow-leaved form of the hop-tree.

ROBINIA PSEUDOACACIA FRISIA This has golden-yellow leaves throughout.

ULMUS CARPINIFOLIA SARNIENSIS A slow-growing form of the Wheatley elm with pure golden coloured leaves. *U. glabra lutescens*, a wych elm with pale yellow leaves; *U. procera vanhouttei*, a golden-leaved form of hedgerow elm.

Conifers

CEDRUS DEODARA AUREA The golden deodar, smaller than the type, is the best golden cedar.

CHAMAECYPARIS LAWSONIANA LUTEA Has golden-yellow foliage; *stewartii* is a free-growing yellow form; *C. obtusa crippsii* is good deep yellow, slowly reaching tree size.

Cedrus atlantica glauca is a graceful conifer with glaucous blue leaves.

CUPRESSUS MACROCARPA 'Donard Gold' A deep yellow and *lutea*, paler yellow, both being of compact growth.

JUNIPERUS CHINENSIS AUREA Young's golden juniper is a small tree of rather narrow form.

TAXUS BACCATA ELEGANTISSIMA The golden yew; *fastigiata aurea* is the golden Irish yew.

Trees with blue (glaucous) and silver foliage

Broad-leaved

ALNUS INCANA Leaves grey underneath.

CRATAEGUS ORIENTALIS Leaves grey on both sides, deeply cut.

EUCALYPTUS The tree has numerous species, but their hardiness over a long period is doubtful; *E. gunnii* is the best known.

POPULUS ALBA The white poplar has white twigs and undersides of the leaves, the best form for the garden being the erect-growing *pyramidalis*. *P. canescens* has grey leaves and makes a large, vigorously suckering tree.

SALIX ALBA The white willow is a large tree unsuitable for most gardens but its variety *sericea* is a smaller, round-headed tree with whiter leaves.

SORBUS ARIA The whitebeam and all its cultivars have a persistent vivid, white underside to the leaves; in *lutescens* the upper surface also is creamy-white.

TILIA PETIOLARIS This has silvery undersides to the large, drooping leaves; in *T. tomentosa* the underneath is quite white.

Conifers

CEDRUS ATLANTICA GLAUCA A large tree with glaucous-blue, and in some specimens, almost silvery leaves.

CHAMAECYPARIS LAWSONIANA Includes a number of glaucous-blue foliaged cultivars, including *allumii*, *columnaris*, *elegantissima*, *erecta alba*, *fraseri*, *glauca* (better known as 'Milford Blue Jacket'), *robusta glauca*, 'Silver Queen' (the foliage turning green in late summer) and 'Triomphe de Boskoop' (tending towards blue).

CUPRESSUS ARIZONICA 'Bonita' has very grey-blue foliage; in *pyramidalis* it is somewhat bluer.

JUNIPERUS CHINENSIS PYRAMIDALIS Has markedly blue foliage; *J. recurva coxii* has blue-green leaves; *J. virginiana glauca* is silvery-blue.

PICEA GLAUCA A large spruce with bluish-green leaves; *P. pungens* has grey-green leaves, the cultivar *glauca* is smaller with grey-blue leaves and *glauca moerheimii* is an even more intensely coloured form.

Trees with white, silver or yellow variegated leaves

These are all sports, perhaps occurring originally on one branch only, of normal trees that have been propagated vegetatively as cultivars. Normally, seedlings revert to the usual form. Suckers arising may not be true.

The deciduous broad-leaved kinds are cheerful in urban areas where smoke pollution is not too bad, but the evergreen conifers on which the foliage persists for several years become drab. Most of these trees fit well into the normal colour scheme of a garden.

Broad-leaved

ACER NEGUNDO The box elder, provides excellent variegated foliage in *elegantissimum*, bright yellow and *variegatum*, conspicuously white. *A. platanoides drummondii*, leaves distinctively margined with white; *A. pseudoplatanus leopoldii*, leaves marked with cream and white.

BUXUS SEMPERVIRENS The following freegrowing cultivars have variegated leaves: *aurea maculata*, leaves marked with gold and *aurea-marginata*, leaves edged with yellow.

ILEX AQUIFOLIUM A number of variegated leaved forms include *argenteo-marginata*, silver-variegated, berrying; *flavescens*, moonlight holly, yellow and gold, berrying; 'Golden King', wide yellow margins, berrying; 'Golden Milkmaid', gold with narrow green margins, not berrying; 'Handsworth New Silver', dark green with white margin, berrying; *laurifolia variegata*, golden margins, not berrying; 'Madame Briot', leaves margined and blotched with gold, berrying; *scotica aurea*, spineless with lustrous, spineless leaves blotched with yellow, berrying; 'Silver Queen', bold creamy-white margins, not berrying.

LIRIODENDRON TULIPIFERA AUREA-MARGINATUM A tulip tree with yellow-margined leaves making a large tree.

ULMUS PROCERA ARGENTEO-VARIEGATA A hedgerow elm having leaves mottled with white. *U. procera argenteo-maculata*, this species has leaves attractively mottled with white.

Conifers

CHAMAECYPARIS LAWSONIANA ALBO-SPICA The tips of branches creamy-white; 'Silver Queen', young foliage silver-white; *versicolor* foliage marked with creamy-white and yellow; *C. nootkatensis argenteo-variegata* has foliage variegated with creamy-white.

SEQUOIA SEMPERVIRENS ADPRESSA The young shoots are greenish-white.

TAXUS BACCATA DOVASTONIANA AUREO-VARIEGATA A golden variegated form of the weeping yew.

THUJA PLICATA ZEBRINA A fine tree, smaller than the type, variegated with bright yellow.

TSUGA CANADENSIS ALBO-SPICATA The tree has white tips to the shoots.

Red and purple foliage trees

Placing trees of these colours needs great care, but their colours mingled with the multitude of others in autumn are effective and of great beauty, they do not blend well with the normal greens, particularly if used in quantity. They should therefore be used sparingly in isolation

1 One of the variegated forms of Ilex aquifolium, the Holly, with broad yellow-green marks on the leaves.
2 The Copper Beech, Fagus sylvatica, a handsome tree for the larger garden.

at points where they will inevitably catch the eye.

A number have clear colours when the leaves unfold but gradually lose this quality and become sombre as the season progresses. Others, not included here, become normal green when the leaves are open.

ACER PLATANOIDES 'Crimson King' ('Goldsworth Purple'), a Norway maple with crimson-purple leaves larger than the type.

BETULA PENDULA PURPUREA The purple-leaved birch is not a vigorous tree.

CORYLUS MAXIMA PURPUREA The purple-leaved filbert is a good colour though not often of tree size.

FAGUS SYLVATICA ATROPUNICEA The dark purple beech, *cuprea* copper beech; and *purpurea*, purple beech, are all well-known, reliable trees reaching a considerable size and quite unsuitable for other than the largest garden. Weeping forms of these coloured variants are also available.

MALUS The flowering crabs provide several kinds with red or purple foliage combined with gay flowers and decorative fruits. All are very hardy and adaptable, well suited to a small garden; *M. x aldenhamensis*, purplish leaves, rich red flowers and crimson fruit. *M. eleyi* is rather more vigorous than the last, the leaves

bronze-green flushed with purple, the fruit hanging longer on the tree. *M. purpurea* has dark purplish-green leaves, crimson flowers and fruits, both tinged with purple. *M.* 'Wisley Crab', larger than the foregoing in all its parts, the leaves bronzy-red, the flowers large, wine coloured, scented and large deep-red fruits.

PRUNUS Several plums have coloured leaves, the best including *P. blireana* (often a large shrub) deep copper with pink flowers. *P. cerasifera atropurpurea,* better known as *P. pissardii,* with crimson-purple leaves, suitable also for hedging; nigra has darker leaves.

QUERCUS PETRAEA PURPUREA Has reddish-purple leaves which become green flushed with red. *Q. robur fastigiata purpurea* has young leaves the same colour.

Trees with early flowers

ACER OPALUS The Italian maple has yellow flowers in early April.

CORNUS MAS This has many small yellow flowers in February.

PARROTIA PERSICA This bears very numerous small scarlet tassell-like flowers in February.

PRUNUS 'Accolade' is a semi-double pink cherry flowering in March; *P. conradinae* is a cherry with scented white or pinkish flowers in late February; *P. davidiana* is a peach flowering in January, *alba* is a white form, *rubra* pink. *P.* 'Fudanzakura' *(semperflorens)* with pink buds and white flowers from November to April. *P.* 'Kursar' a bright pink cherry flowering in March; *P.* 'Okami' a cherry with carmine-pink flowers in March; *P.* 'Pandora' is a single pink, very floriferous March-flowering cherry, giving good autumnal leaf colour; *P. subhirtella autumnalis* carries semi-double white flowers (pink in *rosea*) from November to March.

SALIX CAPREA The goat willow has decorative catkins in March; *S. daphnoides,* the violet-willow, carries them even earlier.

Evergreen trees

Broad-leaved

It is as well to remember that these often drop their leaves untidily in summer.

ARBUTUS All species and hybrids.

BUXUS All species and cultivars.

EUCALYPTUS All species.

ILEX *I.* x *altaclarensis, I. aquifolium* and their cultivars are evergreen hollies.

LIGUSTRUM LUCIDUM A species of privet often reaching tree size, has handsome dark green, glossy leaves, and white flowers in late summer.

MAGNOLIA DELAVAYI This and *M. grandiflora* are evergreens reaching tree size.

PHILLYREA LATIFOLIA A neglected, small evergreen tree with dense, dark-green, glossy foliage.

QUERCUS ILEX The holm oak and *Q. suber,* the cork oak, are handsome trees capable of reaching large sizes, the latter needing mild conditions.

UMBELLULARIA CALIFORNICA The Californian laurel is usually a small tree with aromatic leaves.

Conifers

All conifers are evergreen with the exception of *Ginkgo, Larix* (larch), *Metasequoia* and *Taxodium* (swamp cypress).

1 Libocedrus decurrens, the Incense Cedar, is columnar in form. It has dark green, glossy foliage.
2 Chamaecyparis lawsoniana wisselli has a narrow fastigiate form.

Fastigiate trees

To the botanist, the word fastigiate means with parallel, erect, clustered branches'. It has now become more widely used in a more generalised sense for trees with narrow crowns. All those mentioned are derived from natural sports and do not come true from seed (if that is produced). They are propagated as cultivars. They generally need careful pruning when young to ensure the necessary erect growth.

Their placing needs great care, as they inevitably have an unnatural look. Fastigiate conifers accord well when planted in the regular pattern of formal gardens—the use of the true cypress in the great Italian gardens of the Renaissance. Fastigiate trees can be skilfully used, too, for adding a steadying vertical element to a steeply sloping site. The planting of a pair one on either side of the introduction to a vista can be very effective. Some of the less erect-growing are excellent for planting in narrow roads, or, for example,

at the centre of a lawn where space is limited.

Broad-leaved

ACER SACCHARINUM PYRAMIDALE An upright form of the silver maple, useful for street planting.

BETULA PENDULA FASTIGIATA This is an erect, slow-growing form of the common birch, resembling an erect besom.

CARPINUS BETULUS FASTIGIATA This is a valuable pyramidal rather than truly fastigiate cultivar of the hornbeam.

CRATAEGUS MONOGYNA STRICTA This has a narrow, erect-growing crown.

FAGUS SYLVATICA FASTIGIATA The Dawyck beech is a good erect tree.

LABURNUM ANAGYROIDES PYRAMIDALIS This is an upright laburnum.

LIRIODENDRON TULIPIFERA FASTIGIATUM A narrow-growing form of the tulip tree.

MALUS HUPEHENSIS ROBUSTA This has large white flowers and fairly erect growth. *M. prunifolia fastigiata,* the fastigiate Siberian crab.

POPULUS ALBA PYRAMIDALIS An erect-growing, very effective form of the white poplar; *P. nigra italica* is the common large-growing Lombardy poplar.

PRUNUS 'Amanogawa' A very fastigiate, small-growing cherry with double pink flowers;

1 The Weeping Elm, Ulmus glabra pendula, has a neat shape.
2 Pyrus salicifolia, the Willow-leaved Pear, a dainty tree.
3 The Weeping Cherry, Prunus subhirtella pendula.

P. hillieri 'Spire' reaches 25 feet with pink flowers and good autumn foliage; *P.* 'Umeniko' has single white flowers with leaves colouring in autumn.

PTELEA TRIFOLIATA FASTIGIATA An erect growing form of the hop tree.

QUERCUS ROBUR FASTIGIATA The cypress oak, makes a broadly columnar tree of interesting form.

ROBINIA PSEUDOACACIA ERECTA A narrow form of the false acacia with few leaflets; *pyramidalis* has erect, spineless branches.

SORBUS AUCUPARIA FASTIGIATA A particularly narrow form of the rowan.

ULMUS CARPINIFOLIA SARNIENSIS The Wheatley elm is a large tree of flame-like form excellent for street planting; *U. glabra exoniensis* is a slow-growing erect form of the wych elm, the leaves often being distorted.

Conifers

CEDRUS ATLANTICA ARGENTEA FASTIGIATA A narrowly pyramidal form of the Atlas cedar.

CHAMAECYPARIS LAWSONIANA This provides a number of narrowly erect forms, including the popular *allumii* with bluish foliage; *columnaris* very narrow, glaucous blue; *erecta* bright green; *fraseri* slender, grey-green; 'Kilmacurragh', bright green; *pyra-*

midalis alba with white tips to the branches in spring; and *wisselli* a fine tree reaching considerable size.

CUPRESSOCYPARIS LEYLANDII This is a densely-leaved, quick-growing tree of large size and fairly narrow shape.

CUPRESSUS ARIZONICA PYRAMIDALIS This is very narrow, of moderate size and with almost grey foliage.

GINKGO BILOBA FASTIGIATA This is an upright-growing form of the maidenhair tree useful for street planting.

JUNIPERUS COMMUNIS HIBERNICA The Irish juniper is columnar, but needs supporting.

LIBOCEDRUS DECURRENS The incense cedar makes a distinctive, large columnar tree.

TAXUS BACCATA FASTIGIATA The well-known Irish yew of churchyards, the golden-leaved form being *fastigiata aurea.*

THUJA OCCIDENTALIS FASTIGIATA A slow-growing, very narrow tree.

THUJA PLICATA FASTIGIATA A narrow form of the western red cedar making a tall tree.

Weeping trees

Weeping trees are mostly natural sports that must be propagated as cultivars. They are difficult to place on account of their arresting form, and must stand in isolation since much

of their beauty lies in the manner which their branches sweep down to the ground. Nothing should be grown under them.

Few trees are more frequently planted in an unsuitable place than the weeping willow, attractive when it is a small, slender tree, but becoming mighty in age, when its form often has to be damaged by savage pruning.

BETULA PENDULA TRISTIS A graceful form of the silver birch with steeply drooping branches; *youngii* is smaller, more compact and slow-growing.

BUXUS SEMPERVIRENS PENDULA A good weeping form of the common box.

CARAGANA ARBORESCEN PENDULA An attractive small weeping tree with yellow pea-shaped flowers and fern-like leaves.

CRATAEGUS MONOGYNA PENDULA A weeping hawthorn; *pendula rosea* has pink flowers.

FAGUS SYLVATICA PENDULA The weeping beech, making a big tree; *purpureopendula* is a weeping form of the purple beech.

FRAXINUS EXCELSIOR PENDULA The well-known weeping ash.

GLEDITSCHIA TRIACANTHOS BUJOTI A honey-locust with pendulous branches.

ILEX AQUIFOLIUM ARGENTEO-MARGINATA PENDULA Perry's silver weeping holly, berrying freely.

LABURNUM ANAGYROIDES PENDULUM A gracefully weeping laburnum.

MALUS The following crab-apples have pendulous branches: *M. floribunda* 'Excellens Thiel', a small tree with crimson buds and pink flowers, floriferous but no fruit; *M. prunifolia pendula,* the weeping Siberian crab, with numerous small, scarlet, persistent fruit; *M. pumila pendula* 'Elise Rathke', a weeping form of the native crab.

MORUS ALBA PENDULA The weeping white mulberry is a small tree with perpendicular

135

It is sometimes difficult to decide whether a certain plant is a tree or a shrub, and indeed some plants can be a tree in one garden and a shrub in another, depending on factors such as light, warmth, protection and depth of soil.

Shrub

A shrub may be defined as a perennial woody plant, branching naturally from its base without a defined leader (a single main shoot), and not normally exceeding 30 feet high. Shrubs may be deciduous or evergreen and range from plants no more than an inch or two high, such as some heaths and creeping willows, to huge rhododendrons. Some woody plants may grow either as large shrubs or trees according to circumstances. When the lower part of the plant is woody and the upper shoots are soft, it is referred to as a sub-shrub.

Preparation of the site Just because shrubs *are* so easy to grow, it is a mistake to imagine that you can just stick them into a hole in the ground and then leave them to their own devices. Proper and careful planting is one of the most important operations contributing to their successful cultivation.

The initial preparation of the site should be done, whenever possible, a few months before planting is due to be carried out, in order to give the soil ample opportunity to settle. This may not always be possible, in which case a certain amount of raking and treading may be necessary on light sandy soils, while on heavier clays extra precautions will have to be taken to avoid leaving air pockets round the roots.

Deep and thorough cultivation, either by trenching or double digging, to break up the subsoil, as well as the top spit, is the ideal to be aimed at.

Although the roots of the shrubs will eventually travel far in search of nourishment and moisture, this preliminary cultivation will ensure that they get away to a good start in their first season.

Before the shrubs are put in, the surface soil should be broken down to a reasonably good tilth. Getting it into this condition will provide an opportunity of raking in a slow-acting organic fertiliser, such as steamed bone flour, meat and bonemeal or fish manure. Any of these, applied at the rate of 3–4 ounces per square yard should provide adequate reserves for the first growing season.

With a new garden, on former pasture or woodland, the chances are that the soil will already contain sufficient humus. First, the turf should be sliced off and placed at the bottom of the second spit or, as far as woodland

A border of mixed shrubs selected for either their flower or foliage colour makes a decorative feature.

sites are concerned, all fallen leaves, leafmould, etc., should be collected up and incorporated in the soil as digging progresses.

Where existing beds and borders are being given over to shrubs, it may be necessary to provide humus-forming materials in the form of sedge peat, leafmould, garden compost, spent hops, or rotted down straw, when the site is prepared.

Planting Whether a single specimen shrub is being planted, or hundreds of shrubs are set for a hedge, the actual planting process must be carefully carried out if the plants are to give of their best. Planting holes must be large enough and deep enough to accommodate the roots without bunching or overcrowding, and it is a good idea to leave a slight mound at the base of the hole on which the plant can rest while the roots are spread out and soil is worked among them. On light sandy soils this latter procedure will be simple, but with sticky clays, particularly if planting coincides with a wet spell, it may be necessary to fill in the holes with compost or dry sifted soil. Most shrubs will benefit by being planted in a mixture consisting of equal parts of sifted soil, peat or leafmould and bonfire ash.

Many evergreen shrubs, including rhododendrons, will arrive from the nursery with their roots 'balled' in

1 The Azara species are good shrubs for chalky soil. Azara lanceolata has bright yellow double flowers along the arching stems.
2 The Firethorn, Pyracantha rogersiana, has red berries.
3 Garrya elliptica, excellent in shade.

sacking. When these are planted, the root ball should remain intact. It is not even necessary to remove the sacking, as it will soon rot away, but if it is left in position it is advisable to cut the ties that secure it round the plant.

The shrub should be gently jiggled up and down to ensure that all the roots are in contact with the soil and to prevent air pockets. Planting is usually a job for two—one holding the shrub in position and giving it an occasional shake, the other working the soil round the roots and firming it with the boot, or where small shrubs are concerned, with the hands.

Depth of planting is important. The soil mark on the stem made at the nursery can be used as a guide and shrubs should be planted with the soil slightly above this to allow for the slight sinking that is likely to take place.

Normally, staking will not be necessary, although in positions exposed to strong winds it may be advisable to provide a temporary support for the first season to guard against root damage from wind rock. In any case, it is always advisable to go round newly planted shrubs after a spell of rough weather or prolonged frost to refirm the soil round the base.

The best time to do this is after the soil has had a chance to dry out. Although they like firm planting no shrubs like their roots encased in soil that has been consolidated into a concrete-like consistency, which is what will happen if an attempt is made to firm heavy clay soils when they are still waterlogged.

There are two schools of thought where the initial planting of a new shrub border is concerned. Some garden writers advocate planting at distances sufficient to allow each shrub to develop to its fullest capacity without overcrowding. Others advise planting well in excess of the final requirements and later ruthlessly sacrificing any that are not required.

There are drawbacks to each of these methods. In the latter instance, although it is easy to see when shrubs are beginning to exceed their allotted space above ground, it is difficult to say when overcrowding of the roots starts to take place. Waiting till the branches are jostling one another may cause considerable damage to the roots of those that remain when the unwanted surplus is removed.

On the other hand, in a shrub border with every plant at a distance from the others sufficient to allow room for the ultimate spread of its roots there will be plenty of wide open spaces for several years to come. These can be filled during spring and summer by bulbs and perennials.

The best solution is to provide temporary stopgaps in the form of relatively short-lived shrubs, or common ones of vigorous habit that will not be greatly missed when the time comes to get rid of them to make room for the more permanent occupants of the border.

Brooms are ideal for this purpose. No matter how carefully they are pruned they invariably become leggy and untidy in the course of four or five years. But in their prime they make a colourful display. The many lovely hybrid forms of the native broom, *Cytisus scoparius*, range from white through every shade of cream and yellow to rich mahogany reds and purples. A good representative selection would include 'Cornish Cream', 'Dorothy Walpole', a rich crimson, 'Lady Moore', a bicolor with rich red wings and keel, the lovely apricot and buff 'C. E. Pearson' and the dainty carmine and rose-red 'Johnson's Crimson'. For the edge of the border or the rock garden there are the early-flowering *C. praecox* and the prostrate

C. x kewensis both of which bear masses of cream coloured blossom.

Other 'expendables' include the flowering currants, some of the more rampant mock oranges, such as *Philadelphus coronarius*, as well as the taller forsythias and such coarse-growing shrubs as *Buddleia davidii*.

Winter flowering shrubs By judicious planning and selection it should be possible to have shrubs in flower throughout the year. Winter-flowering shrubs make an invaluable contribution to our gardens, bringing colour and, in many instances, penetrating fragrance during the darkest days of the season.

By mid-November, when the early heavy frosts have stripped the deciduous shrubs and trees of most of their leaves, the first pinkish-white flower clusters of *Viburnum fragrans* will be starting to open. This is one of the loveliest and most useful of winter shrubs; it continues to produce relays of richly fragrant blossoms right up to the end of February. There is a white variety, *candidissima*, with flowers lacking the pinkish tinge of the type, but which contrast even more effectively with the bare, cinnamon-brown twigs.

The witch hazels start to flower towards the end of December and in most seasons it is possible to fill a vase with their curious spidery, cowslip-scented blossoms at Christmas. *Hamamelis mollis*, the Chinese species, with showy golden-yellow flowers—showy by winter standards, at any rate, is the one most widely grown. The form *brevipetala* has shorter petals of orange, while those of *pallida* are a pale sulphur-yellow.

H. japonica comes into flower a little later; the blooms of this species are more striking, their golden-yellow strap-like petals being set off by a purple calyx. They lack, however, much of the scent of the *mollis* varieties.

More fragrant still—half a dozen small sprigs will scent a room—is the winter sweet, *Chimonanthus praecox*, with waxy, pale yellow flowers, the centres blotched with purple. In the

variety *grandiflorus* they are of a pure clear yellow. The plant type starts to bloom in December, the flowers of the latter open a few weeks later and sacrifice some of their scent for showiness.

February will see the bare branches of the mezereon, *Daphne mezereum,* covered in purple, hyacinth-scented blossom. This is a short-lived shrub and might well qualify to fill gaps in the border if it did not make such a valuable winter contribution to the garden. Fortunately, fresh supplies come easily from seed, and provided the scarlet fruits—which incidentally are extremely poisonous—are protected from the birds, which are very partial to them, the task of providing replacements is a simple one as the seed will germinate freely in any good garden soil.

From spring to summer the main display starts with shrubs such as the viburnums, brooms and lilacs and reaches its zenith at midsummer.

With the many plants to choose from, planning and planting for continuity of display should be easy. To obtain a lavish display of blossom for as long as possible it will be necessary to include in the planting plan shrubs such as *Caryopteris clandonensis,* and the tree hollyhock, *Hibiscus syriacus,* the flowering season of which covers the months of late summer and autumn.

Lilacs rank among the favourite shrubs of late spring and the most decorative are the hybrids of *Syringa vulgaris.* Among both singles and doubles, old favourites still reign supreme, with 'Souvenir de Louis Spath' as the best purple and 'Maud Notcutt' most popular as the most outstanding single white. Lesser-known single forms include 'Esther Staley', an unusual shade

of pale lilac verging on pink, and 'Maurice Barnes', the best examples of the true 'lilac' colour.

Many prefer the doubles with their chunky tightly-packed conical flower trusses, although they lack some of the elegant form of the singles. 'Katherine Havemeyer' (soft mauve), 'Madame Lemoine' (white) are all established favourites. All of them, both single and double have the typical enchanting perfume of lilacs and are vigorous shrubs, reaching a height of 15–20 feet.

In the smaller garden there will not be much room for these giants, but some of the lilac species are much more compact and would prove useful where space is restricted. Their flowers may be smaller and less showy than those of the larger hybrids but they yield nothing to these where fragrance is concerned. *Syringa macrophylla,* for example, makes a dainty shrub, only 4–6 feet in height, with elegant purple flower spikes that are extremely fragrant and have an attractive habit of continuing to bloom at intervals throughout the summer. *S. persica alba,* a white-flowered form of the incorrectly-named 'Persian' lilac is a delightful Chinese shrub with narrow leaves and handsome panicles of white flowers.

In late spring the shrub border is redolent with fine perfumes. The mid-season viburnums, with their distinctive clove scent will be in bloom then; also *V. × burkwoodii,* a vigorous cross between *V. carlesii* and *V. utile,* with its large globes of white, *V. × carlcephalum,* another *carlesii* hybrid, with in this instance, *V. macrocephalum* as the other parent, whose large fragrant flowers measure 4–5 inches across and *V. carlesii* itself, still ranking as one of the most popular garden shrubs.

1 The Lilacs, Syringa vulgaris, in a variety of colour, are grown for their flower effect.
2 The berries of Clerodendrum fargesii are of a curious shape.

Midsummer beauty Philadelphus, or mock orange, often wrongly called syringa, will be among the next batch of favourites to come into flower. Its fragrance can be cloying and is too heavy for some tastes. In many of the newer varieties, however, the somewhat funereal smell of *P. coronarius,* is more subdued, and the superb decorative value of their white flowers could never be in dispute. For the smaller gardens of today, there are a number of compact hybrids, much less coarse in habit than the once popular *P. coronarius.* 'Enchantment' is one of the loveliest of these, with elegant, arching branches thickly festooned with double white flowers in June and July. 'Manteau d'Hermine', only 4 feet tall at maturity, also produces its double white blossoms freely. 'Sybille', another delightful shrub of modest dimensions, bears an abundance of dainty white, purple-scented blooms. *P. microphyllus* can be particularly recommended for the small garden. Its leaves are very small and the unusual four-petalled flowers have a distinctive fruity perfume.

Weigelas, still listed sometimes as Diervilla, are useful midsummer shrubs of medium height and girth. Their flowers, borne along the entire length of the previous years' shoots are long and tubular, rather like miniature foxgloves. *W. florida,* a native of Korea and northern China, was discovered by Robert Fortune in the garden of a Chinese mandarin in the last century;

1 The shrub planting at Mount Usher, Eire, includes Azaleas and Malus.
2 Daphne mezereum.
3 Camellia x williamsii 'Donation' at Wisley. Camellia is a superb shrub under the right conditions.
4 Choisya ternata, the Mexican Orange, will tolerate some shade.
5 Cytisus scoparius burkwoodii.

1

3

2

4

1 Many shrubs are included in the garden
for the brilliant colour of their foliage in
autumn. Fothergilla monticola is one of
these.
2 Rhododendrons are among the most
popular of spring-flowering shrubs.
3 The various forms of Hibiscus produce
flowers in August, a month in which
few shrubs flower.
4 The broad green leaves of Sibiraea
laevigata, a deciduous flowering shrub
for summer effect.

it is the hybrids of this attractive species that have produced our popular garden forms.

'Feerie', *W. vanhouttei* and *W. styriaca* are all good, with flowers of varying shades of pink. 'Eva Rathke' and 'Bristol Ruby' have flowers of a stronger colour. 'Eva Rathke' has the longest flowering season. Its deep crimson flowers appear from mid-May until August.

Deutzias, shrubs that deserve wider recognition, will also be in flower at this period. Their habit of growth, narrow at the base but arching elegantly outwards when they attain a height of 4–5 feet, makes them invaluable where ground space is at a premium. The flowers, which are like small tassels, are profusely borne, while in winter the bare cinnamon branches are of great decorative value. *D. elegantissima* is the form most commonly encountered. The pinkish-purple blossoms are profusely borne on arching sprays, while in the variety *pulchra* they are a pearly pink. 'Codsall Pink' is a strong grower and can reach a height of 10–15 feet. This form flowers later than most, starting at the end of June and continuing into July.

No shrub garden would be complete without the summer-flowering viburnums. The snowball bush, *V. opulus sterile,* is the most popular of these. Its globular flowers, green at first, but turning pure white later, make an established specimen of this lovely summer shrub an unforgettable sight when the branches are smothered in white snowballs. It is, however, rather a vigorous grower for small gardens and for these *V. tomentosum plicatum* would be a more appropriate choice. This seldom exceeds 6 or 7 feet in height and the 'snowballs' are in the form of half-globes which are borne in symmetrical pairs along the branches, giving the effect of a stylised Chinese scroll painting. The variety *grandiflorum,* with larger leaves and flowers than those of the type is the best form to grow.

Continuity of display In the rather barren weeks that follow the peak flowering period, hydrangeas are a first-class standby. Apart from the large-leaved species, which require partial shade, they will thrive either in full sun or semi-shade. In the former position, however, copious watering or regular mulching will be required during the first few seasons after planting. *H. macrophylla* is the well-known and deservedly popular pot hydrangea of the florists' shops. It will also do well out of doors in most parts of the British Isles, although in exposed positions and inland districts the blossom buds, which begin to swell very early in the year, may suffer frost damage. This can often be prevented by leaving the previous year's flower-heads on the plants as protection,

but in really cold areas it would be safer to plant one of the completely hardy species such as *H. paniculata, H. villosa, H. serrata* or the oak-leaved hydrangea, *H. quercifolia.*

Another genus of late-flowering shrubs, useful for bridging the gap between the summer and the beauties of autumn leaf colour is represented by the hypericums, or St John's worts, of which, the best-known member is the prolific, weed-smothering *H. calycinum,* the rose of Sharon. For the shrub border, however, the taller species and hybrids are a good deal more useful and decorative. Their flowers, like giant buttercups with a central boss of contrasting stamens, make them among the finest shrubs for a late summer display. 'Hidcote' and 'Gold Cup' are both outstanding forms of *H. patulum,* with large cup-shaped flowers 2–2½ inches across. *H. elatum* 'Elstead' is another attractive form, with oval leaves of a fresh vernal green, and masses of small yellow flowers in July and August that are followed by scarlet fruits.

1 **Cotinus coggygria is good for autumn foliage colour. The colour heightens late in the season.**
2 **Viburnum plicatum tomentosum 'Lanarth' has its horizontal branches covered in creamy-white flowers in June.**

But the outstanding member of the group is undoubtedly the hybrid, 'Rowallane'. Unfortunately, it is not completely hardy in all parts of Britain and needs a sheltered position in many areas. Its magnificent golden chalices are 2½ inches in diameter and well-developed specimens reach a height of 8 feet in milder districts.

To wind up the floral display for the season there is the so-called shrub hollyhock, *Hibiscus syriacus,* together with the blue-flowered *Caryopteris* × *clandonensis,* which is best treated as a herbaceous perennial and cut back almost to ground level each spring.

Shrubs for autumn leaf colour The beauty

of the shrub border is not restricted to its floral display. From September until final leaf fall comes a brilliant cavalcade of coloured foliage, followed by, and sometimes simultaneous with, beauty of winter berry and bark.

Among the shrubs the leaves of which colour so brilliantly, the barberries and cotoneasters play a prominent part. *Berberis thunbergii* has small leaves of a clear green that produce brilliant flame in autumn. The leaves of the variety *atropurpurea*, which are deep purple throughout the summer, assume even more dazzling colours before they fall. *B. verruculosa* is an evergreen species, but many of its dark green leaves turn scarlet, while some of the foliage of the closely related *Mahonia aquifolium*, another evergreen, turns coppery-red in autumn and winter.

Although, botanically, the cut-leaved Japanese maples are not shrubs, but small trees, they have so many of the characteristics of the former that they are usually included in this category.

The Japanese maples are very slow growers and the purple-leaved *Acer palmatum dissectum atropurpureum* and its green-leaved counterpart, *palmatifidum*, both with leaves like the finest lace, never exceed 8–10 feet in height. The leaves of the former turn a vivid deep scarlet, while those of the latter colour to a lighter but no less distinctive hue.

Anyone who gardens on the moist, peaty soils in which rhododendrons and azaleas thrive ought to find room for *Enkianthus campanulatus*, which enjoys similar conditions and puts on a spectacular autumn display in orange and red. The Ghent azaleas, too, can be very colourful in autumn, as also can the common yellow *Azalea pontica (Rhododendron ponticum)*, when its sage-green leaves burst into tints of flame and coral.

One of the most unusual and striking shrubs for autumn colour, is a member of the euonymus genus, of which the spindle tree is probably the most representative. *E. alata* has leaves that turn a bright glowing pink. After they fall, continuing winter interest is provided by the curious corky wing-like excrescences on the stems.

All the cotinus and rhus, related genera, are noted for their brilliant autumn colour. The stag's horn sumach, *R. typhina laciniata*, is particularly spectacular, but this small tree colours rather early for the main autumn display and the display itself is somewhat short-lived. Much more satisfying are the brilliant orange and scarlets of *Cotinus americanus (Rhus cotinoides)*, or the bright yellow of the smoke bush, *Cotinus coggygria (Rhus cotinus)*.

Among wall shrubs and climbers many of the vines and creepers colour magnificently, particularly the giant-leaved *Vitis coignetiae, Vitis inconstans* (syns.

Parthenocissus tricuspidata veitchii, Ampelopsis veitchii), and the true Virginian Creeper, *Parthenocissus quinquefolia*. Where space is restricted, the smaller-leaved and less rampant *Parthenocissus henryana* is useful for providing a wall tapestry of brilliant colour.

On the ground, too, creeping and prostrate shrubs such as *Cotoneaster horizontalis, Gaultheria procumbens* and others will be putting down a red carpet, while the hypericums, that have only just finished their flowering season, will be adding to the autumn colours. *Hypericum patulum forrestii* has the most brilliant foliage of any of these.

Beauty of berry and bark Just as decorative, but with a longer-lasting effect

1 The feathery foliage of Rhus typhina laciniata colours well in autumn.
2 One of the plants grown for its bold red berries is Skimmia japonica.
3 Red berries of Viburnum hupehense.

are the berries of many shrubs. These will continue the display from leaf fall until the New Year—sometimes even later in districts where birds are not numerous.

Once again, the barberries and cotoneasters are well in evidence, with species and varieties bearing fruits of many colours, ranging from the vivid coral red of *Berberis* 'Bountiful' to the grape-purple of *B. darwinii*. Among the striking forms are *B.* 'Buccaneer' and

B. thunbergii, both with bright red berries and both, incidentally, also providing attractive leaf colour. 'Cherry Ripe' has fruits that are salmon-red and pear-shaped; the compact, free-flowering Formosan species, *B. morrisonsienis,* bears larger red fruits than most.

More than a dozen kinds of cotoneaster share this same valuable quality. The better known varieties include *C. horizontalis,* whose herring-bone set branches are packed with scarlet button berries and *C. simonsii,* a popular shrub for hedging and cover planting, with no less brilliant berries the size of peas. Taller forms and species include *C. cornubia* with large berries borne profusely, *C. frigidus* with clustered crimson fruits and *C. salicifolius,* the willow-leaved cotoneaster, that bears heavy crops of bright red fruits. Among the prostrate forms suitable for the rock garden, or for use as ground cover, *C. dammeri* decks its trailing shoots with berries like blobs of sealing wax, while *C. adpressus* has both autumn fruits and bright scarlet foliage.

The pernettyas are a group of attractive small-leaved evergreen shrubs with showy marble-sized berries of an unusual beauty. Not many of them, however, are self-fertile so that a specimen of the type plant, *P. mucronata,* will have to be included to cross-fertilise the more decoratively-berried forms. These last-named include 'Donard Pink' and 'Donard White' (the names are descriptive of the colour of their berries), *lilacina,* with lilac-pink fruits and 'Bell's Seedling' with extra-large, dark-red berries.

The vacciniums, like the pernettyas, are ericaceous plants, and they include the edible North American swamp blueberry, *V. corymbosum,* and others such as *V. macrocarpum,* the American cranberry, a prostrate evergreen, the large scarlet berries of which are used for cranberry sauce traditionally associated with the Christmas turkey. *V. myrsinites,* the evergreen blueberry, is a graceful compact shrub that bears its blue-black berries in May and June when they are of doubtful value for garden decoration.

It is not always realised that certain shrubs are dioecious, for example, the male and female flowers are borne on separate plants, so that a specimen of each sex will need to be planted if berries are to result. Japanese laurels or aucubas all share this specialised sex characteristic, which makes it difficult for the owner of a small garden, with limited space at his or her disposal, to include many of them in the planting plan. But for those with room to spare all of these are well worth growing, not only for the beauty of their berries but also for the year-long decorative qualities of their handsome, evergreen foliage.

Finally, to act as a foil to the winter-flowering shrubs, there are other plants whose main attraction lies in their strikingly-coloured bark or interesting branch formation.

The dogwoods, both the scarlet and yellow-stemmed species, love moisture. They will respond to waterside planting and nothing looks more striking in January sunshine than a group of the scarlet-stemmed Westonbirt dogwoods *(Cornus alba sibirica)* at the edge of a pond or stream, while the curiously twisted stems and branches of *Corylus avellana contorta,* popularly known as Harry Lauder's walking stick, make an unusual and interesting tracery against winter skies.

Pruning It is impossible, in the space available, to lay down principles of pruning in any but the most general terms. As a general rule, however, spring-flowering shrubs can be pruned after they have finished blooming. Those that flower in summer and autumn, on the current year's wood, can have their season's growths cut right back in March of each year.

Shrubs should normally be allowed to develop their natural form and dimensions, but any particularly vigorous growths that appear in the second and third seasons after planting should be tipped when they are between 6 and 9 inches long to induce the formation of laterals to build up a solid framework.

Most shrubs, once established, will need little or no attention as far as pruning is concerned, apart from cutting out weak, straggling, diseased or dead shoots. In any case, drastic pruning is an operation that should always be undertaken with caution and should

normally be resorted to only when shrubs have been neglected or when, like buddleias, forsythias, flowering currants and the larger philadelphuses, they grow too rampantly and exceed their allotted quarters, or trespass on paths and lawns.

Avoid, at all costs, indiscriminate clipping with the garden shears. Such treatment will not only reduce all your shrubs to a monotonous uniformity of shape but will also result in weak, straggling growth. Clearly this would look unattractive.

Propagation This, too, is a vast subject. Many shrubs can be grown easily from seed, although not all of them ripen their seed in this country and it may be necessary to obtain it from specialist seedsmen. Brooms, for example, will germinate as easily and as freely as sweet peas; other shrub seeds, berries in particular, need to be stratified, that is, over-wintered in moist sand, to rot the fleshy seed covering, before they can be sown with any hope of success.

Propagation from hard-wood cuttings is another simple method by which many shrubs may be increased. These cuttings should consist of ripened side shoots that have not flowered, pulled off the parent stem with a heel of bark attached, and inserted in a moist shady bed in July and August. They are left until the end of the following season, when sufficient root and top growth should have developed to enable them to be grown on in a nursery bed.

Shrubs that may be propagated easily by this method include cornus, weigela, deutzia, philadelphus, rhus, cotinus, hydrangea and many other well-known kinds. Hedging shrubs such as privet or *Lonicera nitida* are easier still. Trimmings stuck into the soil almost anywhere will usually root very quickly.

Most modern gardens are comparatively small and it is vital that every inch of space should be employed. One way of doing this and gaining valuable space that might otherwise be wasted is to use vertical surfaces such as walls and fences. Some trees and shrubs can be grown against walls, trained and held in place to cover them with foliage or flowers, and there are also certain plants with special characteristics which make them particularly suited to this task.

Climbing Plants
House walls, garden walls, fences, archways, pergolas, trellises, poles, either single or erected tripod fashion and other vertical or near-vertical features, provide the gardener with another dimension in which to grow plants. There are attractive plants

Many climbing Honeysuckles are well known for their delightful fragrance. They are not difficult to grow in any ordinary soil if trained over arches or bushes as in the wild state.

available for this purpose, many of which benefit from the extra shelter provided by a wall or fence.

Types of plant Suitable plants include those which are true climbers, clinging to some form of support, either by tendrils (e.g. clematis), by twining stems (e.g. honeysuckles) and those known as self-clinging climbers, which adhere to their supports by aerial roots (e.g. the ivies) or by sucker-pads (e.g. the Viriginian creeper and some of its relations). In addition to these true climbers, there are many woody or semi-woody plants wh'ch are not, in fact, climbers but may be trained against walls. Examples of these are the well-known chaenomeles ('japonica'), climbing roses, ceanothus and certain cotoneasters.

Types of support Self-clinging climbers need little in the way of extra support except in their early stages. Once started they cling to walls, fences and the like and need little more attention. Some gardeners are a little wary of the more vigorous self-clinging climbers such as ivies, but, provided they are not allowed to interfere with drain-pipes, guttering, roof tiles or slates, etc., they are unlikely to harm the wall itself. It can be argued that they help to keep the wall dry and the house warm, by providing a leafy covering which keeps off even the heaviest rain.

Tendril climbers and twining climbers obviously need something to which to cling. In the open, garden poles, driven vertically into the ground or set tripod fashion, pergola posts and archways will provide support for twiners, but not for tendril climbers. These will need further support such as wire-netting placed loosely round the poles to which the tendrils can cling. The growths of non-climbers will need tying in to the support as they develop.

Against walls and fences there are various ways of providing support for plants. Trellis-work is a well-tried method and panels may be bought in various sizes. Before they are fixed to the wall they should be treated with a copper naphthenate wood preservative to prolong their lives. Suitable trellis may also be made at home, using lathing, which is obtainable cheaply from builder's merchants or timber merchants. It may be made to a square-mesh pattern or to the traditional diamond mesh. So that the growths of the climbing plants can attach themselves properly the trellis should be fixed an inch or so away from the wall, using wooden distance pieces or spacers. Old cotton-reels are useful because they have a hole through which the fixing screw may pass. All fixing should be done firmly as eventually the mature plant may be quite heavy. Wall

fixings such as Rawlplugs are admirable; an electric drill with a masonry bit is useful but not essential as the necessary fixing holes for the plugs can be made with a hammer and jumping bit. Where walls are painted or otherwise treated it is handy to arrange the trellis in such a manner that it can be easily taken down to enable the wall behind it to be painted. One way of doing this is to hinge the bottom of the trellis to a wooden bar of suitable dimensions fixed to the wall. The top of the trellis is fixed to a similar bar in such a way that it can be undone and the trellis and its plants gently lowered, thus minimising the risk of damage to the plants.

Panels of plastic-covered, heavy gauge wire-netting (Gro-Mesh) are obtainable in various sizes, and these provide excellent support for plants. They may be fixed to the wall in much the same way as wooden trellis.

Wires, preferably covered, stretched across the face of a wall or fence, about an inch away from it, will also provide adequate support for many plants. However, unless the wire is properly strained it may sag in course of time. Vine eyes (drive-in pattern for walls, driven into the perpendicular jointing, screw-in type for wooden posts) are useful devices for fixing wires for climbing plants. Straining bolts, which can be tightened when necessary to take up any slack, are also obtainable. Lead-headed

The garden brought into contact with the house by means of wall plants such as Wisteria and Clematis, flowering in May

1 Polygonum baldschuanicum, the Russian vine, roofs this garden retreat.
2 Vitis coignetiae is superb in autumn.
3 Lonicera sempervirens, the trumpet honeysuckle.
4 Jasminum officinale.

1 Humulus lupulus aureus, the golden hop, is a hardy perennial climber.
2 Lonicera periclymenum is beautiful on the roof, and reaches 10-20 feet.
3 Morning Glory or Ipomoea (a synonym for Pharbitis tricolor).

wall nails, nails with flexible lead tags, are used for individual ties, when it becomes necessary to tie in long, woody growths such as those of climbing or rambler roses.

An unusual way of growing certain climbers such as clematis, honeysuckles, is to let them clamber over dead trees or even up the trunks and into the branches of living trees. It is better to avoid for living trees the very vigorous climbers such as *Polygonum baldschuanicum,* the Russian vine, although this is perfectly suitable for a dead tree, which it will quickly smother with its long, twining growths.

Some climbers may easily be grown in well-drained tubs or other large containers and this method is useful where there is no soil bed near the wall, or in courtyards, patios or on town balconies. John Innes potting compost is suitable but vigorous plants may need regular feeding when in full growth.

Preparing the site Most climbers and other wall plants will grow in ordinary garden soil, but of course, they will grow better and begin to cover their allotted space more quickly if they are given a richer diet. The soil should be deeply and widely dug, adequately drained, and the opportunity should be taken to dig in a good supply of garden compost, well-rotted manure, leafmould, spent hops, and other bulky manures, plus about 4 oz per square yard of bonemeal, well worked into the top 6 inches or so of soil. Sites by walls present certain problems which are not always appreciated by gardeners. The soil in such places is often poor, full of builders' rubble and other rubbish buried when the house was built. It is often dry, protected from rain by overhanging eaves. To ensure that the plants do well it is necessary to carry out considerable soil improvement. In some instances it may pay to remove the existing poor soil and rubble to a depth of a foot or so and replace it with good soil from elsewhere in the garden, adding quantities of rotted manure, compost, leafmould etc., all of which will not only provide plant foods but will also help the soil to retain moisture. Even so, in periods of drought, it may be necessary to water copiously, soaking the site from time to time.

If the soil is replaced it should be allowed to settle for some weeks before planting is done. During this time the wall supports can be fixed in position.

Planting The footings of walls usually project several inches beyond the line of the wall itself and to avoid these and the drier soil at the base of the wall, the plant should not be closer to the foot of the wall than 6 inches. Where there is enough room, a planting hole about 2 feet wide and 1½–2 feet deep should be taken out, to allow sufficient room for the roots to be spread out properly. If the soil is heavy clay it is better not to

replace it but to use instead some specially made up planting soil. The basis of this might be old potting soil or good loam to which should be added generous quantities of garden compost and leafmould plus a couple of handfuls of bonemeal per barrow-load of the mixture to provide slow-acting food.

The roots of the plants should be well spread out round the hole, not cramped up or doubled over. Many climbers arrive in pots and to avoid damaging the roots it may be necessary to break the pot and gently tease out the drainage crocks and spread out the roots. Some plants arrive with their roots 'balled-up' in sacking. With these the root ball should be preserved; it is necessary only to cut the ties, after the plant has been placed in position in a planting hole of suitable size, and pull away the sacking. If this is difficult it may be left in place as it will rot away gradually and the roots will, in any case, grow through it into the soil beyond.

Planting should be done firmly, returning a little soil round the roots first and working this in among them and firming it with the hands. More soil is then added and firmed with the boot, provided the roots are adequately covered, until the hole is filled. The soil-mark on the stem gives a guide to the correct depth to plant, although it is usually best to plant clematis a little deeper than is indicated by the soil-mark generally given.

Some temporary support should be provided for the plants until their growths reach the wire, trellis or other support and can begin to cling or twine. Even though this is temporary it should be firmly fixed to prevent the growths blowing about and being damaged. Short canes, twiggy sticks, strings or wires fixed to pegs driven into the ground, are all suitable.

Training and pruning Left to their own devices many climbers quickly become a tangled mass of growths, new shoots clinging to or twining round older ones, instead of neatly covering the supports provided and filling their allotted spaces. Some initial training may be needed to overcome this tendency. Such training consists in starting the new shoots off in the right direction and occasionally during the season ensuring that they are carrying on in the way they are desired to go. This is particularly necessary where it is required to train the shoots horizontally or nearly horizontally, since the natural growth of the plant is upward.

Shrubs trained flat against walls and fences usually need to have their breast-wood removed from time to time. Very young growths developing from forward-

1 **Passiflora caerulea, a beautiful climber for warm walls.** 2 **Thunbergia alata, black-eyed Susan, an annual**

The climbing form of the rose 'Caroline Testout' is ideal for a pergola. Flowering is almost continuous from June to November

Climbers for Particular Purposes

Annual

Cobaea (P as A)	Maurandya	Rhodochiton
Cucurbita	(P as A)	(P as A)
Humulus (P as A)	Mina	Thunbergia
Ipomoea	Pharbitis	Tropaeolum
Lathyrus		

Tendril

Ampelopsis (D)	Lathyrus (D)	Passiflora (E)
Clematis (D & E)	Mutisia (E)	Smilax (D & E)
Eccremocarpus	Parthenocissus	Vitis (D)
(D)	(D)	

Twining

Actinidia (D)	Jasminum	Pueraria (D)
Akebia (SE)	(D & E)	Schizandra (D)
Araujia (E)	Kadsura (E)	Senecio (D)
Aristolochia (D)	Lardizabala (E)	Solanum (D)
Berberidopsis (E)	Lonicera (D & E)	Sollya (E)
Billardiera (E)	Mandevilla (D)	Stauntonia (E)
Calystegia (D)	Muehlenbeckia	Trachelospermum
Celastrus (D)	(D)	(E)
Holboellia (E)	Periploca (D)	Wistaria (D)
Humulus (D)	Polygonum (D)	

Walls north and east

Berberidopsis	Hydrangea	Pileostegia (E)
(E)	(D & E)	Vitis (D)
Ficus (E)	Jasminum (D & E)	
Hedera (E)	Lonicera (D & E)	

Shrubs, Wall plants (not true climbers)

Abelia (D & E)	Cotoneaster	Indigofera (D)
Abutilon (D)	(D & E)	Itea (D & E)
Adenocarpus	Diplacus (D)	Jasminum (D & E)
(D or SE)	Escallonia	Kerria (D)
Buddleia (D & E)	(D & E)	Magnolia (D & E)
Camellia (E)	Feijoa (E)	Phygelius (E)
Ceanothus (D & E)	Forsythia (D)	Piptanthus (E)
Ceratostigma (D)	Fremontia (D)	Pyracantha (E)
Chaenomeles (D)	Garrya (E)	Ribes (D)
Colletia (D)	Hebe (E)	Rosa (D & E)
Corokia (E)	Hypericum	Rubus (D)
Crinodendron (E)	(D & E)	Schizandra (D)

Key: D Deciduous. E Evergreen. P as A Perennial grown as annual. SE Semi-evergreen.

pointing buds can often be rubbed out to prevent their development; otherwise the secateurs will have to be used judiciously.

Pruning is often needed to keep plants under control or to ensure the production of new flowering growths. Pruning methods for particular plants are discussed under the appropriate article (e.g.

Mulching An annual mulch round the bases of the plants, but not actually touching the stems, will help to prevent the soil from drying out in hot weather, particularly near walls and fences, will keep down weeds and will supply plant foods and improve the soil texture as the mulch is gradually absorbed into the soil by the action of worms and weather. Such a mulch might consist of garden compost, leafmould, partially rotted leaves, or moist peat. Late spring is a suitable time to apply the mulch which should be several inches deep. The covering may be renewed from time to time during the summer if it shows signs of dispersal.

Providing protection Some slightly tender plants may be grown successfully against walls in many parts of the country although in severe weather some protection may be necessary. Bracken fronds may be sandwiched between two layers of wire-netting to make an excellent protection which can be placed round the plant when necessary. Wire-reinforced plastic material can be used to make a roll, stapled together along the edges. This roll can be used to surround the plant but should be fixed firmly to a stake to prevent wind movement. Hessian sacking may be draped over the plants in bad weather but should not be too close to them. In fact, no form of protection should surround the plant too closely and it should be removed as soon as possible to allow light and air to get at the plants again.

Supports Supports will need some attention from time to time as the plants grow and, for vigorous specimens, it may be necessary to provide further supports in course of time. Many plants in full leaf present a good deal of wind resistance and inadequate supports or those which have been weakened through age, may easily be brought down, possibly doing irreparable damage to the plants or at least undoing the work of some years. Any suspect supports should be replaced as quickly as possible.

Feeding In time the plants will exhaust the plant food available in the soil, but before that time arrives some extra feeding will be necessary. Annual mulches will provide a good deal of food in time but spring and summer feeds with sulphate of ammonia, nitrate of soda, Nitro-chalk, all at about 1–2 oz per square yard, or proprietary fertilisers at rates recommended by the manufacturers, are quick stimulants. Over-feeding must be avoided; small doses given at regular intervals are much more effective than large doses given infrequently. Feeding should cease by the end of August to avoid the production of soft, frost-tender growth. Bonemeal stirred into the top few inches of soil at up to $\frac{1}{4}$ lb per square yard in the autumn or winter will release plant foods slowly during the following growing season and possibly for longer.

Annual climbers There are a fair number of annual climbers which may be used to form quick screens if grown against appropriate supports. It almost goes without saying that the quickest results are obtained by growing the plants in rich soils and by feeding them with dilute liquid feeds at regular intervals once they are growing well. The exceptions are the climbing nasturtiums which tend to make foliage at the expense of flowers if grown in too rich a soil. However, even these do better if the soil is not too poor and dry. Deadheading will do much to keep the plants flowering instead of spending their energies on ripening seed. Some of these climbers may be grown from seed sown out of doors in spring where they are to flower, others give the best results if they are grown from seed sown in heat in the greenhouse. The methods of propagation recommended are described under the individual articles on the various genera.

Some climbing plants growing along a fence appear almost to transform it into a hedge, and there is no doubt that in general terms a growing, living hedge is always more attractive as a garden boundary or division than the plain and somewhat stark surface of a fence or wall. There is a much wider selection of plants suitable for hedging than is generally realised and the gardener will be advised to spread his net wider than to choose the somewhat drab and greedy-rooted privet or the commonplace beech.

Where space is unlimited, as in some

parks or large estates, almost any trees or shrubs can be used as a hedge, a shelterbelt or a screen, but where the garden is small the number of plants suitable is somewhat more restricted. The following descriptive list includes almost all the most suitable trees or shrubs so as to give the widest possible choice for all circumstances.

A curving hedge of Lonicera nitida is a feature of this Kentish garden.

Hedging and screening plants described

Shrubs, deciduous and evergreen

Acer (maple) *A. campestre* (common or field maple), makes an attractive deciduous hedge or screen tree which thrives in sun or shade, on clay or chalk soils. Plant 1 foot apart, from October to March. Trim in late summer or winter. Height 5–10 feet. Screens 40–50 feet.

Alder see *Alnus*

Alnus (alder) *A. glutinosa* (common alder) is a hardy, deciduous tree with attractive catkins. It thrives best in a rich soil, dislikes acid, peaty soils. Plant 6–8 feet apart for screens from October to March. Height up to 50 feet.

Arbor vitae see *Thuja* (under *Conifers* below)

Arundinaria see *Bamboo*

Atriplex A. halimus (tree purslane) is a semi-evergreen with silver-grey foliage, which makes a first-class seaside hedge. Plant 18–21 inches apart, from October to April. Trim in early spring. Height

4–6 feet.

Aucuba A. japonica and *A. j. variegata* are evergreens which bear scarlet berries where male and female bushes are planted. Plant 2–3 feet apart during October and November or March and April. Trim in April. Height 6–9 feet.

Bamboo The following genera and species are suitable: *Arundinaria japonica* and *A. nitida, Phyllostachys nigra* and *P. viridi-glaucescens* are useful where a screen or wind shelterbelt is needed. Give them good cultivation and avoid water-logged ground. An annual mulch of leaf mould or rotted manure should be given in the spring, plus 1 oz of sulphate of ammonia per square yard. Plant 3–4 feet apart in May. Trim when required from April to mid-May.

Barberry see *Berberis*

Beech see *Fagus*

Berberis (barberry) Suitable evergreen species and varieties are *B. darwinii*, with orange-yellow flowers followed by plum-coloured berries, height 6–8 feet; *B. stenophylla*, golden yellow flowers, height 8–10 feet. Plant both at 1½–2 feet apart. Trim after the flowers have faded. *B. verruculosa*, golden-yellow flowers, height 3–4 feet. Plant 15–18 inches apart from October to March. Trim after flowering. Deciduous species: *B. thunbergii, B. t. atropurpurea*, height 3–4 feet. Plant 15–18 inches apart from October to March. Trim in February. *B. t. erecta*, height 2½–3½ feet, makes an excellent dwarf and compact hedge. Plant 12–15 inches apart from October to March. No trimming is needed.

Betula (birch) *B. alba* (silver birch) makes a useful deciduous screen or shelter tree. Plant 8–10 feet apart from November to March. Birches can also be planted as hedge shrubs, spaced at 1½–2 feet apart. Height as a hedge 8–10 feet, as a screen 40–50 feet.

Birch see *Betula*

Box see *Buxus*

Buckthorn see *Hippophae*

Buxus (box) *B. sempervirens* (common box) makes a superb evergreen hedge with a pleasant musky fragrance. It does well in any soil, likes chalk soils and succeeds by the sea. Plant 1½–2 feet apart during March and April or September and October. Trim in summer or, where hard cutting back is necessary, in April. Height up to 9 feet for hedges, screens 15–18 feet. *B. suffruticosa* (edging box). One nursery yard will plant 2–3 yards of edging. Plant during March and April or September and October. Trim two or three times during the summer. Height not usually more than 3 feet.

Calluna (ling) *C. vulgaris* makes a good low hedge on acid soils. Plant 1–1½ feet apart during April and May or September and October. Trim in spring. Height

1 Erica vulgaris makes a low hedge.
2 A hedge of Fuchsia magellanica.

$1\frac{1}{2}$–2 feet. There are many varieties and cultivars in a good colour range.

Carpinus (hornbeam) *C. betulus* is a hardy, deciduous shrub or tree. Its beech-like leaves have a rougher texture than those of beech. It is excellent for exposed places and it mixes well with hawthorn or quickthorn. One hornbeam should be planted to six quickthorn. Plant either in double rows, 15 inches between the plants and 8 inches between the rows or in single rows 1 foot apart, from October to March. Trim in July. Height 10–20 feet.

Castanea (chestnut) *C. sativa* (sweet or Spanish chestnut) is a hardy, deciduous shelterbelt tree for inland planting. It does best on sandy loam. Plant 3–6 feet apart from October to March. Trim in winter. Height 60–80 feet.

Chaenomeles *C. japonica* (Japanese quince) is a deciduous, flowering and fruiting hedge shrub. There are many varieties in varying shades of pink and red. Plant 1–$1\frac{1}{2}$ feet apart from October to March. Trim at the end of April or early May. Height 2–10 feet.

Cherry laurel see *Prunus laurocerasus*
Chestnut, Sweet see *Castanea*
Conifers see separate list below

Corylus (hazel) *C. avellana* (common hazel), a deciduous shrub which thrives in any soil. It is good for a mixed hedge of hawthorn, holly, hornbeam and elm. Plant 1–2 feet apart, from October to March. Trim in late February or March. Height 10–20 feet.

Cotoneaster There are many suitable evergreen and deciduous species and varieties, including *C. frigida, C. rotundifolia, C. simonsii, C. wardii* and *C.*

watereri, all with white and pinkish flowers or orange-red berries. Plant $1\frac{1}{2}$–2 feet apart from October to March. Trim between the end of February and the end of March. Height 6–9 feet.

Cotton lavender see *Santolina*

Crataegus (may or quickthorn) *C. oxyacantha*, the common hawthorn, is a hardy, deciduous small tree, a most popular hedge plant for garden and farm. It mixes well with holly, beech or hornbeam and will thrive in any soil and grow in sun or shade. Plant in single or double rows 12–15 inches apart, 8 inches between the rows, from October to March. Cut back newly planted hedges in March or April to within 6–9 inches of ground level. Trim from June onwards. For formal hedges several clippings can be given during the summer. Farm hedges are usually trimmed in the winter months. Height 5–20 feet.

Cypress see *Chamaecyparis* (under *Conifers* below)

Erica (heather) Several species and many varieties are ideal for dwarf hedges. Plant 9–18 inches apart, according to variety, during April or May or September and October. Trim in early spring. Height 1–4 feet. Most ericas need an acid soil, though *E. carnea, E. mediterranea* and *E. × darleyensis* will grow in chalky soils.

Escallonia These are hardy and half-hardy evergreen and deciduous flowering shrubs bearing pink or red flowers. They make ideal hedge shrubs for coastal areas, the best being *E. macrantha* or one of its varieties such as 'Crimson Spire' or 'Red Hedger'. Plant

1–$1\frac{1}{2}$ feet apart, in September or during March or April. Trim after the blooms have faded, in late summer. Height 4–10 feet.

Eucalyptus *E. gunnii* the hardiest species makes a good screen in milder counties. It has attractive evergreen glaucous grey-green foliage and thrives in well-drained soils. Plant 6 feet apart in spring. Trim in April when necessary. Height up to 30 feet.

Euonymus (spindle tree) *E. japonicus* is an evergreen, ideal for coastal planting as it does well in wind-swept areas. It makes a good town hedge and it will thrive on any soil. Plant $1\frac{1}{2}$ feet apart in September or April. Trim once or twice in the summer; any hard pruning should be done in April when necessary. Height 8–12 feet.

Fagus (beech) *F. sylvatica* (common beech) is a hardy, deciduous tree, its leaves richly coloured in autumn, and hanging on well into the winter or spring. Little is to be gained by planting bushes more than 3 feet high. The ideal size is $1\frac{1}{2}$–2 feet. For single rows space them 15 inches apart in the rows and 8 inches between the rows. Plant from October to March. Height: hedges 5–10 feet, screens 10–18 feet. *F. s. purpurea*, the purple beech, has attractively copper-coloured foliage which mixes well with green beech.

Forsythia These deciduous shrubs which will thrive in any soil, make good flowering hedges. Plant $1\frac{1}{2}$–2 feet apart from October to March. If trimmed annually as soon as the flowers have faded, a neat flowering hedge will be maintained. Height 4–7 feet.

Fuchsia Some fuchsias make fine deciduous flowering hedges, best suited in Britain to the south coast and the west country. As they are liable to early frost damage they are best planted with the base of the shoots 4 inches below ground level. Plant at $1\frac{1}{2}$–2 feet apart in May. Trim in spring by cutting back lightly or severely, depending on frost damage during the winter. After severe winters cut back the hedge to ground level. Height 3–8 feet. *F. magellanica* and its varieties are chiefly used for hedge purposes, though some of the larger flowered, so called florists' varieties, can be used. Most fuchsia hedges are treated fairly informally.

Griselinia *G. littoralis* is an evergreen which does well in London and also as far north as the Yorkshire coast. It is an excellent shrub for a wind-break or for providing shelter. It thrives in any soil. Plant $1\frac{1}{2}$ feet apart in March or April. Trim between May and July. Height: hedges 5–7 feet, screens 7–10 feet.

Hawthorn see *Crataegus*
Hazel see *Corylus*
Heather see *Erica*

Berberis darwinii, from Chile, provides a splendid flowering hedge.

The Variegated Holly is a good evergreen to use for a permanent hedge.

Hebe (syn. *Veronica*) Hardy and slightly tender evergreen shrubs. There are many species and cultivars, some of the most colourful being varieties of the somewhat tender *H. speciosa*. Hebes are good for coastal areas. *H brachysiphon* (syn. *traversii*) is hardy anywhere. Plant 1½ feet apart in September or April. Trim in April. Heights vary from 2–5 feet.

Hippophae (sea buckthorn) *H. rhamnoides* is a deciduous, hardy and dioecious (i.e. male and female flowers on separate plants) shrub and only when both sexes are planted will berries be produced; one male to five or six female bushes is most satisfactory. It is an excellent seaside hedge or wind shelter shrub. Plant 2–3 feet apart, from October to March. Trim in late March or early April. Height 10–15 feet.

Holly see *Ilex*

Holm Oak see *Quercus ilex*

Honeysuckle see *Lonicera*

Hornbeam see *Carpinus*

Ilex (holly) *I. aquifolium* (common holly). This is one of our oldest evergreens, hardy and dioecious, and like *Hippophae*, there must be a male bush planted if berries are to be obtained. There are many fine varieties, including golden and silver variegated forms. Holly is very wind-hardy, but resents severe exposure. Plant 1½–2 feet apart in September, April or early May. Trim during August or September. When overgrown or neglected hedges require to be cut back, do this in April. Height 5–20 feet. Worthwhile varieties are: *I. a. polycarpa laevigata*, a very free berrying form, 'Golden King' (a berrying form),

No plant is more striking for a low flowering hedge than Lavender.

'Silver Queen', a male form which, therefore, does not berry. One of the most vigorous is *I. a. altaclarensis*, a male form.

Japanese Quince see *Chaenomeles*

Larch see *Larix* (under *Conifers* below)

Laurel see *Prunus*

Lavandula (lavender) These evergreen shrubs, which produce sweetly scented flowers are suitable for low hedges. *L. spica*, English lavender, 3–4 feet high, *L. s.* 'Twickel Purple', rich purple 2–3 feet, *L. s. nana atropurpurea* (syn. 'Hidcote Variety'), deep purple-blue flowers, 1–1½ feet high, are among the best of several species and varieties. Plant 2–2½ feet apart for the tall varieties and 1 foot apart for the dwarf varieties, in March to early April.

Lavender see *Lavandula*

Lavender Cotton see *Santolina*

Ligustrum (privet) This is the most freely-planted of any evergreen. *Ligustrum ovalifolium* (oval-leaved privet) should be planted in single rows, 1 foot apart, or in double, staggered rows 15–18 inches apart, with 8 inches between the rows, from October to March. Trim at least twice a year, in May and September. Overgrown hedges can be cut hard back in April. Height 2–10 feet. The golden-leaved form is *L. o. aureum*, height 4–6 feet.

Lilac see *Syringa*

Ling see *Calluna*

Lonicera L. nitida (Chinese honeysuckle) is an evergreen, with small, box-like leaves. It is not as hardy as privet, but is neater and denser in habit. Plant 1 foot apart, from October to April. Cut back hedges, after planting, to within

9–12 inches of ground level. Trim two or three times during the summer. Height 4–4½ feet.

Mahonia M. aquifolium (Oregon grape) is a hardy evergreen of the berberis family, with holly-like leaves, dark, glossy green, turning in autumn to a purplish-crimson. It does well in shade and in draughty places, such as, between houses and is also useful for covering banks. Plant 1½–2 feet apart from October to April. Trim as and when required in April. Height 3–4 feet.

Maple see *Acer*

Metasequoia see *Conifers* below

Monterey Cypress see *Cupressus macrocarpa* (under *Conifers* below)

Myrobalan Plum see *Prunus cerasifera*

Norway Spruce see *Picea* (under *Conifers* below)

Olearia The daisy bushes are evergreen shrubs, wind-hardy and excellent in coastal areas. *O. haastii* has small, grey, box-like foliage. Plant 1–1½ feet apart in September or October or April or May. Height 3–4 feet. *O. macrodonta*, holly-like leaves, dark glossy grey-green above, with silvery white felt underneath. Space 2–2½ feet apart. Height 10–15 feet. Both have white daisy flowers.

Oregon Grape see *Mahonia*

Osmarea O. × burkwoodii is an evergreen with dark green, box-like foliage, and white, sweetly scented flowers. Plant 15–21 inches apart from October to March. Trim in April. Height 9–12 feet.

Phyllostachys see *Bamboo*

Pine see *Pinus* (under *Conifers* below)

Pittosporum P. tenuifolium, is an evergreen, for hedges or screens, especially useful for coastal areas. It grows best

in a rich loamy soil, but will grow in sand or chalk soils. Plant 2 feet apart in September or April. Trim in April. Height 10–20 feet.

Poplar see *Populus*

Populus (poplar) *P. alba* (white poplar) is a very hardy, deciduous screen tree, resistant to salt winds and suitable for wind-swept cliffs. Plant young trees 5–15 feet apart from November to March. Height 80–100 feet. *P. nigra italica* (Lombardy poplar) is a hardy deciduous tree with a fastigiate or pyramidal habit. Plant 5–10 feet apart from November to March. Height up to 100 feet.

Portugal Laurel see *Prunus lusitanica*

Privet see *Ligustrum*

Prunus This genus includes the ornamental plums such as the deciduous *P. cerasifera* (myrobalan or cherry plum) and its varieties, the common laurel, *P. laurocerasus,* and the Portugal laurel, *P. lusitanica. P. cerasifera* is often grown as a farm hedge, planted 1½–2 feet apart from October to March. Trim in July or August. When severe cutting back is needed do this in December. Height up to 20 feet. *P. c. pissardii* and *P. c. p. nigra* are two good purple and very dark purple-leaved shrubs or small trees. Plant as for *P. cerasifera*. Height up to 20 feet. *P. × cistena.* This fairly dwarf growing hybrid with *P. cerasifera pissardii* as one of its parents, has been known since 1910, but it was not put on the market as a hedge shrub before about 1960. It has purple foliage and large single, white flowers with purple centres. Plant 1 foot apart from October

to March. Trim immediately after flowering. Height 5–7 feet. *P. laurocerasus* (common or cherry laurel). Plants of this large-leaved evergreen should be set out at 1½–2 feet apart during September and October or March and April. Trim with secateurs in April or July. Height 5–20 feet. *P. lusitanica* (Portugal laurel). This is an evergreen with handsome rich, dark green, glossy leaves. Height 10–20 feet. Other remarks as for the common laurel.

Pyracantha (firethorn) An evergreen shrub, usually grown against a wall or fence for its berrying qualities. However, it makes a first-class evergreen hedge. There are several species. One of the best is *P. atalantioides,* very hardy, a vigorous grower, with crimson-scarlet berries. Plant 1½–2 feet apart in September, October or April. Trim in April, where possible with secateurs. Another good kind is the hybrid *P. × watereri*, with red berries, and a very twiggy habit. It will reach 8–10 feet, though a hedge 5–6 feet tall is preferable. It makes an excellent town hedge. Other remarks as for *P. atalantioides.*

Quercus (oak) *Q. ilex* (evergreen or holm oak). This is an evergreen, with dark green, holly-like but not prickly leaves. It excels on poor sandy soils, is very hardy and does well in coastal areas. It is good as a hedge or screen. Plant 1–2 feet apart for hedges, screens 10–15 feet apart, in September. April

1 **Potentilla fruticosa used as a hedge.**
2 **Rhododendrons give a permanent flowering hedge at Lynch, Allerford**

or early May. Trim in April. Height as a hedge 15 feet, as a screen 20 feet. *Q. robur* (common oak). A hardy, deciduous tree. Useful for planting in mixed screens. Plant 5–10 feet apart, from October to March. Height up to 30 feet (considerably taller in maturity).

Rhododendron R. ponticum (common rhododendron) makes a first-class evergreen flowering hedge. It is very wind hardy, good in coastal areas, and in London and industrial areas. It does well in acid, peaty soils, and equally well in clay soils, although it will not succeed in chalky or limey soils. In June its purplish-pink flowers are carried above dark glossy leaves. Plant 1½–2 feet apart or where larger plants are used 3–4 feet apart, during September and October or March and April. Trim in April or directly after the flowers have faded. Height 8–15 feet.

Ribes (currant) *R. aureum* (buffalo currant) is a hardy deciduous flowering shrub, fine for an informal hedge, its golden-yellow flowers spicily fragrant. Plant at 1–1½ feet apart from October to March. Trim after flowering. Height 5–8 feet. *R. sanguineum* (flowering currant). The variety 'Pulborough Scarlet' is the best: it makes a fine hedge. Plant at 1½ feet apart from October to March. Trim after flowering. Height 8–10 feet.

Rosa (rose) When considering the planting of a rose hedge one must first decide whether it is to be kept moderately formal or be allowed to grow naturally with the minimum of attention. In the latter instance the wealth of

The Rose is a good hedging plant. Rose 'Penelope' forms a flowering boundary.

flower or hips, where this applies, will of course, be much greater. The most popular roses are the *Rosa rugosa* types and the hybrid musk roses, which are especially fragrant. Many of the floribundas are vigorous growers and very free flowering. Many of the shrub roses have very fragrant flowers and shapely hips.

Preparation of the ground for all rose hedges should be thorough. It should be well-dug and enriched with well-rotted farmyard manure or well-rotted garden compost. When actually planting the hedge, cover the bare roots with a mixture of peat and bone-meal—2 good handfuls of the latter to 3 gallons of peat—which should be thoroughly moist before it is mixed and used. Having sprinkled the roots with a good covering, place some fine soil over this followed by coarser soil, afterwards firming it well with the feet. Plant at any time from November to March at the following distances apart.

Low and medium-sized rose bushes, 2–3 feet apart, more vigorous kinds 4–5 feet apart. Pruning of the species roses and the floribundas should be carried out in February and March. The following species and varieties are a

few of the many suitable for rose hedges.

'Great Maiden's Blush' (*Rosa alba* hybrid), a strong grower, warm blush-pink, fading to cream, fragrant, 6–8 feet. 'Commandant Beaurepaire' (a Bourbon rose). Strong grower, crimson, striped and splashed with pink and purple, flowering June to July, 5 feet. 'Zephirine Drouhin' (Bourbon). Thornless, cerise-pink, from early June onwards. Very fragrant, 8–12 feet. 'Kathleen Harrop' (Bourbon). Clear pink and crimson, thornless, 8–10 feet. 'Cecile Brunner' (China rose). Dainty salmon-coloured flowers, shaded rose. Tea-scented, 3–4 feet. 'Nathalie Nypels' (China rose). Double shell-pink, sweetly scented free flowering, 3–4 feet. 'Old Blush' (common monthly rose) (China rose). Silvery-pink, flushed crimson. June to October, 5 feet. *R. eglanteria* (syn. *R. rubiginosa*) sweet briar or eglantine), single pink flowers, 5–8 feet.

'Penzance Hybrids' (sweet briars). Vigorous, single to semi-double pink flowers, attractive hips, 5–8 feet. 'Georges Vibert' (*R. gallica* hybrid). Carmine-pink with white stripes, 2–3 feet. *R. officinalis (R. gallica maxima)*

(red damask, apothecary's rose, red rose of Lancaster) Bushy habit, bright crimson, sweetly scented, June, 3–4 feet. *R. gallica versicolor (Rosa mundi)* Bushy habit, light crimson, striped and splashed pink, 3–4 feet.

Hybrid musk roses 'Cornelia', double coppery-apricot, flushed pink, delicious scent, June to October, 6–9 feet. 'Felicia', silvery-pink, richly scented, June to September, 6–9 feet. 'Penelope', semi-double, large, shell-pink blooms, richly fragrant, June to September, 6–8 feet. 'Prosperity', bushy habit, semi-double, creamy-pink, richly fragrant, June to September, 6–8 feet. 'Vanity', single, rosy-carmine, sweetly scented, June to September, 6–8 feet. 'Wilhelm', vigorous habit, rich crimson, June to October, 5–6 feet. *R. rugosa*. Single pink flowers in July, with pleasing fragrance, large red hips and yellow and orange foliage, in autumn. Suckers freely, 5–7 feet. 'Roseraie de L'Hay' (*R. rugosa* hybrid). Crimson-purple, June to September, 5–9 feet. 'Sarah Van Fleet' (*R. rugosa* hybrid). Semi-double, light pink, fragrant, 5–6 feet. 'Schneezwerg' (*R. rugosa* hybrid). Compact, upright habit, with rosette blooms. May to October, 3–4 feet. 'Stanwell Perpetual' (*R. rugosa* hybrid). Double flesh-pink, fading to white.

June to October, 2–3 feet.

Floribunda roses Since the second World War the floribunda rose has become extremely popular. Many varieties are very vigorous and exceptionally free-flowering, which makes them ideal for hedges. One variety is better than a mixture, but where the latter is wanted the variety 'Masquerade' can be planted, as its flowers are a mixture of yellow, pink and red. Usually a single row is sufficient, planted at about 15 inches apart, from November to March. In their first year prune the bushes back to within 6–9 inches of soil level to encourage plenty of growth from the base. In subsequent years prune sufficiently to keep the hedge neat and the plants in good condition.

The following dozen is a good representative selection of floribundas including the 'Grandiflora', 'The Queen Elizabeth'. 'Chinatown', deep golden-yellow, edged cherry, scented, 4–5 feet. 'Dainty Maid', large single blooms, shaded warm rose and gold, 4–5 feet. 'Florence Mary Morse', large rich scarlet flowers which make a continuous show, 4–5 feet. 'Iceberg', the greenish-white blooms are produced right into the early winter, 4–5 feet. 'Korona', beautiful semi-double, flame-scarlet flowers of great size, 4–5 feet. 'Masquerade', this harlequin-like variety has buds which are at first yellow but the open flowers gradually change and deepen to shades of salmon pink and flame red. Height 3–4 feet. 'Orange Triumph', though the rich reddish-orange dusky coloured flowers of this 1937 variety are smaller than those of present-day floribundas, they are quite outstanding. Height 4–4½ feet. 'Rosemary Rose', attractive flat rosette, currant-red to crimson blooms quartered and sweetly scented, 3–4 feet. 'Shepherd's Delight', large clusters of semi-double orange-scarlet blooms touched with gold at the base. Slightly fragrant, 4–5 feet. 'Silberlachs', with its large clusters of warm pink flowers, replaces 'Else Poulsen'. Height 4–5 feet. 'The Queen Elizabeth', very upright, tall-growing variety with rose-pink flowers on very long stems. Height a good 5 feet or more.

Rose see *Rosa*

Rosemary see *Rosmarinus*

Rosmarinus (rosemary) This evergreen with aromatic leaves is useful where a small informal hedge is needed. *R. angustifolius* 'Corsican Blue', is an upright bushy shrub, with porcelain-blue flowers from April to June. Height 3½–4½ feet. *R. officinalis* (rosemary) has bluish-mauve flowers. Plant at 12–15 inches apart, from mid to late April; trim after flowering. Any hard cutting back needed should be done in April. Height 6–7 feet, though 3–4 feet is usually tall enough.

Rue see *Ruta*

Ruta (rue) Where an alternative to lavender is wanted, rue is ideal. *R. graveolens* 'Jackman's Blue', makes an attractive low evergreen hedge with glaucous-blue foliage. Plant 12–15 inches apart in March. Trim in April. Height 2–3 feet.

Santolina (lavender cotton or cotton lavender) *S. chamaecyparissus* is a hardy, dwarf evergreen, with silver-grey foliage and yellow button-like flowers. Plant 1 foot apart from September to April. Trim off old flower heads, when faded, with shears. To keep hedge neat clip in April. Height 1½–2 feet.

Senecio S. laxifolius is an evergreen, with silver-grey leathery leaves and yellow daisy-like flowers. It makes an informal

1 Rosemary is a plant that can be used for an informal hedge. It is fragrant and likes the sunshine.
2 Climbing Roses need the support of a fence or trellis to provide a screen.

hedge. It does well in coastal areas, also in industrial cities. Plant 15–18 inches apart in October or March. Trim in April. Height 3–4 feet.

Sorbus *S. intermedia* (Swedish whitebeam). This is a hardy, deciduous tree, useful for hedging or screening. It has dull white flowers followed by red fruit in autumn. Plant from October to March, as a hedge 2–3 feet apart, for screening purposes 8–9 feet or 16–20 feet apart. Trim in late winter or early spring. Height 20–40 feet.

Spiraea These are hardy deciduous flowering shrubs. Plant 1–2 feet apart from October to March. Trim spring-flowering kinds after blooms have faded, summer and autumn flowering ones in February or March, at the same time hard pruning can be carried out on either group. *S. arguta* has white flowers in April and early May. Plant 1½–2 feet apart. Height 4–5 feet. *S.*

japonica 'Anthony Waterer' has deep carmine flowers from July to September. Plant 1½ feet apart. Height 3–4 feet. *S. menziesii triumphans* has purple-rose bottle-brush like blooms from June to end of September. Plant 2–3 feet apart. Trim in winter or spring. Height 4–6 feet. *S. thunbergii* has bright green foliage, and sprays of white flowers from mid-March to mid-April. Plant 1½–2 feet apart. Height 4–5 feet.

Syringa (lilac) *S. vulgaris* (the common lilac) is a deciduous shrub usually planted for its colourful, scented flowers. It does, however, make a very useful spring and summer hedge, its foliage changing from green to yellow in the autumn. If trimmed formally it will not flower, but if left to grow informally it will. Plant 2½–3 feet apart, October to

Tamarix is a first class plant for a hedge or screen in a seaside garden.

March. Trim after flowering or in early April. Height 5–10 feet. Other species which can also be planted as hedges are: *S. chinensis* (Rouen lilac), with graceful foliage and lilac-coloured, fragrant flowers. Height 6–10 feet. *S. c. rubra*, purplish-red, fragrant flowers. Height 9–12 feet. *S. persica*, lilac-coloured, scented flowers. Height 4–6 feet. *S. p. alba,* white, scented flowers. Height 4–6 feet. All bloom in May.

Tamarisk see *Tamarix*

Tamarix (tamarisk) These are deciduous shrubs, much used in coastal areas, as they stand up to salt spray. They will grow in poor sandy soil and also in limey soils. All have attractive feathery foliage and long slender spikes of white or pinkish flowers. Plant 1½ feet apart from October to March. Trim in late February or March. Species available are *T. anglica*, white-tinged, pink flowers, in late summer, and early autumn. Height up to 10 feet. *T. gallica* (common tamarisk), pink flowers in late summer and early autumn. Height up to 10 feet. *T. pentandra*, rosy-pink flowers in late July and August, height 12–18 feet. *T. tetrandra,* reddish-pink flowers in May, produced on the previous year's growth. Trim after flowering. Height 10–15 feet.

Viburnum *V. lantana* (wayfaring tree) is a deciduous shrub with white flowers in May and June, followed by red fruit in late summer and autumn which eventually turn black; the foliage often colours well in autumn. Plant 2–3 feet apart from October to March. Trim in the winter. It does well on chalky soils. Height up to 8 feet, sometimes more. *V. opulus* (guelder rose) is a deciduous shrub with flat bract-like white flowers in early June, followed by bright red berries and colourful foliage in autumn. Plant 2–3 feet apart from October to March. Trim in winter. Height 8–10 feet. *V. tinus* (laurustinus) is a most popular evergreen hedging shrub, especially in south coast areas. It thrives equally well on chalk or non-chalk soils. Its white flowers with pink stamens are produced throughout the winter and often throughout the spring. Plant 1½ feet apart in early autumn or even in spring. Trim in April. Height 6–10 feet.

Weigela *W. florida variegata*, makes an attractive deciduous hedge with silver variegated foliage and strawberry-ice-pink flowers in May and June. Height 6–8 feet. *W. × hybrida* and its many varieties are all equally suitable. Plant 2–3 feet apart from October to March. Trim all species and varieties, after flowering. Height 6–9 feet.

Whitebeam, Swedish see *Sorbus intermedia*

Conifers All the conifers recommended are evergreen except *Larix* (larch) and *Metasequoia* which are deciduous. Conifers, like other evergreens, have the advantage that they provide a permanent screen for twelve months of the year. Many also have attractive colour forms which include varying shades of green, gold and silver through the glaucous blues. The genus with the greatest variety of forms is *Chamaecyparis*, especially *C. lawsoniana*, Lawson's cypress. The two most recent conifers planted as hedges are × *Cupressocyparis leylandii* and *Metasequoia glyptostroboides*.

Chamaecyparis C. lawsoniana (Lawson's cypress). The foliage of this conifer ranges through the palest to the darkest greens to glaucous green and blue. Plant at 1½–2 feet apart in late September to October, or March to April. Trim in May or June. When severe pruning is necessary this is done in April. Height 10–18 feet. *C. l. allumii* has glaucous blue foliage. Height 10–12 feet. *C. l. erecta* 'Jackman's Variety' has green foliage and is conical in habit. Height 5–8 feet. *C. l. fletcheri* has bluish-grey, feathery foliage. Height 4–10 feet. *C. l.* 'Green Hedger' is a very rich green. Height 5–15 feet. *C. l. lutea* has golden foliage. Height 5–8 feet. *C. l. pisifera plumosa aurea* (syn. *Retinospora pisifera plumosa aurea*) has soft, golden feathery foliage. Height 5–12 feet. *C. l.* 'Triomphe de Boskoop', has glaucous blue foliage.

Cryptomeria C. japonica elegans has feathery juvenile foliage, which is permanently retained; it is a glaucous green in summer, changing from rich bronze to rosy red in autumn and winter. Plant 1½ feet apart in September or October, or March or April. Trim in April and again in August. Height 5–6 feet.

Cupressocyparis × *C. leylandii*. This bigeneric hybrid has, since the end of the Second World War, become very popular, and has in fact superseded *Cupressus macrocarpa* which is one of its parents, the other being *Chamaecyparis nootkatensis*. This tree has the speed of growth of *C. macrocarpa* with the hardiness of *C. nootkatensis*, which is a native of western North America from Alaska or Oregon. It makes a fine hedge or first-rate screen tree. Plant 1½–2 feet apart, in September or October or March or April. Trim in July and August. Height for hedges 5–8 feet, for screens 50–60 feet.

Cupressus C. macrocarpa (Monterey cypress) is a fast growing conifer which is a bright green when young, later turning darker and less bright. It was introduced in 1838 and for 100 years was, apart from *Thuja occidentalis*, *T. plicata* and *Chamaecyparis lawsoniana*, the most popular conifer planted for hedges, particularly in coastal areas in the south. However, in recent years its popularity has waned because of its tender habit and unreliability in frost, coupled with its dislike of regular clipping. Ten to fifteen years is a good average life span for a macrocarpa

The various forms of Chamaecyparis are useful for an evergreen screen. Here a golden form adds decorative interest.

hedge. Plant 1½–2 feet apart in late March or April. Trim during the middle of April. Height 8–15 feet.

Larix (larch) *L. decidua* (syn. *L. europaea*) (common larch) is a deciduous conifer with fresh green foliage. It is useful as a screen tree in a mixed planting. It thrives best on chalk or sandy soils. Plant 4 feet apart, eventually thinning the trees to 8 feet. A double row makes an effective windbreak. Plant from October to March. Height up to 50 feet.

Metasequoia M. glyptostroboides (the dawn cypress) is an ancient, deciduous conifer introduced to this country in 1948. Its habit of growth and foliage is remarkably like that of *Taxodium distichum*, swamp cypress. The dawn cypress makes an upright tree with soft-green, feathery foliage in spring which changes to a rich pinky-brown in autumn. It makes a beautiful hedge or an excellent screen tree. Plant 2 feet apart in September or October or March or April. Trim three or four times a year between spring and late summer. Height for hedges could be anything from 5–10 feet. The eventual height for screening purposes is at present unknown, but is likely to be at least 50–60 feet.

Picea (spruce) *P. abies* (common or Norway spruce) is a hardy conifer with deep glossy green needles or leaves, the tree usually grown as the Christmas tree. It is a useful conifer to plant among deciduous trees. Plant 4–8 feet apart in September or October, or March or April. Height up to 100 feet.

Pinus (pine) *P. laricio* (Corsican pine) is a very hardy tree, with dark green foliage. It is a good wind resister, but

1 At Waddesdon Manor, Bucks. Yew hedges emphasise the terrace and stairway. 2 At Ammerdown Park, Somerset, the tall Yew hedges are clipped formally.

does not transplant well, and it is best to plant 1 foot high specimens. Plant 3 feet apart in September or April, thinning them later. Height 80–100 feet. *P. l. nigricans* (Austrian pine) has dark green foliage, is very wind-hardy, and thrives on chalky or poor soils. Plant at 1 foot high, 3 feet apart in September or April, thinning later. Height 80–100 feet. *P. radiata* (syn. *P. insignis*) (Monterey pine) has beautiful grassy-green foliage, is very fast growing, does best in maritime area and is wind-hardy. It prefers deep, rich well-drained soils. Plant 4–5 feet apart in September or April. Height 80–100 feet. *P. sylvestris* (Scots pine) is one of the most beautiful and stately conifers when mature. It

has a rugged reddish-brown trunk, grey-green needles and small brown cones. Plant at 3 feet apart in September or April, thinning as and when needed. Height 80–100 feet.

Taxus T. baccata (common yew). This is without a doubt the oldest and most revered conifer which we plant for hedging purposes. It makes a wonderful wall-like hedge, is excellent for topiary and can be grown in any soil, lime, clay or sand; and for full measure it flourishes in coastal areas, and is equally accommodating in industrial areas. Yew is not slow growing as it is so often thought to be and a well established hedge will make as much as 1–1½ feet of growth a year. However, you have to be patient with a yew hedge; young bushes transplant better than older ones and they usually make quicker growth. Yews must have good drainage, they also require ample humus in the soil. Before planting, bastard trench or double dig the ground. When preparing the soil, add rotted farmyard manure, or good garden compost, plus bonemeal at the rate of 6 oz per square yard. Bushes should be 1–3 feet high. Plant them 1–2 feet apart, in September or early October or late March or April. Trim in August or September. When hard pruning is needed do this in April. Height for hedging 10–15 feet; for screens up to 20–30 feet.

Thuja T. occidentalis (American arborvitae) is a useful, pleasantly scented conifer, greenish leaved during the summer, turning a brownish-green colour in autumn and winter. Plant at 1½–2 feet apart, in late September or October or March or April. Trim in late summer. Young hedges need trimming in early life, though the top is best left until it reaches the required height. Height for hedging 5–12 feet, as a screen 30–40 feet. *T. plicata* (giant thuja). For a time between the two world wars this thuja was not much planted because of a fungus disease to which it was prone, but fortunately this trouble became less evident in the 1960s. Its dark, glossy green foliage makes it a most handsome hedge. Plant 1½–2 feet apart in late September or October or March or April. Trim in late summer. Height as a hedge 5–12 feet, for a screen 50–60 feet. *T. p. zebrina,* a golden variegated form requires the same treatment as *T. plicata.* Height for hedging 6–12 feet, screens 30–40 feet.

As we have seen, an attractive hedge or screen can be made from roses, and the wild dog rose of our countryside, twined through the heterogeneous foliage of the wild or farm hedge, suggests that this is natural. The great majority of roses, however, are grown in our gardens as shrubs rather than as hedges. No other plant gives such colour and beauty for such a long period, with so little trouble.

The rose, often styled the 'queen of

Rosa banksiae lutea is a climbing Rose best grown on a warm wall.

flowers' is the most long-esteemed genus of flowering shrubs. The cultivars run into many thousands. For convenience, the following three groups may be distinguished: wild species, old garden roses and modern roses.

Wild species group These include their varieties and interspecific hybrids. The wild species bear single flowers in nature, although double-flowered sports are known for at least a third of the species and are best grouped here. The flowering season is short (June to July mainly) but followed by plentiful, often showy hips in autumn. Several are worth growing as specimen shrubs (e.g., *R. multibracteata* and *R. hugonis*), as climbers (e.g., *R. banksiae*), as hedges (e.g., *R. rubiginosa*), as carpeters (e.g., *R. luciae wichuraiana*).

Old garden roses group These are shrubs and some early climbers, distinguished by the same short flowering season as for species, but with larger, mostly double flowers. They are typified by the gallicas with many-petalled, saucer-shaped flowers in pink, mauve or maroon or variously mottled. Like the species they suit the shrub garden, wild garden and the backs of borders.

Modern roses group These, for the most part, have a long flowering season or marked recurrence of flowering in the autumn. They are typified by the few-petalled conical bud of the hybrid tea, with clear unfading colours. They are *par excellence* the group for cut and exhibition blooms. It is rarely desirable to mix roses of the modern roses group in the same bed as roses of the wild species or old garden roses groups because of the clash of colours and different habit and pruning requirements.

Many of the old-fashioned roses make such large bushes that they cannot be accommodated in the small gardens of today. Many of them, again, have a relatively brief flower period compared with modern varieties, and for this reason the lists and descriptions that follow are concentrated on the popular modern types which can be bought so easily and so inexpensively from garden stores, garden centres and nurseries everywhere.

Roses and their cultivation

Almost no garden subject has been written about at greater length, or with more enthusiasm, than roses and their cultivation. Nevertheless, there is plenty that can be said on the matter, and the fact that roses grow easily in most parts of Britain only makes the keen gardener

Hybrid Tea Roses are the most popular of all types of rose and new varieties are being added every year.
1 Hybrid Tea 'Super Star'.
2 Hybrid Tea 'Peace'.

more than ever determined to think of everything in order to cultivate the flower to its greatest perfection.

Certainly roses will repay your attention. Whether they are grown on a fairly large scale, as, for example in the Italian rose garden at Trentham, Staffordshire, or in smaller groups in the home garden, roses provide tremendous pleasure at a reasonably small cost and minimal effort.

In an article which concentrates on the technical side of the subject it would be wrong to forget entirely the historical and romantic associations of the flower. Chaucer's *Romaunt of the Rose*, with its associations of courtly love, and the Scene in the Temple Garden, London, in Act II of Shakespeare's King Henry VI, Part 1, when the rival factions in the 'Wars of the Roses' plucked the red or the white rose,

are just two examples of how the rose from the earliest times has come to symbolise the deepest feelings of countless men and women.

Modern roses fall mainly into the following groups: hybrid tea, floribunda, shrub, climbing and rambling, polyantha pompon and miniature.

Hybrid tea These include the large flowered, shapely bedding and exhibition roses, many with a strong fragrance. The group merges the few remaining hybrid perpetuals in general cultivation and what used to be known as 'Pernetianas', representing all the original pure yellow, orange, flame and bicolor varieties. The first hybrid tea varieties were obtained crossing the hybrid perpetuals with the tea-scented roses.

Floribunda These include all the original hybrid polyanthas evolved by the rose breeder Svend Poulson of Denmark. He

There are hundreds of Hybrid Tea Roses from which to make a selection including dwarf and climbers. A few of the best are recommended on this page. It is now possible to find Hybrid Teas in almost any colour other than a true blue, or a green. All the following are Hybrid Tea varieties:

3 'McGredy's Yellow'.
4 'Miss Ireland'.
5 'Silver Lining'.
6 'Ena Harkness'.
7 'Margaret'.
8 'Piccadilly'.
9 'Grand mère Jenny'.
10 'Lady Seton'.

Fifty first-class hybrid tea roses

Name	Habit of growth	Colour	Fragrance	Name	Habit of growth	Colour	Fragrance
Anne Watkins*	T/U	Apricot, shading to cream	S	Mischief*	T/B	Rich coral-salmon	S
Beauté	M	Light orange and apricot	S	Miss Ireland*	M	Orange-salmon, reverse peach	S
Belle Blonde	M/B	Deep tawny gold	M	Mme L. Laperrière	D	Dark crimson	M
Blue Moon	M	Lavender-mauve	R	Mojave*	T/U	Burnt orange and flame	S
Buccaneer*	T/U	Rich golden-yellow	S	Montezuma	T/B	Rich reddish-salmon	S
Caramba*	M/U	Crimson, with silver reverse	S	My Choice	M	Pale carmine-pink, reverse buff-yellow	R
Chrysler Imperial	M/U	Dark velvety crimson	R	Peace*	T/B	Light yellow, edged pink	S
Diorama*	M/B	Apricot yellow, flushed pink	M	Perfecta	T/U	Cream, shaded rosy red	S
Doreen*	M/B	Chrome-yellow, shaded orange	M	Piccadilly*	M/B	Scarlet, reverse yellow	S
Dorothy Peach*	M	Golden-yellow, shaded peach	S	Pink Favourite*	T/B	Deep rose-pink	S
Eden Rose*	T	Rose-madder, paler reverse	R	Prima Ballerina*	T/U	Deep carmine-rose	R
Ena Harkness*	M/B	Velvety scarlet-crimson	R	Rose Gaujard*	T/B	White, shaded carmine-red	S
Ernest H. Morse*	M/U	Rich turkey-red	R	Sarah Arnot	T	Deep rosy-pink	S
Fragrant Cloud*	M/B	Scarlet changing crimson-lake	R	Signora*	T	Flame, pink and orange shades	M
Gail Borden*	T/B	Peach and salmon, shaded gold	S	Silver Lining	M/U	Silvery rose, paler reverse	M
Gold Crown	T/U	Deep gold, shaded red	M	Spek's Yellow*	T/U	Rich golden-yellow	S
Grand'mère Jenny*	T/U	Light yellow and peach-pink	S	Stella	M/B	Carmine-pink, shading to white	S
Grandpa Dickson*	T/U	Lemon yellow, paling to cream	S	Sterling Silver	M/U	Lavender-mauve, shaded silver	R
Helen Traubel*	T	Pink and apricot blend	M	Summer Sunshine	T	Intense golden-yellow	S
Josephine Bruce	M/S	Dark velvety crimson	R	Super Star*	T	Light pure vermilion	M
Lady Belper	M	Light orange	M	Sutter's Gold*	T	Orange-yellow, shaded pink and red	R
La Jolla	M	Pink, cream and gold blend	S	Tzigane	M	Scarlet, reverse chrome-yellow	M
Lucy Cramphorn*	T/B	Geranium-red	S	Virgo	T/U	White, tinted pale pink	S
Margaret*	M/B	China-pink, paler reverse	M	Wendy Cussons*	M/B	Rich cerise	R
McGredy's Yellow*	M/U	Light yellow without shading	S	Westminster	T	Cherry-red, reverse gold	M

Key *Habit of growth* T=tall U=upright M=medium B=branching D=dwarf S=spreading
Fragrance S=slight M=moderate R=rich *Exceptionally good in autumn

1 'Blue Moon'.
2 'Helen Traubel'.
3 'Ernest Morse'.

Fifty first-class floribunda roses

Name	Habit of growth	Colour
Allgold	D	Rich golden-yellow
Anna Wheatcroft	M	Light vermilion
Arabian Nights	T	Deep salmon-red
Arthur Bell	T/U	Deep golden yellow, paling to cream
Chanelle	M	Peach and buff
Circus	M	Yellow, pink and red
Copper Delight	D	Bronze-yellow
Daily Sketch	T	Pink and cream
Dearest	T	Coral-rose
Dorothy Wheatcroft	T	Bright orange-scarlet
Elizabeth of Glamis	M	Light salmon
Elysium	T	Pale rose, shaded salmon
Evelyn Fison	M	Bright scarlet
Europeana	M	Deep blood-red to crimson
Faust	T	Yellow shaded pink
Fervid	T	Bright poppy red
Frensham	T	Scarlet-crimson
Golden Slippers	D	Orange and yellow shades
Golden Treasure	M/B	Deep yellow, non-fading
Goldgleam	M/B	Canary yellow, unfading
Gold Marie	T/S	Deep tawny gold, tinged red
Highlight	T	Orange-scarlet
Iceberg	T	White flushed pink
Joyfulness	M	Apricot shaded pink
Korona	T/U	Orange-scarlet, fading deep salmon
Lilac Charm	D/B	Silvery lilac, single flower
Lilli Marlene	M	Scarlet-crimson
Lucky Charm	M	Yellow, pink and red
Manx Queen	M	Orange-yellow shaded pink
Masquerade	M	Yellow, changing to pink and red
Meteor	D	Orange-scarlet
Orangeade	M	Orange-vermilion
Orange Sensation	M	Vermilion-scarlet
Paddy McGredy	D/B	Deep carmine-pink
Paprika	M	Bright turkey-red
Pernille Poulsen	D/B	Salmon-pink, fading lighter
Pink Parfait	M	Pastel shades of pink and cream
Queen Elizabeth	T/U	Rose-pink
Red Dandy	M	Scarlet-crimson, large flowers
Red Favourite	D	Dark crimson
Rumba	M	Orange-yellow, edged scarlet
Ruth Leuwerik	D	Bright scarlet shaded crimson
Scented Air	T/B	Rich salmon-pink
Shepherd's Delight	T/U	Scarlet, flame and orange
Sweet Repose	T	Soft pink shaded apricot
Tambourine	T/U	Cherry-red, reverse orange-yellow
Toni Lander	M/U	Coppery salmon-red
Vera Dalton	M	Medium rose-pink
Violet Carson	M	Peach-pink, reverse silvery pink
Woburn Abbey	T	Tangerine-orange and yellow
Zambra	D	Rich orange and yellow

Key T = tall　M = medium　D = dwarf　S = spreading
U = upright　B = exceptionally branching

A wide selection of Floribunda Roses is available for garden decoration:
1 'Iceberg'.
2 'Queen Elizabeth'.

crossed poly-pompons with hybrid teas, and all the many-flowered roses (other than the poly-pompons), the climbing and rambling groups and the Pemberton, so-called 'hybrid musks'. The term 'hybrid polyantha' was discontinued soon after the Second World War, because varieties were being added to the group each year with little or no true polyantha 'blood', resulting from crossing hybrid teas with various groups of shrub roses.
Shrub This group covers a very wide range of modern hybrids of species and also includes all the old types of garden roses, often referred to as 'old-fashioned' roses.
Climbing and rambling Practically all rambling and climbing roses derive from the Synstylae section of the genus. They include hybrid tea climbing sports.
Polyantha pompon These have largely been superseded by modern floribundas and the miniatures. They are compact-growing, cluster-flowered bedding roses, with small rosette type flowers similar in appearance to those of the old wichuraiana ramblers.
Miniature These are tiny replicas of the hybrid teas and floribundas, with flowers, foliage and growth scaled down in

'Telstar'.

proportion. They are mainly hybrids from *R. chinensis minima* and may never exceed 6–12 inches in height.

Selecting and ordering It is important to order your roses early in the season, that is between June and August, when most of the rose shows are held. During this period the roses may be seen in flower at the nurseries and by ordering promptly you can be sure of the most popular varieties being available.

It is advisable to order from a rose specialist, and from one who buds his own plants, rather than from a man who is not a producer. This is because the grower selling under his own name has a reputation to maintain, and no well-known rose specialist can afford to sell plants which do not give satisfaction. When you visit the nursery, or display garden adjoining it, watch for the habit of growth, disease and weather resistance and freedom of flowering of any of the species provisionally selected.

There is a great deal of variation in the quality of maiden rose plants supplied from various sources, and cheap offers are often the dearest in the long run, as the quality is normally very inferior. Bearing in mind that a healthy rose, when once properly planted, may last from 12 to 20 years or more, with reasonable treatment, it is false economy to attempt to save a few shillings on the initial cost when this may mean the difference between success and failure. It is essential to obtain plants from a reliable source. This is because of the need for them to be hardy and well-ripened, true to name, budded on a suitable rootstock which will transplant readily and not sucker freely and free from disease spores.

Bare root roses are sometimes still on offer in overheated departmental stores, but nowadays these are normally offered packed in individual polythene bags. The trouble with these roses is that they are frequently subjected to this overheated atmosphere for considerable periods, with consequent dehydration

showing in bone-dry roots and shrivelled stems. A rose purchased in this condition is unlikely to flourish unless measures are taken to plump up the wood again by burying the entire plant for about ten days in moist soil, before planting it in its permanent quarters. Another disadvantage of these pre-packaged roses is that each package acts as a miniature greenhouse, and the stems are forced into tender premature growth while they are awaiting sale. This tender growth receives a severe check when the plants are taken out of their packages and exposed to the hazards of the open garden.

Container-grown roses are offered at many nurseries and garden centres. These enable the planting season to be extended throughout the year, as no root disturbance should occur in planting from containers into the permanent beds. They may even be planted when in full bloom.

Although it is unwise to succumb to cheap offers in end-of-season sales, nearly all rose specialist firms offer collections, their selection of varieties, at an all-in price lower than the aggregate cost of ordering the same varieties individually. For the beginner who is not fussy about varieties he starts with, provided that they are popular, this is as good a way as any of placing a first order, as the quality of the plants should be equal to the nurseryman's normal standard.

Soil Ordinary well-drained soil which has grown good crops of vegetables will suit most roses. Ideally a medium heavy loam, slightly acid (pH 5.5 to 6.5) is best. The site should be open and away from large trees and buildings, but not in a draughty position between two houses. On poor soils plenty of old chopped turf, compost, hay and straw and vegetable waste should be added to the subsoil when preparing the beds by double digging, together with any animal manure available. The top spit will be improved by adding granulated peat, compost and bonemeal (at the rate of 4 ounces per square yard) and hoof and horn meal (at 2 ounces per square yard). These should be thoroughly mixed with the soil and not left on the surface or in layers. On heavy land the beds should be raised a few inches above the general level, but sunk slightly on sandy soil. Perfect drainage is vitally important.

Planning and design The planning of a rose garden is essentially a matter of personal choice depending on individual requirements. The first question to settle is whether the layout is large enough to take roses grown in beds and borders on their own, or whether the roses must fit in with other plants in mixed borders. In a formal rose garden there are separate beds for individual varieties, whether of hybrid tea or

'Ambrosia'.

floribunda type. These beds are cut in lawns with the possible inclusion of several standard or half standard roses of the same variety to give added height.

Although well-kept turf is the best setting for roses it involves a great deal of labour to maintain in first-class condition and it is always advisable to have at least one dry path crossing the rose garden, so that barrowing can be done in wet weather without cutting up the turf. Crazy paving or formal stone paving slabs are best for this dry path, with cement run between the crazy paving stones to provide a firm surface and to reduce the labour of weeding. Normally rose beds about 5 feet wide are to be preferred to rose borders against a wall or fence, on the grounds of accessibility for weeding, pruning and cultivation generally. A bed of this width will accommodate three rows of plants, 18 inches between the rows with 1 foot at each side between the outside rows and the edge. This will be sufficient to avoid an overhang with nearly all varieties, which would otherwise interfere with mowing and trimming the edges, if the setting is grass.

'Irish Mist'.

The shape of the rose beds is a matter for personal taste, but a simple design is normally best, and it involves less labour for maintenance. It should always be borne in mind that numerous small beds cut in a lawn, apart from looking fussy, require the edges trimming regularly and also slow down the operation of mowing the lawn.

Few amateurs can afford the space to have beds confined to one variety, but mixed beds should be selected carefully, and the varieties chosen for either tasteful colour blending or for similar habit of growth. Alternatively, the centre of the bed should be planted with a variety of taller growth and the perimeter with one of more compact habit. It is far better to plant six or more of the same variety in a group than to dot them about in ones and twos, and this holds good whether beds or borders are being planted.

In a rose border or a mixed border featuring roses and other plants, bold groups are essential for maximum display. In a deep rose border, the grading of groups of varieties according to height will be desirable, with the tallest at the back, although monotony may be avoided by breaking up the gradings with an occasional group of taller varieties running towards the front, or a single pillar or tripod with recurrent-flowering climbing roses about the middle.

Colour grouping with roses is again a matter of personal taste. Some people delight in the extreme contrast between a pure scarlet and a deep golden yellow, whereas others might find this garish, and prefer colour harmonies in blends of soft pink, apricot and orange shades. Some may prefer to group the same, or similar, colours together. The object of colour blending, of course, is to bring out the best in each colour by careful association of adjacent colours. Thus, white and orange-scarlet next to each other will emphasise, by contrast, the purity of the white and the brilliance of the orange-scarlet. On the other hand, orange-scarlet next to deep carmine pink would be an unhappy combination, as the blue in the carmine pink would look crude and harsh by contrast with the orange-scarlet.

As a general guide shades of yellow will associate well with shades of red. Orange, flame and apricot contrast well with dark crimson. Deep pink, especially carmine pink and cerise, is safest with cream, primrose yellow or white, and the same is true of lilac, lavender and mauve. These shades in roses are often dull in the garden and may need enlivening with bright yellow close by. Scarlet, orange-scarlet, crimson, deep pink and cerise are better separated from each other by using buffer groups of the soft pastel shades of cream, flesh, amber and off-white.

'Sweet Repose'.

The question of whether to use other plants for carpeting rose beds often arises, bearing in mind that the roses do not normally provide much colour until June. Violas as ground cover or border plants add colour in the spring. Low growing plants, such as aubrieta, arabis and the 'mossy' saxifrages may also be used for edgings, but they will need shearing back after flowering. There is no reason either why shallow-rooted annuals should not be used, such as eschscholtzias, love-in-a-mist and night-scented stocks.

Slow growing conifers may also be used for effect. These have the advantage of being evergreens, and will improve the appearance of the rose garden,

although the rank growers should be avoided. The Irish juniper, *Juniperus communis hibernica*, is excellent and takes up little space with its narrow, erect growth. The same is true of *Chamaecyparis lawsoniana columnaris glauca* in blue-grey, and the Irish yews, *Taxus baccata fastigiata*, and the golden *aurea*. Two very splendid slow-growing forms are *Chamaecyparis lawsoniana ellwoodii* and *fletcherii*. Both of these will remain below or about 5 feet in height for many years. Clematis may also be planted either by themselves or with recurrent flowering pillar roses, and will often be outstanding, introducing colours not found among roses. *Clematis jackmanii* in rich violet-purple will make a splendid pillar when planted with roses 'New Dawn' or 'Aloha'.

Planting This may be done safely from late October to the end of March whenever the soil is friable and free from frost. Autumn planting usually gives the best results, provided the soil is not too wet for planting firmly; otherwise it will be better to wait for suitable conditions. On receipt of the bushes they should be heeled in temporarily in a trench, throwing plenty of soil over the roots and treading firmly. When the soil in the bed is friable, a large bucket of moist granulated peat, into which a couple of handfuls of meat and bonemeal have been mixed, should be prepared. The position of each bush in the bed is marked with a stick. Distance apart will depend on the vigour

'Zambra'.

'Evelyn Fison'.

and habit of the variety, but on an average soil about 18 inches each way will be about right for most. Exceptionally vigorous kinds, such as 'Peace', which need light pruning, may be better at least 2 feet apart. The roots should be soaked for a couple of hours before planting. A shallow hole is taken out wide enough to take roots when fully spread. The plant should be inspected carefully for suckers emerging from the root system, and any found should be pulled off. Damaged and broken roots must be trimmed and unripe or damaged shoots removed, also all leaves and flower buds. The prepared plant is then tested in the hole for correct depth; the union of the stock and scion should be just covered with soil. A few handfuls of the peat mixture are thrown over and between the roots and the hole half filled with fine soil and trodden firmly before filling up to the correct level. Standard roses are staked before covering the roots to avoid possible injury. It is beneficial to mulch new beds with 2 inches of granulated peat, to conserve moisture.

Pruning All dead or decadent wood should be cut out as soon as it is noticed at any time. Full-scale pruning should be done when the bushes are dormant, or nearly so. This may be done at any time from January to mid-March, depending on the weather and the area. In the first spring after planting all groups, except climbing sports of hybrid tea roses, should have weak or twiggy shoots removed entirely, together with any sappy growth. The remainder should be cut back just above a dormant shoot bud pointing away from the centre of the plant and not more than 6 inches from the base. Spring planted roses may be pruned in the hand just before planting. Climbing sports of hybrid teas should just be tipped and the main shoots bent over by securing the ends to canes or wires, to force the lower buds into growth. On light hungry soils it may be advisable not to prune any groups the first year, but to encourage as much new growth as possible by mulching and watering.

Subsequent years Pruning of hybrid teas may be hard, moderate or light, according to circumstances. Light pruning is generally preferable on poor sandy soils which do not encourage a lot of new wood. This means cutting back new shoots formed in the previous season to about two-thirds of their length and removing all weak or twiggy growth. On average soils moderate pruning may be done, involving cutting back all new wood about half way and removing entirely the weak and twiggy shoots. Hard pruning is seldom necessary for modern varieties, but some will respond to it on a good soil with ample feeding. It requires the cutting out of all but two or three of the main growths and reducing these to just above a dormant bud about 6 inches from the base.

Floribundas require different treatment. The object is to ensure as continuous a display of colour during the season as possible. This requires the application of a differential pruning system, based on the age of the wood. Growth produced from the base in the previous season should merely be shortened to the first convenient bud below the old flower truss. The laterals on two-year-old wood should be cut back half way and any three-year-old wood cut hard back to about three eyes from the base. As with all groups, all dead, decadent, unripe and twiggy wood should be removed entirely.

Shrub roses and the old garden roses in general do not require much pruning. Apart from the cutting out of dead and exhausted wood and cutting back a main growth near the base occasionally to encourage new basal growth, pruning is mainly confined to remedying overcrowding and ensuring a shapely outline.

The treatment of climbers varies with the group to which they belong. Generally, the more recurrent flowering the variety, the less rampant is its growth and the less the pruning required.

'Daily Sketch'.

The once-flowering wichuraiana ramblers, which renew themselves with new canes from the base each season after flowering, should have all old flowering wood cut out and the new canes tied in to take its place. Climbing sports of hybrid teas and other climbing hybrid teas require little pruning, but should be trained fanwise or horizontally to force as many dormant eyes into growth as possible. Flowers are borne either on laterals or sub-laterals. Recurrent flowering pillar roses, such as 'Aloha', 'Coral Dawn' and 'Parade', require only the removal of dead or exhausted wood and any which is weak or twiggy, plus sufficient thinning out of the remaining wood to avoid overcrowding.

General cultivation Suckers must be removed before they grow large. They may come from any point below the inserted bud and with standards they may appear either on the standard stem below the head or anywhere on the root system. The roots of roses should not be disturbed any more than is essential to the removal of weeds and suckers.

Where light or moderate pruning is practised, summer thinning or de-shooting may be necessary, and this will be routine procedure for the keen exhibitor. All side shoots appearing before the terminal buds have opened should be pinched out as soon as they are large enough to handle. While watering is not a practical proposition on a large scale, newly planted roses may need the roots soaking thoroughly at weekly intervals during hot weather. Roses planted in dry positions, against walls or close-boarded fences, will also require regular watering in the summer.

Removal of spent flowers is essential if a later crop is to be produced and seed pods should never be allowed to develop. Dead-heading should be a routine operation throughout the season.

'Arthur Bell'.

In the first summer after planting merely the flower and foot of the stalk, without any leaves, should be removed, but in subsequent years the growth from the pruning point may be reduced to half way, to ensure a fine second display. Disbudding will also be necessary for the keen exhibitor and those who insist on high quality blooms. Not more than three buds are left on hybrid tea stems for garden display or a single bud for exhibition. In the autumn any long growths should be shortened to minimise possible gale damage.

Feeding Before embarking on a feeding programme you should find out whether your soil is naturally acid or alkaline. There are a number of soil-testing kits available. Lime, if required, is best applied in the form of ground chalk (calcium carbonate) during the early winter months, at 3 or 4 ounces per square yard, sprinkled evenly over the surface of the beds and left for the winter rains to wash it down. By the time the spring mulch is due, the lime should have done its work. As roses prefer a slightly acid soil, it may be necessary to apply lime every year, though never on chalky soil.

During February and March it is beneficial to apply a dressing of meat and bonemeal at 4 ounces per square yard, pricking it just below the surface. If this proves difficult to obtain in small quantities sterilised bonemeal may be used instead. About the middle of April

A bold and satisfactory effect is always obtained from Roses when varieties are planted in groups.

a complete rose fertiliser can be applied to established beds, according to the makers' instructions. There are many of these available, or a useful compound fertiliser may be made up quite cheaply from 16 parts of superphosphate of lime, 10 parts of sulphate of potash, 5 parts of sulphate of ammonia, 2 parts of sulphate of magnesia (commercial Epsom Salts) and 2 parts of sulphate of iron. These parts are in terms of weight, and the ingredients must be mixed thoroughly, any lumps being crushed. The fertiliser should be sprinkled evenly at about a *level* tablespoonful per plant, afterwards hoeing and watering in if necessary. The temptation to use a double dose in the hope of obtaining spectacular results should be resisted.

Alternatively, for those who do not wish to go to much trouble, many firms market a rose fertiliser to the well-known 'Tonks' formula, which was based originally on the chemical analysis of the ashes of a complete rose tree after burning it in a crucible. The formula comprises 12 parts of superphosphate of lime, 10 parts of nitrate of potash, 8 parts of sulphate of lime, 2 parts of sulphate of magnesia and 1 part of sulphate of iron. It should be applied at the rate of 3 or 4 ounces per square yard and pricked in with a border fork.

About the middle of May, when the soil will have started to warm up, a mulch of animal manure or, if this is unobtainable, compost, granulated peat, leafmould or spent hops should be applied evenly to the beds, preferably 2 inches deep. If peat, leafmould or spent hops are used they should be well moistened and fortified with a further application of the compound rose fertiliser, at the same rate as in mid-April. It is a good plan to wash this in with a hose jet applied at pressure to the mulch. The keen grower, with ambitions to produce excellent specimen blooms, may wish to try liquid stimulants from the stage of bud formation. Apart from liquid animal manures, which should *always* be applied in very dilute form (no stronger than a pale straw colour) and at intervals of ten days or so, soot water and soluble blood are useful nitrogenous fertilisers. Nitrate of potash (at ½ ounce per gallon) and superphosphate of lime (at 1 ounce per gallon) may also be used safely at these strengths. The important points to watch in liquid feeding are: to use the feed in very dilute form only; to ensure that there is already plenty of moisture in the soil before applying and to stop application at the end of July.

About the end of August, especially in a wet season, it is a good plan to apply a dressing of sulphate of potash to the rose beds at the rate of 3 ounces per square yard. This will help to ripen and harden the wood in readiness for the winter. It should be pricked in along with what remains of the mid-May mulch.

Chapter 6

GROWING IN POTS AND CONTAINERS

You do not need a garden to be a gardener. Almost all plants will grow inside a container of some sort, which means that if you have a town flat you can still grow plants on a balcony, on the roof or even in a window box. If you have a concreted yard you can grow plants in containers there and even if you have a magnificent garden, there are still places where plants in pots or tubs can add colour.

Plant containers

A wide diversity of design is to be found in plant containers, ranging from the humble and familiar flower pot to the sophisticated, automatically watered plant trough. Materials range in age and type from the old stone trough to the very latest plastic. They include asbestos, cement, clay, metal, plastics and fibre-glass and wood. They may be adapted for indoor or outdoor use depending on appearance and strength.

Plastics and fibre-glass Extruded polystyrene is used by some manufacturers to produce plant containers which are very light and attractive with their speckled or marbled tone finish. A considerable advantage these containers have is that they rapidly assimilate warmth. This in turn keeps the compost in the containers much warmer than that in clay or stone ones. They have several other advantages. They keep the plants evenly warm and retain moisture for some time. As the material is smooth, the containers will not scratch and they are particularly useful for placing on furniture. Finally, they are weatherproof and rotproof.

Several shapes and sizes are available from terrace type pots which are large enough to hold small shrubs or a mass of bedding plants to bulb bowls and troughs. They are ideal containers for the woman gardener as they are light and pleasant to handle. They must be used with care, however, as they are fairly fragile when filled. For example, it is not wise to pull a large trough, when filled, by its rim, as this can break off easily. A long trough must be supported underneath with a piece of timber if it has to be moved when filled. Usually, however, containers should be placed in their correct positions first and then filled and planted.

Some window-box or plant trough designs are manufactured from strong plastic materials which result in light-weight, rot-proof articles. They also have particular appeal to the woman gardener as they are attractively decorated by relief designs. Suitable plastic and fibre-glass shallow plant troughs can be obtained for indoor use. These are ideal for placing pot plants in, especially on the window ledge. A few small pebbles in the bottom plus a regular supply of small amounts of water will provide the ideal moist atmosphere for growing many plants. There are several fibre-glass plant tubs on the market. These

are made from special high-quality fibre-glass in various colours, such as red, yellow and green. The material used in their construction is light, so the containers are easy to handle. As their colouring is permanent, there is no need to paint them and they will not rot or warp.

Fibre-glass is also used for troughs, window-boxes, urns and other types of plant container. One range consists of facsimile reproductions of antique originals with exquisite motifs accurately copied. Of typical design in the style of these reproductions is a substantial square plant container dating back to an original made about 1550.

1 Well-stocked plant tubs on a brick paved terrace.
2 An old wine barrel sawn in half makes two large plant containers. Holes must be drilled in the base for drainage purposes and plenty of brick rubble or other similar material put in the tubs to ensure sharp drainage.
3 A 'Chilstone' reproduction of a Regency basket plant container.
4 Old tubs, because of their depth, are ideal for such shrubs as Hydrangeas.
5 Plant tubs such as this were once used for growing Orange trees. They are fitted with lifting rings at the corners to enable them to be moved under cover before the first frosts.

A 'Chilstone' urn, a reproduction of a Regency design.

Its size makes it suitable for a tree or large shrub. Another example is an attractive window box of narrow proportions with a lead finish from an original of the same period. A King George II period tub, dated 1757, with high reliefs of a ship in full sail, shells, starfish and mermaids and a Queen Anne style urn, dated 1710, with griffon handles and cherubs reliefs, are other examples of originals reproduced in this series. The facsimiles are so good that it is virtually impossible to detect that they are made of fibre-glass, except that they are very much lighter in weight than the lead originals. An attractive container of this kind can be bought for a reasonable price, some are very fine and the choice is wide enough to cater for most tastes.

Wood Elm, oak, teak and cedarwood are natural materials which are used by the manufacturers of many types of attractive container. They may take the form of square or long troughs, and several have been specially designed for indoor use. Sizes of troughs vary considerably, but popular dimensions are from $24 \times 12 \times 12$ inches to about $60 \times 12 \times 12$ inches. Some plant troughs can be purchased in 'do-it-yourself' kits, and are very easy to assemble. There are also matching sets of tubs and troughs, especially useful where these containers are to be used on a patio. For indoor use, containers should be as attractive as

possible and many manufacturers have paid particular attention to finish. One range of Burma-teak tubs has tapered screw-in legs and a beautiful high gloss, tarnish-proof finish of three coats of a special lacquer.

Cement A particularly useful plant container range is manufactured from a mixture of asbestos and cement. This process results in containers which are extremely durable and not liable to damage by even the severest of frosts. They are a little heavy to handle but their other qualities more than make up for this. Some are made in very unusual shapes. They may have hour-glass-like outlines, others are similar to ice-cream cones. These new shapes add considerably to their attractiveness. They may be particularly useful as water containers for small fountain or waterfall effects. They can be used for plant displays indoors and for outdoor work; it is a simple matter to drill holes in their bases.

There is much to commend the use of concrete containers and there are several attractive designs available. Some specialist stone craftsmen produce quite ornate examples, some of which are very expensive. For the average small garden, the smaller designs should be selected. Tudor or Italian style vases which are about 20 inches high and 16 inches in diameter are quite suitable. For the larger garden and where an informal design is required, pieces such as a large fluted vase, or one in the manner of design developed in the Regency period, about 3 feet high, would blend better with the more spacious surroundings. They can be obtained fairly easily.

Hand-made pots This type of pot for garden decoration is increasing in popularity and some very beautiful designs are available. Shapes and sizes are diverse. Some take the form of 'Ali-Baba' jars, others are quite squat with a diameter of some 18 to 24 inches and a depth of 7 to 10 inches. For larger plants such as trees and shrubs there are much deeper designs. Several specialists in this type of wheel-thrown pottery will make pots to customer's special order or design. Among the choices available there are some very charming wall pots which have holes for fixing to walls. All these pots have ample drainage and, provided they are well crocked and filled with a good, well-drained or open compost, they are frost-proof.

Holders or supports For indoor use there are several types of metal pedestals which provide very attractive supports for plant containers. The use of wrought iron for garden display work seems to be increasing in popularity too, especially for patios, paved areas, etc. These pedestals have a plant container or a platform top for alternative displays. In one or two designs the height is adjus-

table. Wall units and table pieces are also available, the latter are very useful as they are only about 8 inches high and enable the flower arranger to produce small arrangements most effectively. Various wrought iron bases or stands are made for automatically watered pots and troughs and there is also a special wall support for some of the troughs.

The metal stand supporting the plant containers, which may be pots or a trough, sometimes takes the form of scroll-work, or it may consist of short or long legs, perhaps with a magazine or newspaper rack between or an encircling metal 'cage' for pot or trough or a hanging basket. Some of the scroll-work may be covered in white polythene, both to make it more attractive and weatherproof. Some fibre-glass plant tubs are provided with a supporting metal tripod as an optional extra.

Hanging baskets An attractive way of displaying plants outdoors is by the use of hanging baskets. These are available in the form of simple wire baskets which, when lined with a piece of perforated plastic sheet or moss, hold soil and plants neatly. More modern wire baskets are coated with plastic. The usual sizes are 10 inches, 12 inches, 14 inches and 16 inches in diameter. A special half-basket for walls is available in sizes of 14 inches and 16 inches

Inventive ideas If you cannot afford to spend a great deal on ornamental vases or urns, a wide range of other objects, not originally intended as plant containers, may be pressed into service. Old wine barrels are often obtainable from wine merchants or other sources and the barrels, when sawn in half carefully, make two excellent plant tubs. A number of holes should be drilled in the bottoms for drainage purposes. A poker is possibly the most useful tool for this purpose. It will be easy to drive holes through the wood when the tip is red hot. The tubs should be treated with a copper-based wood preservative before they are used.

Builders' yards can provide many unusual containers, particularly for the imaginative gardener. Old chimney-pots, plain or decorated may often be picked up quite cheaply. They can easily be provided with concrete bases and allowance may be made for drainage holes by putting in wooden plugs before the concrete has set. These may be knocked out afterwards. Old domestic water tanks of various shapes and sizes make perfectly acceptable containers, particularly if they are painted on the outside and holes are knocked in their bases. Old wash coppers are not difficult to find. Many have rounded bases, which tend to make them a little unstable, but this can be overcome by beating the base more or less flat with a hammer or mallet. Drainage holes are easily provided. The range of sizes is quite considerable; some from old country houses may be 3 feet in diameter and as much in depth. Exposed to the elements they take on a pleasant greenish-bronze patina. Some are made of cast iron and this is more difficult to drill for drainage purposes, though it can be done. On no account try to knock holes in the base of a cast-iron wash 'copper', as the material is brittle and you may ruin the container.

From the greengrocer, in spring, it is sometimes possible to obtain tall split-cane baskets in which new potatoes are imported. At best these must be considered as temporary containers, with a life of one or two seasons, although they will last a little longer if they are lined with polythene sheeting before they are filled with drainage material and soil.

Farm sales are worth attending by the gardener in search of less usual containers. It is often possible to pick up quite cheaply such things as feeding troughs, which make suitable long low containers. It does not matter if their bases are corroded; it merely makes it

easier to provide the necessary drainage holes. A coat of paint helps to make them more acceptable in the garden. Disused hay-racks may also be found and, when fixed against a wall, as they were originally, make unusual features. Before they are filled with soil they should be lined with fine-mesh wire-netting or perforated plastic sheeting, both of which will retain the soil yet allow surplus water to escape freely.

The day of the heavy wooden wheelbarrow is almost over as modern barrows are made of metal or heavy-duty plastic. If you have an old wooden barrow or can obtain one, do not consign it to the

1 'Panniers' carried by this old statue are filled with Ivies, making unusual containers for a corner of a town garden.
2 A modern container, made from pre-cast concrete, suitable for a large garden or a municipal garden.
3 A low container of classical design forms an excellent focal point here.

bonfire, for after holes have been drilled in the bottom it makes an unusual and well-adapted container for all sorts of plants. You can either leave it in its natural state and treat it with a wood preservative, or paint it with a good quality lead paint, to give it a new lease of life.

It is occasionally possible to find examples of the large earthenware pots used for forcing rhubarb, when they were inverted over the crowns to exclude most of the light. These already have a hole in the 'base' (actually the top when they are used for forcing) and this will act as a drainage hole when they are used as plant containers.

There is practically no limit to what may be used for growing plants in. Old baths, including hip baths, have been used in town gardens, while it is not at all unusual to see, in country gardens, hollowed-out tree-stumps used as informal plant containers.

A point to remember, particularly as far as deep containers are concerned, is

only that pests of all kinds will have been killed, but that disease will not be present and, even more important, that when we use the seed compost, for example, we will know that any seed germinating will be the seed we have sown, not some weed seed dormant in the soil. This can be a great help, but it is a luxury for which we must pay and it is not always worth while.

Obviously the steam sterilisation of large quantities of loam can be an expensive business and the expense must be passed on to the gardener, but it is a comparatively simple matter to sterilize our own soil in small quantities. Small electric soil sterilization containers can be bought for a few pounds and will last almost for ever, given reasonable care. Most will take about a bushel of soil and require merely to be plugged in to an electrical supply for a few hours. The soil is baked and made quite sterile. Alternatively, it is even possible to tie a comparatively small quantity of soil into a piece of cloth and suspend this in a normal domestic boiler or steamer for a few hours, where the steam will effectively sterilize the contents.

We must not allow our desire for a sterile soil mixture to overwhelm us, for there are many occasions when it will be a complete waste. We have just discussed sterilizing our own soil but this is not the end of the process. The soil must be blended with a graduated proportion of sand and peat, and the ingredients of the fertiliser must also be gathered together, mixed and added to the base. In other words, we must go to very considerable trouble to provide ourselves with what is admittedly a helpful – even a foolproof – growing medium.

This compost, although it could never be called too good, is perhaps often unnecessarily good. Just as we do not use a French bottled Burgundy to prepare *coq au vin*, because its finer qualities would be wasted, so by using John Innes compost for all our plantings we would be throwing away money, materials and time.

Although some of the smaller garden stores or ironmongers who stock the John Innes compost may not have supplies of other soils, most will get it on request. Any garden centre worth its name will carry supplies as a matter of course. Several lines may be available as well, probably, such as leafmould, but more frequently to be found are various mixtures incorporating manures or other fertilizers of various types: these are nearly always useful, although it is sometimes a valuable experience to compare

that ample provision should be made for drainage. To prevent the drainage holes from being blocked and to prevent worms and slugs from entering through them, it is wise to stand the containers on bricks or pieces of wood, so that their bases are clear of the ground.

Because each vessel is individual and separated from any other container, it is possible to fill them with different types of soil particularly suited to special plants. Where in the garden we may have limy clay, we can fill a pot with a sandy acid soil and so grow plants unsuited to our native earth. But these are exceptions and most of our plants will grow best in an average soil mixture. Artificially blended soils are usually known as composts.

Standard mixtures in small or large quantities can usually be bought from garden stores, ironmongers and even many chain stores throughout the country. These are the John Innes composts we discussed in some detail on pages 24 and 25. These composts however, can be treated as the basis only, and by adding sand to the mixture we can make it more porous; by adding lime or peat, we can make it more alkaline or acid. So it is a relatively simple matter to alter the "single" average composition of the soil mixture to suit our own requirements.

One of the greatest benefits of the John Innes soil composts is that if they are made of a properly processed recipe they will have been sterilised. This means not

Tomatoes can be raised in soilless compost in a cool greenhouse.

An electric steam-sterilising unit. The bucket base is made of wire mesh.

packed sizes and prices.

Of course, if we have a garden of our own it is a simple matter to fill our containers from it with natural soil direct from the border. Otherwise we can get it from one of our usual sources of supply.

We should be fully aware of the benefits of making our own garden compost, and today very few gardeners are foolish or wasteful enough not to do this, but in addition it is always helpful to have seperate sources of more specialised soil – for example, when the leaves fall in autumn and winter they should be collected together and allowed to rot down, rather than be put with the remainder of the compost material. Of course, if the garden is small and the leaf supply, therefore, severely restricted, it will probably be wiser to add the collected leaves to the compost heap. Again, each time a tree is planted or a bite is taken in the lawn, the turf removed should be carefully stocked, grass down, to rot down into a most valuable source of friable and humus-rich soil.

It is true that even home produced soils may contain weed seeds, even some pests, but these are minor problems when the soils are to be used only for planting say, a fuchsia, in a setting for the decoration of the terrace. In such circumstances any weeds that appear can easily be removed

and pests dealt with in a matter of moments. Any tendency towards acidity or alkalinity is probably minimal or will have been noticed earlier in the garden, and dealt with.

Cutting composts The compost into which cuttings are put to root must provide a suitable medium for encouraging the quick formation of roots. It is not designed to feed the plants and thus it is good gardening practice to pot up rooted cuttings into a potting compost once good roots are formed.

The essential qualities of a cutting compost are hygiene (freedom from soil-borne pests and diseases), air and good drainage combined with the ability to hold sufficient moisture. Therefore a gritty and porous texture is best.

Silver sand is the most reliable rooting medium for most cuttings but does not provide any plant food at all and so the cuttings once rooted must be moved on to a compost containing plant nourishment. Sand and peat mixed in equal parts probably gives the best results and gives the gardener a better margin of time before potting up is required because this mixture does provide food.

The John Innes cutting compost is composed of:

1 part by loose bulk of medium loam
2 parts of peat
1 part of coarse sand.

This compost can generally be brought from sundriesmen ready made up. Proprietary rooting media such as vermiculite, No-soil compost and Rootine are also available from sundriesmen and all ensure good results.

Under certain circumstances it is sometimes preferable to use a compost which contains no soil. There are several types of proprietary mixtures now available. Most of these are based on peat and incorporate carefully measured quantities of plant foods. One of their advantages is their lightness.

Soilless peat-based composts These new seed and potting composts are already widely used commercially and may well replace the older John Innes mixtures. Experimental work in recent years shows that tomatoes, cucumbers, many garden flowers and even cacti grow well in peat-based composts containing plant nutrients. These are proprietary composts developed by leading horticultural suppliers. The composts should be used according to the instructions supplied with them. Failures may occur if the gardener omits an initial thorough watering, compresses the compost excessively, or permits the compost to dry out when in use. It is advisable to purchase a fresh supply of soilless composts for each season's work. The composts are clean to handle and are recommended for the raising of plants in the greenhouse or in containers in cold frames.

The most vital factor to bear in mind with all container grown plants, regardless of the compost or soil mixture, is that because of the relatively small quantity

Coloured paving slabs of various shapes, sizes and colours and pierced screen walling.

of the rooting medium this will quickly dry out and necessitate frequent watering. It is possible to grow plants successfully in containers without drainage holes, but this requires a considerable layer of drainage material at the base of the tub or pot and constant care over watering. It is much easier and always recommended that all types of container have efficient drainage holes in the base, or sometimes low in the sides.

In hot, dry weather some containers may need watering twice a day and if this is not done the compost will sometimes dry out to the extent that subsequent waterings will fail to be completely absorbed and the plants will suffer. If the drainage system is efficient and the compost is maintained at a suitable moisture, then each time the compost surface is watered the water should quickly disappear through the soil and trickle out at the base.

This means two things: first that as the water runs through the compost it will drag air with it, vital to the health of the plants, and second that this coursing of water through the compost is bound to leach out the plant foods at a faster rate than if the plants were growing in the natural soil. This means that plants in containers must be fed regularly and frequently.

Frequent feeding means that plants in containers can look particularly lush and handsome and no position in the garden suits them more than a paved area such as a patio or terrace. Here the tubs or pots seem to sit naturally and not only is there an affinity of artificiality, but the growing plants serve to break up and informalise the somewhat stark areas of bare stone or paving.

Because of the limitations on its size the owner of the town garden can sometimes grow most of his plants only in containers. One advantage of this is that the growing plants can frequently be changed according to season to give a constant flow of colour and interest and to overcome the damaging effects of atmospheric pollution.

Often a "town garden" consists just of window boxes. These are helpful in creating an atmosphere of cool green or colourful growing material, and there is tremendous scope in their use.

Window-box gardening

Although window-boxes can be had ready-made, a made-to-measure job of teak, cedar or oak will look better than an ill-fitting affair made of artificial materials. Hardwoods look better unpainted and may be either oiled or varnished. Softwoods should be treated with preservative and may be painted. The timber should be at least ½ inch

1 Round slabs, used in conjunction with in-filling pieces, are used to pave this patio garden.
2 A formal patio where a dripping fountain provides a sense of coolness.

thick and the inside depth should be from 7 to 10 inches. If the window sill exceeds 5 feet you may make two boxes, each half the required length to make fixing and handling easier. If the front of the box slopes at a slight angle outwards it will be easier to grow trailing plants in the box. It is best to use screws of galvanised iron or brass to hold the various sections of the box together. Drainage holes are essential and should be about ½ inch in diameter. Make a double row of holes with about 6 inches between the holes in each row.

Fixing A window-box on a high sill that is not securely fixed can be dangerous, so use long hasps and staple fittings to secure the box to the window frame. The eye can be screwed to the side of the box and the hook to the window frame. This makes it easy to remove the box. Where the window ledge has a downward and outward slope use a batten of wood to level up the box.

Ready-made boxes Wood, galvanised iron, aluminium, plastic and fibre-glass are all materials used, and many types have galvanised containers which can be planted and then just dropped into position. This makes it easy to switch containers with plants newly-flowering to take the place of containers in which the plants have finished flowering. This advantage can also be obtained by using the boxes for pot plants, which can be placed on shallow trays within the box.

Preparation The soil should have a good texture and be rich in humus and plant nutrients. It is better to prepare the box actually sited on the window ledge, as this saves carrying a box full of soil to the ledge and siting it in what is often an awkward position. Lay broken crocks on the bottom of the box at about ½ inch deep to prevent soil being washed out of the drainage holes and at the same time give adequate drainage. On top of this a fibrous material such as peat should be laid at a depth of 2 inches. To within a ½ inch of the rim the soil proper should be John Innes No 2, or you can mix up 3 parts loam (or good garden soil), 1 part of peat or leafmould and 1 part of sharp sand. To each bushel add two or three handfuls of bonemeal. The soil should be changed every two or three years, or the top two or three inches should be replaced with fresh soil or compost.

Planting Pelargoniums or fuchsias, in association with alyssum or lobelia, together with foliage plants, such as coleus, or the grey-leaved *Senecio cineraria,* will provide a summer display

1 Concrete slabs are used in contrasting colours to provide a formal pattern for this patio.
2 Rectangular tiles make a clean entrance path to the house.
3 A patio in a town garden where colour is provided by plants in a variety of containers.
4 Planting up a window-box.

requiring little maintenance. Hardy and half-hardy plants, including stocks, zinnias and verbenas, all give a long-lasting display if the dead flowers are picked off regularly. Tobacco plants, French and African marigolds also make a good effect.

Less orthodox planting includes begonias (both tuberous and fibrous-rooted species), ferns, fuchsias, creeping Jenny *(Lysimachia nummularia)* with periwinkles, *Tradescantia fluminensis,* and the smaller ornamental ivies, all of which are suitable for a north-facing aspect. Where there is partial shade only (north-east and north-west aspects) begonias, pelargoniums, lobelia, alyssum and phacelias all do well. French and African marigolds, *Salvia splendens,* such pelargoniums as 'Paul Crampel', 'Gustav Emich' and 'Henry Jacoby', contrasted with the silvery foliage of *Helichrysum frigidum* or *H. angustifolium,* or the scarlet petunia 'Comanche' with the paler zinnias, are all suitable for full sunlight. By using shrubs, conifers and pot plants it is possible to obtain a more rapid display. Cyclamens, cinerarias, schizanthus and primulas are excellent, but the first three need a sheltered south-facing aspect. Pot chrysanthemums are tougher, provided they have been hardened off. These can be used in the box from April to November or December.

Trailing plants and climbers   Creeping Jenny, canary creeper, ivy-leaved geraniums and nasturtiums are decorative, and on south-facing aspects the trailing *Campanula fragilis* can be induced to give a fine display in late summer. Climbing plants should be planted at the ends of the box and allowed to climb up the walls on either side of the window with suitable supports. *Cobaea scandens* is an outstanding half-hardy climber which will scale 30 feet in one season the golden leaved hop, *Humulus japonicus aureus*, is another interesting and attractive climber.

Climbing nasturtiums will cling to strings or wires, and good varieties include the scarlet 'Lucifer' and the rich red 'Indian Chief'. *Ipomoea rubrocaerulea* 'Heavenly Blue' (morning glory) is another half-hardy climber that likes a sheltered, sunny position. The convolvulus-type flowers open in the mornings and are finished by noon and have intensely blue trumpets.

More permanent climbers are the compact ivies, such as *Hedera helix aureo-variegata* or the smaller-leaved 'Buttercup'. Vines, also the Virginian creeper, *Parthenocissus quinquefolia,* or the smaller-leaved, more compact *P. henryana, Vitis vinifera purpurea* and *V. coignetiae* are all suitable.

Bulbs One of the best times of year for a window-box is early in the year when daffodils, tulips, hyacinths, scillas, chionodoxas and other bulbs are flowering. Plant closely as soon as the summer display has ended, or plant bulbs at the point of flowering after Christmas. Make sure that the latter are hardened off and do not put them outside until early March.

Equally suited to town or country decoration, at home just as much on a balcony or roof garden as on a terrace or patio, is the delightful hanging basket, a type of decoration which until recently appeared to be disappearing but has happily achieved popularity again.

Hanging baskets
The use of hanging baskets is a simple but very attractive way of decorating a porch or terrace during the summer– and indeed most of the year. They can be bought in sizes from 10–18".
inches in diameter and 6–9 inches deep.

Baskets are made of stout galvanised wire in an open mesh or a weave design or of green, plastic-coated, rustproof wire, in the same patterns. Polythene baskets are also available in green, red, white, yellow and blue and baskets made entirely of alkathene can be purchased with a special drainage device. In green-

1

2

1 Pelargoniums make fine window-box decoration.
2 A window-box planted for summer effect with coloured foliage plants requires a minimum of attention.

1

2

3

4

5

6

1 The basket is balanced on the rim of a bucket to keep it firm while planting is done. The first lining of sphagnum moss is packed into place.
2 An interlining of polythene is put in place, and holes punched half way up to draw off the surplus water, each time watering is done.
3 Compost is put into the basket, so that the finished level will be just above the polythene lining.
4 Small plants are knocked out of pots and planted at an angle in the centre of the basket.
5 Smaller plants are put around the sides and positioned horizontally to give a better finished effect.
6 The plants are watered in once the basket is complete, and either hung up to drain, or left over the bucket.

houses, square wooden containers made of slats are often used, particularly for orchids of trailing habit, such as *Stanhopea*.

For safety's sake baskets should be hung from strong hooks, well above eye level where they cannot obscure the light or a view or be knocked about as people pass under them.

Planting up the basket For outdoor use plant up during the latter half of May or very early June, wedging the basket in the top of a large bucket, bowl or box to hold it firm while the planting is done. Line it with damp sphagnum moss; about half a gallon of this will be required to make a good lining. Alternatively thickish polythene can be used to

line the basket, when holes will need to be punched in the base for drainage although it is possible to purchase perforated polythene which is quite suitable. Polythene does not look as decorative as sphagnum moss but holds the moisture better and if the basket cannot be given daily attention it is probably better to use this material, although a thin layer of peat packed within the sphagnum moss lining will help considerably with water retention.

If sphagnum moss is not available, hay packed tightly round the interior of the basket, is an adequate substitute.

Some gardeners like to put a small plastic saucer in the base to catch and retain some of the water, and to reduce drip to some extent.

A reasonably rich compost is best because the small amount that can be accommodated has to provide sustenance for a fairly extensive root system. John Innes potting compost No. 2 is suitable, especially if a little leafmould is incorporated. Do not attempt to get too many plants into one basket. A 12 inch diameter basket will hold three plants from 5 inch pots, plus several smaller or trailing plants between them and around the edge.

Choose plants that are just coming into flower, turn them out of their pots and fill the well of the basket with compost, firming it with the fingers. Place the larger plants in position, angling them slightly towards the edge. At this stage small plants such as lobelia and alyssum can be tucked between the mesh of the basket so that eventually the flowers will clothe the sides. Continue to pack in the soil round the root balls and make it firm, leaving a slight depression or well on the surface of the soil, another trick to conserve moisture and to prevent water from overflowing when the basket is watered. The surface should be about 2 inches below the rim of the basket. Seeds of nasturtiums can be pushed into strategic positions at this stage. Immerse the basket in water, then allow it to drain before hanging it up.

Maintenance Avoid positions in full sun or deep shade; the former dries out the arrangement too quickly and the latter discourages showy flowering, although such positions are suitable for baskets planted up with ferns for foliage effect. Water three or four times a week, daily or even twice daily during very hot weather, adding a flower fertiliser to the water at the recommended rate once a week, after flowering has started. Water from above, allowing the basket to drain if possible to avoid leaching out the plant food; otherwise immerse it for a few minutes in a tub of water and allow surplus water to drain away before hanging it up again.

Watering a hanging basket from above can be difficult unless one stands on steps. It can, of course, be lifted off its hook but a large basket full of earth and plants can be quite heavy and awkward. Two methods of dealing with this problem are worth mentioning. One is to fix a small pulley in place of the hook. Strong cord, or preferably strong pliable wire or chain, is fixed to the suspension ring of the basket and passed over the pulley. The other end is attached to a roller blind hook fixed on the nearest wall. The basket may then be lowered for watering and easily raised again. The other method is to use a device, obtainable commercially, known as a 'Tommy Longarm'. Basically this is a small watering can mounted on a swivel on the end of a long pole. A length of string fixed to the can runs through a hook and down the pole. Pulling on the string tips the can thus enabling the basket to be watered easily from below. Wash the leaves occasionally and snip off dead flower heads to keep a well-groomed appearance.

Suggested plants. The following plants are highly recommended for growing in hanging baskets.

Flowering plants for summer display: Achimenes; Ageratum; Begonia 'Gloire de Lorraine' and pendulous kinds such as 'Mrs Bilkey', 'Fleur de Chrysantheme', 'Golden Shower', 'Lena', 'Meteor'; *Begonia semperflorens* for mild localities; Calceolaria; *Campanula isophylla* and *C. isophylla alba*; *Chrysanthemum frutescens* (marguerite); *Columnea banksii* (G); Fuchsia, drooping varieties such as 'Cascade', 'Golden Marinka', 'La Bianco', 'Marinka', 'Thunderbird'; Heliotrope; *Hoya bella* (G); *Lantana camara* for mild localities; *Lobelia pendula* and *L. tenuior; Lobularia maritima* (sweet Alison); Pelargonium, upright zonal kinds for top of basket, ivy-leaved varieties for draping the sides, such as 'Abel Carriere', 'Edward VII', 'Galilee', 'L'Elegance', 'Madame Crousse', 'Madame Morrier'; Petunia especially 'Bal-

1 A small hanging basket, planted with Fuchsias and Pelargoniums.
2 Browallia, a greenhouse flowering annual makes a decorative trailing plant for a hanging basket.
3 A floriferous Begonia in a basket.

cony Blended' strain; Tropaeolum (nasturtiums), especially climbers or trailers; Verbena, dwarf and trailing.

Perennials: Aubrieta; *Campanula portenschlagiana; Cerastium tomentosum; Cymbalaria muralis; Glechoma hederaefolia; Lysimachia nummularia; Vinca minor.*

Foliage plants: Hedera (ivy) in variety; *Saxifraga stolonifera* (syn. *S. sarmentosa*).

Bulbs: (for late winter and spring display) Crocus, *Narcissus* (daffodil), *Galanthus* (snowdrop), Tulip (double).

As frankly artificial as hanging baskets and just as charming are some of the miniature gardens, differing widely in style and content and depending largely on the taste and talent of the gardener for their individual charm.

Miniature gardens can take a number of forms. In the very small plot, you can share the pleasures of those who work on a broader canvas by restricting your planting, not only to single specimens of your favourite plants, but also by growing those that are compact in habit with a slow rate of increase.

The miniature garden proper, however, will not be able to rely on such measures. For its impact, it will have to depend mainly on dwarf plants, some of which may be miniature replicas of their taller counterparts while others will display their own individual characteristics.

A good way of getting horticultural quarts into pint pots is to garden in

A simple indoor miniature garden can be made in a clay seed-pan, using small perennial plants from pots and is a delightful and fascinating source of interest.
1 The base of the seed pan is covered with large crocks to ensure sharp drainage, and these are covered with moss and peat to keep the compost open and porous.
2 Compost is added to about half the depth of the pan and levelled.
3 Suitable stones, not too large and not too small, are put in position and firmed in place with a dibber.
4 and 5 Small plants are put into position and planted with a small trowel.
6 The finished garden is permanent.

sinks and troughs. Several of these plant containers, each with its separate planting scheme, can be accommodated in a minimum of space. Many a town forecourt, backyard or balcony could benefit from the inclusion of a feature of this kind.

Unfortunately, genuine stone troughs and sinks are fast becoming collectors' items and, in consequence, increasingly difficult and expensive to come by. The stone sinks of Victorian kitchens and sculleries have long ago been replaced by vitreous enamel and stainless steel, while the larger troughs, formerly used for watering cattle and horses, have given place to galvanised iron tanks.

The occasional specimen still turns up

at country sales and in junk yards, but dealers are aware of their value and prices have risen astronomically. As an alternative, concrete or old glazed sinks can be adapted for the purpose. But neither of these will have the charm of the genuine article which, if it has been out-of-doors for any length of time, will be weathered and decorated with mosses and lichens.

Particular attention must be paid to drainage before planting up any of these containers. A piece of perforated zinc should cover the existing drainage hole and the base of the trough or sink should be covered with broken crocks or stone chippings to a depth of 2–3 inches. On top of this goes a layer of peat moss or chopped turves, the latter grass side down.

The planting mixture should consist of 2 parts of loam to 1 part of peat and 1 of sharp sand, with a dusting of lime or the addition of mortar rubble. The lime content must be omitted where ericaceous plants, dwarf rhododendrons, or other lime-haters are to be planted.

Among the many plants that can be grown successfully in a sink or trough garden are the hardier small saxifrages, sempervivums (houseleeks), thrift and other alpine plants of tough constitution. In a shady situation, mossy saxifrages, hardy cyclamen and miniature ferns will flourish.

For more permanent effects, use can be made of some of the dwarf shrubs and conifers mentioned below.

Miniature rose gardens Miniature roses have become generally popular in recent years. One of their main attractions lies in the opportunity that they afford of enjoying the beauty of roses where space would not permit the planting of a rose garden of the orthodox kind.

Sometimes known as fairy roses, many of these delightful dwarfs bear a strong resemblance to popular hybrid tea roses and floribundas. Others have equally delightful individual characteristics.

1 Small succulents have been planted in a two-inch shell to make a really miniature garden.
2 Miniature gardens made up of Saxifrages, Sedums, Campanulas, Arenarias, Lewisias and miniature Conifers.
3 Androsaces, Houseleeks, Lewisias, Dwarf Conifers and other alpine plants make an interesting small garden.

1

Little interest was shown by gardeners in these pygmy roses until after World War II, when scarcity of garden help and a swing from houses to flats and maisonettes brought their many useful qualities into prominence. These, apart from their compact habit, include permanence and a very long flowering season.

Many of the miniature roses stem from the dainty *Rosa rouletti*, a tiny rose that was discovered in a Swiss cottage garden by a Dr Roulet and named in his honour. From this charming miniature have evolved, directly or indirectly, many of the loveliest miniatures available today, including 'Tom Thumb', 'Pixies' and 'Midget'.

Miniature roses are extremely hardy. They come into flower early—often by the middle of May—and continue to produce their flowers throughout the summer and autumn. They are best planted from pots as they do not like root disturbance. This makes it possible to plant them at almost any time of year although March and April are the best months for this operation. Those planted in summer should be given plenty of water during dry spells in their first season.

The many named forms now available can be used to create a complete rose garden in miniature or can be incorporated as a separate feature of a larger garden. They are also useful for permanent dwarf bedding schemes.

All the features of a full-sized rose garden can be incorporated, scaled down, of course, to suitable dimensions. Pygmy pergolas, trellises and small rustic screens can be used to support climbing varieties, while miniature standards will emphasise focal points and act as central features of miniature bedding schemes.

Miniature roses need only a minimum of attention where pruning is concerned. This operation is best carried out with a sharp pair of nail scissors. It consists mainly of removing weak growths and cutting back dead or diseased shoots to healthy wood. It is carried out in spring.

These small roses thrive best in similar types of soil to those in which the hybrid tea roses and floribundas do well. They like a fairly heavy, slightly acid loam, rich in humus. Lack of humus can be remedied by forking in well-rotted animal manure or garden compost, a few weeks before planting. If neither of these is available, peat or leafmould, laced with bonemeal, make satisfactory substitutes.

These dwarf roses will also flourish and look well in the old stone troughs already mentioned; the sinks are too shallow and there would be a danger of the roots drying out. They can be used, as well, for another kind of miniature garden, the window box, provided that the latter is at least 9 inches deep.

Among those most widely grown are 'Baby Gold Star' (golden yellow), 'Bit O' Sunshine' (gold), 'Humoreske' (deep

2

3

pink,) 'Little Buckaroo' (scarlet with white centre), 'Sparkle' (single scarlet) and the midget rose that started it all, *Rosa rouletti*.

'Baby Masquerade', a newer introduction, is a perfect replica, in miniature, of the favourite floribunda of the same name, with clusters of flowers that produce the typical kaleidoscope of colour of the latter.

This rose, together with 'Cinderella' (pale pink edged white), 'Coralin' (coral-pink) and 'Maid Marion' is obtainable in standard form. There are climbing forms of the bright pink 'Perla Rosa', the yellow and orange 'Little Showoff', which is practically perpetual-flowering and 'Baby Crimson', which is also known as 'Perla d'Alcanada'. 'Pink Cameo', too, makes an attractive climber. None of these climbing miniatures exceeds 4–5 feet in height.

A garden of dwarf conifers Another way of making a miniature garden, of interest the whole year through, is to use dwarf conifers. Many of these are replicas of their taller counterparts and can be used to obtain similar effects on a reduced scale.

First and foremost are the various forms of Lawson's cypress, which share the useful characteristics of the larger kinds. *Chamaecyparis lawsoniana minima glauca*, with blue-grey foliage and whorled branchlets makes an interesting focal plant in a garden of dwarf conifers. It reaches an ultimate height of 4–6 feet,

but this only very slowly. Similar in habit is *C. l. obtusa coralliformis*, with red twisted branches and close-packed bright green foliage. *C. pisifera* 'Boulevard' is a comparatively new introduction with blue-grey sprays of feathery foliage while *C. p. filifera aurea* is practically a golden counterpart of the former.

There are two charming little cryptomerias that will not exceed 2–2½ feet. Both *Cryptomeria japonica pygmaea* and *vilmoriniana* are slow-growing and make dense globular bushes whose form contrasts well with the pyramidal shape of the dwarf cypresses.

One of the most outstanding of these miniature conifers is the dwarf juniper, *Juniperus communis compressa*. This makes a dense blue-grey column, only 2 feet tall. There are also two dwarf spruces with a conical habit in the same pygmy category as this juniper. They are *Picea abies pygmaea*, with close-set dark green needles and *P. a. albertiana conica* whose foliage is a softer green. *Pinus sylvestris beauvronensis* is a dwarf Scots pine, only 4–4½ feet at maturity, that can be planted to simulate a large

1 Dwarf Conifers of many kinds are ideal for miniature gardens.
2 At the RHS Garden, Wisley there is a splendid collection of trough gardens, each one planted up in an individual way with succulents and miniature conifers.
3 One of the troughs, which contains a selection of Houseleeks.

tree in the scaled-down dimensions of a garden of dwarf conifers.

The remaining space can be filled by the very slow-growing bun-shaped dwarfs such as *Chamaecyparis lawsoniana juniperoides*, a variety that grows only 4–6 inches tall, with a spread of similar dimensions or *Picea abies gregoryana*, which makes a 1½-foot hummock of grey-green foliage and is broader than it is tall.

179

Chapter 7

GOODNESS FROM THE GARDEN

Where there is space in the garden most people like to grow fruit and vegetables, better flavoured, fresher and less expensive than those from the shops. If they are to be grown at all it is worth growing them really well. So before planting make sure that your soil is deep, well dug, clean of weeds, moist, open to sun and air and free as possible from frosts. Choose your plants with care from a reputable supplier and seek advice about the most suitable varieties for the soil and space available.

Many fruits require fertilisation from another tree or bush if they are to give generously of their produce, so wherever possible plant more than one of a type, choosing another that flowers at the same time. Tables of flowering times follow where necessary.

Probably the most popular of all home grown fruits is the apple, a comparatively easy fruit to grow in this country and giving the bonus of beautiful blossom in the spring.

Apples Some varieties set no fruit at all when self pollinated, while others under favourable conditions set a fair crop. Yields are better when there are enough varieties for cross-pollination. There are a number of popular varieties which are poor pollinators (triploid varieties) but most are diploid, which pollinate each other very well. It is important to have at least two diploid varieties in a collection, unless the pollinator chosen is sufficiently self-fertile alone. When choosing varieties select those which will flower about the same time or overlap by a few days with others. There is some variation in the flowering periods of varieties but on the whole the times are very consistent. Winter temperatures and district can affect flowering periods.

In the following tables varieties are in seven flowering groups. Select if possible varieties within the same group for pollination. The old very late variety 'Crawley Beauty' is sufficiently self-fertile to set a crop.

A number of small trees in a range of varieties covering a long season is preferable to a few large trees each giving an excessive quantity of fruit at one season and with one flavour. On average, a cordon tree gives 3–5 pounds of apples, pyramids 6–8 pounds, bush trees on Malling IX rootstock 25–30 pounds, bush trees on Malling II 80–100 pounds, and larger trees according to size.

Alternatively, a 'family' tree having several varieties grafted on the one trunk can be grown or additional varieties be grafted on to an established tree which is yielding glut crops.

Apple trees have a long expectation of life and may remain fruitful and healthy for 50 years or more.

Cultivation Apples prefer deep loams but can be grown on sandy soils and heavy clays, if care is taken to drain wet soils and irrigate dry ones.

Cordons (planted 2½ feet by 6 feet),

Apple 'Granny Smith' a firm green eating apple.

espaliers (10–18 feet apart), and arcure trained trees (3 feet by 6 feet), are grown against walls, fences or on post and wire supports; dwarf pyramids (3½ feet by 7 feet), spindle bushes (6 feet by 13 feet), pillars (5–6 feet by 10 feet), bush (12 feet by 12 feet), and half-standards (15–18 feet by 15–18 feet), on an open, but sheltered, site. Provide wind-breaks if natural shelter is not present.

Plant in November, if possible, or up to the end of March whenever the soil is sufficiently friable. It is best not to incorporate farmyard manure before planting into any except the poorest of soils. Plant as firmly as possible, ramming the soil round the roots with the square end of a stout post, and tie the tree to a substantial stake. Mulch the root area to conserve moisture in the soil during the first season, thereby minimising the transplanting check to growth.

Subsequently, control the vigour balance by applying farmyard manure annually as a mulch in the spring and fertilisers according to the tree's needs

Trained trees respond to being summer pruned in July or August, the side shoots being shortened to five leaves, the leaders remaining unpruned. Winter pruning consists of shortening summer-pruned shoots to two buds and reducing the lengths of the leaders by a third. Bush and half-standard trees are not summer pruned: in winter, the dead and crossing shoots are cut out and also sufficient branches to keep the head of the tree to an open habit. The leaders are shortened by a third for the first four years only—leaving them unpruned from then onwards induces the branches

Flowering times for apples

Very early
Aromatic Russet (B)
Gravenstein (T)
Keswick Codlin (B)

Early
Adam's Pearmain (B)
Beauty of Bath
Ben's Red (B)
Bismark (B)
Cheddar Cross
Christmas Pearmain (B)
Discovery
Egremont Russet
George Cave
George Neal
Golden Spire
Irish Peach
Laxton's Early Crimson
Lord Lambourne
Lord Suffield
McIntosh Red
Melba (B)
Michaelmas Red
Norfolk Beauty
Patricia (B)
Rev W. Wilkes (B)
Ribston Pippin (T)
St Edmund's Pippin
Scarlet Pimpernel
Striped Beefing
Warner's King (T)
Washington (T)
White Transparent

Early mid season
Arthur Turner
Belle de Boskoop (T)
Blenheim Orange (TB)
Bowden's Seedling

Early mid season cont.
Bramley's Seedling (T)
Brownlee's Russet
Charles Ross
Claygate Pearmain
Cox's Orange Pippin
D'Arcy Spice
Devonshire Quarrenden (B)
Early Victoria (Emneth Early) (B)
Emperor Alexander
Epicure
Exeter Cross
Fortune (B)
Granny Smith
Grenadier
Howgate Wonder
James Grieve
John Standish
Jonathan
King's Acre Pippin
Kidd's Orange Red
Lord Grosvenor
Merton Pippin
Merton Prolific
Merton Russet
Merton Worcester
Miller's Seedling (B)
Ontario
Peasgood's Nonsuch
Red Victoria (B)
Reinette du Canada (T)
Rival (B)
Rosemary Russet
Sturmer Pippin
Sunset
Tydeman's Early Worcester
Tydeman's Late Orange
Wagener (B)
Wealthy
Winter Quarrenden (B)
Worcester Pearmain

Mid season
Allington Pippin (B)
Annie Elizabeth
Chelmsford Wonder (B)
Cox's Pomona
Delicious
Duke of Devonshire
Ellison's Orange
Golden Delicious
Golden Noble
Herring's Pippin
Lady Henniker
Lady Sudeley
Lane's Prince Albert
Laxton's Superb (B)
Monarch (B)
Orleans Reinette
Sir John Thornycroft

Late mid season
American Mother
Coronation (B)
Gascoyne's Scarlet
King of the Pippins (B)
Lord Derby
Merton Beauty
Newton Wonder
Northern Spy (B)
Royal Jubilee
William Crump
Winston
Woolbrook Pippin (B)

Late
Court Pendu Plat
Edward VII
Heusgen's Golden Reinette

Very late
Crawley Beauty

B=biennial or irregular flowering varieties. T=triploid varieties with poor pollen. Those not marked T are diploid varieties. Coloured sports eg Red Millar's Seedling usually flower at the same time as the parent.

'Lord Lambourne', a sweet dessert apple

to droop and become more fruitful. Putting the soil down to a mixture of fine grass and clover, which is kept cut short, retards tree growth and induces fruitfulness. In addition, dessert apples take on a better colour when grown in grass than under clean cultivation and have a longer storage life.

Many varieties set an excessive number of fruitlets and hand thinning is necessary if the apples are to grow to a worthwhile size. Many fruitlets fall naturally to the ground during the "June Drop" but additional thinning is necessary in June and July. Each cluster of dessert fruit must be reduced to two fruitlets, always removing the largest one— the 'king' fruit—first, and the clusters reduced to at least 3 inches apart. Thin cookers to single fruits 6–8 inches apart.

Apples are ready for harvesting when well coloured, with the seeds becoming brown in colour, and when they part readily from the fruit spurs. Test for fitness for picking by raising each apple to a horizontal position, giving a slight twist—if the stalk separates readily from the spur, without tearing, the apple is fit to pick.

Eat early maturing varieties direct from the tree or within a few weeks after being harvested. Store keeping varieties in a cool, dark, moist and frost-proof place.

Forms of apple trees: 1 maiden 2 fan-trained 3 dwarf pyramid 4 espalier 5 cordons 6 bush 7 Apple 'Scarlet Pimpernel'

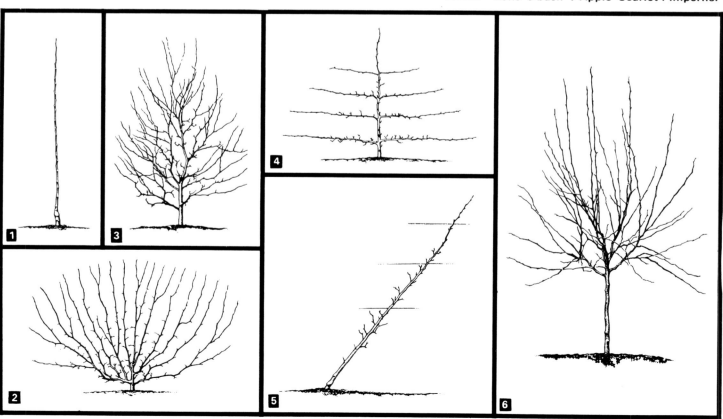

Apples for the garden—dessert

Variety	Pick	Eat	Flavour	Texture	Crop
*American Mother	Late Sept.	Oct.–Nov.	Very good,	Crisp, juicy	Irregular
*Ashmead's Kernel	Oct.	Nov.–March	Excellent, very aromatic	Firm	Light, occasionally heavy
*Beauty of Bath	July	Aug.	Good for season	Very soft	Sometimes irregular
Brownlees' Russet	Mid.–Oct.	Jan.–April	Good	Tender	Irregular
Claygate Pearmain	Mid.–Oct.	Dec.–March	Choice, aromatic	Crisp	Abundant
Court Pendu Plat	Early Nov.	Dec.–May	Acidly sweet	Firm	Very good
*Cox's Orange Pippin	Late Sept.	Oct.–Feb.	Excellent	Tender	Good to fair, depending on soil
*Crimson Cox	Mid.–Oct.	Nov.–Feb.	Not as good as Cox's Orange	Firm	Very good
D'Arcy Spice	End Oct.	Nov.–April	Aromatic	Firm	Medium, sometimes biennial
Discovery	End July	Aug.	Good for an early, pleasant aroma	Firm	Regular, precocious
Duke of Devonshire	Oct.	Feb.–March	Very good	Crisp	Good
*Egremont Russet	Late Sept.	Oct.–Dec.	Choice, nutty	Firm	Very good and regular
Ellison's Orange	Late Sept.	Sept.–Oct.	Good	Crisp	Very good, sometimes biennial
Epicure	End Aug.	Sept.	Very good	Firm	Prolific
*Fortune	Early Sept.	Sept.–L. Nov.	Sweet, aromatic	Crisp, tender	Good, sometimes biennial
George Cave	Mid.–July	early Aug.–Sept.	Pleasant for early sort	Firm at first	Regular and heavy
Granny Smith	Leave until first frost	Dec.–May	Moderate	Crisp	Free, tending to be biennial
Gravenstein	Late Sept.	Oct.–Nov.	Rich, aromatic	Soft	Good
Ingrid Marie	End Oct.	Dec.–April	Moderate	Firm	Good
Irish Peach	July	Aug.	Good straight from tree	Soft	Irregular
*James Grieve	Early Sept.	Sept.–Oct.	Very good, refreshing	Soft	Very good, regular
*King of the Pippins	Mid.–Oct.	Oct.–Nov.	Medium	Crisp	Good, regular
Lady Sudeley	Early Aug.	Aug.–Sept.	Good straight from tree	Soft	Good
*Laxton's Superb	Mid.–Oct.	Nov.–Feb.	Very good, aromatic	Soft	Good, sometimes biennial
*Lord Lambourne	Late Sept.	Oct.–Nov.	Excellent	Soft	Very good
*May Queen	Oct.	Jan.–May	Dry, nutty	Crisp	Very good
Melba	Early Aug.	Mid.–Aug.–Sept.	Distinctive aroma	Soft	Heavy, tending to be biennial
*Merton Beauty	Early Sept.	Sept.–Oct.	Rich, slight aniseed	Tender	Moderate
*Merton Charm	Mid.–Sept.	Sept.–Oct.	Excellent	Soft	Regular, good
Merton Prolific	Mid.–Oct.	Nov.–Feb	Acceptable	Firm	Exceedingly fertile
*Merton Russet	End Oct.	Dec.–March	Acid	Crisp	Good
*Merton Worcester	Mid.–Sept.	Sept.–Oct.	Sweet, aromatic	Firm	Excellent, liable become biennial
Orleans Reinette	Mid.–Oct.	Nov.–Feb.	Excellent, aromatic	Crisp	Fair
*Red Ellison	Mid.–Sept.	Sept.–Dec.	Aniseed	Crisp	Heavy and regular
*Ribston Pippin	Mid.–Oct.	Nov.–Jan.	Excellent, aromatic	Firm	Moderate
Scarlet Pimpernel	End July	End July–Sept.	Sweetly acid	Soft	Heavy
Spartan	Mid.–Oct.	Nov.–Feb.	Acceptable	Firm	Heavy
*St Cecilia	Early Oct.	Dec.–March	Excellent	Solid	Good
St Edmund's Russet	Sept.	Sept.–Oct.	Excellent from tree	Tender	Heavy, regular

(continued from first column)

Variety	Pick	Eat	Flavour	Texture	Crop
St Everard	Late Aug.	Sept.	Very good	Crisp	Irregular
*Sturmer Pippin	Leave until first frosts	Jan.–June	Very good	Firm	Good
*Sunset	Oct.	Oct.–Feb.	Very good	Medium firm	Heavy
Tydeman's Late Orange	End Oct.	Feb.–April	Excellent	Firm	Heavy
Winston	End Oct.	Jan.–April	Good	Very firm	Good
Worcester Pearmain	Early Sept.	Sept.–Oct.	Very good	Firm	Very good and regular

Apples for the garden—culinary

Variety	Pick	Eat	Flavour	Texture	Crop
Annie Elizabeth	Mid.–Oct.	Nov.–June	Good, acid	Cooks to froth	Good when settled down
Arther Turner	July–Sept.	July–Nov.	Good, acid	Firm	Regular and abundant
Bramley's Seedling	Late Sept.	Oct.–April	Excellent, acid	Firm	Very good
Crawley Beauty	Mid.–Oct.	Dec.–April	Good	Firm	Prolific and consistent
Edward VII	Mid.–Oct.	Dec.–April	Exceptionally good	Firm	Moderate
Emperor Alexander	Mid.–Sept.	Sept.–Nov.	Good	Tender	Fair
*George Neal	Sept.	Sept.–Oct.	Rich, slightly acid	Frothy cooked	Very free and regular
Golden Noble	Sept.	Sept.–Jan.	Excellent, acidly sweet	Tender	Good and regular
Grenadier	Mid.–Aug.	Aug.–Sept.	Good, acid	Frothy cooker	Very good and reliable
Howgate Wonder	Sept.–Oct.	Oct.–Feb.	Slightly acid	Cooks to froth	Heavy
*Lane's Prince Albert	Early Oct.	Nov.–March	Very good, acid	Soft	Very good
Lord Derby	Late Sept.	Oct.–Jan.	Excellent, sharp	Soft	Very free
*Monarch	Sept.	Oct.–March	Good, acid	Soft	Very good
Newton Wonder	Mid.–Oct.	Dec.–May	Very good, medium acid	Crisp	Irregular
Rev. W. Wilks	Early Oct.	Oct.–Nov.	Good	Cooks frothily	Very fertile
Warner's King	Late Sept.	Nov.–Feb.	Good	Tender	Moderate
Wellington	Mid.–Oct.	Nov.–March	Briskly acid	Solid	Moderate

Apples for the garden—dual purpose

Variety	Pick	Eat	Flavour	Texture	Crop
Allington Pippin	End Oct.	Oct.–Jan.	Good, acid	Firm	Very good
Barnack Beauty	Mid.–Oct.	Dec.–March	Good	Crisp	Fair to heavy
Belle de Boskoop	Mid.–Oct.	Dec.–April	Good, acid, aromatic	Firm	Moderate to heavy
Blenheim Orange	Mid.–Oct.	Nov.–Jan.	Excellent, nutty, acid	Crisp, cooks to pulp	Good and regular when settled down
*Charles Ross	Sept.	Oct.–Nov.	Moderate, sweet	Tender	Good and regular
Cheddar Cross	Mid.–Aug.	Late Aug.–early Sept.	Refreshing, slightly acid	Soft	Good
Cornish Gilliflower	Oct.	Dec.–April	Rich, sweet	Firm	Light
Herring's Pippin	Early Oct.	Oct.–Nov.	Good, spicy	Soft	Very good and regular
Mutsu	Early Oct.	Oct.–early April	Mildly sub-acid	Crisp	Heavy and regular
*Peasgood's Nonsuch	Early Sept.	Sept.–Nov.	Good	Soft	Irregular
*Rival	Early Oct.	Oct.–Dec.	Moderate	Firm	Fair
Wagener	Early Nov.	Dec.–	Fair	Firm	Very regular

**Particularly good as cordons.

Pears

In the opinion of most people dessert pears have a flavour superior to that of apples; it is more pronounced and the pears themselves are frequently much juicier. The best dessert pears have a melting consistency like butter (and hence the French word *beurre* applied to many varieties), although, for texture, many people prefer a crisp apple.

Although pear trees are longer-lived than apples, they tend to spur more freely forming too many clusters of buds. They are less prone to pest and disease attack, they flower earlier and therefore are more vulnerable to spring frosts. A few varieties only are suitable for growing in the open in most parts of Britain. Others need the protection of a

wall, and some not only require such shelter but will thrive only in our warmer districts.

Although all dessert pears can be cooked if they are picked while still slightly unripe, particular varieties are usually grown for this purpose. Special varieties, too, are grown for the making of perry, a fermented drink made from the juice in much the same way as cider is from apple juice.

A slightly acid soil suits pears best and a very alkaline soil should be avoided as, in such conditions, pears suffer badly from iron deficiency.

Compared with apples, pears are more likely to withstand poor drainage, but are less able to tolerate dryness. A very light sandy soil, therefore, must be

liberally enriched with humus-forming and moisture-holding materials. The ideal soil is a deep, rich loam somewhere between light and heavy.

Standard or half-standard trees take many years to come into bearing and eventually become too large for the average garden. Bush-type trees, pyramids, cordons, fans or espaliers are, therefore, more appropriate for small gardens, and these are usually grown on 'Malling Quince A' rootstocks.

The form of tree to be grown depends rather on the space available. For the open garden, bushes, pyramids or cordons are the usual choice. Bushes take up most room but their maintenance takes least time. Pyramids come into bearing more quickly and their small

Pears which suit the garden (Dessert varieties unless otherwise stated)

Variety	Season	Fruit quality	Crop	Special remarks
Baronne de Mello	Oct–Nov	Excellent, very juicy	Heavy	
Beurré d'Amanlis	Aug–Sept	Melting, sweet, very juicy	Heavy	Succeeds almost anywhere
Beurré Clairgeau	Nov–Dec	Faint musk flavour, firm flesh	Very heavy	Cooker
Beurré Diel	Oct–Dec	Delicious when quite ripe	Heavy	
Beurré Hardy	Oct	Good, flesh tinged with pink	Very heavy	Very hardy, succeeds almost anywhere
Beurré Superfin	Oct	Sweet, very melting, delicately perfumed	Moderate	Dessert variety but good for bottling and canning
Bristol Cross	Oct	Quite good, juicy and melting	Very heavy	
Catillac	Dec–Apr	Firm white flesh cooks red	Very heavy	Best of cookers
Clapp's Favourite	Sept	Fair sweet, juicy but gritty	Heavy	
Conference	Oct–Nov	Melting, juicy and sweet	Heavy	Succeeds almost anywhere. Dessert but good for bottling and canning
Doyenné d'Ete	July–Aug	Melting, sweet and very juicy	Heavy	Regular cropper
Doyenné du Comice	Nov	Tender and juicy delicious	Fair	One of the best dessert varieties but good for bottling and canning
Dr Jules Guyot	Aug–Sept	Melting, very juicy, slight musk flavour	Heavy	
Durondeau	Oct–Nov	Sweet, juicy, good flavour	Heavy	Succeeds almost anywhere
Easter Beurré	Feb–Apr	Sweet, melting with rich musk flavour	Moderate	
Emile d'Heyst	Oct–Nov	Juicy and very sweet	Heavy	Succeeds almost anywhere
Fertility	Oct	Little flavour, juicy and crisp	Heavy	Succeeds almost anywhere
Glou Morceau	Dec–Jan	Delicious flavour, melting and very sweet	Regular	Needs a warm wall
Gorham	Sept	Sweet, juicy, with musk flavour	Moderate to heavy	
Hessle	Oct	Slightly sweet	Very heavy	Cooker, succeeds almost anywhere
Improved Fertility	Sept–Oct	Fruit larger and better quality than 'Fertility'	Heavy	Self-compatible
Jargonelle	Aug	Sweet, juicy, slightly musky	Good	Tip-bearer, does well in north
Joséphine de Malines	Dec–Feb	Good flavour, pinkish-white, juicy flesh	Heavy	Tip-bearer
Louise Bonne of Jersey	Oct	Excellent flavour, melting and sweet	Heavy	Regular cropper but very vulnerable to spring frosts
Marguerite Marillat	Sept–Oct	Juicy but flavour only moderate	Good	
Marie Louise	Oct–Nov	Sweet, juicy, good flavour	Moderate	
Merton Pride	Sept–Oct	Sweet, juicy, excellent flavour	Good	
Packham's Triumph	Nov	Sweet, very juicy, good flavour	Good	Tip-bearer, also good for bottling and canning
Passe Crasanne	Mar–Apr	Sweet, very juicy, good flavour	Fair	Needs wall protection
Pitmaston Duchess	Oct–Nov	Pale yellow flesh, melting, very juicy but flavour only fair	Good	Dual-purpose
Santa Claus	Dec–Jan	Moderate, sweet but gritty	Good	
Seckle	Oct–Nov	Very sweet, rich flavour	Moderate	
Souvenir de Congrès	Sept	Sweet and very juicy, musky flavour	Heavy	
Thompson's	Oct–Nov	Very melting, delicious, rich flavour	Moderate	
Triomphe de Vienne	Sept	Juicy, good flavour but inclined to be gritty	Good	
Vicar of Winkfield	Nov–Jan	Firm flesh, sweet	Good	Cooker
William's Bon Chrétien	Sept	Very juicy, excellent flavour, musky	Good	Popular dessert variety but good for bottling and canning
Winter Nelis	Dec–Jan	Sweet and very juicy, good flavour	Good	Should be eaten while still yellowish-green

1 Pear 'Conference', a reliable variety.
2 'Uvedale's St Germain' is a dessert Pear.

size makes spraying, picking and protection from birds easier. Their pruning, however, takes rather more attention. Cordons require posts and wires for support but have the merit of taking up little room individually so that a single row can comprise a collection of varieties providing a succession of fruit. A row of cordons, too, can sometimes be planted on the southern side of a wall or close-boarded fence, so that full advantage is taken of the wind shelter thus provided.

Fans (trained specimens) can be grown in the open, with suitable posts and wires for support, but this is the best type of tree to grow against walls. Espalier-training may also be used against walls and espalier pears may be planted as a decorative yet useful edging to vegetable plots. The latter idea used to be more popular than it is today; the drawback is that fruit planted on the edge of the vegetable plot is liable to receive too much nitrogen so that growth is encouraged rather than fruiting, and suitable spraying is sometimes difficult where the drift may be harmful to other crops.

Planting should be done between leaf-fall and March—the sooner the better, and provided the soil is friable, following normal lines of procedure. It is particularly important that the union between scion and rootstock should be well above soil level (at least 4 inches). If this point is not observed and roots are formed by the scion, the dwarfing effect of the rootstock will be obviated and the tree will not only grow too large but will be many years coming into bearing. It should be noted, too, that where trees have been double-worked (because of incompatibility between quince and the chosen variety), there will be two unions and it is the lower one which must be quite clear of the soil.

After planting, staking and making firm, it is advisable to put down a 2-inch deep mulch of garden compost, well-rotted stable manure, peat or leafmould which will help to keep the soil moist in the event of a dry spring. Newly-planted pears should be inspected regularly in dry weather and watered liberally if there is any tendency to dry out.

For quality fruit the following planting distances should be regarded as the minimum: cordons (3 by 6 feet), fan-trained and espalier on 'Quince C' (12 feet apart), on 'Quince A' (15 feet apart), dwarf pyramids (4 by 7 feet), bush on 'Quince C' (12 feet each way), on 'Quince A' (15 feet each way), standard and half-standard (35 feet each way).

The subsequent manuring of pear trees should be adjusted according to performance.

In many cases pears will be maintained in good health by an annual (spring) application of rotted dung—a dressing on the surface about 2 inches deep—this mulch then being gently pricked into the soil surface with the fork in autumn. As an alternative or where no dung is available, a mixture of chemical fertilisers should be given early in February; 2 ounces of superphosphate of lime, 1 ounce of sulphate of ammonia and ½ ounce of sulphate of potash per square yard sprinkled as far as the roots extend (approximately the same as the spread of the branches or the height of the tree, whichever is greater) and raked into the surface.

In general the pruning of pears follows similar lines to that of apples (see Fruit pruning), and so does the spraying to control pests and diseases.

In harvesting pears it is particularly important to pick at the right moment. With early varieties it is preferable to pick a little too soon than to wait too long, but with mid-season and late-keeping sorts the pears should be picked only when they separate easily from the spur on being lifted just above the horizontal in the palm of the hand and then given a very slight twist

In choosing pear varieties to plant it is necessary to consider not only the purpose (dessert, cooking, bottling) and personal taste, but also the provision of suitable pollinators which must flower at the same time as the variety to be pollinated.

Flowering of pears

Early	Mid season	Late
Beurré Anjou	Belle-Julie	Beurré
Beurré	Beurré	Bedford (MS)
Clairgeau	d'Amanlis	Beurré Bosc
Beurré Diel (T)	Beurré Six	Beurré Hardy
Comtesse de	Beurré Superfin	Bristol
Paris	Conference	Cross (MS)
Doyenné d'Eté	Dr Jules Guyot	Catillac (T)
Duchesse	Duchesse de	Clapp's
d'Angoulême	Bordeaux	Favourite
Easter Beurré	Durondeau	Doyenné du
Emile d'Heyst	Fertility	Comice
Louise Bonne	Fondante	Glou Morceau
of Jersey	d'Automne	Gorham
Marguerite	Jargonelle	Hessle
Marillat (MS)	Joséphine de	Laxton's Victor
Passe Crasanne	Malines	Marie Louise
Précoce de	Merton Pride	Nouveau Poiteau
Trévoux	Packham's	Pitmaston
Princess	Triumph	Duchess (T)
Seckle	Souvenir du	Santa Claus
Uvedale's St	Congrès	Winter Nelis
Germain (T)	Thompson's	
Vicar of	Triomphe de	
Winkfield	Vienne	
Winter Orange	Williams' Bon	
	Chrétien	

T = Triploid   MS = Male Sterile

The varieties 'Jargonelle', 'Joséphine de Malines' and 'Packham's Triumph' are tip-bearers and on that account should be avoided for pyramids, cordons, fans, or other forms of trained tree.

Plums

Plums are popular for cooking, jam-making and bottling or canning, but the sweeter varieties are among our most delicious dessert fruits. Damsons ripen a little later than most plums. The fruits are small, oval and richly flavoured, but not really sweet enough for the general taste for eating raw. They are, however, excellent for cooking, preserves and bottling. Bullaces are small round fruits which ripen even later and are useful on that account to lengthen the season. Bullaces can be eaten raw but are excellent for cooking. Gages are simply a class of plum with a characteristic, and particularly delicious, flavour. Gages, bullaces and damsons are all grown in the same way as plums.

Plums will grow in most parts of the country but as they flower early they are very vulnerable to spring frosts. The choicer kinds deserve the protection of a wall where protection from frost (and birds) can more easily be given. They do

1 The Damson 'Merryweather' has purple skin and yellow flesh, and ripens in late September and October.
2 Plum 'Denniston's Superb' crops well in mid-August and has a golden skin and flesh, being one of the hardiest and most reliable of gages.

best in districts where the annual rainfall is between 20 and 35 inches. Damsons will succeed in areas having higher rainfall, and less sunshine, than plums will tolerate.

Plums need a well-drained soil and one containing plenty of humus to hold moisture during the growing season. A very acid soil should be limed, but an alkaline soil should not be planted with plums. Plums (and other stone fruits) do need calcium but they will not prosper in an alkaline soil. Plum trees planted in thin soils overlaying chalk often suffer seriously from lime-induced iron deficiency.

No really satisfactory dwarfing rootstock has yet been found for plums. The two least vigorous are common plum and St Julien 'A'; the former, however, is only compatible with certain varieties. Trees grown on these rootstocks are sometimes described as 'semi-dwarf' but, even so, a standard or half-standard would be too large for the average garden, and even a bush-type tree requires a spacing of 12–15 feet (on Brompton or Myrobalan 'B' rootstock, 18–20 feet).

Because plums do not produce fruiting spurs as apples and pears do, they are not so amenable to training, and are seldom satisfactory as cordons or espaliers. They may, however, be grown as fans, for wall-training or with the support of posts and horizontal wires, but root-pruning will probably be necessary every five years or so to restrain growth and maintain fruiting (see Root pruning). A fan tree on St Julien 'A' rootstock should be allotted at least 15 feet of wall space.

Plums may also be grown as semi-dwarf pyramids on St Julien 'A' rootstock and this is a form which is best for the small garden. Such a tree requires a spacing of 10 feet and, as it will never be allowed to grow much over 9 feet in height, it is possible to arrange some kind of cage or netting over the top of the tree to keep off birds, which will otherwise damage the fruit. An additional advantage is that the branches of a pyramid seldom break and there is thus less likelihood of infection by disease.

For training as a pyramid a maiden should be planted in the usual way and the following March it should be headed back to 5 feet. Any laterals above 18 inches from soil level should be shortened by half and any arising lower down the stem should be cut off entirely. Towards the end of July or early in August, when new growth has finished, cut back branch leaders to 8 inches, making the cut to a bud pointing downwards or outwards. Cut laterals back to 6 inches. Repeat this procedure annually. Leave the central leader untouched in summer but in April of the second year cut it back to one-third of its length. Repeat this annually, cutting the new growth back by two-thirds until a height of 9 feet is attained. After that shorten the new growth on the central leader to 1 inch or less each May.

Plant plums in the usual way between November and March, the sooner the better, always provided the soil is friable (see Planting). Stake securely and put down a mulch to preserve soil moisture.

An established plum needs plenty of nitrogen but, until good crops are being carried, on most soils it will be sufficient to give a light mulch of rotted farmyard manure or garden compost in spring, and prick this lightly into the surface the subsequent autumn. When good crops are being borne, the yearly mulch may be supplemented with 1 ounce per square yard dressing of Nitro-chalk and ½ ounce per square yard of sulphate of potash, given in February. Every third year, add 1 ounce per square yard of superphosphate. Where no manure or garden compost is available, peat may be used as a mulch and the dose of Nitro-chalk doubled.

The wood of plum trees naturally tends to be brittle and branches often break in late summer gales when the crop is heavy. Thinning of the fruit will help to prevent this form of breakage, and it is also advisable to arrange some kind of support for extra-heavily laden branches on bush-type trees. Wooden props may be fixed beneath branches (well padding the point of support) or a tall, strong central pole can be erected

Plums for the garden

Variety	Season	Fruit quality	Crop	Special remarks
Belle de Louvain, red to purple skin, yellow flesh	Late Aug	Fair flavour when cooked	Good	Cooker. Slow to start bearing
Black Prince, blue-black	Early Aug	Slight damson flavour	Heavy	Cooker. Very early flowering and therefore vulnerable to frost
Blaisdon Red, dark red skin, yellow green flesh	Late Aug	Acid. Good for jam	Reliable	Cooker. Picking may continue over three weeks
Bountiful, plum-purple skin, yellow flesh	Mid-Aug	Resembles 'Victoria' but lacks its quality	Heavy	Cooker. Resistant to silver leaf
Bryanston, greenish-yellow skin and flesh	Mid-Sept	Gage flavour but less pronounced than greengage	Good	Dessert. Large fruits
Cambridge Gage, green to yellow skin and flesh	Late Aug	True gage flavour	Fair but regular	Dessert, cooking or preserving. Fruits small
Coe's Golden Drop, yellow skin and flesh	Late Sept–Oct	Sweet, rich flavour	Moderate	Does best on a wall. Will cook well but generally held to be the finest dessert plum
Count Althann's Gage, dark crimson skin, yellow flesh	Mid-Sept	Excellent. Sweet and juicy	Good	Dessert. Good on walls
Czar, dull red skin, yellow flesh	Early Aug	Poor quality. Cooks with red juice	Heavy, regular	Cooker. Very hardy and reliable
Delicious (Laxton's Delicious) Bright red skin, golden yellow flesh	Mid-Aug	Sweet and very juicy. Good flavour	Good, regular	Dessert. Keeps well after picking
Denniston's Superb, greenish-yellow skin	Mid-Aug	Fair gage flavour	Good	Dessert. Hardiest and most reliable of gages
Diamond, blue-black skin, yellow flesh	Early–mid-Sept	Prune flavour	Irregular	Cooker, Very good for bottling
Early Laxton, yellow skin with red flesh	Late July	Sweet and juicy, first-class cooked	Moderate	Dual-purpose. Earliest of all for dessert
Early Orleans, reddish-blue skin, yellow flesh	Late July–August	Sweet. Cooks with deep red juice	Heavy	Cooker
Early Transparent, orange-yellow skin, yellow flesh	Mid-Aug	Very sweet, rich gage flavour	Heavy	Dessert. Repays thinning. Excellent on walls.
Farleigh Damson, purple skin, yellow flesh	Mid-Sept	Good flavour	Very heavy	Cooker
Giant Prune, deep red skin, golden flesh	Mid-Sept	Little flavour	Good, regular	Cooker
Golden Transparent, golden yellow flesh and skin	Early Oct	Very sweet, rich gage flavour	Prolific	Dessert. Best grown as fan on a wall
Goldfinch, golden flesh and skin	Late Aug	Sweet and juicy. Fair flavour	Good	Dessert
Jefferson, golden skin and flesh	Early Sept	Very good gage flavour	Good	Dessert
Kirke's Blue, dark reddish-purple, greenish and yellow skin	Mid-Sept	Choice flavour	Irregular	Dessert. Sometimes known simply as 'Kirke's'
Langley Bullace, black skin, greenish-yellow flesh	Early Nov	Really more a damson than a bullace	Prolific	Cooker. Self-compatible

Flowering of plums

Compatibility

Group A	Group B	Group C
Early		
Black Prince	Utility	Golden Transparent*
Jefferson		
Early mid season		
Black Diamond	Farleigh	Denniston's Superb
Coe's Golden	Damson	Monarch*
Drop		Ontario*
Late Orleans		Warwickshire
President		Drooper*
Mid season		
Bryanston Gage	Early Laxton	Bountiful
Kirke's Late	River's	Brandy Gage
Orange	Early	Czar*
Washington	Prolific	Laxton's Cropper
	Goldfinch	Laxton's Gage
		Merryweather
		Damson*
		Pershore
		Purple Pershore
		Severn Cross
		Victoria*
Late mid season		
Count Althann's	Cambridge	Blaisdon Red*
Gage	Gage	Early Transparent
Delicious	Early	Giant Prune
Pond's Seedling	Orleans	Oullins' Golden
Wyedale		Gage
Late season		
Late Transparent		Belle de Louvain*
Old Greengage		Belle de Septembre
Red Magnum Bonum		Marjorie's Seedling*
		Shropshire Damson

Choice Cherries for the Garden

Variety	Class	Flavour	Colour	Crop	Flowers	Fruits
Amber Heart (Kentish Bigarreau)	D	Rich	Yellow and red	Prolific	Mid	Mid July
Archduke	D & C	Sweet	Dark red	Good	Late	July
Bigarreau Gaucher	D	Rich	Almost black	Good	Mid	Late July
Bigarreau Napoleon	D	V. Fine	Yellow and red	Good and Regular	Late	Late July
Bigarreau de Schrecken	D	Good	Black	Good	Mid	Late June
Bradbourne Black	D	Rich	Black	Heavy	Late	Late July
Early Rivers	D	Delicious	Black	Good	Mid	Mid June
Emperor Francis	D	Richly Aromatic	Dark red over yellow	Productive	Mid	Late July
Frogmore Early	D	Good	Yellow and red	Heavy and Regular	Late	Early July
Géante de Hedelfingen	D	Rich	Black	Good	Late	Late July
Governor Wood	D	Good	Yellow and red	Good	Late	July
Kentish Red	C	Acid	Red	Good	Late	Early July
Late Duke	D & C	Fair	Deep Red	Good	Late	August
May Duke	D & C	Fair	Black	Good	Late	June
Merton Bigarreau	D	Winey	Purplish-black	Heavy and Regular	Mid	Late July
Merton Bounty	D	Sweet	Dark crimson	Good	Mid	Early July
Merton Favourite	D	Rich	Black	Good	Early	Early July
Merton Glory	D	Good	Cream and crimson	Good	Mid	Mid July
Merton Heart	D	Rich	Dark crimson to black	Heavy	Early	Early July
Morello	C	Acid	Dark red to black	Prolific	Late	August to September
Noir de Guben	D	V. good	Black	Fair	Early	July
Roundel Heart	D	Sweet	Deep crimson	Heavy	Mid	Early July
Waterloo	D	Rich	Black and red	Slightly biennial	Early	Late July

D Dessert C Culinary V Very

and branches supported from this by ropes, maypole fashion.

Dessert plums should be left on the tree until quite ripe and then picked by taking hold of the stalk so that the 'bloom' is not spoiled. The season of the best dessert varieties can be extended slightly by storing a few fruits, wrapped individually in paper, in a cool, airy place. They will keep for a couple of weeks or so.

Cherries

Two main groups of cherries are cultivated for the merit of their fruit, the 'sweet', dessert (Prunus avium) and the 'sour', culinary (Prunus cerasus); a third group, the 'Duke' cherries, form an intermediate class. The sweets are subdivided into the 'black' and 'white' varieties. All fruiting cherries are hardy in the British Isles, though the blossom may be damaged by spring frosts.

Named varieties are propagated on to rootstocks by budding in July and August, or by grafting in March, which would be rather unusual. Seedling Gean Mazzard and the clonal Malling F 12/1 rootstocks are used. Unfortunately, as yet, a dwarfing rootstock is not available and a mature sweet cherry tree may be up to 30 feet tall with a corresponding spread—too large for the average modern garden. Bush Morello (sour) trees rarely exceed a height of 15 feet.

Sour cherries do well in almost any situation and are particularly valuable for training as fan trees against a north-facing wall unsuited to other fruits. Although sweet cherries can also be grown as fans, they dislike hard pruning and are happiest as standards or half standards given minimum pruning. Plant standards 30 feet apart,

A good flavoured Cherry 'Late Duke' grown for culinary and dessert use. It ripens in mid-June.

half standards 25 feet, bush and fan trees 15 feet. Cherries as a class dislike poorly drained, heavy soils. The sweet varieties do well on deep, light to medium loams while the sour ones will tolerate poor soils, provided they are not waterlogged. Lime in the soil is not an essential as is commonly supposed.

Morello cherries are self fertile and will pollinate any sweet cherry flowering concurrently. Most sweet cherries are infertile with their own pollen and often with certain other varieties also. The John Innes Institute has classified the sweets into a number of groups but not with their companions (see table above). It is important to select varieties for interplanting whose blossom period coincides or overlaps. A few varieties called universal donors are compatible with all groups flowering at the same time. The dessert cherry season extends from mid-June to mid-August; culinary kinds are used throughout the year for cooking, bottling and making into jam or cherry ale.

Cultivation Young trees, not exceeding five years old, transplant best. Planting can be carried out at any time from mid-October to mid-March, whenever the soil is sufficiently friable to be worked between the roots.

Excavate a wide hole just deep enough to allow the roots to be covered with 4–5 inches of soil (see Fruit in the garden). Plant firmly and stake securely. Shorten the previous season's

Peach 'Dr Hogg' is a variety producing large velvety fruits with a rich apricot-coloured flesh.

growth on the leading branches by half, and side shoots to 3 inches. In the spring, mulch the soil surface over the root area with composted vegetable refuse or decayed straw. Do not let weeds encroach for the first few years.

Sweet cherries fruit chiefly on the spurs formed freely on the older wood. Pruning consists in maintaining the tree to an open habit with an evenly balanced head, together with the removal of dead, crossing and rubbing branches. This minimal pruning should be confined to the spring and early summer when infection from silver leaf disease is least likely.

Sour cherries fruit on shoots formed the previous season. After the basic fan of branches has been built up by shortening the leaders annually as for sweet cherries, annually replaced sidegrowths are tied in parallel to the permanent branches. The replacement shoots are selected during May to August—one near the base of a fruiting shoot and another at its tip to draw sap to the fruit; all others are pinched out when quite small. The tip of the terminal shoot itself is pinched out when 3–4 inches of growth has been made.

After the cherries have been gathered, the fruited shoots are pruned back at their junction with the selected replacement shoots. The latter are then tied in neatly as before.

Cherries appreciate a spring mulch of farmyard manure at the rate of 1 cwt to 10 square yards, or 2–3 oz per square yard of Nitro-chalk if manure is unobtainable, plus an autumn application of 1–2 oz per square yard of sulphate of potash. Trees on walls respond to being fed with liquid manure.

Protecting the fruit from bird damage is necessary, using fish nets or rayon spider's web material on trees of a suitable size, or by bird scaring where trees are too large to net.

Sweet cherry pollination groups
Group 1. 'Early Rivers' (e), 'Bedford Prolific' (e), 'Knight's Early Black' (e), 'Roundel Heart' (m).
Group 2. 'Bigarreau de Schrecken' (e), 'Waterloo' (e), 'Merton Favourite' (e), 'Frogmore Early' (m), 'Merton Bigarreau' (m), 'Merton Bounty' (m).
Group 3. 'Bigarreau Napoleon' (m), 'Emperor Francis' (m).
Group 4. 'Merton Premier' (m), 'Amber Heart' (m).
Group 5. 'Merton Heart' (e), 'Governor Wood' (m).
Group 6. 'Bradbourne Black' (l), 'Gèante de Hedelfingen' (l).
Universal Donors: 'Noir de Guben' (e), 'Merton Glory' (m), 'Bigarreau Gaucher' (l).
Flowering period: (e) early; (m) mid-season; (l) late.
N.B. A variety will not set fruit with its own pollen nor when cross-pollinated by another variety in the same group. It will, however, set fruit with any other variety from the other groups, or with a universal donor provided that their blossoming periods coincide or overlap.

Peaches and Nectarines
The peach, *Prunus persica*, is closely related to apricots, cherries and plums. It was introduced into England in the early sixteenth century via Europe and Persia from China. The nectarine is a natural sport of the peach with smaller, more delicately flavoured fruits, which are smooth-skinned, whereas peaches have a rough skin.

Bush peaches are hardy in southern England; the protection of a south or south-west wall is needed further north. Nectarines invariably are grown on walls. Both fruits need abundant sunshine and crop to perfection under glass. A well-drained, deep, medium loam soil gives the best results. Soils with a high lime content are disliked; but acid soils should be dressed with mortar rubble. An application of ½ lb per square yard of coarse bonemeal should be given at planting time and an annual summer feed of a balanced fertiliser at the rate of 4 ounces per square yard should be applied. Give the trees a spring mulch of

Peaches for the greenhouse or outdoors

Variety	Flavour	Colour	Size	Fruit
Bellegarde	Rich, very juicy	Yellow and crimson, white flesh	Large	Early September
Duke of York	Very sweet	Crimson, white flesh	Very large	Mid-July
Erly Redfre	Rich	Creamy-yellow with crimson flush white	Large	Early August
Hales Early	Sweet, aromatic	Yellow with red flush	Medium to large	Late July
Peregrine	Juicy delicious flavour	Bright crimson	Large	Early August
Rochester	Rich, sweet juicy	Yellow, mottled red	Good size	Mid-August
Nectarines				
Early Rivers	Tender, juicy	Bright scarlet	Large	Mid-July
Lord Napier	Brisk, rich and delicious	Yellow and crimson	Large	Early August
Pineapple	Delicious and melting	Orange and red	Fairly large	Early September

decayed dung if the material is available. Plant one to three-year-old trees between mid-October and mid-March, preferably in October or November. Trim any damaged roots, cover them with no more than 4–6 inches of soil, tread firm and ensure that the graft union is above ground. Keep the trunks of wall trees 4 inches away from the walls. Fan trees should be tied temporarily until the soil has settled, bush trees should be staked, putting the stake in the planting hole before the tree. Planting distances are: for fan trees 15 feet apart, and for bush trees 15–20 feet. Mulch either with compost or strawy manure in March, and rub off the first season's blossom buds.

Frosty sites are unsuitable as the trees flower in February or early March, and wall trees should be protected with hessian or tiffany at night, though this should be removed by day to allow pollinating insects access to the flowers. Although both fruits are self-fertile, hand pollination ensures a full set. Fan trees, however, often set an excessive crop, and the fruitlets should be thinned progressively so as to leave peaches at one per square foot and nectarines at one per 9-inch square. Give copious waterings while the fruits are swelling. Leave the crop to ripen fully on the tree, and check daily for ripe fruits by palming off —finger pressure causes bruises. They should be used promptly, for dessert, bottling, canning or jam making.

When pruning it should be remembered that peaches and nectarines fruit on the previous season's shoots, so prune them hard enough to induce plenty of new growth, at least 12 inches in length annually. However, do not go to the other extreme as excessive pruning induces lush growth and diminished cropping. Cut out any dead wood, crossing branches and a third of the old growth of bush trees in May, cutting always at a strong sideshoot. Disbud the fruiting shoots of fan-trained trees during April, May and June, retaining one new shoot at the base, tip and middle. Pinch out the growing tips of the last two at five leaves, but allow the basal shoots to grow to their full length. Cut out the fruited shoots after harvest and tie in the replacements in fan formation at 3 inches apart. Over-vigorous trees should be root pruned.

Strawberries

Stocks Strawberries are subject to several serious virus diseases, and at one time these threatened to make commercial cultivation quite uneconomic and garden culture most disappointing. However, there has been considerable improvement in the general health of strawberry stocks since the introduction of a government scheme of inspection.

It is of the utmost importance to start with disease-free stock and one should purchase from a grower with a good

reputation to maintain. Where possible one should buy from a grower who has been given a Ministry of Agriculture 'A' Certificate for his stock and will quote the number. Unfortunately not all varieties are eligible for the ministry scheme and in such instances one can only patronise growers who have gained 'A' Certificates for their eligible varieties in the hope that they may be equally careful with their non-eligible stocks.

Site Although the strawberry is of woodland origin, the modern fruit requires all the sun it can get. On the other hand, the site for the strawberry bed needs to be sheltered, for cold spring winds can very seriously check growth. The garden sloping gently towards the south, unshaded but sheltered, will yield the earliest crops.

Although strawberries may be grown in most parts of Britain, late spring frosts may be a limiting factor. This can be quite a local problem and if your garden lies in a frost-pocket there is not much you can do about it except to be ready to give some kind of protection with cloches or plastic to plants in flower or to sidestep the difficulty by growing only the so-called perpetual-fruiting types, removing the first trusses of blossom and concentrating on late summer or autumn fruits.

Soil Strawberries do best in a rich medium loam with a high humus content. Well-rotted leafmould is an excellent material to incorporate in soils deficient in organic matter, but any other decayed vegetable matter can be used. The site needs to be well drained.

Heavy clay, peaty and very light, sandy soils should be prepared well in advance of planting time.

Soils with a very high lime content are unsuitable for strawberries.

Preparation Early preparation will not only assist soil improvement but will also ensure freedom from perennial weeds, which can be a considerable nuisance. When digging, rotted farmyard or stable manure should be worked in, 10 lb per square yard being regarded as a normal 'dose' and twice this rate is recommended for poor, sandy soil. Follow with a surface dressing of 1 ounce per square yard of sulphate of potash.

Where no natural manure or garden compost is available 1 ounce per square yard each of superphosphate, sulphate of ammonia and sulphate of potash should be sprinkled over the bed after digging and lightly raked in. If the soil is not already rich in humus, add up to half a bushel of peat per square yard.

Planting Strawberries are usually planted in beds, the rows being 2½ to 3 feet apart, the plants 15 to 18 inches apart in the rows, according to the richness of soil. One reason for early soil preparation is that the soil should be firm.

Summer-fruiting strawberries may be planted either in the late summer to early autumn or even in the spring, provided that in the latter instance all blossom is removed the first summer. The earlier plants can go out, the bigger and stronger plants they will make their first year—so, if you can obtain plants so early, plant in July, August, or even September, but October is late.

The perpetual-fruiting varieties can also be planted in autumn but rooted runners are not available so early. However, as they have time to catch up in spring, October planting is quite satisfactory, provided the soil is properly workable and will break down to a friable tilth. On cold, heavy soils the planting of perpetual strawberries is probably better deferred until spring.

When ordering, for preference stipulate plants which have been rooted in pots. These will be slightly more expensive but they will transplant more readily, with less root damage, and they will have better root development.

Use a trowel for planting and take a hole out for each plant deep enough to accommodate the roots without bending them. Then return a little soil at the centre of the hole to make a mound on which the strawberry plant can 'sit' with its roots spread evenly around it.

The base of the crown should be just at soil level: if it is too high, roots are exposed and dry out, resulting in eventual death of the plant; while if the crown is half buried, it will either produce unwanted weak secondary growths or rot away entirely.

Plant firmly, using the handle of the trowel as a rammer. As you proceed, see that the roots of plants awaiting their turn are not exposed to the wind. Finally, rake the bed smooth and give a good watering to settle the soil.

Follow-up Keep an eye on the weather and the state of the soil because many strawberry plants are lost or seriously retarded by the effect of drought during the weeks immediately after planting. Also inspect the bed after hard weather, and refirm with your boot any plants which have been lifted by frost action.

In the early spring scatter fertiliser dressing down the rows at the rate of 2 ounces per square yard. This is made

1 The blossom is removed from a Strawberry runner to encourage it to make a better root system.
2 When the berries have formed it is necessary to put some protective material beneath them.
3 Clean dry straw can be spread around the plants, and the fruit lifted above it, to ripen.
4 'Cambridge Vigour' grown on straw.

up of 1 part of sulphate of potash, 1 part of sulphate of ammonia and 2 parts of superphosphate (all parts by weight). Be careful that these fertilisers do not go on the leaves, and gently rake them into the surface soil. Then apply a light mulch of well-rotted farmyard manure, garden compost or peat to help to preserve soil moisture in the event of a spring drought but be prepared to water as well when necessary.

Timing the fruit When, in the spring following planting, the first blossom buds appear, you have to make a major policy decision. First-year flowers on maiden plants will give the earliest crop and the largest individual berries, but if you remove this first year's blossom and wait until the second crop, the yield will then probably be greater than the total of two years' crops on plants fruiting in their first season.

If you are very anxious to secure early fruit and if you are going to protect them with cloches or polythene tunnels, then first-year blossom should be left on. Indeed, where earliness is considered all-important, the strawberries may be treated as an annual crop and a fresh batch of earlies planted every year, to be dug up and burned immediately after harvesting. In such instances, strawberries may take their place in the regular annual rotation of the vegetable garden.

Where size of crop is considered more important than earliness, and the plants are deblossomed in their first year, there is every prospect of the strawberries continuing to yield well for three years, possibly for four.

The perpetual-fruiting varieties, in fact, bear at least two distinct crops. In the first year after planting, the first batch of blossom should be removed to give the plants a chance to gain size and

strength. Blossom appearing after the end of June is allowed to develop and the fruit will be ripe from late summer onwards. In subsequent years, you have the choice between two crops, one in June and one in autumn, and one, larger crop, earlier in autumn or in late summer.

Not long after the berries begin to develop, runners will appear. Unless these are required for propagation they should be cut off at once with scissors so as not to waste the plant's energies. With early-rooted plants set out early, runners may even be produced in the first autumn and these should certainly be removed. Perpetual-fruiting varieties tend not to produce runners so freely as the summer-fruiting kinds, but nevertheless these, too, should usually be removed unless required for increase.

Protection Before the first ripening strawberries are heavy enough to weigh the trusses down to the soil, some kind of protection is necessary to prevent the berries being splashed by mud. The traditional method is to lay straw on the soil, barley straw being more easily tucked close to the plants than the

stiffer wheat straw and less liable to be a carrier of pests than oat straw. Before putting down the straw, weed by gentle hoeing, handweeding, or spot application of weedkiller.

You should not be in too much of a hurry to put down the straw because, as it is light in colour, it loses heat rapidly and increases the risk of radiation frost damage to open blossom or tiny fruitlets.

Straw, however, is not always easy to obtain, and you can buy patented strawberry mats or specially made wire supports which hold the berries clear of the soil. Even a scattering of peat is better than nothing.

Slugs can do much damage in a strawberry bed and slug bait pellets should be scattered freely among the plants and kept renewed as necessary during the fruiting season.

Picking Out of doors the first berries are likely to ripen between four and six weeks from when the blossom opened. The fruit should be picked by taking the stem about $\frac{1}{2}$ inch behind the berry between finger and thumb. In this way the berry can be broken off without being touched.

1

Raspberries

Most raspberries bear red fruit but a few have white or yellow berries. Most ripen in July, some in September or October, and some in either season according to when they are pruned. For varieties fruiting in summer, pruning is carried out immediately picking has finished, the old canes being cut out completely and replaced by the new canes from the perennial rootstock which will then fruit the next year. With autumn-fruiting varieties the fruited canes are cut back during the dormant season (usually in February) and the new canes which appear in spring will fruit in the autumn of the same year (for individual varieties see table: 'A selection of raspberries'.

Raspberries are very subject to virus diseases but the health of commercial stocks has been greatly improved in recent years by the scheme of inspection and certification carried out by the Ministry of Agriculture, Fisheries and Food. For this reason it is particularly important to start by planting only canes obtained from a completely reliable source.

Raspberries do best in full sun but this condition is not always easily provided in a small surburban garden and, if necessary, the fruit will tolerate some slight shade. The most important requirements are that the soil should be free of lime and not subject to waterlogging. All fruits need slightly acid conditions but raspberries will stand a more acid soil than most. In an alkaline soil, raspberries are seriously affected by iron and manganese deficiency.

Preparing the bed Although a well-drained soil is essential for success, a sandy soil will need to have plenty of organic matter incorporated in preparation. Raspberries need a plentiful supply of moisture throughout the growing season.

It is sound practice to dig over the prospective raspberry bed during the summer prior to planting, taking particular care to pick out the roots of all perennial weeds which may be encountered. Bindweed' and couch grass are often a cause of much trouble and, because raspberries are shallow rooters, deep cultivation after planting is inadvisable.

A generous amount of rotted garden compost or farmyard or stable manure should be worked in as digging proceeds —up to 10 lb per square yard, more on sandy soils. Provided the soil is definitely acid, matured mushroom bed compost may be used with advantage but this material is slightly alkaline and should, therefore, be avoided if the soil is already neutral or nearly so. To insure against any possible shortage of phosphates, also dig in a dressing of 1 ounce per square yard of superphosphate.

Feeding the bed After planting the supply of organic matter and plant foods in the soil will be maintained by an annual mulch of farmyard or stable manure at a rate of about 5 lb per square yard. Where natural manure is unobtainable peat or straw may be used instead to supply organic matter plus a spring dressing of 1 ounce of sulphate of ammonia, 1 ounce of superphosphate and ½ ounce of sulphate of potash, per square yard, to provide necessary nutriment. An excess of nitrogen will stimulate the growth of the canes but without any corresponding increase in the crop. A deficiency of potash, on the other hand, will soon show itself in reduced yield.

Incidentally, the site, soil and manurial requirements of the raspberry apply equally to all other cane fruits.

Planting Raspberries may be planted either in the open or against a fence or wall. In the latter case, the canes can be secured simply by lengths of strong string tied to staples at the ends of the row and at intervals of 18 inches or so. A free-standing row, however, will require substantial posts at each end of the row and these should be put in before planting. Concrete or angle-iron posts make a good permanent job and should be embedded in concrete. Struts should be arranged on the inner sides of the posts to take the strain. Two lengths of gauge 12 or 14 galvanised wire will be required at 2 feet and at 4 feet from the ground (or 5 feet where very vigorous varieties are planted). The canes should be planted 2 feet apart in the row and, if more than one row is wanted, rows should be 6 feet apart.

Early autumn is the best time to plant but planting is permissible at any time between autumn and spring, always provided the soil is dry enough to be friable and is not frozen. Should the soil be too wet when the canes arrive from the nursery, heel them in temporarily, in as dry a spare spot as may be available.

If they arrive when frost prohibits planting, keep them wrapped up, and store in a cool shed where the roots will not dry out. Plant them or heel them in out of doors as soon as conditions permit. If the roots appear at all dry when planting, soak them in a bucket of water for an hour or so.

Too deep planting is a common error with raspberries: the roots should be covered by no more than 3 inches of soil. If the canes have just arrived from the nursery, it is usually possible to see the old soil mark on the stem, indicating the correct depth.

The quickest way to plant a row of raspberries is to take out a shallow trench the width of your spade. As you set the canes in position, spread out the roots evenly and trim off any damaged parts. Replace the soil in the trench, holding each cane erect in turn as the soil is placed over its roots and made firm. When planting as shallowly as this, however, it is unsafe to use one's heel as a rammer—gentle pressure with the sole of the boot will be sufficient. Immediately after planting cut back the canes to a height of 2 feet and finally lightly rake the soil to break up the surface.

In February, mulch the bed with a good layer of rotted garden compost, rotted dung or mature mushroom bed compost (again, provided the soil is already definitely acid).

Subsequent pruning In spring, as soon as the growth buds on the raspberry canes may be seen to be swelling, cut back the canes still further—to a visibly live bud about 10 inches above soil level. The idea of this is to leave just sufficient top growth to keep the roots active. No cropping must be permitted the first season and, after this cutting back, new suckers will spring up from the roots and these shoots are the ones which will fruit in the second season. Once these new shoots are growing well, the old 10-inch high pieces should be cut down to soil level.

In the second summer, when the fruit has been picked, cut down all the fruited canes right to soil level. These should be replaced by new canes now springing up. If there are more than five or six, select the best of even size, removing any odd extra-vigorous canes and any growing up between the rows at a distance from the main rootstocks. All prunings should at once be burned to prevent the spread of disease or pests.

The new canes should be tied in to the horizontal wires individually as they grow.

In the following February the canes should be tipped, making the cuts to growth buds some 6 inches above the upper wire. This will stimulate better growth lower down where the berries are less liable to suffer wind damage.

Autumn-fruiting varieties should have fruited canes cut out in February and

1 Raspberry 'Malling Exploit' has fairly large fruits and crops heavily.
2 The method most commonly adopted in gardens for tying Raspberry canes to support wires is to fasten each cane individually with raffia or twine.
3 An alternative method is to let them grow to their full height, tie them in to the wires, and loop back the extremities forming an arch.
4 Raspberry 'Malling Landmark'.

A selection of raspberries

Variety	Season	Colour of berry	Description
Malling Exploit	Summer Early to mid-season	Red	Fair flavour. Larger fruits, heavier cropper than Malling Promise, to which otherwise very similar
Malling Jewel	Summer Early to mid-season	Red	Vigorous. Heavy cropper. Good flavour
Malling Promise	Summer Early to mid-season	Red	Very vigorous. Large fruits of good flavour
Lloyd George	Summer Mid-season, or autumn if cut down in spring	Red	Outstanding flavour. Specify 'New Zealand' strain
Yellow Antwerp	Summer Mid-season	Yellow	Moderately vigorous. Fairly large berries of good flavour
Malling Enterprise	Summer Mid-season to late	Red	Vigorous. Large fruit, good flavour
Newburgh	Summer Mid-season to late	Red	Fairly vigorous. Very fair flavour. Some berries large. Good variety for heavy land
Norfolk Giant	Summer Late	Red	Very vigorous. Heavy cropper. Fruit firm with acid flavour. Good for preserving
Hailsham	Autumn	Red	Vigorous. Large berries
September	Autumn	Red	Vigorous. Good cropper. Pleasant flavour. Bright red berries of medium size

2

3

4

the new growths will then fruit the same year.

Loganberry

The loganberry is, perhaps, the supreme bramble type of berry, as it is ideal for stewing, jam- and jelly-making, bottling, canning, juice extraction and wine-making. The berries can also be eaten as dessert when fully ripe, but may be too tart for some palates.

Opinions are divided as to whether the loganberry is a red-fruiting form of the common Californian blackberry, *Rubus ursinus vitifolius,* or a seedling from a cross between the 'Red Antwerp' raspberry and the American blackberry 'Aughinburgh'. The plant appeared in 1881 in the garden of Judge J. H. Logan of Santa Cruz, California, from whom it takes its name. It has been cultivated in England from 1897.

The loganberry produces vigorous, prickly canes carrying 3- to 5-lobed leaves. As flowering is late, the plants may be grown in low-lying situations; spring frosts rarely damage the blossom, though severe winters may affect the canes. Loganberries are self-compatible and yield heavy crops of blunt, firm, very juicy, deep red berries of a rich flavour,

from August to September. The yield may be sustained for 15 years or more. The berries do not plug, so are picked complete with core. Picking is best done when the berries are quite dry.

Heavy, rather than chalky and light and dry, soils are preferred—chalky soils induce iron and manganese deficiencies. Well-drained loams and brick earths are ideal. Loganberries love rich soil and respond to generous manuring. Nitrogen is the most important plant food requirement. Mulch annually with farmyard manure in late autumn or feed with 2 ounces of fish manure and 1 ounce of sulphate of potash per square yard.

A sunny and open but sheltered site is best with protection from north-east winds. The rows should run north–south.

Propagation is usually by tip-layering between June and mid-August. The tips of young canes are pegged down 2–3 inches deep (or weighted with a flat stone), into small pots filled with a rooting compost and sunk in the ground. The young plants are severed from the parent canes when well-rooted in the following February. Alternatively, leaf bud cuttings are rooted 2 inches apart in a bed of sandy soil in a closed and

shaded garden frame in July or August. Each cutting consists of a leaf and bud with a 1-inch length of cane bark devoid of pith. Roots are produced in three to four weeks; the young plants are hardened off a month later and transplanted the following spring.

Rooted tips or cuttings are planted 6–10 feet apart in February or March against fences, north or east walls, and up arches. Post and wire supports with wires at 2, 4 and 6 feet from soil level are used on open sites. Shorten the young plants to 9 inches after planting, to encourage the production of strong new shoots on which fruit will be borne the following year. To reduce disease infection from the older canes, the young canes are trained fan-wise on the opposite side from the old canes. The two ages of cane occupy alternate sides annually. Ten to 12 fruiting canes are retained per plant. Fruiting is on one-year-old canes which are cut down to ground level in October after fruit harvest.

Pests and diseases are the same as those which attack raspberries.

Two good varieties are the following: 'LY 59', which is a virus-free clone available since the late 1950s. It is free from the debilitating viruses which reduce the crop of infected loganberries. It is the heaviest cropper—it may yield $17\frac{1}{2}$ pounds of fruit per bush; 'American Thornless', a prickle-free mutation found in 1933. It is a pleasure to prune it. Slightly less vigorous than the common loganberry, it is an ideal variety for the smaller garden and may yield up to 15 pounds of fruit per bush.

Currants

Of the three kinds of currants, black currants derived from *Ribes nigrum* are grown more commonly than red currants (derived from the intercrossing of three *Ribes* species) or white currants (derived from red currants). All three are self-fertile, fruit prolifically and take up only a relatively small area. They all thrive in most districts and start cropping early in life.

No soil is too rich for black currants; they can be fed lavishly with nitrogenous fertilisers. They prefer soils with good drainage but retentive of moisture—black currants will absorb copious amounts of water. Poor growth on thin soils can be improved by applying deep mulches.

Red and white currants withstand drought better than black currants and are less greedy for nitrogen. Otherwise, their requirements are very similar. Red and white currants blossom early and so must not be planted in low-lying frost pockets. Black currants tolerate

The Loganberry is a vigorous plant, producing long whippy runners and big juicy berries with a distinctive flavour.

1 Red currant 'Red Lake' produces heavy crops of large fruits. 2 Black currant 'Mendip Cross'. 3 White currant 'Transparent' fruits on permanent spurs

being partially shaded by trees or buildings though this delays ripening a little. A sheltered site is desirable to encourage pollinating insects to work if flowering time coincides with bad weather. The bushes have a productive life of up to twelve years.

Black currants are in season from July to early September, fruiting on the previous season's shoots. Red and white currants ripen from late June to late July and fruit on spurs formed on the old wood.

Cultivation The modern method of planting black currants is to insert three cuttings 4 inches deep at each planting position and allow them to fruit *in situ*. Plant at 6 × 3 feet intervals. Cuttings 12 inches long, are taken in the autumn from well-ripened shoots of the current season's growth—it is unnecessary to make the cuts directly below the nodes as the cuttings root readily wherever the cuts are made.

Alternatively, plant one to two-year old bushes between October and mid-March, the earlier the better. The soil should be dug deeply prior to planting and have 1 cwt of well-rotted farmyard manure dug in every 10 square yards.

Do not allow the fibrous roots to become dry while awaiting planting; heel them in until planting can be carried out. The roots should not have more than 2 inches of soil above them when planted in their permanent positions.

Cuttings rooted *in situ* can be allowed to fruit the first season but transplanted one-year-old bushes should be pruned to help them recover from the transplanting check and induce strong growth, by shortening the shoots to four buds.

Prune established black currant bushes as soon as their crop is harvested. Remove about a third of the older branches to maintain vigour and to induce sucker shoots to form below ground. Retain a good supply of last year's shoots, spaced evenly over the bush. Mulch the bushes in April with hop manure, matured deep litter poultry manure or decayed farmyard manure.

Feed black currants in the spring with 2 oz per square yard of sulphate

of ammonia or Nitro-chalk and in the autumn with 1 oz per square yard of sulphate of potash. Red and white currants manage with 1 oz of sulphate of ammonia per square yard in the spring and the same amount of potash in the autumn.

Generally, red and white currant bushes are grown with a short leg, 4–5 inches in length, sucker growths being removed; on dry gravel soils, die back may be severe and a multi-stemmed bush may be more practical. Bushes with a leg are obtained by first removing the buds from the bottom half of each cutting before insertion.

Single or double cordon red or white currants, planted against a wall, give extra-large berries and are easily netted against birds. Plant bushes 5 feet × 5 feet, single cordons 1 foot apart in the row, double cordons, 1½ feet apart in the row; rows 4 feet apart.

Prune red currants in the winter by shortening the leading shoots by a third and the sideshoots to two or three buds. Summer pruning in July promotes fruit bud formation. Shorten the sideshoots to five leaves; leave the leading shoots unpruned.

OVATE
Oval-shaped. Examples: Parrot tree, Parrotia persica, with coloured foliage; holly, Ilex aquifolium; poplar, Populus serotina (triangular ovate)

Leaf portraits

The guide identifies 18 leaf forms ranging from ovate and lanceolate to digitate and fleshy, showing examples of each form

LINEAR
Long, thin, grass-like. Schyzostylis. Daffodils (Narcissus species). Carnations (Dianthus species). Iris species

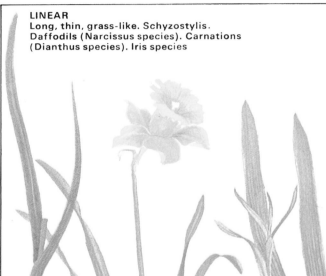

LANCEOLATE
Lance-shaped. The willow (Salix species)

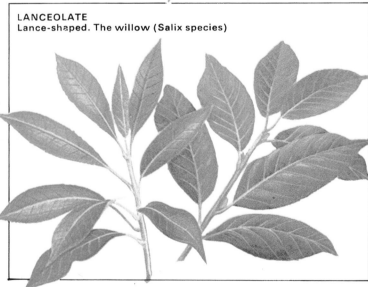

RENIFORM
Kidney-shaped. Pelargonium species. Often with attractive zones of colour

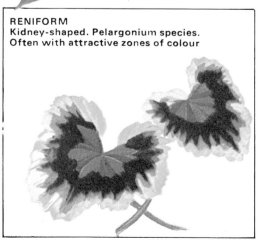

CORDATE
Heart-shaped. Cyclamen persicum. Other examples: violets

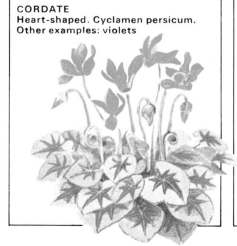

ELLIPTICAL
Spindle tree. Euonymus europaeus

ATULATE
oon- or spatula-shaped.
p: London Pride, Saxifraga
brosa. Haberlea species.
 right:
mula
cies

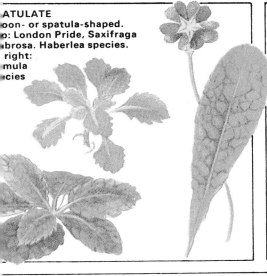

TRIFOLIATE
Three leaves together as in
clover. Oxalis species

FILIFORM
Thread-like. Coreopsis verticillata.
Nigella damascena

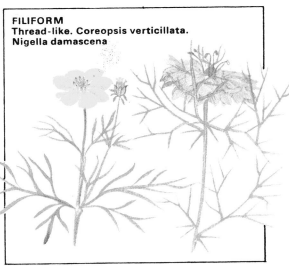

CICULAR
edle-like. Spruce.
e (Pinus species)

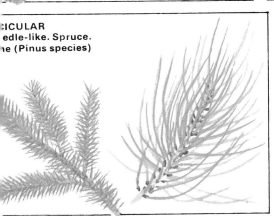

SQUAMOS
Sheathed,
stem-clinging.
Chamaecyparis
species

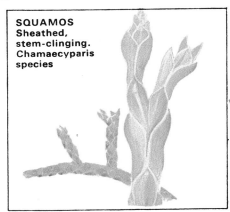

SAGITATE
Arrow-like. Caladium bicolor

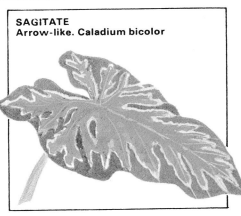

BOVATE
nerally oval but blunted slightly at
d away from leaf stalk.
agnolia obovata

PELTATE
Shield- or target-shaped.
Canary creeper,
Tropaeolum
speciosum

DIGITATE
Finger-like. Lupin. Horse chestnut,
Aesculus hippocastanum

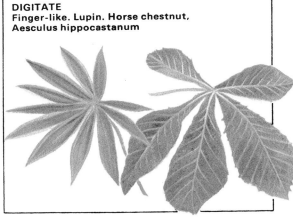

RBICULAR
attened form of obovate.
der, Alnus glutinosa

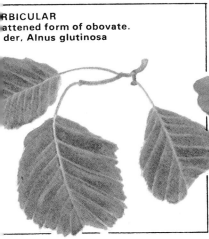

PALMATE
Palm-like. Fig, Ficus carica. Ivy (Hedera
species). Vine (Vitis species)

FLESHY
The form of many cacti and
succulents. Houseleeks
(Sempervivum species)

197

Gooseberry varieties

Variety	Colour	Season	Habit	Flavour	Notes
Careless	white	mid	drooping	good	not under trees
Cousen's Seedling	yellow	very late	drooping and spreading	sweet	rather prickly
Crown Bob	red	mid	drooping	good	prone to bullfinch attack
Early Sulphur	yellow	early	upright	good	one of the best earlies
Golden Drop	yellow	mid	upright	strong	needs mildew control
Green Gem	green	late	upright	fair	heavy cropper, prone to mildew attack
Keepsake	green	early (cooking) late (dessert)	drooping	excellent	heavy and certain cropper
Lancashire Lad	red	mid	upright	fair	excellent all-rounder, resists mildew
Lancer	green	mid	upright—spreading	superb	heavy crops
Leveller	yellow	mid	drooping	very good	immense fertility plus quality
Whinham's Industry	red	mid	spreading	very good	does well under trees
Whitesmith	white	mid	upright—spreading	good	excellent all-rounder

Gooseberries

The gooseberry, *Ribes grossularia*, is native to Britain where it has been cultivated since the thirteenth century at least. Being self-fertile and productive, it is ideal for the small garden. Gooseberries excel in the cooler areas of the Midlands and North.

They are tolerant of most soils but not of waterlogging. Growth may be weak on poor gravel soils or soft and disease-susceptible on heavy clays. Both these extremes benefit from enrichment with garden compost, peat or leafmould. Gooseberries are very sensitive to potash deficiency.

A position in full sun is best for early ripening; bushes can be planted against north or east walls to give extra-late crops. As gooseberries flower early in the spring it is important not to plant them in low-lying, frosty areas. For economy of space, they may be planted between plum trees as both appreciate generous manuring.

Besides the more usual bush forms, single, double, or triple cordons can be grown for special dessert or exhibition berries. Standard goosberries are easier for elderly people to grow and pick.

Cultivation Gooseberries are propagated from hardwood cuttings in mid-October, choosing well-ripened shoots 8–9 inches long. The lower buds are removed to prevent suckers from forming. The prepared cuttings are planted 4 inches deep in a slit trench with sand or grit in the bottom. Standard gooseberries are formed by grafting scions on to *Ribes aureum* rootstocks with stems of the required height.

Planting is carried out from November to February on ground previously enriched with farmyard manure. Bushes should be set out 4–6 feet apart each way; single, double and triple cordons at 1 foot, 1½ feet and 2 feet respectively; standards at 4–6 feet apart.

Bushes and cordons should have a 6 inch stem devoid of roots and shoots to prevent suckering. Cut off the topmost roots if need be.

Plant firmly, covering the roots with 3–4 inches of soil. Shorten the leading shoots by a half and side-shoots to two buds. Give a generous mulch in the spring and thorough waterings in dry spells during the first summer. Keep the soil weed free by hoeing shallowly—deep cultivation damages the surface roots.

Gooseberries demand an ample supply of potash, particularly on light soils; potash deficiency induces poor growth and premature defoliation. Feed annually in the spring with 1–2 oz per square yard of sulphate of potash, not muriate

1 Gooseberry 'Rote Preisbeere' at the green stage in early June, when the berries are hard and bitter, before they are ready for picking.
2 Gooseberry 'Careless' when fully ripe is rather transparent.

Bunches of white grapes, grown on the cordon system, are harvested.

of potash which causes leaf scorching. Scatter bonfire ash round the bushes to give extra potash. Avoid promoting lush growth susceptible to American gooseberry mildew disease by excessive use of nitrogenous fertilisers.

Summer prune the sideshoots to six leaves in July to promote blossom bud formation and to remove mildew-infected tips. Tear out suckers—cutting only induces more to develop.

Thinning the crop produces larger berries. Defer thinning until the small berries are worth being picked for cooking (about Whitsuntide). Late varieties mature about the end of August. Harvest the berries when they are under-ripe for cooking or when fully coloured and soft for dessert use.

Winter prune the bushes in November or defer pruning until the spring where bird damage to the buds is known to be severe. Shorten leading shoots by one third. Spur prune sideshoots to 1½ inches for heavy crops or to two buds for large dessert berries. Prune upright bushes to outward-pointing buds, weeping bushes to upward-pointing buds. Keep the centres of the bushes open.

Grapes

Grapes can be grown quite successfully out of doors in the southern part of the country, preferably given the protection of a warm wall. Plant between October and February in a rich, deep soil.

Plant firmly and immediately after planting, prune the young plant to within 12 inches from its base to encourage a strong shoot to grow.

Plants out of doors can be grown as cordons, espaliers, fans or bushes.

The bush method is the simplest and consists mainly in cutting the branches of the plant back each year to within 1 inch of the main stem. The straggly habit of the bush form makes it a nuisance in the garden and the berries may be spoilt by trailing on the ground.

The cordon is the most common form. It consists of a rod trained to a wire framework about 4 feet high. The rod is encouraged to grow in the same way as an indoor plant.

The laterals from the rod are trained 12–15 inches apart and cut back each winter to one bud. Horizontal cordons can also be grown and these have the advantage that they can be covered with tall cloches in late summer to help to ripen the berries.

Espaliers are grown by developing pairs of branches 12 inches apart from the main stem. Two- or three-tier espaliers are quite sufficient.

Fan shapes can be grown quite easily by training 5–8 shoots from the main stem to grow on a wire framework.

The general pruning treatment is the same as for indoor plants, but of course,

Varieties of grape

For the open border

Gamay Hâtif des Vosges	Black, small, early
Madeleine Royale	White, medium, early
Perle de Czaba	White, small, very early, muscat
Noir Hâtif de Marseilles	Black, small, early, muscat
Seyve-Villard 5–276	White, very prolific, late

For walls

Golden Chasselas	White, medium, late, prolific
Chasselas Rose	Red, medium, fairly late

Under cloches

Any of the above, also:	
Muscat Hamburgh	Black, exquisite flavour, muscat
Madeleine Noir	Black, early
Reine Olga	Good
Millenium of Hungary	Good
Ascot Citronelle	Good but uncertain cropper

much less growth will be made during the summer months. In August, cut away as many of the side shoots as possible, so that light and air will get to the berries and ripen them properly.

Planting distances for the various types are: Cordons, 3 feet apart; Espaliers, 6 feet; Fans, 8 feet; Horizontal cordons, 4 feet.

Each winter give the soil round the plant a dressing of good general fertiliser, together with a mulch of farmyard manure. Once again prune in November.

Propagation Vines can be propagated by eyes or cuttings. Cuttings should be 12 inches long and inserted to half their length in good soil in November or December. Vine eyes can be propagated in a greenhouse or warm place.

Vines are self fertile and there is no problem with pollination.

There are a number of lesser known fruits which can also be grown, such as medlars, quinces, figs, mulberries and others. They are not included here because they are of specialist interest only and full information concerning their culture can be obtained from the supplier of stock.

Chapter 8

VEGETABLE AND HERB GARDENS

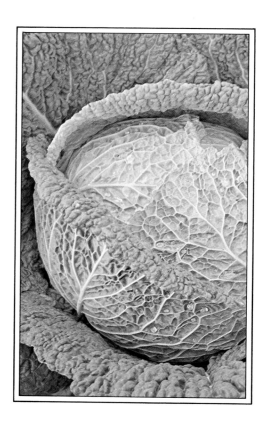

The days are gone when every garden gave half or more of its space to fruit and vegetables. Gardens today are too small for this and at the same time commercial production and distribution of fresh foods has improved to such an extent that normal table necessities can be bought easily, frequently ready-processed, in every part of the country.

The flavour of freshly dug or picked vegetables is so exceptional, however, that even with limited space it is worthwhile trying to grow just a few. In this case it is wise to concentrate on those vegetables which are either difficult to buy in the shops or are particularly delicious when home-grown.

Planning starts in January when the seed catalogues are studied and orders placed for seeds and seed potatoes. Variety is of great importance and the good gardener is always able to harvest something fresh at any time of the year. During the winter, home-grown produce generally consists of cabbage and allied greens together with fresh or stored roots. The owner of a fairly large garden should consider buying a deep freeze cabinet in which surplus summer vegetables and soft fruits may be stored for winter use so that the diet is more varied. The forcing of such crops as seakale, chicory and endive is another way of preventing monotony in winter fare.

No vegetable garden is complete, nor can the diet be so varied, without the use of at least one form of glass (or possibly plastic) protection. These are frames, cloches or greenhouse. Their uses are described later in this book.

With these principles outlined in Chapter two for kitchen gardens in mind, it is possible to plan ahead and decide which vegetables are to be grown.

Edible Asparagus

This delicious vegetable is expensive to buy but easy to grow. The shoots are cut below soil level when they are about 4 inches long, but all cutting must cease soon after the middle of June to allow the plants to develop over the summer and build up the crowns for the following spring. Asparagus plants must not be cropped until they are at least three years old and then only moderately until they are well established.

An asparagus bed will last for a good many years, so it should be dug to a depth of 2 feet, incorporating manure in the second spit, and if the soil is heavy add some cinders or other material that will break up the soil and improve the drainage as the crowns are liable to rot in heavy, wet soils. It is advisable on heavy, ill-drained soils, to raise the level of the beds about 6 inches to improve the drainage. The beds are usually made about 4 feet wide with an alley of 2 feet or so between them.

Crowns are planted in spring or seed may be sown. If planting crowns make

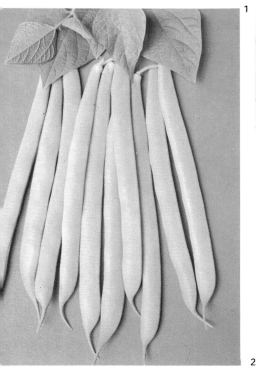

1 Dwarf Bean 'The Prince'.
2 Dwarf French Bean 'Cherokee'.
3 Broad Bean 'Gillett's Wonder'.

sure the roots are spread out well and then cover them with 3 inches of soil. They should be spaced about 1 foot apart. in rows 15 inches apart.

Seeds may be sown either directly into the permanent beds or in a seed bed or frame and then thinned out eventually leaving the plants 9 inches apart. They will be ready for planting into their permanent bed the following spring. Female plants, which are berry-bearing, do not produce such good crops as the male plants and should be discarded, replacing them with male plants. It is not possible to distinguish between them until the plants are two years old so the rogueing must be done when the plants are in their permanent beds, or the seedlings can be kept in the seed bed and planted out as soon as they can be sorted out.

Topdress the beds in the spring with a thick layer of well-rotted manure and keep them weeded but do not use a hoe as the roots are so near the surface. The top growth must be cut down in the autumn when it turns yellow.

Broad Beans

These were certainly known to the Ancient Egyptians and are probably natives of northern and western Asia. They are extremely hardy.

Cultivation A good rich loam suits these beans, though they are not difficult to grow on any soil. This crop may well follow cabbages and potatoes, or manure may be dug in sparingly. A certain amount of chemical fertiliser may be added as follows: 3 oz per square yard of superphosphate and 1 oz per square yard

of sulphate of potash. These beans prefer a neutral or alkaline soil to one which is acid.

In January or February seed may be sown in boxes or individual pots and started under glass. In April the young plants are set out and the crop becomes mature in June. Another method is to plant outdoors in April for the main summer crop or a May sowing becomes ready in September. At one time autumn sowing was popular, but a number of bad winters in succession has made this method unpopular.

In sowing, the seeds are spaced at 6 inch intervals in rows 2 feet apart. The beans may be put $1\frac{1}{2}$ inches deep or, on clay soil, be placed on the surface and soil ridged up to cover them. When the first bean pods are showing the tip of the main shoot should be broken off and removed.

Named kinds include: 'Green Windsor', 'Saville Longpod', 'Early Longpod', 'Masterpiece', 'Green Longpod', 'Bunyard's Exhibition' and 'Harlington White'.

Haricot beans and french beans (*Phaseolus vulgaris*) The difference between the french bean and the haricot bean is merely that in the former the pod containing immature seeds is eaten, while the haricots are the ripe seeds without the pods. The details of cultivation are the same for both french and haricot forms of the bean.

Though in Britain the runner bean is more often grown than the french, on the continent the reverse is true. It is not always known that a climbing form of the french bean is available though the dwarf kind is certainly more popular and has some advantages.

Cultivation Soil should be rich and light and well dug, with a dusting of superphosphate of lime at 3 oz per square yard and manure at the rate of 1 cwt to each 8 square yards. For early crops seeds may be sown in boxes during April and started under glass to be hardened off and planted out in May. Outdoors it is unwise to sow before the end of April.

The secret of a good crop of succulent beans is speedy raising without check. Water freely and mulch if dry weather occurs. It is essential with this bean to begiń picking while the beans are still tender and not more than 4 inches long. It seems a British trait to produce the heaviest crop of the largest vegetables, and this is why the best qualities of flavour and texture are sometimes lacking from our vegetables.

The outdoor beans should be spaced 6 inches apart in drills 1 inch deep, 18 inches apart.

At the end of the season the plants may well be allowed to ripen their remaining seeds as these when shelled and dried are really the haricots of commerce. They may be used as seed for next year's crop, but as long as they are kept dry they may be kept for over a year for use in cookery.

French beans may be forced under glass to have them at a time when they are unobtainable in the shops. From a January sowing under glass with a maintained temperature of 60° F (16° C) beans may be had by May. Early March sowings give beans in June. Soil should be as for tomato culture and an even temperature and state of moisture must be maintained throughout.

Named kinds include: 'Brown Dutch', 'Canadian Wonder', 'Cherokee', 'Fin de Bagnols', 'Masterpiece' and 'Black Prince'.

Runner beans (*Phaseolus coccineus*) This plant is a native of tropical America, and when first introduced into Britain it was grown for the beauty of its bright scarlet blossoms. It is actually a tender perennial, but is commonly grown as an annual; though it is possible to take a plant and overwinter it, nothing is gained.

Those who use the railways running into London will, in late summer, have noted in almost all the suburban backyards abutting upon the line thriving plants of the beloved scarlet runner, and it is notable that this is often the only vegetable grown. All of which speaks eloquently of the merits of this most popular amateur's plant.

Cultivation It would be most unwise to plant runner beans before May as they will not take the least frost. Should an early crop be required the same method may be used as advised for the french bean and sow the seed in boxes under glass. It is not necessary to sow these seeds before April since they may not be put out before late May or the beginning of June.

The method of planting for those plants which will be staked is that of two double rows 10 inches apart separated by a space of at least 5 feet. It is in this central area that the strong supports must be placed. The individual seeds must be placed at 8 inch intervals.

The poles or stakes should be quite 8 feet long and should be connected by a strong horizontal structure firmly lashed to the uprights. The rest of the framework is merely a net or an arrangement of strings. The weight of a row of runner beans in full growth is considerable and they present a large surface to be shaken by the wind. To avoid all this scaffolding it is quite possible to convert the plants into shrubby masses by a routine of pinching out the growing shoots. However, when this plan is adopted the individual seeds must be spaced at 2 foot intervals, with a distance of 3 feet between the rows. Naturally a given number of plants will occupy considerably more ground space under these conditions.

When runner beans are in full production pick them frequently. As with french beans, they should be picked when they are young and tender.

Named kinds include: 'Best of All', 'Giraffe', 'Kentucky Wonder', 'Painted Lady', 'Prizewinner', 'Streamline' and 'Princeps'.

Beetroot

This sweet salad-vegetable has a high food value. It needs good deep soil, and is best suited to occupy a place where a previous non-root crop has been grown. Do not add fresh manure as this is inclined to cause forking of the root. If, instead of growing vegetables in the kitchen garden, they are grown in the old-fashioned cottager's way interspersed with flowering plants, the beetroot is a most suitable plant, since the round or

Runner Bean 'Prizewinner Enorma', a new variety

turnip-shaped beet has generally fine decorative crimson leaves. In addition to the round beet there are two other forms obtainable, a long-rooted, and an intermediate type, called tankard or canister-shaped. Good named kinds are: 'Crimson Globe', 'Veitch's Intermediate', 'Cheltenham Green Top' and 'Nutting's Red Globe'. All are forms of *Beta vulgaris.*

Cultivation The soil must be of an open well-worked, but not recently manured type. Ammonium sulphate should be given at the rate of 1 oz. per square yard, potassium sulphate at the same rate, and 4 oz of calcium superphosphate also to each square yard.

Sow the globe-rooted beet in April; the others may follow in May. Make drills, 12 inches apart, space seeds 5 inches apart. A point to note is that each so-called 'seed' is, in fact, a 'seed-ball' containing several seeds and more than one may germinate. It is necessary to single the seedlings to one at each point when they are 1 inch high.

Another most important point to remember with this crop is the extreme care required when the roots are harvested. On no account should root or top growth be damaged, or the result is quite likely to be a most unpalatable ,anaemic-looking thing instead of the rich wine-red and appetising vegetable it should be. The roots should be only shaken free of soil as they are dug in August or September, and then stored in a shed, giving some cover in the form of dry soil, peat or leaves. Top growth may be carefully twisted off to avoid damage. Do not leave the roots to get hard and woody before digging them. After the beets have been cooked they may be cut without damaging the appearance of them, but if they are cut before cooking their appearance will certainly be spoiled.

Broccoli, Sprouting

This is another variety, *italica*, of *Brassica oleracea*. Both purple and white sprouting produce a profusion of young shoots invaluable for prolonging the supplies of winter greens. Purple sprouting is the most hardy and will safely overwinter in most open situations. Young shoots may be produced for Christmas, but it is in March and April that the vegetable is most useful. White sprouting is perhaps a little less strong in flavour, not so hardy and can only be grown in sheltered gardens. The small curds which sprout forth in profusion are white instead of purple. Seed should be sown thinly in the open from the middle of April, in drills ½ inch deep and 9 inches apart. Thin seedlings when they are large enough to handle. Plant out in June or July 2 feet 6 inches apart, in rows allowing 3 feet between the rows. This is a useful crop to plant in July after an early crop of potatoes. The ground must be in good heart, preferably well manured for the previous crop. Otherwise, dig in decayed manure or compost with the addition of extra phosphates and potash, for example 3 oz of superphosphate and 1 oz of sulphate of potash. Really firm ground will help to keep the plants upright through spells of severe weather, but it may be found necessary to draw soil towards the stems to give extra protection or even to stake the largest of the plants. Varieties are named by type, such as Early or Late Purple or White Sprouting.

Brussels Sprouts

This important member of the cabbage family, known botanically as *Brassica oleracea* var. *gemmifera (Cruciferae)*, originated in Belgium. The popularity of the vegetable is due not only to the fact that picking can be extended over a long period, but it can stand up to severe winter weather. It is indeed one of the most valued of brassica crops. Brussels sprouts need a deeply-worked, rich, firm soil, plenty of room for development and a long season of growth.

Cultivation To produce compact, firm sprouts, it is essential to have firm ground and an attempt should be made to follow a crop for which the ground has already been well manured. Alternatively, dig in well-decayed manure in the autumn. Late preparation, loose soil or fresh manure results only in lush growth and loose sprouts. If manure is not available apply 3 oz of superphosphate and 1 oz of sulphate of potash per square yard prior to planting. Even when manuring has been carried out the addition of half the recommended quantities of fertiliser will be found beneficial. For early or late varieties, sow in a

Above Globe Beetroot, harvested when still young and tender, before they have become old and 'woody'.

Below Young shoots of Purple Sprouting Broccoli, ready in spring, help to prolong the supplies of winter greens.

Cambridge 5 is a good modern variety of Brussels Sprout. It is a late kind, tall-growing, its stems covered from the ground with large, firm green sprouts. Seed is sown in March; plants are set out in late May.

prepared seed bed in a sheltered position in the middle of March. Transplant to permanent positions in late May and firm well. Under normal growing conditions allow 2½ feet between the plants and in the rows, but with vigorous growing varieties on good growing soil allow 3 feet between the rows and 2½ feet between the plants. As a precaution against cabbage root maggot and club root disease, dip the washed roots of the young plants into a thin paste using 4 per cent calomel dust and water. Water the young plants if the weather is hot and dry. Hoe the soil frequently to keep down weeds. Apply 1 oz of Nitro-chalk in September or October. In open windy areas it is as well to stake plants in the autumn if growth is at all vigorous.

Remove yellow leaves as they appear. Pick the sprouts as they are ready. Do not remove the tops until the end of the winter as this helps in the formation of sprouts and gives protection during severe weather.

Varieties 'Cambridge No. 1' (early); 'Cambridge No. 2' (mid-season); 'Cambridge No. 5' (late); 'Harrison's XXX', a good heavy cropping early; 'Jade Cross', a newer F.1. hybrid, very early, producing a heavy crop of dark green sprouts; 'The Aristocrat', an excellent mid-late variety producing medium-sized sprouts with perfect flavour.

Cabbages

Cultivation Cabbages are gross feeders and require adequate quantities of manure dug in well before planting. Firm ground is essential. Apply 3 oz of superphosphate and 1 oz of sulphate of potash prior to planting. A slightly alkaline soil with a pH 7·0 or over is best. On an acid soil apply lime, but never at the same time as manure. Apply a good basic dressing for autumn planting, such as 4 oz of basic slag and 1 oz of sulphate of potash. A dressing of 1 oz of nitrate of soda per square yard in early spring will provide the necessary tonic to start the plants into active growth. The earliest sowing may be under glass in January or early February, and the seedlings pricked off into a protected cold frame 2–3 inches apart. Plant out when hardened off in early May and apply 1 oz of nitrate of soda six weeks later. Cutting should begin in late June. When the ground is in a suitable state in March or early April make a main sowing, using two varieties, one for autumn use and the other for winter cutting. Sow thinly in drills ½ inch deep. Plant these out when ready in early June to 18 inches apart in the rows and 2 feet between the rows. Plants for autumn planting to produce spring cabbages should be sown from the middle of July to the middle of August depending on weather, soil, and locality. Two separate sowings a fortnight apart can prove helpful if the precise sowing time is doubtful. Plant out in September and firm well. Plants must be hard and sturdy. Distance of planting for spring cabbage should be 18 inches apart each way, or 18 inches between the rows, cutting alternate plants first as spring greens. A useful spring crop may be obtained by planting 12 inches between the rows and 9 inches in the rows using the crop as spring greens.

Varieties Early frame sowing, 'Primo' and 'Greyhound'. April sowing for summer and autumn cutting, 'Winningstadt' and 'Wheeler's Imperial', or for winter cabbage 'Christmas Drumhead' and 'January King'. Sowing July–August for summer cutting, 'Harbinger', 'Early Offenham' and 'Flower of the Spring'.

Red cabbage, also known as pickling cabbage, is usually sown in July or August, and thereafter treated in the same way as spring cabbage, although it is better to plant out at 3 feet apart to get better heads. Alternatively it may be sown in March. There are few varieties: those that are available have 'Red' as part of their name e.g. 'Red Drumhead', 'Large Bloodred', although 'Stockley's Giant' is an exception.

Cultivation Carrots do best in deep, well-cultivated sandy loam, preferably well manured for the previous crop. Fresh manure causes forking and excessive top growth. Apply a good compound fertiliser 7–10 days prior to sowing. This may be fish meal or 3 parts of superphosphate, 2 parts of sulphate of potash and 1 part of sulphate of ammonia, applied at 3 oz. per square yard. Sow early crops thinly in drills ¼ inch deep and 9 inches apart from November onwards in heat or under cloches in January or February as soon as the soil is workable. Thin the seedlings as required, using the young roots as they become fit for use. Outdoor sowing may begin in early March or when the ground is suitably dry. Successive sowings of short-horn and stump-rooted types made at 3 week intervals until the middle of June provide a continuous supply of young carrots throughout the summer. Make drills for the main crop ½ inch deep and 12–15 inches apart. Postpone sowings of main crop for storing until late May or June where carrot fly is troublesome. Thin main crop to 2 inches when the seedlings are large enough to handle, finally thinning to 6 inches. As a precaution against carrot fly, draw soil towards the rows after thinning, and lightly dust with lindane. Lift for the winter storing in October. Carefully lift the roots with a fork and cut the tops to ½ inch above the root. Store in layers of dry sand or ash in a cool shed or where the quantity is large, use the clamp method as for potatoes. The store must not be damp or soft rot will result. Where cloches or frames are available, make a sowing of a stump-rooted variety in August out of doors and place the cloches in position in October for pulling November and December. Hoe throughout the season to keep down weeds and to keep the soil surface crumbly. Careful watering throughout the season obviates root cracking which occurs when a period of drought is followed by heavy rain. As a result slugs and millipedes find their way into the root, and are blamed for the severe damage. With good crop rotation and cultivation there should be little difficulty with pests or diseases.

Among the reliable varieties are: *Short-horn:* Earliest French Horn and Early Nates. *Stump-rooted:* Red Coned Early Market. *Intermediate:* St. Valery. *Main crop:* James's Scarlet Intermediate.

Cauliflower

Cultivation A deeply-dug well-manured soil in an open sunny position is best,

but the ideal condition is when the crop follows a heavily manured one such as early potatoes. Apply a dressing of super-phosphate at 2 oz per square yard prior to planting. As for other brassicas the soil must be well firmed. The earliest cauliflowers for June cutting are raised from seed sown in boxes in a heated greenhouse in January or February. Prick off the seedlings into boxes, or pot up individually and gradually harden off until plants are ready for setting out in rows 18 inches apart with 18 inches between the plants in April or May as weather and locality permit. If heat is not available sow seed in a cold frame in September, prick out seedlings at 3 inch intervals and plant out in the spring. Caterpillars rarely attack this early crop. Sow seed for the main crop in March in drills $\frac{1}{4}$ inch deep and 9 inches apart in a sheltered seed bed and plant out in May, 2 feet apart and $2\frac{1}{2}$ feet between the rows. An adequate supply of water, and continuous hoeing to keep a surface dust mulch, will go a long way to ensure a good crop. As soon as a head or curd appears a leaf may be broken over it to provide shade or the curd is likely to become discoloured. As with broccoli there is a wide choice of varieties with varying periods of maturity, but careful planning is required to ensure a succession of heads throughout the season. Among the best-known varieties are 'Early Snow-ball' and 'Delfter Market', for cutting during June or July; 'Early London' and 'Dwarf Mammoth', which mature in August; 'Majestic', which is ready in September; 'Walcheren', an old variety, ready October to December; 'Veitch's Self Protecting', for late October cutting; 'Canberra' a newer Australian variety, maturing in November and December.

Celery

Cultivation Sow celery thinly in pots or boxes in heat in March for early varieties, or in a cold house in mid-April for the main crop. Prick off into deep seed boxes as soon as the seedlings are large enough to handle, at 2 inch intervals. After hardening off, plant out from mid May to the end of June, in prepared trenches. This is not only helpful in earthing but enables watering to be carried out by flooding the trench.

Prepare the trench some time before planting by removing soil 8–12 inches deep, depending on the situation, placing the soil in equal amounts on either side of the trench. Keep the sides of the bank as upright as possible patting them with the back of the spade. This forms neat ridges on which lettuce,

1 A well-grown head of cabbage. It is not difficult to produce a succession of these useful vegetables throughout the year.
2 Carrot 'Amsterdam Forcing', splendid for early forcing, it grows to about 5 inches with excellent quality and texture.

spinach or radish can quite easily be grown. Place a good depth of manure in the trench and dig this into the bottom soil. Firm well by treading and leave the trench as long as possible to settle before planting. For single rows plant 10–12 inches apart, 12 inches each way for double rows staggering the plants. Immediately after planting, flood the trench and repeat this operation in dry weather. Feed occasionally with weak manure water or dried blood, and also apply two dressings of superphosphate at 1 oz per 6 foot run, by mid August.

Start to earth up when the plants are fully grown in August or September, after removing any sideshoots and low-growing leaves which would otherwise be completely covered. Tie the stems with raffia and place soil from the side bank around the plants up to the base of the leaves. Slugs can cause much damage and it is wise to scatter slug bait round the plants before earthing up, especially if paper collars, black plastic or drainpipes are used, as they sometimes are, to ensure long, well-blanched stems. Pat the sides of the ridge to encourage rain to run down, rather than penetrate into the celery hearts. Celery fly can cause serious damage from May to September if precautionary measures are not taken.

Digging may begin six to eight weeks after earthing.

'Clayworth Prize Pink' produces a good crisp head. Good white varieties include 'Sandringham White' and 'Wright's Giant White'. White varieties which need no earthing up include 'Golden Self Blanching' and 'Tall Utah'.

Kale

Also known as borecole, this hardy vegetable is a member of the brassica family. Varieties include the Scotch kales, cottager's kale, thousand-headed and asparagus kale. All are grown for winter supplies of greens. They are particularly recommended to gardeners in very cold areas where winter cabbage and sprouting broccoli are difficult crops.

Sow seeds in the open on a well prepared seed bed in an open position in April or early May. The drills should be no more than an inch deep and 6 inches apart. If the plants tend to become rather large whilst in the seed bed, they may be transplanted and set a few inches apart until being moved to their final growing positions in June. Suitable spacings are 18 inches between the plants in staggered rows at 24 inches apart. Dwarf Scotch curled does not need such generous spacing.

Prepare the ground and plant as for winter cabbage. Kale does well on ground from which potatoes have been lifted. The plants may also be set between rows of early potatoes, provided that these are not too close. Where possible, the plants should be top-dressed with well-rotted dung or garden compost in mid July. Soil is then drawn from between the rows over the dung or compost to form a low ridge around the stems of the plants. This encourages good root growth and helps to prevent the plants from being blown down in winter gales.

As far as Scotch kale is concerned, it is the leaves which are eaten, and picking should start at the base of the plants. With the other kinds, the plants are beheaded, following which short side-shoots are produced, as on sprouting broccoli. When these shoots have been harvested, more grow for use during the spring months. Unless the shoots are picked for use when quite young they are inclined to be rather bitter.

1 Dwarf curled Kale.
2 Celery is grown in trenches to facilitate the blanching of the stems. 3 It is later earthed up.

Leeks

The leek is a valuable vegetable for winter and spring use and is often grown to replace onions when the last of the stored crop has been eaten. Sow the seeds outdoors in late March or early April on a prepared bed. A seed bed prepared for cabbage and lettuce sowings is suitable. Prevent annual weeds from smothering the grass-like seedlings, and water, should May be a dry month. The seedlings are dug up and moved to their growing positions in June or July. June planting is preferable.

For leeks of good size, a well-manured or well-composted soil is necessary. Mark the rows with the garden line at 18 inches apart. The usual planting tool is a blunt-nosed dibber, such as may be made from an old spade handle. Make the planting holes 9 inches apart in the rows and sufficiently deep so that only the

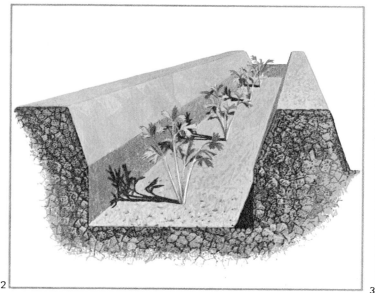

tops of the plants show above the soil when one plant is dropped into each hole. After planting, simply fill the holes with water. This washes sufficient soil down on to the roots; more loose soil fills the holes when the rows are hoed a week or two later. Following planting, inspect the bed for a day or two and replant any plants which may have been pulled out of the holes by birds. Mulching with sedge peat or, on rich soils, with weathered sawdust, in late July, saves all further cultivation.

Leeks are left in the soil throughout the winter in the same way as parsnips. Should the ground be needed for another crop in February or March, any leeks still in the soil may be lifted and heeled into a trench. All leeks should be used before May.

The leek is a favourite vegetable among exhibitors and for this purpose, seeds are sown in gentle heat in the greenhouse during January or February. The seedlings are pricked off into fairly deep trays and each seedling is allowed 1½ square inches of space. The seedlings are hardened off gradually in the cold frame for planting out in early May. Some keen showmen prefer to prick the seedlings into small clay pots and to pot on into the 5-inch or 6-inch sizes.

To obtain leeks blanched to a length of 2 feet or more, the plants are grown in trenches prepared similarly to those in which single rows of celery are grown (see Celery). The preparation of the trenches calls for deep digging and the addition of well-rotted manure or alternatives such as garden compost or spent mushroom compost. The trenches are spaced 3 feet apart with 12 inches between the plants. Soil from between the rows is drawn up towards the plants as they grow to form a steep ridge. Liquid manure feeds are given as well as frequent top-dressings.

'Musselburgh' and 'The Lion' are good standard varieties. The pot leek is a northern speciality.

Lettuce

Lettuces fall into three groups—cabbage, cos and loose-leaf. The cabbage kinds are subdivided into crispheads and butterheads. Those sold by the greengrocer are almost always butterheads because crispheads do not travel well and wilt rather quickly after harvesting. The cos varieties have long, boat-shaped, very crisp leaves and they are preferred by many for their fine flavour. Loose-leaf lettuces are more popular in the United States than here, although one American variety, 'Salad Bowl', is liked by many gardeners.

Any check to steady growth is liable to result in rather poor lettuces. Water is very important, but the soil must be sufficiently porous to allow for good drainage. Although late summer lettuces will tolerate the shade cast by rows of taller vegetables, earlier sowings demand

an open, unshaded site. The soil should have been dug well during the winter digging programme and organic manures in the form of farmyard manure, garden compost or spent hops applied generously. These manures are invaluable in helping to retain soil moisture. If he is able to have use of greenhouse cold frames and cloches, the good gardener is able to raise lettuces for at least six months of the year. The production of winter and early spring lettuces is not easy and these crops are a challenge to the gardener. Certain hardy varieties for April cutting may be over-wintered in the open in favourable areas, but much depends on the winter weather following the autumn sowing.

Outdoor sowings may be made in March in the south-west and during the first two weeks of April in other areas. Here again, cloches are useful. Sow as thinly as possible in 1-inch deep drills spaced 15 inches apart. Keep down weeds by hoeing and thin the seedlings to 1 foot apart when three or four leaves have formed. The thinnings from March, April and May sowings may be used to make further rows.

A sowing made in late July provides lettuces in November and December but here again, the weather plays an important part. The rows need cloche protection from October onwards. For early spring supplies, sow in the cold frame in September and, subsequently, replant the seedlings in the greenhouse or in frames. Alternatively, sow in the greenhouse in early October and transplant when the plants have four leaves. Deep planting at any time is unwise. It is particularly dangerous where lettuces are to be over-wintered. Over-crowding must also be avoided and correct ventilation is very important.

Birds often peck at lettuce seedlings and plants. A few strands of black cotton fixed above the rows prevents this trouble. Although present-day cos varieties are reputed to be self folding, better hearts form if the plants are tied rather loosely with raffia or soft string. Loose-leaf varieties are less prone to bolt than cabbage and cos plants. Instead of cutting the whole plant, leaves are picked as and when required from loose-leaf varieties.

Among the very many varieties on offer, the following may be relied upon for worth while crops.

For outdoor sowings from March until July 'Sutton's Improved', 'Unrivalled', 'Trocadero', 'Webb's Wonderful', 'Giant White Cos', 'Salad Bowl'.

To stand the winter out of doors 'Stanstead Park', 'Arctic King', 'Brown Cos'.

Marrows

A very rich bed is essential for a regular supply of marrows between late July and the autumn. Soil which has received a generous dressing of well-rotted farmyard manure or garden compost is ideal. Planting distances depend on the type of plant. A bush variety needs almost one square yard of surface area; a trailer needs a great deal more if allowed to roam at will over the ground. Trailing or vining marrows may also be trained on tall supports. These may be bamboo canes or even the garden fence.

Water is essential and the plants must on no account be permitted to become dry at the roots. Liquid manure feeds should be given weekly when the first marrows begin to swell. To ensure that both water and liquid manure reach the roots, many gardeners sink a clay pot alongside each plant. The water and the liquid feeds are poured into the pots and

1 Well-blanched specimens of Leek 'Musselburgh', a good variety both for exhibition and for culinary use.
2 'Salad Bowl' is a loose-leaf variety of Lettuce. Instead of cutting the whole plant, leaves are picked as and when required, from such varieties.

Mustard and Cress

This is a useful, easy-to-grow salad crop which may be grown throughout the year provided that a temperature of 50–60°F (10–16°C) is given. Cress takes a little longer to germinate than mustard so cress seeds must be sown in a separate container three days earlier than mustard in order to be able to gather the two together. Bulb bowls or seed trays should be filled with fine, sandy soil or with bulb fibre. Water well, using a very fine rose on the can, and then sprinkle the seeds evenly and reasonably thinly on to the moist surface. Firm the seeds into the soil or fibre with a block of wood. No covering of soil, fibre or sand is necessary. Stand the containers in a dark place or cover the pots or trays with pieces of wood until the seeds germinate. Water carefully if necessary. After germination, allow full light. Both mustard and cress grown indoors are ready for use within two to three weeks of sowing. Cut the 3-inch high seedlings with scissors. For successional crops, sow weekly between October and April.

For the first crops out of doors, sow on an open, south-facing site in early April. After forking the soil lightly, firm it well and then rake so that the soil is very fine indeed. Sow as for under glass. Early sowings may be damaged by heavy rain which beats the tender seedlings to the ground. This may be prevented by providing glass protection; sowings may also be made earlier in the cold frame in soil similar to that recommended for plants grown in bowls or seed trays, or under cloches. For sowings made between late May and September, choose a north-facing border.

Onions

When the seeds are to be sown directly in the soil where the plants are to grow, the bed should be well prepared. Digging and manuring will have been carried out during the late autumn or winter and the soil needs raking before sowing so that the bed is level, even and free of large clods and stones. Sow thinly in 1-inch deep drills, spaced 1 foot apart. After sowing, fill in the drills and firm. Do not tread heavily on a clay soil. Keep the seedlings free of weeds by hoeing between the rows during April and May, and pull out any weeds in the rows. Start thinning the plants in mid-June and continue thinning until mid-July by which time those which are to remain should have at least 6 inches of row space. When thinning, take great care not to break roots or foliage and never leave either on top of the soil. The odour of the broken plants attracts female onion flies and their small maggots ruin many onion crops. If the soil is on the dry side, water both before and after thinning. Use the immature onions in salads.

Continue weeding the onion bed until July. During that month, or in

run directly to the root area. Weeding is necessary until the large leaves shade the surrounding soil and inhibit weed growth.

The plants bear male and female flowers. Bees, flies and other insects transfer ripe male pollen to the female blooms. Where female flowers fall off without setting fruits, natural fertilisation is not occurring. In such cases, hand pollination is advisable. Do this before noon. Pick a male flower for each female to be hand pollinated. Strip the petals from the male and twist its core into the centre of the female. The females may be recognised quite easily because they carry an embryo marrow behind them.

Bush plants need little attention. Trailers may be guided between other crops or, if they are to be trained to supports, the main shoot must be tied in regularly. Cut the marrows when they are young and tender. They are old if the thumb nail does not pierce the skin easily. Marrows for jam or for storing are allowed to ripen on the plants until September. The storage place should be cool and dry. The marrows are some-

Above **the male and** *below* **the female flowers of the Marrow, with the immature vegetable behind it. Marrow flowers have to be fertilised by hand, in order that the fruit can form.**

times hung up in nets for storage purposes. Smaller marrows are now preferred. Up-to-date varieties include 'Zucchini F₁ Hybrid' (bush), 'Productive' (bush), 'Prolific' (trailer), 'Cluseed Roller' (trailer). 'Rotherside Orange' is a prolific variety of excellent flavour. 'Cocozelle' (the Italian vegetable marrow), a bush variety, produces dark green, yellow-striped fruits up to 2 feet long.

Courgettes, or French Courgettes, have become increasingly popular in recent years. In the natural course of events the fruits do not grow very large but, in any case, to obtain the best results, they should be cut when not much bigger than thumb size and cooked unpeeled. Constant cutting will ensure the steady production of fruits throughout the summer. Cultivation is otherwise the same as for the larger marrows. For exhibition purposes, 'Sutton's Table Dainty' is a popular variety.

Maincrop onion varieties

'Ailsa Craig' Large, globular, handsome. Suitable for both spring and late summer sowing. One of the best for exhibition.

'Autumn Queen' Flattish shape. Good keeper. For spring and late summer sowing.

'Bedfordshire Champion' Large, globe-shaped, straw-brown skin usually tinged with pink. For spring sowing only.

'Big Ben' (A) Large, semi-flat shape, golden skin. Practically non-bolting. Exhibition quality. Good keeper. Sow in August.

'Blood Red' Medium-size, deep red skin, flat, pungent. Very hardy and especially recommended for cold areas. Good keeper.

'Crossling's Selected' A globe onion much liked by exhibitors.

'Early Yellow Globe' Flattish-round, medium-sized, golden skinned, quick maturing and reasonably good keeper. For spring sowing only.

'Excelsior, Cranston's Selected' Pale-skinned, large, round exhibition variety.

'Giant Rocca' (Brown) (A) Brown-skinned, flattish globe. For August sowing only. Does not store well. There is also 'Yellow Rocca'.

'Giant Zittau' (A) Medium to large, semi-flat, golden-brown skin. Good keeper. Strongly recommended for August sowing.

'James' Long Keeping' Oval, brown skin, medium size, stores well.

'Marshall's July Giant' (A) Large, semi-globe shaped, early maturing. For August sowing.

'Marshall's Leverington Champion' Globe-shaped, pale golden skin, very large, fairly good keeper. Recommended for exhibition use.

'Red Italian' (A) Medium-sized, red-skinned, flat bulbs. Sow in August.

'Reliance' (A) Large, flattish, golden skin. Sow in August.

'Rijnsburger Globe' Large, pale-skinned, globe-shaped, long-keeping.

'Rousham Park Hero' White Spanish type, semi-flat, greenish-yellow skin, mild flavour. Can crop well on light soils.

'Sutton's A1' Large flat bulbs, a good keeper. For spring or August sowing.

'Sutton's Solidity' (A) Large, flattish bulbs. Plants do not bolt. A good keeper. Especially recommended for August sowing.

'Superba' A new F₁ hybrid. Medium-sized globular bulbs with smooth golden-brown skin. Early maturing and noted for uniformity. Stores well.

'The Sutton' Globe-shaped, early-ripening, excellent keeper.

'Up-to-Date' Globe-shaped, straw-coloured skin, remarkably good keeping qualities.

'White Spanish' Flattish onion, golden skin, mild flavour, good keeper.

'Wijbo' An early maturing selection of 'Rijnsburger'. Noted for uniform appearance of the crop.

(A) = Recommended for August sowing. Onions from this sowing are referred to as Autumn-sown among exhibitors.

August, the foliage becomes yellow and topples to the soil. Here and there it may be necessary to bend the foliage of a plant downwards. No further weeding is necessary and the crop is left to ripen. When the foliage is brown and brittle, choose a dry, sunny day, pull up or dig the onions from the soil, and spread them in the sun to complete the drying process. In wet weather, spread the onions on the greenhouse bench or under cloches. When the onions are quite dry, rub off soil, dead roots and dry, loose scales. Store the ripe onions in trays in a cool dry place, or better still, rope the crop. Hang the ropes in an outhouse or in the garage.

Onion sets These are small onions grown by specialist nurserymen. The crop is dug and dried in the previous summer and offered for sale in the early winter and spring. One pound of sets is sufficient for the average garden. Small sets are considered of better quality than large ones. Do not leave onion sets in bags after purchasing them, but spread them in a tray in a cool place before planting them in March. Prepare the bed as for seed sowing and plant the sets 6–8 inches apart in 1-inch deep drills.

1 Towards the end of the summer, the foliage of the Onion is bent over to allow light and air to get to the bulbs.
2 Onions can be roped together and stored by hanging them up in an outhouse or garage or potting shed, where dry air can circulate.

Except for hoeing to keep down weeds, little in the way of cultivation is necessary. The feeding of the plants with fertilisers may result in 'bolting'. In late July, loosen the soil around the swelling bulbs to expose them to the sun. This must be done carefully because the plants may be blown down by strong winds if the roots are broken. The foliage will topple to the soil in August and from then on harvesting and storing are as for onions from seeds.

Spring onions Where maincrop onions are raised from sets, 'spring' or salad onions are grown by sowing seeds of 'White Lisbon' in August or in March. In colder parts, the August sowing needs cloche protection from October until the spring. Although the bed should not be a rich one, it must be well-drained. Sow quite thickly and hoe to remove weeds in September and again in March. Start pulling the small onions for salad use in May and continue to pull until July. The March sowing provides salad onions from July until the autumn.

Onions for Pickling 'Marshall's Super Pickle' is a new onion with the round shape and size as favoured by the commercial pickler. Seeds of this variety or of any maincrop suitable for spring sowing are sown rather thickly in ½-inch to 1-inch deep drills spaced at 9 inches apart in soil of low fertility during March or April. Weeding must be attended to regularly but the onion plants are not thinned. Harvesting is carried out when the foliage is dead, brown and brittle.

For white cocktail onions seed of 'Silver Skin' or 'Pearl Pickler' is sown quite thickly in April or early May. The soil should be reasonably fertile. If grown in a poor soil the onions are liable to be too small for use. Apart from weeding no cultivation is necessary and the plants are not thinned. The crop is harvested when the foliage dies. Unless harvested promptly, the bulbs produce fresh foliage.

Onion Fly

The adult flies of this pest (*Hylemyia antiqua*) appear in spring and lay eggs in clusters on the necks of the onions. The white maggots feed inside the onion, causing the foliage to collapse and the bulb to be destroyed. Pupation takes place in the soil. Another generation of flies emerges in July and yet another by late August. The larvae from these overwinter in the pupal stage.

The pest is controlled by trichlorphon applied according to the maker's instructions or by gamma-BHC dust applied at the 'loop' stage (when the young leaves form a 'loop')and again a fortnight later.

Parsley

Cultivation The point to remember about parsley is that it is certain to be needed by the cook at all times of the year. To allow for this, frequent (at least three) sowings should be made between March and September. Large beds of parsley will not be required by the average family and so the plants may be used as an edging to a vegetable plot, or even, as the leaves are decorative, they may well be used to edge the flower border. If larger quantities are required the seed should be sown thinly in 1-inch deep drills, spaced 1 foot or so apart and the seedlings should be thinned eventually to 6 inches apart. Plants will grow in any ordinary soil, provided it is not too acid. The best results are obtained if the soil is dug deeply and a fair amount of garden compost or other organic material is incorporated.

Parsley seed is rather slow and irregular in germination and it is not at all unusual for nothing to appear for a month or six weeks. Thinnings of parsley may, of course, be used for garnishing, and when your plants are well grown it will be necessary only to cut part of the foliage for use, leaving the plants to make fresh growth.

To make sure of your winter supply it is as well to give the plants cloche protection before the frosts occur, but generally no cover is needed at least until November. If you care to pot up a few plants of parsley and bring them into the greenhouse in winter you may have excellent leaves to cut at all times, even when frost is severe. The seedsmen offer a few named kinds such as 'Dwarf Perfection', 'French', 'Green Velvet', 'Moss-curled'.

Parsnips

Cultivation It is essential if you expect to produce good-sized specimens to trench the soil deeply so that the desirable, long, straight, unforked roots are produced. The large seeds are sown in 1-inch deep drills in small groups at intervals of 4 inches, the drills spaced 1½ feet apart. Choose a calm day for sowing as the seeds are light and liable to blow away in windy weather. Do not try to transplant as this will generally result in some injury to the essential tap root. Should all your seeds germinate you may remove alternate plants in the drills leaving the remaining ones at 8-inch intervals.

The best soil is one which has been well manured for a previous crop, and no animal manure should be applied later. However, a stimulant may well be given in the form of a mixture of 3 ounces of superphosphate, 1 ounce of sulphate of ammonia and 1½ ounces of sulphate of potash per square yard. The roots will be ready for use at the end of October but, since they are frost resistant, they may be left in their rows until they are needed; or, if the soil has to be dug in preparation for further cropping, the roots may be lifted and packed away in a shed or cellar with a covering of dry soil or sand. In any event it is always wise to lift and store a few roots in case the ground freezes hard, making it impossible to dig up the roots.

Peas

There are dwarf and taller pea varieties. Although plants of the short, dwarf varieties may be grown without supports it is the custom to provide all garden peas with supports of some sort.

Long Parsnip roots, the results of good cultivation.

Peas sowing times and varieties

First Early

Sow			For use	
	November	Give cloche protection in cold areas	For use	May–June
	February	Under cloches except in the south-western areas		June
	March–April	Open garden		June–July
	Late June	Open garden		September

Name		Height of plant in ft
	Early Bird	2
	Feltham First	1½
	Foremost	3
	Forward	2
	Gradus	3
	Kelvedon Triumph	1¾
	Kelvedon Viscount	2¼
	Kelvedon Wonder	1½
	*Little Marvel	1¼
	Meteor	1½
	Pilot Improved	3
	Progress (Laxton)	1½
	Sleaford Phoenix	1½
	*Topcrop	2½

Second Early

Sow	April	For use	July

Name		Height of plant in ft
	Achievement	5
	*Early Onward	2½
	Giant Stride	2
	Kelvedon Climax	2½
	*Kelvedon Monarch	2½
	Kelvedon Spitfire	2
	*Shasta	2½
	*Sutton's Chieftain	2½
	Sutton's Phenomenon	2
	*Sutton's Show Perfection	5

Maincrop

Sow	April–May	For use	August

Name		Height of plant in ft
	Alderman	5
	Histon Kingsize	3½
	Histon Maincrop	2½
	Lincoln	2
	Onward	2

Late

Sow	May	For use	August–September

Name		Height of plant in ft
	Autocrat	4
	Gladstone	4
	Lord Chancellor	3½

*Also recommended for Quick-Freeze
The height of plants varies by several inches due to soil and seasonal climatic conditions

Twiggy brushwood of the height the plants will attain is much liked by gardeners. Bamboo canes linked together with strong thread or garden twine often replace the traditional brushwood. Garden netting for pea growing is offered at garden shops and by horticultural retailers. The tall supports needed by tall growers should be augmented by several strong, tall stakes to prevent strong winds in summer from blowing down the plants when bearing their heavy crops.

Seed is sown in a 2-inch deep furrow, which is 6 to 8 inches wide, made with the draw hoe. The seeds are sprinkled thinly into the furrow so that each seed is between 2½ to 3 inches from the next. Should the soil be dry, the furrow should be flooded with water and sowing

Garden Pea 'Kelvedon Advance' is an excellent early variety producing long straight pods with a blunt end. It grows about 2½ feet in height.

undertaken when this has drained away. After sowing, the seeds are covered with soil raked over them. During the raking any large stones should be removed. The distances between rows of peas vary. It is generally accepted that the distances between the rows should be the same as the height of the variety being grown, but with very dwarf peas 30 inches between rows is the rule. Supports, if to hand, should be set in position immediately after the seed has been sown. The tendrils of the pea plant cannot grasp thick supports and where these are in use young pea plants are encouraged to climb by the insertion of short pieces of twiggy wood on either side of the row. The twigs also afford some protection to the young plants by breaking the force of cold winds.

Pea seeds and pea seedlings are attractive to birds and black cotton or small mesh chicken wire are useful protectors. The wire mesh should be removed when the seedlings are a few inches tall. The old-fashioned scarecrow is a useful bird deterrent as are large polythene bags fixed to tall stakes. Where mice are known to take freshly-sown seeds, traps should be set or a proprietary poison used with care and according to the manufacturer's instructions. Slugs are a great nuisance in some gardens and a slug bait may have to be laid down. Weevils also attack pea seedlings. Weevil damage may be distinguished from that caused by slugs. Leaves bitten by weevils have a scalloped-like shape. Hoeing around the rows regularly and the dusting of the plants when dry with derris powder or soot are ways of combating weevils.

Potatoes

The principal requirements of the potato plant are adequate available food, sufficient water, good drainage and the type of soil in which tubers may swell easily. An open, unshaded site is very necessary. Light soils are considered very suitable, provided they have been dressed with large quantities of moisture-retaining organic matter. A heavy soil may also be improved structurally by the addition of organic material. A reasonably light, easily worked loam is probably the ideal. Where farmyard manure is available, it may be dug in during winter digging at the rate of up to 1 cwt to 6 square yards. Garden compost may be applied even more generously during winter digging or as a mulch after planting. If a compound potato fertiliser is raked into the soil before planting, use it at the rates advised by the manufacturer.

Potato plants are raised from seed tubers taken from plants grown in parts of Britain which are free of virus-carrying aphids. The potato fields are visited by Ministry of Agriculture officials who issue certificates regarding the freedom from disease of the plants. Tubers from these plants are known as 'Certified Seed'. It is unwise to plant any but certified seed tubers. They should be purchased in January or February and sprouted in trays housed in a light but

frost-proof room (a process known as 'chitting'). It is believed that sprouted potatoes result in earlier crops. The gardener may also see which tubers have not sprouted and these are not planted. At planting time—in late March or April—each potato has two or three short, sturdy sprouts. The actual planting date depends on the condition of the soil and on the weather.

There are many planting methods. Perhaps the simplest is to make 8-inch deep trenches with the draw hoe or with the spade. First Earlies are planted at 12 inches apart with 2 feet between rows. Other varieties need more space; 15 inches between the tubers and 30 inches between the rows are satisfactory distances.

The black plastic method of growing potatoes is favoured by many gardeners because it obviates almost all cultivation. The planting holes are made with the trowel. A tuber—with its sprouts uppermost—is set in each hole. The holes are then filled in and the black plastic sheeting is unrolled over the row. It is important to ensure that the sheeting is securely anchored into the soil. One way of doing this is to make slits with the spade on either side of the row and also at each end of the row. The edges of the 3-foot wide sheet are tucked into the slits when the material is unrolled. When growth starts in May, the shoots of the potato plants are drawn through small holes (made with scissors) in the polythene sheeting.

Rows not treated in this way need weeding now and then. Many gardeners earth up the plants, too. This process consists in drawing soil up and around the plants, using the draw hoe. Earthing up is done in two or three stages. Finally, the plants appear to be growing on low hills. Earthing up is no longer considered necessary but the practice is advantageous on heavy soils where the plants benefit from the improved drainage provided.

There is only one way of ascertaining when First Earlies are ready for use. This is by examining a root. Scraping away some earth may reveal reasonably large tubers. If this fails, dig up a root in late June. If some of the potatoes are as large as a hen's egg, continue digging as and when required. If the potatoes are far too small for use, wait a fortnight before starting to dig.

Radishes

Seeds of this quick-growing vegetable may be sown for salads at intervals from

1 Seed Potatoes are prepared for planting, to encourage the buds to break.
2 When planting Potatoes, the tubers are placed in the drill.
3 Once growth progresses the soil is drawn up at each side of the plants, an operation called 'earthing up'.
4 Lifting Maincrop Potatoes.

early March to October. It is generally treated as a catch crop, being sown on a piece of ground which is intended for cabbages or some other crop to be planted subsequently. A rich, moist soil and cool conditions yield the most succulent radishes. Slow growth may cause them to have a rather hot, unpalatable taste.

Sowings in March or early April may be made in the cold frame or under cloches. Sow the seeds in 1-inch deep drills, the drills being six inches apart. Sow thinly to avoid having to thin out. Remember each radish needs at least 1 square inch of surface area. Sow similarly in open ground. Prevent annual weeds from smothering the seedlings and soak the rows with water if the soil is on the dry side. There are many varieties and 'French Breakfast' is probably the most popular. 'Sutton's Red Forcing' is suitable for cloche and frame sowings. The long, white radish, 'Icicle', is liked for its flavour.

Winter radishes are large and may have a black skin, as in the variety 'Black Spanish', or a red skin such as 'China Rose', or a white skin like 'All Season'. Do not sow winter radishes until June and space the rows 1 foot apart. Thin the seedlings to 9 inches apart, and keep the rows free of weeds. Water well in dry summer weather. Lift the roots in October and store them in slightly moist sand.

Rhubarb

Because the roots continue to crop for up to ten years after planting, special attention should be given to choosing a suitable site for rhubarb and preparing it well. The bed should not be shaded and should be dug deeply. Any roots of perennial weeds must be removed when digging. Where dung is available, this should be dug in at the rate of 1 cwt to 10 square yards. Otherwise garden compost may be incorporated into the soil or spread over the bed after planting; a barrowload to the square yard is not excessive. Plant the roots 3 feet apart, using the spade. November, February or March are suitable planting times. Plant firmly and leave the pink buds at soil level. Supplies of rhubarb are appreciated early in the season. This is why 'Timperley Early' is favoured. 'Hawke's Champagne' is better known but this variety crops later and the flower stems which the plants make in June or July should be cut away as soon as they are noticed. 'Glaskin's Perpetual' may be raised from seed. Sow seed in the cold frame in March or April and thin the seedlings to 6 inches apart. A year later, set the plants in the specially prepared bed.

Do not pull any sticks in the first season after planting and, in subsequent years, do not over-pull as this weakens the plants. Hand weeding should be carried out during the first summer but,

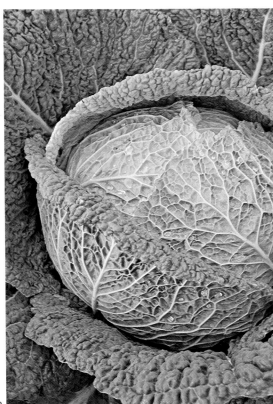

1 Radish 'French Breakfast'.
2 Remove the flowering stems of Rhubarb to encourage the production of stems the following spring.
3 The Savoy Cabbage has thick puckered leaves. It is a useful vegetable as it matures in winter.

in future seasons, no weeding is necessary because the large leaves inhibit weed growth. To ensure that the plants continue to crop well, mulch the bed each autumn with well-rotted farmyard manure or garden compost.

Savoy

This hardy plant, a type of cabbage, has been grown in Britain since the seventeenth century. The leaves are quite distinct from those of other cabbages, being very puckered or crimped. Although there are early varieties, most gardeners prefer those which are of use during the winter and early spring. Successional crops are obtained by choosing drumheads for cutting between November and April. Its botanical name is the tongue-twisting *Brassica oleracea bullata sabauda*.

Cultivation Cultivate as for winter cabbage—the seeds being sown in the seed bed in April for plants to be set out on fertile soil in June. Allow 2 foot of space between the rows, setting the plants from 15–18 inches apart. If the soil is on the dry side, water the planting holes and plant very firmly when the water has drained away. During July and August, hoe or mulch to prevent weeds. Particular care must be taken to prevent cabbage caterpillars from estab-

lishing themselves in savoys. Varieties to grow to provide a succession for cutting include 'Ormskirk Medium', for cutting from November to February; 'Ormskirk Late Green', very hardy and the solid, medium-sized heads are cut between January and late March; 'Ormskirk Extra Late', a large, flattish, dark green savoy for use in March and April.

Shallots

Some people prefer the milder flavour of the shallot, *Allium ascalonicum*, which they grow in place of onions. Generally, however, shallots are grown for pickling. When stocks of non-bolting onion sets were not available, many gardeners found shallot growing far easier than onion growing. The soil in which they are to be grown must be well-drained and, unless very large bulbs are required, without manure or fertilisers. A very poor soil is greatly improved by being mulched with garden compost just prior to planting time.

Traditionally, shallots were planted on the shortest day in December and lifted on the longest day in June. The soil is seldom suitable for planting during the winter, and planting between late February and early April produces good results. Simply press the bulbs

213

into the ground at intervals of 8 inches in the row, and allow 12 inches between rows. Birds, earthworms and severe frost may loosen the bulbs so, about a week after planting, inspect the bed and replant or replace where necessary. If birds continue to pull out the bulbs the bed should be netted.

Unless the plants are to be fed with liquid manure for the production of very large shallots, little is needed in the way of cultivation. Weeds may be removed by hand or hoeing. Alternatively, use sedge peat as a mulch around the plants in late April.

In early June, draw a little of the mulch or surrounding soil away from the bulb clusters to allow more sunlight to reach them. The foliage will yellow in July, when the clusters should be lifted with the garden fork and spread out to dry. In fine, sunny weather dry them in the open; in wet weather under cover. The greenhouse staging, the cold frame or under cloches are suitable places.

When quite dry, split the clusters into separate bulbs and store them in a cool, airy place for use when required. The bulbs are best stored in Dutch trays or in vegetable nets. Do not store in sacks or polythene bags. Some of the medium-sized bulbs may be set aside for planting in the following season. There are both yellow and red shallots. These include 'Giant Long Keeping', yellow; and 'Giant Long Keeping', red; and 'Giant Red'. 'Hâtive de Niort' and 'The Aristocrat' are favoured by exhibitors.

Spinach
It has been estimated that a 30-foot row of spinach supplies just about

1 Spinach is a useful summer vegetable which can be grown with little trouble.
2 Swedes provide a good winter root vegetable that stores well.

the right amount for a family of four during the summer months. But one sowing is not sufficient. Fresh young foliage is demanded and where spinach is much appreciated, successional sowings should be made fortnightly between late March and mid July. For later autumn supplies and for pickings in the following spring, a sowing should be made in a sheltered position in mid-August.

Spinach needs a rich, well-dug soil and one which retains moisture during the summer months. For the leaves to be really succulent, the plants need soaking with water during dry spells. Some gardeners find that their plants need less water if rows sown in May, June and July are partially shaded by other, taller vegetables.

Well-rotted farmyard manure or garden compost should be used in the preparation of the bed. A suitable dressing for sandy soils is 1 cwt of manure to 6 square yards. Garden compost may be used more generously. Provided the soil contains sufficient plant nutriments, no feeding of the plants is necessary. Rows of August-sown spinach are sometimes fed with nitrate of soda, applied at the rate of 1 ounce to each 10 feet of row, in early April.

Sow the seeds as thinly as possible in 1 inch deep seed drills spaced 9 inches to 1 foot apart. Thin the seedlings to 3 inches as early as possible and start

harvesting the leaves as soon as they are of usable size. Do not wait until they are on the tough side. Regular hard picking is essential for summer spinach and almost all of the leaves of a plant may be removed at any one time. Plants from the August sowing should not be treated in this manner. Take only the largest leaves from them.

'Round Seeded' and 'Long Standing' are popular kinds for spring and early summer sowings. 'Long Standing Prickly' is hardier and is sown in August. The word 'prickly' refers to the seeds and not to the smooth leaves.

Perpetual spinach or spinach beet is less well known. Those who know it prefer it for its larger leaves. Sow in April, allowing 15 inches between the rows. Thin the seedlings to 8 inches apart. Successional sowings are not necessary because leaves may be pulled from the plants on and off between early summer and September.

Swedes
Garden swedes, such as 'Bronze Top' and 'Purple Top Improved' often replace winter turnips. Swedes are hardy, and the large roots may be left in the ground until Christmas at least. You can also lift the roots in October, cut off the foliage and store the swedes indoors in dry sand.

Swedes do best in an open, sunny site, and the soil should have been well manured or composted for the previous crop. A sprinkling of a general compound fertiliser may be made before sowing if the soil is not too fertile. Sow very thinly in May or early June in 1-inch drills spaced at 15 inches apart. Thin the seedlings to 12 inches apart and, if growth appears rather slow during the summer, topdress and hoe into the ground nitrate of soda at the rate of 1 ounce to a row of 10 feet. This fertiliser should be watered in, if the season is a dry one. Hoe to keep down weeds. Alternatively, mulch with chopped straw or sedge peat in late July.

Sweet Corn

Zea mays rugosa is known in Britain as sweet corn. This cereal is a native of America and is boiled as a vegetable. The John Innes hybrid varieties remain popular, but 'Kelvedon Glory' is a newer introduction of merit.

In the south, seeds may be sown out of doors in May. Choose a sunny position and in areas exposed to gale force winds in August, provide a windbreak. The soil should have been well dug and dressed with dung or garden compost. These organic fertilisers not only supply plant foods but assist in providing good drainage on heavy soils and in retaining moisture on lighter ones. Sow the seeds 1 inch deep in rows 15 inches apart. Several short rows are preferable to one or two long ones. When the plants are grown in compact blocks wind pollination is more effective.

In other parts of the country, sow two or three seeds in 3½-inch pots in the cold frame or under a cloche in early May. Reduce the seedlings to leave one strong plant in each pot. Set the plants in the open when all danger of frost has passed or protect the rows with cloches until early July.

In dry summers, water as necessary and feed the plants with liquid manure if the soil was not supplied with sufficient organic matter before sowing or planting. Hand weeding is safer than using the hoe which is liable to sever surface anchorage roots. Mulching the bed with straw in July saves weeding.

Harvest the cobs when the silks which hang from them are brown-black in colour and quite brittle. A check on the state of maturity may be made by carefully opening the top of the green sheath and by pressing a grain with the finger nail. If a watery juice exudes, the cob is too young. If the grain contains paste, it is too old. At the correct stage a creamy liquid spurts out. Cobs are twisted from the plants. The sooner the cobs are cooked after harvesting, the higher the sugar content.

Tomatoes

Outdoor Tomato growing Provided that an early-ripening variety is chosen, worthwhile crops of tomatoes may be grown in the garden in most parts. 'Outdoor Girl' is outstanding for its early-ripening quality. In colder parts frames and cloches give protection to the plants during June and early July. Plants may be raised from seed in a cold frame, in an unheated greenhouse, or under a cloche during April in warmer areas.

Many gardeners prefer to buy plants for outdoor growing but this limits the choice of variety and most plants on sale are of varieties which are more suited to greenhouse conditions. The tomato plant is not only killed by frost but is adversely affected by sudden temperature changes and in most parts it is seldom possible to set plants outdoors without protection until early June. About 15 inches should be allowed between plants in rows 30 inches apart. Before planting, the planting holes should be filled with water and planting done when this has drained away. Supports for the plants may be bamboo canes, stakes or a wire trellis. Weeds must be controlled. Growing the plants in a black plastic substitute for mulch saves time and work, a straw mulch may be laid down in mid-July. The plants need tying in regularly to the supports and the central growing point of each plant is removed in late July, when three or four trusses of fruit will have set. Remove all side shoots.

Where a very early-ripening variety was not chosen a great part of the crop may not have ripened by mid-September. Plants may then be defoliated and cloches placed over them. Untie them from the supports and lower them on to clean straw. The cloches are then set over the bed and pickings continue until late October. Where no cloches are to hand all tomatoes on the plants should be harvested during the latter half of September. Most of the fruit will ripen off well in a drawer in a warm room. Any small green tomatoes may be used for chutney.

Turnip

This root vegetable, *Brassica campestris rapa* (syn. *B. rapa*), has been grown in Britain since the sixteenth century. The roots are global or flattish round. A well-drained sandy loam is suitable for

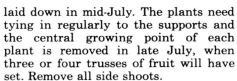

1 Tomato side shoots are removed as soon as seen.
2 Cordon-trained Tomatoes are taken 'round the corner' at the row's end.
3 Black plastic can be used as a mulch substitute for Tomatoes.

Cordon-trained Tomatoes which have been layered once.

both types—summer and winter. But if the soil is light and sandy, it dries out rapidly and turnip flea beetles flourish. A heavy soil is unsuitable for summer turnips but is usually suitable for the winter type. Both very light and heavy soils are improved by regular winter dressings of manure, etc. A site that was manured for a previous crop should be chosen. If liming was not carried out during the previous winter, ground chalk should be dusted on to the surface at the rate of 4 ounces to the square yard before seed sowing.

The first sowing, out of doors or under cloches, may be made from mid-March to mid-April with a second successional sowing in May. Sow seed thinly ½ inch deep in rows 1 foot apart. Dust seedlings with derris to control flea beetles and hoe to keep down weeds. Thin the seedlings to 4 inches or so apart and water in dry spells. Quick growth with no checks at all is essential for succulent summer turnips. Start pulling for use when the turnips are sufficiently large. If left to age they become coarse and fibrous. Sow seed of winter turnips similarly, in late July or early August. Water seed drills if the soil is dry and sow after the water has drained away. Dust the seedlings with derris and thin to 9 inches apart. Winter turnips are

often left in the ground and pulled when wanted. In colder parts the roots are best lifted in the autumn when the outer leaves are yellowing. Cut back the foliage to about ½ inch from the crown and shorten long tap roots by a few inches before storing the roots in moist sand or ashes.

For a supply of turnip tops for 'greens' in spring sow seed of a suitable variety in August quite thickly in ½-inch-deep drills spaced at 18 inches apart. In colder areas the plants benefit from cloche protection during the winter. When picking leaves for use take but one or two from each plant.

Turnip varieties *Summer* 'Early Snowball', 'Early White Milan', 'Red Top Milan', 'Golden Ball'; *winter* 'Manchester Market'; *for turnip tops* 'Hardy Green Round', 'Green Globe'.

Herb gardens

The form and size of a herb garden is determined by the interest these plants hold for the individual. It can be a tiny border of commonly used culinary herbs such as mint, parsley, sage and thyme or an elaborate garden designed to house a wide collection of herbs. Many plants could legitimately be included in one of these large gardens, so that the decorative effect can be the primary consideration when drawing up the plan. For success, a sheltered part of the garden should be chosen. Herbs are always at their best in warm still air and a hedge can be planted to provide both seclusion and decorative completeness to the garden. Choose rosemary, lavender, sage or roses for this hedge. A good temporary shelter can be provided quickly for a season or two by annual sunflowers, until the newly-planted hedge attains a useful size. A gently sloping site often affords the best position as drainage is essential unless a bog garden proper is to be a feature of the herb garden.

Borders Small herb borders, as part of the vegetable garden, to provide flavourings for culinary use, are best treated like vegetable borders. The plants should be set in rows so that the hoe can run between them as regularly as it is in the remaining part of the kitchen garden. In its widest sense the herb border can be virtually a herbaceous border and include verbascum, chicory, catmint, delphinium, artemisia, tansy and foxglove; then it needs to be planned just as carefully as a perennial border is planned. The herb borders near the alpine house at the Royal Horticultural Society's garden at Wisley, Surrey, provide good examples of the medium-sized border and are confined to sage, balms, thymes, alliums, rue, mints, salvias, borage, marjorams and angelica. It is obvious that the decorative value is less than when the choice of plants is

Mature roots of Turnip 'Early White Stone'.

extended to include many flowering plants. The decision as to what to include, or exclude, is determined by personal choice as well as available space.

Natural orders The natural order garden is a favourite way of assembling herbs and examples can be seen at many botanic gardens, including Kew and Oxford. The principle is to arrange plants of one natural order in each bed, making a representative collection as a whole. The idea can be extended according to the selection of plants and each bed can be designed as a small island border, though naturally this is difficult for the *Umbelliferae* and labiates, which all seem to have such strong family resemblances.

Collections The collection may be limited to medicinal herbs, such as belladonna,

digitalis, aconitum, betony, comfrey, or may be a cook's corner, or merely include the sweetly-scented and aromatic plants beloved of bees and preserved as pot-pourri. Similarly one may build up a Bible garden, growing only plants mentioned in the Bible, or a Shakespeare garden including only those plants the poet mentioned.

Designs for herb gardens Individual beds lend themselves to a checkerboard effect where small square beds are formed in staggered rows, the alternate

1 Rue, Ruta graveolens 'Jackman's Blue', is a glaucous-leaved form.
2 Chives, the leaves of which are used in cooking to impart a delicate onion flavour to food.
3 Lovage, Ligusticum officinale, a plant with many old world associations, is not much grown these days.

spaces between being paved or set with chamomile to form carpets. This draught-board design makes a good foundation for many kinds of herb garden and is effective when each bed contains a single kind of plant. This sort of herb garden is to be seen at Lullingstone Castle near Eynsford in Kent and was planned by the late Miss Eleanor Sinclair Rohde. Larger gardens can be planned on a more ambitious scale. A favourite approach is to have a central feature such as a sundial or bird bath, bee hive or even a circular chamomile or thyme lawn forming the hub of a wheel and long narrow beds of individual plants forming the spokes. In a plan such as this, the juxtaposition of various plants requires a little forethought, otherwise ill-assorted neighbours can mar the general charm of the idea.

1

2

3

Some plants to include in the herb garden

Alkanet (Anchusa)	Curry plant *(Helichrysum angustifolium)*	Lavender Cotton (Santolina)	Rue *(Ruta graveolens)*
Angelica *(Angelica archangelica)*	Dandelion *(Taraxacum officinale)*	Lime *(Tilia europaea)*	Saffron *(Crocus sativus)*
Aniseed *(Pimpinella anisum)*	Dill *(Anethum graveolens)*	Lovage *(Ligusticum officinale)*	Sages *(Salvia officinalis)*
Artemisias	Elder *(Sambucus nigra)*	Mace *(Achillea decolorans)*	Salad Burnet *(Sanguisorba minor)*
Balm *(Melissa officinalis)*	Elecampane *(Inula helenium)*	Mallow (Malva spp)	St John's Wort (Hypericum)
Basil, bush *(Ocimum minimum)*	Fennel *(Foeniculum officinale and F. vulgare)*	Marigold *(Calendula officinalis)*	Savory *(Satureja hortensis)*
Basil, sweet *(Ocimum basilicum)*		Mignonette *(Reseda odorata)*	Senna (Cassia)
Bay *(Laurus nobilis)*	Feverfew *(Chrysanthemum parthenium)*	Mints (Mentha spp)	Sorrel (Rumex spp)
Belladonna *(Atropa belladonna)*		Monkshood *(Aconitum anglicum)*	Southernwood *(Artemisia abrotanum)*
Bergamot *(Monarda didyma)*	Figwort *(Scrophularia nodosa)*	Mulberry *(Morus nigra)*	
Bistort *(Polygonum bistorta)*	Foxglove *(Digitalis purpurea)*	Mullein *(Verbascum thapsus)*	Spearmint *(Mentha spicata)*
Borage *(Borago officinalis)*	Fumitory *(Fumaria officinalis)*	Musk (Mimulus)	Sunflower *(Helianthus annuus)*
Broom (Cytisus spp.)	Garlic *(Allium sativum)*	Nasturtium *(Tropaeolum majus)*	Sweet Bergamot (Monarda)
Caraway *(Carum carvi)*	Germander (Teucrium spp)	Nettle *(Urtica dioica)*	Sweet Cicely *(Myrrhis odorata)*
Catmint (Nepeta)	Good King Henry *(Chenopodium bonus-Henricus)*	Orache *(Atriplex hortensis)*	Tansy *(Tanacetum vulgare)*
Celandine *(Ranunculus ficaria)*		Orris Root *(Iris florentina)*	Tarragon *(Artemisia dracunculus)*
Chamomile *(Anthemis nobilis)*	Ground Ivy *(Glechoma hederacea)*	Parsley *(Carum petroselinum)*	Thymes (Thymus spp)
Chervil *(Anthriscus cerefolium)*	Hellebore *(Helleborus niger)*	Pennyroyal (see Mint)	Valerian *(Valeriana officinalis)*
Chicory *(Cichorium intybus)*	Henbane *(Hyoscyamus niger)*	Peppermint (see Mint)	Verbena *(Verbena officinalis)*
Chives *(Allium schoenoprasum)*	Horehound *(Marrubium vulgare)*	Periwinkle *(Vinca major and V. minor)*	Vervain *(Verbena officinalis)*
Comfrey *(Symphytum officinale)*	Horseradish *(Armoracia rusticana)*		Violet *(Viola odorata)*
Coriander *(Coriandrum sativum)*	Hyssop *(Hyssopus officinalis)*	Purslane (Portulaca spp)	Woad *(Isatis tinctoria)*
Corn salad *(Valerianella locusta)*	Juniper *(Juniperus communis)*	Raspberry *(Rubus idaeus)*	Woodruff *(Asperula odorata)*
Costmary *(Chrysanthemum balsamita)*	Lady's Mantle *(Alchemilla vulgaris)*	Rhubarb *(Rheum rhaponticum)*	Yarrow *(Achillea millefolium)*
Cumin *(Cuminum cyminum)*	Lavender *(Lavandula officinalis)*	Rose (Rosa spp)	
		Rosemary *(Rosmarinus officinalis)*	

1

1 The Herb Garden at Sissinghurst, Kent is bordered by a hedge to provide the shelter from wind and weather that herbs require.
2 Mint, one of the commonest of herbs.
3 Comfrey, or the old fashioned Knit-bone, is a decorative perennial.

2

3

Harvesting and drying The art of harvesting and drying herbs to retain the flavour and aroma is one that can be acquired only by practice. The essentials are to harvest at the right time and in the right condition that part of the plant to be used, say seed, leaf or root, and to dry the material at the correct rate. Our climate is too humid to allow for drying in the open without deterioration. The object in drying is to dehydrate the plant by good ventilation. The process is, therefore, best undertaken in a well-ventilated, shaded or dark place where a temperature of not less than 70°F (21°C) can be maintained.

The part of the plant required should be collected when it is ready, handling a small portion only at a time. Put the material into flat boxes or garden trugs when it is cut in the garden and never collect more than there is time to spread out for drying immediately. Material left about in heaps starts to deteriorate immediately because the essential oils escape. Many umbelliferous plants, notably sweet Cicely, flag at once and cannot really be dried. In general the best time to harvest leaves is usually just before the flowers are fully open and a sufficient number of leaves must be left on the plant for it to continue to function. Flowers such as lavender and bergamot are at their best when they are fully open, but to catch the essential oils, gather them just before maturity, and

select unblemished ones. Seed is ready when it is mature and needs merely to be cleaned of seed pods and husks when dry. Roots, naturally, are lifted at the end of the season. By gathering on a dry day, as soon as the dew has gone, the least amount of moisture adheres to the plant material. One kind of material should always be kept separate from another and a minimum amount of handling is important to avoid bruising.

Some plants such as sage can be hung in small bunches in an outhouse or porch to dry, but it is far better to treat all material to a quicker drying method. Domestically the most suitable places are airing cupboards, darkened greenhouses, the plate-warming compartment of a cooker, a slow oven (with the door left ajar), a clothes drying cabinet or a spare room provided with electric heater and ventilator fan. All these places need to be dust free. Flat cardboard boxes without lids, sheets of brown paper, hessian, muslin or nylon tacked to wooden frames to make a tray, may be used to hold the herbs during the process. Wire netting is not suitable, unless it is covered with muslin, because the metal can damage the plant material. The ideal temperature is between 70 and 90°F (21 and 32°C) and ought not to exceed 100°F. An air thermometer is a help and indeed a necessity where any quantity of herbs are to be treated. The ideal is not to have the temperature so high that the plants blacken (parsley does not seem to lose its colour in this way).

A minimum of handling should be the rule during the drying process; a daily turning should be enough because the amount of material being treated should be small in relation to the drying accommodation available. Maintain a temperature around 90°F (32°C) for the first twenty-four hours then reduce it to around 70°F (21°C) until the process is complete. There should be only a faint aroma; if the scent becomes strong this is a certain indication that the temperature is too high. Fresh material ought not to be introduced into the drying chamber before one operation is complete because this increases the humidity, although sometimes this cannot be avoided. The exact time taken over the process is difficult to estimate and will vary according to the space, ventilation and amount of material being treated. Leaves and stems should be brittle and rattle slightly when touched but they should not be so dry as to shatter to powder when handled. Should the stems bend and not break

under the fingers then they are not quite dry. Roots need to be brittle right through and not have a fibrous or spongey core. The amount of water in a growing plant is as high as 80 or 90 per cent. So to obtain an appreciable amount of dried material for winter use a comparatively large amount of the fresh plant needs to be harvested over a period.

Storing The essential requisite is that the dried herbs are stored in such a way that reabsorption of atmospheric moisture is impossible. This can present quite a problem in our climate. First

1 Bay leaves come from the evergreen shrub Laurus nobilis, which is a useful addition to the herb garden.
2 Caraway and Woad at Sissinghurst.
3 The Common Sage can be had in this attractive variegated form, Salvia officinalis aureo-variegata.
4 The Broad-leaved Garlic is native to Britain, a plant as much at home in the herb border as in the kitchen garden proper.
5 A good plant of Balm, Melissa officinalis, which has soft aromatic leaves.
6 Bistort, or Esterledges, a native plant with pungent bitter leaves.

allow the herbs to cool after drying, then chop, rub or sieve them as required, discarding stems and other chaff. Pack them away at once to prevent dust from being collected. Glass jars with screw tops are suitable only for small quantities of material destined for immediate use. Otherwise, metal containers or foil lined boxes are suitable, but wooden jars with either tight-fitting lids or screw caps are ideal. Plastic bags firmly closed with a sealer can be stored in boxes, but it is always a good plan to keep each kind of herb absolutely separate from another.

Freezing Several culinary herbs, particularly the soft-leaved ones such as mint and balm can be successfully stored in the deep freeze. Treat them separately, and store in plastic bags after blanching. Chives, mint, balm, fennel, parsley and sorrel can all be kept in this way. Wash the plants well under running water, plunge them for about thirty seconds into boiling water, cool them under the cold water tap, put them into plastic bags, seal and store until required in the deep freeze. They require very gentle thawing before use.

Chapter 9

PLANT PROTECTION IN THE GARDEN

Greenhouse gardening

Few gardeners do not at some time or another have an urge to grow plants in a greenhouse. It extends the range of plants that can be grown so that those too tender for our winter climate can be cultivated and it is a branch of gardening that can be enjoyed whatever the weather.

Before purchasing a greenhouse you should decide what plants you wish to grow and choose a design which is suitable for them. For instance, if you wish to grow mainly tomatoes in the summer and lettuce in the winter you could well choose a greenhouse glazed almost to the ground as both these crops need maximum light and they benefit from the extra glazing. If you are mainly interested in growing pot plants the greenhouse could have partly glazed side walls, the lower half being of wood or brick with staging for the plants level with the side walls. It is also possible to have a greenhouse glazed to the ground on one side and with a low wall on the other side to enable plants to be grown in a border on the glazed side and pot plants on the staging on the other side.

Heating Before a heating system is installed you should give careful thought not only to its initial cost but also to how much it will cost each year to maintain the desired minimum winter temperature. As a rough guide, to heat a greenhouse to a minimum temperature of 50°F (10°C) will cost twice as much as one heated to 45°F (7°C); three times as much for a temperature of 55°F (13°C) and four times as much for a temperature of 60°F (16°C).

Management In a greenhouse you are able to control the 'climate' to a great extent and provide the most desirable conditions for the type of plants being grown. You do this by providing a suitable temperature, ventilation, moisture and shade as and when required.

Without a heating system a greenhouse can be difficult to manage, particularly in the winter. Damp, stuffy conditions must be avoided when temperatures are low and the roof ventilators should be opened whenever possible. Watering should be done very sparingly and it is better to keep the soil slightly dry rather than wet.

A heating system is of value not only in maintaining the desired temperatures but also in preventing excessively damp conditions from developing, particularly when the weather is very damp. For instance, in early autumn, when the air is often very damp at night, a little heat with some roof ventilation will help to overcome the dampness.

In hot weather in the summer the situation is reversed. To prevent temperatures rising too high inside the greenhouse the ventilators should be opened fully and some shade given with blinds or a special distemper applied to the outside of the greenhouse. In addition, water is sprayed on the floors and stagings to create a humid atmosphere around the plants—hot and dry conditions encourage red spider mites and plants lose moisture too rapidly. Watering should be done freely, particularly with plants that have well filled their pots with roots.

Soil composts To grow plants well they need good soil. This is not simply ordinary soil from the garden; it should consist of a mixture of fibrous soil—preferably obtained from decaying turves—moist granulated peat and coarse sand with fertilisers added. The John Innes Seed and Potting Composts (see Composts, Soil) have been scientifically devised for the cultivation of plants under glass and, made up strictly according to the formulae, they give very good results. Soil-less composts are being used more extensively these days since they do away with the need for sterilising the loam and their value does not depend upon the quality of the loam as does the value of soil composts.

Hygiene Pests and diseases spread very rapidly in the warmth of a greenhouse and a careful watch should be kept for the first signs of their presence. Fortunately many can be controlled effectively by using insecticidal or fungicidal smokes and sprays.

Growing plants in the same border of soil year after year brings problems, and root diseases can set in. Sterilising the soil with steam is effective in combating these disorders but, in a small greenhouse, steaming a large quantity of soil is hardly practical. One way out of the problem is to grow tomatoes, for example, on the ring culture system. The plants are grown in bottomless pots stood on a base of coarse weathered ashes (see Tomato cultivation).

Seedlings are very vulnerable to soil-borne diseases and for seed and potting composts it is well worthwhile sterilising the soil before mixing the other ingredients of the compost. Should diseases, such as damping-off, appear among seedlings, Cheshunt Compound will help to arrest the disease. Having done all one can to provide 'clean' potting soil, pots and boxes should also be washed whenever possible and dipped in a good disinfectant. This also applies to the interior of the greenhouse. Once a year all the wood and glass should be scrubbed down with disinfectant. The outside of the greenhouse should also be washed, particularly in industrial areas, as soot and grime can exclude light.

Unheated greenhouses What can be grown in a greenhouse depends on the

1 A well-stocked greenhouse using various electrical aids.
2 One of the many forms of Camellia japonica.

1 Melons are among the fruits that may be grown in a greenhouse even without artificial heat.
2 Tomatoes ripening in an unheated greenhouse.

minimum temperature that can be maintained in the winter. A great deal of interest can, however, be had from a greenhouse with no heating equipment and if you are working to a small budget an arrangement of this sort is a good beginning; heating equipment can be installed later on as you become more experienced and wish to experiment with a wider range of plants.

An attractive display can be had in an unheated greenhouse by growing mainly hardy plants in pots. These will flower a little earlier than those in the open but the flowers will not be spoilt by inclement weather. Other plants that are usually started into growth early in warmth for summer flowering, can also be grown by starting them later when outside temperatures are higher.

Shrubs The camellia is often thought to be tender, possibly because the flowers, which appear early in the year, are sometimes damaged by frost. For this reason the protection of a greenhouse is valuable. All the varieties of *Camellia japonica* will grow happily in pots of lime-free soil, but they should not be cossetted as if they were hot house plants. *Prunus triloba flore pleno* has double pink flowers and is another fine flowering shrub for the cold greenhouse. The yellow-flowered forsythia and rosy-purple *Rhododendron praecox,* lilacs as well as winter-flowering heathers *(Erica carnea)* will all give a bright display. For flowering in the summer *Hydrangea paniculata grandiflora* produces enormous white flower trusses. It is easily grown in pots and the stems should be cut back severely each spring. The 'hortensia' hydrangeas will flower earlier than the species mentioned above and really good blue flowers can be had if the soil is treated with a blueing powder.

Bulbs These can provide a wonderful display early in the year. The earliest to flower are 'prepared' daffodils in January followed by 'Paper White' narcissi, the dark blue *Iris reticulata* and named varieties of snowdrop. Other small bulbs well worth growing are miniature daffodils, such as *Narcissus cyclamineus, N. bulbocodium* and *N. triandrus albus,* winter-flowering crocuses and *Eranthis hyemalis,* the winter aconite with buttercup-yellow flowers.

For flowering in the summer, lilies such as *L. auratum* and *L. speciosum* look superb grown in pots. Gloxinias and tuberous-rooted begonias are popular plants and the tubers of these can be started into growth in early April.

Other flowers for a spring display, which can be purchased or lifted from the open garden in the autumn and potted up for the cold greenhouse, are wallflowers, dicentras, astilbes, forget-me-nots, polyanthus, lily-of-the-valley and Christmas roses *(Helleborus niger).*

Fruit and vegetables Even in a cold greenhouse, grapes will succeed but it is important to choose suitable varieties such as 'Black Hamburgh' or 'Foster's Seedling'. The vines can be grown in large pots or tubs with the stems trained up a supporting framework, or they can be planted permanently in a border of good soil.

To have tomatoes fruiting under glass in June the seed has to be sown soon after Christmas in a hot house. They can also be grown in an unheated greenhouse but fruit will not be ripe until late summer. Young plants can be purchased for setting out in a border at the end of April.

There is no reason why melons and cucumbers should not be grown in a greenhouse without artificial heat. As with tomatoes, early fruits cannot be expected but all the same they taste much better when picked fresh from one's own garden.

Peach trees can be grown in the open garden but they flower early in the year and their blossoms are likely to be damaged by spring frosts. Given the protection of a greenhouse this hazard can be avoided. Peaches make luxuriant growth and they can easily 'swamp' a greenhouse. For this reason they should be grown as fan-trained trees with all the stems neatly trained out up the roof or against one end of the greenhouse. Good varieties for a cold greenhouse are 'Peregrine' and 'Duke of York'.

Where there is a vacant border of soil in an unheated greenhouse during the winter, lettuce can be grown. Seed may be sown in October, and will produce seedlings ready for planting in November or December, and they should be fit for cutting in April and May.

It must not be thought that all these flowers, fruits and vegetables can be grown together in a small greenhouse. If you prefer flowers it is best to grow little else although a vine or a peach tree could be grown with them. Tomatoes do not like heavy shade and so it would be unwise to have a vine, which produces a heavy coverage of foliage in the summer, with them. Cucumbers and tomatoes should also be kept separate for the best results. Tomatoes like plenty of light and air in hot weather, whereas cucumbers like tropical conditions—heavy shade, high temperatures and high humidity.

Cool greenhouses Although great interest can be had from an unheated greenhouse a wider range of plants can be grown and earlier fruit and vegetables can be had if the greenhouse has a minimum winter temperature of 50°F (10°C). With the aid of artificial heat it is also easier to maintain a good growing atmosphere or climate for the plants.

Shrubs As in the cold greenhouse, hardy shrubs such as forsythia and *Prunus triloba* can be brought into the greenhouse in winter for flowering much earlier than those in the open. Camellias will thrive, provided the temperature is not allowed to shoot up too high in the day—this causes the flower buds to drop—and hydrangeas in pots can be made to flower early. Indian azaleas are popular florists' pot plants. These can be kept from year to year in a heated greenhouse, provided they are fed regularly. They flower in winter and early spring and can be put outside for the summer. *Acacia dealbata,* or mimosa, with yellow fluffy flowers and a heady scent can be enjoyed in early spring. There are also a great many ornamental climbers that will enjoy the warmth. The passion flowers, the brightly coloured bougainvilleas, the soft blue *Plumbago capensis* and *Lapageria rosea* with rose pink, waxy bells, all flower in summer.

Bulbs All the popular bulbs such as daffodils, hyacinths and tulips, can be made to flower in the dark days of winter in a heated greenhouse, but after the pots and bowls are removed from the plunge beds they should be given cool conditions at first and gradually acclimatised to warmer conditions.

Hippeastrums, often mistakenly called amaryllis, have large, handsome flowers and the bulbs may be started into growth in February for spring flowering. Freesia corms, started into growth in August, produce their colourful and scented flowers in February and March; they will grow well in a minimum temperature of 40°F (4°C).

Arum lilies are not true bulbs—they have tuberous roots—but in a heated greenhouse they will flower in the spring. An easily grown and handsome bulb is the Scarborough Lily, *Vallota speciosa.* It can be stood outside for the summer and in August it will produce its vermilion trumpet flowers on stout stems. Flowering a little later, nerines have delightful, glistening flowers in pink, red and white; they differ from many bulbs in that they need to be rested and kept dry in the summer.

Begonia and gloxinia tubers may be started into growth in March for flowering in the summer. Achimenes can be treated similarly, grown in pots or in

1 'Bellegarde' is one of a number of varieties of Peach which do well in a greenhouse with slight heat.
2 Grape 'Black Hamburgh' is a popular variety for the greenhouse.

hanging baskets.

Other flowers that will flourish in a greenhouse with a temperature of 50°F (10°C) in winter are perpetual-flowering carnations—they like light and airy conditions and will flower for most of the year; chrysanthemums for autumn and winter flowering; and fuchsias for the summer.

Pot plants that can be raised from seed in spring and early summer for a display in winter and spring are: *Primula obconica, P. malacoides* and calceolarias. Some gardeners, unfortunately, are allergic to *P. obconica* and if they handle plants it sets up an unpleasant skin irritation.

Cyclamen can be grown successfully from seed sown in August, to provide plants for flowering 16 months later. The poor man's orchid, schizanthus, is also easily raised from seed in August for flowering the following spring.

Regal pelargoniums are becoming more popular and they are useful for their handsome flowers borne from June onwards; these are best propagated from cuttings taken in late summer.

Fruit and vegetables Cucumbers and melons need a temperature no lower than 60°F (16°C) to grow well and it is not wise to make sowings before April. Tomatoes also need a temperature of 60°F (16°C) for germination and seed should not be sown before early April in the cool greenhouse.

Peaches and nectarines can be started

into growth early with a little artificial heat but it is important to remember that the trees are given a rest in cool conditions in the winter. Suitable varieties are: Peaches—'Early Rivers', 'Royal George' and 'Hales's Early'; Nectarines—'River's Orange' and 'Early Rivers'.

In a moderately heated greenhouse grape vines can be started into growth early and a little heat in early autumn helps to complete the ripening of the grapes. Suitable varieties are 'Black Hamburgh', 'Foster's Seedling' and 'Madresfield Court'.

Given good light, lettuce is a useful winter crop in a moderately heated greenhouse. From a sowing in mid-October the seedlings are pricked out in

1

2

boxes and planted in prepared beds in November; the lettuce should be ready for cutting in February. A suitable variety is 'Cheshunt Early Giant'.

In addition to those already mentioned, other vegetables and salad crops well worth growing in a cool greenhouse are mustard and cress, radishes and aubergines. Rhubarb and seakale can also be forced under the greenhouse staging in complete darkness.

Warm greenhouses To be able to heat a greenhouse to a minimum temperature of 55°F (13°C) on the coldest night in winter is an expensive undertaking but it is also rewarding. A great many fascinating tropical or 'stove' plants can be cultivated in addition to those already mentioned.

Shrubs Among the shrubby plants with handsome foliage for a warm greenhouse, most of which are rarely seen, codiaeums (crotons) are outstanding. They have leaves of various shades, brightly marked with green, red, yellow and orange. Dracaenas also have attractively coloured leaves and they include *D. godseffiana* with green, white-spotted leaves and *D. fragrans victoriae* with long green and yellow striped leaves.

The poinsettia, *Euphorbia pulcherrima,* a popular plant at Christmas time with red rosettes of bracts, needs a warm greenhouse to grow well and so does its close relative *E. fulgens,* which has small orange-red flowers on arching stems in winter.

Gardenias, which are prized for their pure white fragrant flowers, do best in a warm greenhouse. Less commonly seen is *Brunfelsia calycina,* an evergreen

1 Tapping a pot to see whether it requires watering.
2 Hot air is blown through plastic tubes to warm the greenhouse.

shrub with purple flowers.

For training up the greenhouse roof there are numerous exotic climbers. The Madagascar jasmine, *Stephanotis floribunda,* has thick leathery leaves and clusters of white scented flowers. There are also several clerodendrums with colourful flowers; *C. thompsoniae* has crimson and white flowers and *C. splendens* produces clusters of red flowers.

Bulbs Begonias, gloxinias, hippeastrums and smithianthas can all be started into growth in January or early February; seed of begonias and gloxinias can also be sown in January. Apart from these popular types, *Eucharis grandiflora* with beautiful, white and fragrant flowers will revel in a warm greenhouse. The tuberose, *Polianthus tuberosa,* is another bulbous plant well worth cultivating for its white, fragrant flowers. Caladiums have tuberous roots and they are grown for their handsome foliage. The tubers can be started into growth after resting in the winter.

Other plants that enjoy a warm greenhouse include coleus and *Begonia rex,* both of which have highly ornamental foliage. Winter-flowering begonias, provide a wonderful display of colour in white, pink and red. Saintpaulias, so popular as room plants, do best in a well-heated greenhouse.

Fruit and vegetables Most of the kinds already mentioned can be grown in a

warm greenhouse. Cucumbers and melons enjoy high temperatures and a humid atmosphere. Peaches and nectarines do not require high temperatures and the same applies to vines, although that very fine grape, 'Muscat of Alexandra', a tricky variety to grow, enjoys warmer conditions, particularly at flowering time and when the berries are ripening. Strawberries, put in pots in late summer will produce early fruit if they are gradually introduced into warmer conditions in February. 'Royal Sovereign' is a good variety for forcing. Figs are not often grown under glass but they can be cultivated in pots and, gradually given warmth in January and February, will produce ripe figs in late spring.

Heating methods

With so many different forms of heating appliance available, it is often a little difficult for the amateur to make an easy selection or decision. The three main types of heating are electricity, solid fuel and oil. Each has its own particular merits and drawbacks. The final decision as to the best type to use can be simplified if certain points are carefully considered. The first must be the amount of money which is available, not only for the initial purchase but the running of the apparatus afterwards.

Oil The cheapest to purchase and maintain is the paraffin oil burner. Many different types are available, from the very small model which could be used for heating a frame, to the large types which are quite capable of keeping the temperature inside big greenhouses (20 feet × 10 feet) well above freezing point. Whilst there are some very good models available, there are some which are very cheap and poorly made. It is very important that the purchase of an oil heater is made only from a specialist firm who use good quality metal and provide a suitable burner or wick. The best type of heater incorporates a blue-flame burner which, if properly trimmed and used with a high grade oil, should burn without causing fume damage to plants inside the greenhouse. There is a range of excellent heaters manufactured from solid, hand-rolled copper. These should provide many years of faithful service and will not corrode.

The capacity or performance of a heater is also ascertained by the number of B.T.Us per hour the burners are capable of (B.T.U. stands for British Thermal Unit which is the quantity of heat required to raise the temperature of 1 lb of pure water one degree Fahrenheit). Several of the smaller oil heaters have a B.T.U. output of approximately 2,900 whereas the larger models have a B.T.U. output of 5,800. Certain types are so adaptable that the heat output can be increased simply by replacing the existing burner with a more powerful one.

The amount of paraffin required to keep a heater working will depend on its size and capacity of its burners. Here are some examples: 2,900 B.T.Us, 60 hours burning on one gallon of paraffin; 3,500 B.T.Us, 54 hours and 5,800 B.T.Us, 34 hours per gallon. Some of the small heaters will burn for approximately 120 hours per gallon of fuel. It should be borne in mind, however, that the fuel tank capacity of some of the small types is only 3 or 4 pints.

The correct burning of an oil heater depends on the amount of oxygen it receives. If a greenhouse is completely shut down it is quite possible that the burners will not receive sufficient air and consequently may produce fumes. A very small amount of air can be supplied if a ventilator is opened not more than ½ inch on the sheltered side of the greenhouse. It is also necessary to keep the wick trimmed regularly and a high-grade oil used.

The positioning of the heater is important if the greatest benefit is to be gained. In a small house the heater can be placed at the far gable end, away from the door and on the central path. It is essential that the heater is placed on a level foundation so that the wick receives a regular amount of oil and also that the fuel gauge indicates accurately.

In a larger house it will be necessary to place the heater in the centre of the greenhouse and on the pathway. To

A Camplex thermostatically controlled glasshouse fan heater.

maintain higher temperatures in the larger houses two heaters may have to be used, placing one a little way away from the plain gable end and the second one about halfway along the path. Avoid at all costs a direct draught to a heater as this could cause the flames to flare and set the apparatus on fire.

Oil heaters demand regular attention to filling, wick trimming and adjusting. A heater should be checked about 20 minutes after it has been lit, as it is quite possible that the flames will have increased a little from the first setting and it will be necessary to readjust their height.

Oil heaters are invaluable in the garden shed where they will give frost protection to tubers (e.g. dahlias or potatoes), which have been placed there for winter storage. They also add considerably to your comfort when you are busy in the potting shed during the cold, early part of the season.

It is now possible to provide a measure of automation to oil heaters by feeding fuel from a large drum by gravity to the heater's supply tank via a length of pipe. The large drum can be placed outside the greenhouse and the feed pipe taken inside.

Solid fuel This is a very popular system of heating a greenhouse: it provides the maximum amount of heat for a low consumption of fuel. Like the paraffin heater, however, it is necessary to attend to it regularly. Great advances have been made with designs and many labour-saving gadgets have been introduced.

Although solid fuel boilers require stoking and cleaning, some of the latest are designed to burn unattended for 14 hours or more. Their fuel consumption, too, is surprisingly economical for the amount of heat generated. For a

temperature of about 50°F (10°C) in an 8 foot × 6 foot greenhouse only ½ cwt of fuel is required weekly. Built-in thermostats considerably improve the performance of solid fuel boilers.

Smokeless zone restrictions do not affect the modern greenhouse solid fuel boilers as they can burn most of the recognised smokeless fuels. One problem that arises with these boilers is that of fuel storage. In large gardens it may be possible to allocate an area conveniently close to the boiler for a fuel dump. This enables you to buy in all the fuel you require for the winter period, often at reduced summer prices. The problem of room in the smaller gardens might be troublesome and you may have to have a standing order for fuel so that you receive small amounts regularly.

The maintenance of solid fuel equipment is very easy as there are few parts which are liable to cause trouble or wear out. Everything about these systems is robust and the thermostatic controls are very strongly constructed and extremely simple. Pipes are made from steel or high duty aluminium. The pipe joints are easy to connect by means of special expansion joints which are simply bolted tight when in position. Pipes are usually fastened to the walls or sides of the greenhouse by means of special holders. In this way they occupy the minimum amount of room.

Electricity Electrical heating scores heavily over other systems if complete automation is required. It is, however, one of the most expensive methods to install and run.

Before any form of electric heating can be installed it is necessary to bring the supply of electricity to the greenhouse site. This can be costly if the greenhouse is situated some way away

from the source of supply. When siting a new greenhouse it is important to bear this point in mind. There are two ways in which the supply can be brought to the greenhouse; by underground cable or overhead. The former is the best method as the cable is unobtrusive and safely out of harm's way. Underground cable is specially protected against mechanical and chemical damage. It is expensive and should be installed where it cannot be damaged by garden tools. Usually the cable is buried beneath the lawn or close by a path. In certain districts it is permissible to take the mains cable overhead or against a wall, but you must seek the advice of the local electricity authority beforehand.

Where maximum internal working room is important, tubular electrical heaters are ideal as they are fastened to the sides of the greenhouse. Banks of tubes can be quickly installed to maintain any desired temperature. Usually a hand-operated or preferably a rod-type thermostat should be wired to these heaters to ensure automatic and economic running.

Fan heaters can be moved around and are extremely efficient in that they blow warmed air to all parts of the greenhouse. This system ensures that there are no cold corners in the greenhouse. During the summer months the heating elements can be switched off and the fan used for air circulation only. Most fan heaters have a thermostat built in and although not as sensitive as the rod type they ensure reasonable running costs. A fan heater should be placed near the door and at least 2 feet away from the side or other obstructions. If there is the possibility of drips of water from the staging, the heater must be placed away from it. In a small greenhouse this type of heater may take up valuable working room, although it could be placed to one side while work is carried out. It is also necessary to make quite sure that there are no plants in the direct line of the hot air.

Convector heaters draw air in at the base, warm it and send it out hot at the top. They take a little longer to heat up the greenhouse as their warmth is concentrated just round the unit. This heater should be situated at one end of the house if it is a small one, or towards the centre in the larger ones.

A great deal of expense can be saved if small areas of the greenhouse can be heated. This can be accomplished in several ways, one of which is to partition part of the greenhouse and install heating in it. This section can be used as an intensive propagation section. If a small cabinet is made, air heating cables can be installed. These are specially designed and can be connected to a thermostat to provide automatic running.

Electric propagators are available in many sizes and these, too, are an ideal form of confined heating. Usually these propagators are made from easily cleaned fibre glass and the heating is supplied by a length of heating cable which in turn is connected to a control box and thermostat. High temperatures of 65–80°F (18–27°C) can be maintained easily and economically.

References have been made in this article to thermostats. The inexpensive types are suitable for loads from 1200 to 2000 watts. They can be regulated to control temperatures between 35 and 75°F (2–24°C). These are hand operated models and are usually accurate to within 4–6°F. The rod types are more expensive but very much more accurate. Usually there is only a differential of 1°F. These models are capable of controlling loads up to 4000 watts. The temperature range is usually wider, 30–90°F. A thermostat must be used with any form of electric heating so that the equipment can be left unattended and running costs kept to a minimum.

With the advent of central heating it is possible for the gardener to make use of the domestic supply if a lean-to greenhouse is purchased. The greenhouse can be placed against a warm sunny wall of the house and a radiator or two can be taken into the greenhouse from the domestic supply. It will be necessary to damp down the greenhouse floor frequently if the floor of the greenhouse is concrete. Central heating is a dry type of heat and a humid atmosphere must be provided to ensure a good growing condition for the contents. The garden frame is less effective than the greenhouse, but it can still be most useful and occupies less space and is considerably less expensive both to buy in the first place and to run.

Frames

The protection which frames afford seeds and plants can be put to good use in several ways. A frame can be a safe harbour for tender plants during the wetter and colder winter months. Such shelter encourages quicker and earlier growth enabling the gardener to force certain crops out of season. Plants raised in the warmth of a greenhouse and intended for outdoor planting need to be inured gradually to more robust conditions and must, therefore, spend a little time in a frame where, by gradually admitting more air, cooler conditions obtain. This process is known as hardening off.

Heating frames Frames are usually unheated but with the advent of safe electric warming cables it is quite easy to convert an unheated frame. The use of warmth in this way extends the versatility of the frame considerably and converts it into a miniature greenhouse.

Propagating frames Another type of frame is the propagating model which is much smaller than the outdoor ones and is intended for use in the greenhouse on the staging. Most of the modern ones are manufactured from fibreglass and are compact in shape and attractive in appearance. To provide the essential germinating temperature, heat is supplied in the form of bottom heat. Special electric cables are used which are placed in a sand base. The more expensive models are equipped with sensitive rod thermostats which can be set to a wide range of temperatures. This ensures accurate, labour-saving use. Two or three sheets of glass are provided so that the top of the propagator can be covered. When necessary, the glass sheets can be opened to provide ventilation.

The site for the frame It is very important to place the frame in the best possible position for good plant growth. Ideally, a frame should face south, but if this is not possible it must be situated where it is sheltered from cold prevailing winds and where it will receive the maximum amount of sunlight. A frame is an important adjunct to the greenhouse where it is used as a place to harden off plants which have been raised under glass. Used in this way, the frame should be placed as close as possible to the greenhouse so that the plants need not be carried far.

The frame should be positioned on well-drained ground, never where water tends to lie. If it is to be used without a greenhouse and is to be heated, it is advisable to site it close to the electricity supply to minimise installation costs. Many of the modern frame designs are attractive and do not look unsightly placed close to the dwelling house.

The soil and site for the frame need careful preparation. The area should be excavated to about 12–16 inches deep and a 3–4 inch layer of small rubble and weathered cinders incorporated. If the sub-soil is heavy, it should be broken up well beforehand with a fork. The remainder of the site should be refilled with a specially prepared compost. The various John Innes formulae are the best and can be made up at home or purchased ready mixed (see Compost). The formula to be used will depend on whether the frame is required for seed raising or for the cultivation of plants to maturity. In a small frame it is a good idea to use seed boxes, pots or pans for the seed raising and to grow plants to maturity directly in the prepared frame.

Frame gardening It is surprising what can be done in a frame with a little preliminary planning. It is excellent as a propagator for a large number of seedlings and cuttings. Seeds can be sown thinly broadcast in the frame soil, in neat rows, or in pots or boxes placed inside the frame. The time to start must depend on whether the frame is heated or not. If the frame is heated work can begin as early as mid-February; in an

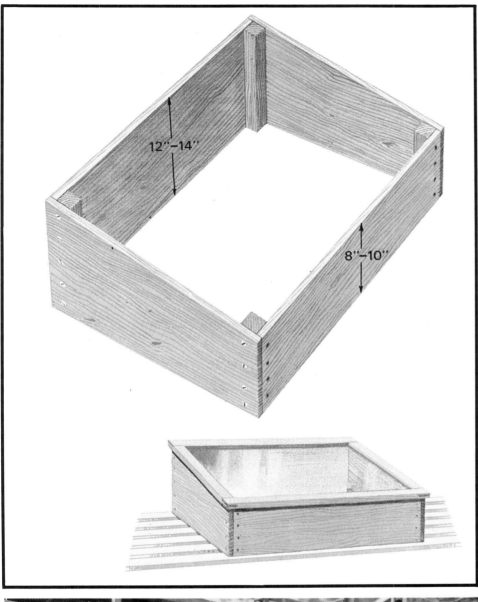

1

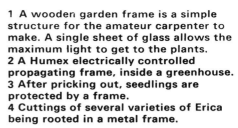

2

1 A wooden garden frame is a simple structure for the amateur carpenter to make. A single sheet of glass allows the maximum light to get to the plants.
2 A Humex electrically controlled propagating frame, inside a greenhouse.
3 After pricking out, seedlings are protected by a frame.
4 Cuttings of several varieties of Erica being rooted in a metal frame.

3

4

227

A frame of galvanised steel affords maximum light. It can be portable.

unheated frame it is better to delay until about mid to late March.

The hardy and particularly the half-hardy annuals are ideal for frame sowings, to produce sturdy plants for planting out in the late spring and early summer. The following are worth a trial; salvias, nemesias, China aster, antirrhinums, stocks, lobelias, petunias and *Phlox drummondii*. Late spring sowings may be made of perennials; polyanthus and delphiniums are especially good for this purpose. Polyanthus sown in March and delphiniums sown in May, potted on into 3–4 inch pots make fine, sturdy plants for planting out into their flowering quarters in the autumn.

Cuttings can be raised in a frame to provide a wide variety of flowers. Good examples are chrysanthemums and dahlias. Chrysanthemum cuttings will be available from February until late April, depending on whether the frame is heated or not. Dahlia tubers boxed up in late March will also produce abundant cuttings. Protection from frost is necessary and a heated frame is better for this type of work.

The simplest possible way to aid and protect plants is to use cloches, in effect a kind of movable, unheated frame which is available in various shapes and materials, but is normally tent-like and made of glass or clear plastic.

Cloche gardening

Cloches are designed to give protection and this feature can be made use of in several ways. During wet or cold weather the soil can be covered with cloches and kept dry and warm. This enables the gardener to sow or plant much earlier than usual. Protection from cold winds and low temperatures encourages earlier

1 Diagram of a barn cloche illustrating how rain water moves laterally from the sides into the root zone of the crops.
2 Two rows of lettuce under barn cloches with strawed paths.

and quicker growth and many plants can be started several weeks earlier than normally. In the colder northern counties and elsewhere many valuable winter crops can be brought through severe conditions successfully. Cloches stood securely on edge or wrapped around tender, larger plants, afford protection from cold prevailing winds and will promote healthier growth.

Two or three cloches placed together with their ends sealed with glass, make ideal propagators or miniature frames. If the larger type of cloche is used a number of seedlings can be raised in a comparatively small area.

Cloches protect plants from bird damage. Many seedlings are attacked by birds, especially pigeons, in town gardens. Seedlings raised under cloches are given complete protection. Strawberries are not only forced earlier but are also kept in good condition by the glass. Plants grown to maturity under cloches, particularly flowers, are protected from weather damage, and the keen exhibitor will quickly appreciate this fact.

Planning and Preparation Cloche cultivation is an intensive form of gardening and from a small piece of ground a wide variety of produce can be gathered. Cloches are used in continuous rows or strips, which must be sealed at the ends by a sheet of glass, retained in position

by a piece of cane or strong wire. The number of rows or strips which are used will depend on the amount of ground available.

One of the best ways to use cloches is to lay down a double row on a 6 foot wide strip of ground with a 4–6 inch gap between the two cloche rows. This 6 foot wide strip will also include a 2 foot wide path. The rest of the cloche garden is marked out into several of these 6 foot wide strips. If the plot is laid out in this way, the cloches will not have to be moved far when they are transferred from one crop to another.

The basic system of cropping is as follows: a double row is planted or sown and covered with cloches. Later on the vacant double strip near them and separated by the 2 foot wide path is sown or planted. The cloches from the first double strip are moved over to cover this newly cropped strip, leaving the de-cloched crop to mature in the open. As soon as this crop has been cleared, the ground is prepared and another crop sown or planted. In due course, the cloches on the second strip are moved back on to the first strip and the crop just de-cloched is either gathered or allowed to mature in the open. This to and fro movement keeps the cloches continually in use. It is possible to devise more ambitious cropping schemes which require more strips and rows of cloches.

The intensiveness of cropping can be increased still further if inter-cropping is practised. This means the cultivation of a quick maturing crop in the same strip as a slower growing main crop. The former is gathered several weeks before the latter is ready. An example of this is the cultivation of a centre row of sweet peas under a row of cloches, with a row of lettuce on either side of the peas. The lettuces grow rapidly and will be cleared before the sweet peas become tall.

Crop selection Intensive gardening such as this cannot be successful unless the crops and their varieties are selected with some care. Most of the cloche crops can be divided into these three sections:
(a) Hardy plants which crop in early spring. Sowings are made under cloches in late autumn and winter and are kept covered until early April.
(b) Half-hardy plants which are covered during April and May.
(c) Tender plants which require cloche coverage during the summer.

Soil preparation Soil moisture must be conserved under cloches as the ground is covered for long periods and protection from rain and the higher temperatures produced under the cloches can cause rapid drying out. To combat this, as much humus material as possible is worked into the ground to act as a sponge which retains moisture for long periods.

The humus can take the form of well-rotted manure worked in at the rate of a barrowload to 8 yards of strip; horticultural peat at a barrowload to 5 yards a strip or composted vegetable waste at a barrowload to 6 yards of strip. The strips are marked out with a line and dug over as deeply as possible to ensure good drainage. As the strip is prepared the humus material is worked into the bottom of each short trench. Where soils are light, some additional peat should be worked into the top 3–4 inches. This is also done when a small cloche seed bed is prepared.

Each year, at a convenient time in the planning of a new rotation system, the 2 foot wide path should be dug over and used as part of a growing strip. In this way, over the years, a very rich area of cloche ground is maintained.

Growing vegetables A week before sowing or planting takes place a well-balanced or general fertiliser is given at 3 oz per square yard. This is raked in thoroughly and the raking action will also break the soil down ready for sowing or planting. If cloches are placed over the prepared strips a week before sowing or planting takes place, the

1 The clear, rigid almost unbreakable plastic type cloche for which the manufacturers claim a life-span of about 10 years. 2 A Poly-Tunnel cloche being used experimentally for strawberries

ground will be warmed slightly and will be maintained in a suitable condition despite bad weather.

Given the protection and the extra warmth of a greenhouse, frame or cloche, many seeds germinate more surely and at greater speed even where there is no artificial heat.

The sowing of seeds in a cold frame is largely the same as for outdoor sowings. The soil mixture in frames is usually one well suited to good germination. In early spring the frame sash should be set on the frame at least a week before sowings are carried out. The covering of the frame in this way traps any available sun heat and the frame bed is warmed and dried.

Where seeds are to be sown on ground given cloche protection warm the soil by placing the cloches in early spring. Seed rows in frames and under cloches may be set quite closely together so that maximum use is made of the surface area. If you water protected seed rows before germination use a very fine rose.

In the greenhouse seeds are generally sown in receptacles (see Seed boxes). For some specialised sowings and for limited sowings clay seed pans are often used. Pots, now offered in a wide range of materials, are most useful for those plants which resent the root disturbances which occurs when pricking out seedlings raised in boxes or pans. New clay receptacles should be soaked in water for several hours before being used. Used wooden boxes should be washed in mild disinfectant.

Where the sowing is made in a seed box some compost is placed in the box, firmed with the fingers and levelled with a ruler or strip of wood to within a half inch of the top. A wooden presser simplifies this task. The compost is then watered thoroughly, using a very fine rose on the can, and set aside to drain. The seed is then sown thinly on the moist surface. Large seeds are spaced at an inch or so apart. The seeds are normally covered after sowing by sieving a ¼-inch layer of the compost over them. Sowings in pans and pots are carried out in the same way.

The containers are then covered with a sheet of glass on which a sheet of brown paper is laid. The glass prevents evaporation and lessens the need for further watering. The paper provides dark conditions.

Although growing plants from seed can

1 Leaf cuttings can be made of several plants, including **Streptocarpus**. Slits are made in the leaf veins, and the leaf is pegged down on to sandy compost.
2 New plants appear at the incisions.
3 The new plants are seen here complete.
4 The new individual plant.
5 Leaf cuttings from a **Saintpaulia**.
6 Use a small pot and sandy compost.
7 and 8 The cutting and new shoots.

1

2

5

6

3

4

7

8

be speeded up by means of the protection of a greenhouse, frame or cloche, it is still quicker and frequently more certain to raise new plants from cuttings.

Cuttings There are various different types of cuttings which are widely used for propagation purposes. The parts of a plant used may consist of young, green stem-growths, semi-ripe wood, hard-wood, single leaves, buds and roots. Stem cuttings may be taken about 3–4 inches in length of half-ripe shoots in July or August of such plants as cistus, hydrangeas, hebes and the like. Some, such as those of camellias, may have a heel of the old wood attached ('heel' cuttings), though most cuttings are prepared by trimming them just below a node or joint ('nodal' cuttings) with a sharp knife or razor blade. The cuttings should be inserted to about a quarter of their depth in pots of moist sandy soil, or John Innes cutting compost, or a mixture of sand and peat, or in a sandy propagating bed in a cold frame. Such cuttings should be shaded from the direct sunlight and be lightly sprayed over with tepid water each morning until roots have formed. Any cuttings that show signs of damping off should be removed.

In the spring young shoots may be taken from the base of such plants as chrysanthemums and dahlias which have been brought into early growth in a warm greenhouse or frame. These are known as soft stem cuttings and after they have been prepared by trimming them cleanly below a node or joint and removing the lower leaves, they should be inserted to a quarter of their depth in moist, sandy soil in a propagating frame with a temperature of about 55°F (13°C). Delphiniums, lupins, heleniums and many other plants, such as the somewhat tender lemon-scented verbena *(Lippia citriodora)*, may be treated in this manner. Cuttings of the more tender plants such as dahlias may be rooted more quickly if the propagating frame is supplied with bottom heat and a very moist atmosphere is maintained, by inserting the cuttings in pots of moist sand or other rooting mixture, and plunging the pots in moist peat in the frame, and spraying them overhead each day. However, as far as the hardier plants, such as lupins and delphiniums are concerned, too much heat and too moist an atmosphere may easily result in the loss of cuttings through damping-off disease or other fungus diseases. Once such soft stem cuttings have rooted they should be potted singly, or in some instances they may be planted out in the open, provided they are not neglected. They should be protected from direct sunlight and drying winds while they are becoming established.

Leaf cuttings Healthy, well-developed leaves of numerous plants provide a useful means of propagation. Those that root particularly easily by this means include various begonias, such as *Begonia rex,* gloxinias, saintpaulias, streptocarpus, and some ferns, both tender and hardy. After removing a leaf from the parent plant make a few light incisions with a sharp knife across the veins on the underside and then lay the leaf on the surface of moist compost, consisting of peat and sharp sand. Peg the leaf down gently; hairpins are useful for this purpose. Leaf cuttings should be shaded from direct sunlight and have a reasonably warm and moist atmosphere. Begonia leaves, among others, will produce roots quite quickly, even when just placed in a saucer of water, but the difficulty is that the roots are so tender that potting on the young plantlets is quite a problem.

Camellias are frequently increased by means of leaf-bud cuttings, which are similar, except that the leaf is taken from the current year's growth, complete with a plump, dormant bud with a small piece of stem wood attached. Such leaves are inserted in sharp, moist sand in pots or in a propagating frame in March in gentle heat. With the aid of mist propagation it is possible to deal with much larger numbers of cuttings over a longer period and the percentage that root is usually greater.

Rooting cuttings in polythene film An interesting way of rooting hard-wood or semi-hard-wood cuttings without inserting them in the normal rooting compost, is to use polythene film. The cuttings are prepared in the normal manner and a piece of film about 8–9 inches wide and, say, 1½ feet long, is placed on the propagating bench. On one half of this, along the length, is placed a layer of damp sphagnum moss. The cuttings are then placed on this (their bases may first be dipped in hormone rooting powder if desired) about ½–1 inch apart, their tops projecting over the edge of the polythene strip. The lower half of the strip of film is then folded up over the moss and the cuttings. Then, starting at one end and working towards the other, the strip of film with the moss and cuttings is rolled up tightly and tied top and bottom with raffia or fillis. Roots should eventually form and these will be visible through the clear polythene. When all or most of the cuttings have rooted the roll can be untied and the cuttings potted up or planted out, taking care not to break the brittle young roots.

The advantages of this method are

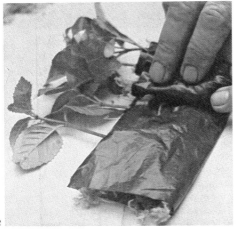

1 Placing hard-wood cuttings on sphagnum moss for rooting in polythene.
2 The polythene is folded over.
3 It is then rolled over from one end to the other.
4 Rubber bands are used to make a neat parcel of the cuttings.

Mist propagation provides the right conditions of humidity and bottom heat, to encourage and hasten rooting.

that once the roll has been tied up no further watering is needed as moisture will not evaporate through the film (the roll should, however, be kept out of direct sunshine, on the greenhouse shelf or bench, or even on a window-sill), and that a number of cuttings can be rooted in a quite small space.

Hygiene When preparing cuttings, particularly soft stem cuttings which are liable to be attacked by soil-borne diseases or by virus diseases transmitted by insect vectors, it is advisable to take precautions against such attacks. Always use a clean razor blade or knife, if necessary sterilising the blade in a sterilant or disinfectant such as a weak solution of Jeyes Fluid. When a batch of cuttings of, say, dahlias or chrysanthemums is being prepared for rooting it is essential to ensure that they do not flag while they are waiting to be inserted in the compost. As soon as each cutting has been taken from the chrysanthemum stool or dahlia tuber, drop it in a container of aired water to which a few drops of Jeyes Fluid has been added.

Virus diseases may be transmitted by sucking pests such as aphids. For this reason, when quantities of cuttings are to be rooted, it is advisable to fumigate the greenhouse beforehand and also to spray stools and tubers with a suitable insecticide and to dip cuttings in an insecticidal solution before they are rooted. Trouble with damping-off diseases can be prevented by watering John Innes cutting compost with Cheshunt Compound. This is less necessary with pure sand or sand/peat mixtures as both these should be reasonably sterile.

Mist Modern electrically controlled mist propagation units are fitted with jets that emit a fine mist spray to envelop cuttings with moisture in order to raise the relative humidity. This used to be done with the aid of a hand syringe but it is much more accurately carried out by the 'electronic leaf' which is placed among the cuttings. As soon as the 'leaf' becomes dry the spray is turned on for a predetermined period. Cuttings inserted in a sandy propagating bed heated by electric soil-warming cables will root more quickly than in a cold frame, and with a mist unit installed it is not necessary to shade cuttings, except during very hot, sunny weather.

Soft stem cuttings rooted under mist must be potted at an early stage and grown on in a greenhouse before being hardened off. Semi-hard-wood cuttings can be left in the mist for a longer period as they do not usually make so much top growth, and hard-wood cuttings can remain in the cutting bed until the spring, if necessary. Mist propagation is not the answer to all the problems of rooting cuttings, but it is particularly useful with large-leaved evergreens, such as camellias, and it has also proved successful with acers (maples), large-flowered clematis hybrids, various conifers, dahlias, daphnes, hibiscus, ilex (holly), magnolias, mahonias, pittosporums, pyracanthas, rhododendrons and azaleas, syringas (lilacs) and viburnums.

Rooting compounds Chemical substances, known as rooting hormones, are available both in liquid and powder form, and are useful for accelerating the rooting of cuttings that may otherwise prove difficult. They are not the answer to the rooting of all types of cuttings but when used according to the maker's instructions can prove to be a valuable aid. With the powder the cutting is prepared and then the base is dipped into the powder before being inserted in the rooting compost. When using the liquid formulations the prepared cuttings are stood in a container with an inch or two of the liquid in the bottom for some hours before being inserted in the rooting compost.

The garden room or modern conservatory is a place for relaxation and leisure pursuits. Sir Cecil Beaton's conservatory at his home at Broadchalke, Wiltshire.

The actual substances are used in minute quantities. For instance, one of them, naphthoxyacetic acid is used at the rates of between 2 parts and 25 parts per million. Three other substances, alpha-naphthalene-acetic acid, indolyl-butric acid and beta-indolyl-acetic acid, are used at rates ranging from 10–200 parts per million, depending on the type of cutting which is being rooted.

A conservatory is a means of mixing the practical and the decorative together to get the best of both worlds.

Conservatories

Conservatories really include lean-to greenhouses, glass corridors and perhaps glass-covered courtyards. They are joined to the house and can contain a variety of pot and climbing plants for all-the-year-round decoration.

Conservatories of reasonable size are not expensive to build. They are easy to look after, and give remarkable scope for the gardener to grow a variety of hardy and not so hardy plants.

Near-greenhouse conditions, ideal for growing and rejuvenation, can easily be arranged by installing simple heating systems. Sometimes, in the warmer, more southerly parts of the country or where the conservatory has a warm aspect in a sheltered position, the

Plants are remarkably adaptable and some can be persuaded to tolerate even quite dark corners in badly heated rooms. Given the garden room, now being built onto so many modern houses, the selection of plants that can be grown with little trouble is suprisingly extensive. Anyone in search of ideas for garden room or conservatory plants should visit one of the national botanic gardens such as that at Cambridge at which this picture was taken. Sinningias (gloxinias), Campanulas, Marantas, Aphelandras and Chlorophytums are a few of the pot plants that can be seen. Others, deciduous and evergreen, can be trained up the walls

heat circulating from the house is sufficient.

A solid floor makes it possible to keep a thriving, humid atmosphere by the simple means of damping down. Heat without humidity can be fatal to plants; moist, warm conditions help to keep most of them at the peak of condition.

Where there is staging to stand the pots on, it should be strong enough to carry a layer of shingle.

Strictly speaking, conservatories are display houses for plants which have been raised and grown elsewhere, though there is not the slightest reason why the conservatory should not be

pressed into service for simple propagation and other jobs for which an ordinary greenhouse might be used. The only trouble is that used in this way, clutter can spoil the effect.

To go even further you leave both the greenhouse and the conservatory behind and enter the living rooms of the home, where with no more than reasonable care a wide range of decorative, even glamorous, plants can be grown.

House plants

There are two kinds of plant that we bring into our houses. The more spectacular are the flowering plants, cyclamen, azaleas or African violets. Unfortunately their season of attractiveness is limited. All too soon the flowers will fade and the plants then have little attraction. If you have a greenhouse, you can keep the plant going and prepare it for another season, but we usually do not feel inclined to keep it in the house; certainly not in a conspicuous position. The other kind of plant is less spectacular; its beauty is centred in its foliage rather than in its flowers, but it has the advantage that, provided you treat it properly, it will grow permanently in your rooms and increase in size and effect from year to year. These plants, grown for permanent

A collection of house plants which includes *(Back left to right)* **Hedera canariensis, Ficus elastica, Sansevieria,** *(Front left to right)* **Croton, Dieffenbachia, Begonia masoniana, Maranta, Peperomia and Aphelandra.**

effect, are commonly known as house plants.

Most of us do not live in glass houses; therefore the plants we can grow in our rooms are limited in number. Even a room that appears well lit to us, will seem shady to a plant and, as a result, the majority of houseplants are those that can tolerate shade. If a plant is to be permanently attractive, it should be evergreen. We can visualise exceptions, such as the bonsai dwarf trees, where the outline of the tree is attractive even when no leaves are visible, but there are not many of these exceptions to the demand for evergreen plants. Again most of us live in rooms of only moderate size and we require plants of moderate dimensions. We also do not want them to grow too quickly. Re-potting is a tedious operation for those who live in flats or in houses without gardens and we do not want to have to undertake it more than once a year at the most. Although plain green leaves are attractive enough, particularly if they have interesting shapes, leaves that contain some colour are usually regarded as more attractive. Colour in leaves occurs in two forms. Some leaves are naturally coloured; for instance those of Rex begonias and *Cordyline terminalis,* but there are other plants which produce coloured forms of their normally green leaves. These are described as variegated and the variegation may be due to a Number of varied causes, from a virus infection to a periclinal chimaera. Whatever the cause, the result is that some part of the leaf lacks chlorophyll, the substance that makes leaves green. If the chlorophyll is completely lacking, the area appears white, while, if there is very little present, the area appears golden or yellow. Although some plants appear naturally variegated, nearly any plant can occasionally produce a variegated form. Variegation is an exceptional occurrence and the plant can be perpetuated only by vegetative propagation, normally by rooting cuttings or layers. Seeds are very unlikely to transmit the variegation. By no means all people find variegated leaves attractive, but very many do and, as a result, many plants are popular because of their variegated leaves that would otherwise be little regarded. The popular variegated forms of *Tradescantia fluviatilis* and *Chlorophytum capense* may be cited as examples. With half or more of the chlorophyll lacking, the leaves of variegated plants can only do half the work of normal green leaves and so variegated plants tend to grow more slowly than the unvariegated forms. This is not unexpected; a more surprising result of variegation, though it is not always the case, is that the plants are often more tender than the normal forms. There seems to be no very obvious explanation for this.

We can now summarise the qualities that we require for a house plant. It must be compact in habit of growth, tolerant of shade and evergreen. The leaves should be attractive, either by reason of their shape or their colour: if we can have attractive flowers as well, so much the better, but with the emphasis to be laid on the permanence of the attraction, agreeable flowers are obviously a bonus. In fact the combination of handsome flowers and handsome leaves is somewhat rare in any branch of gardening. Among the house plants many of the bromeliads provide an exception to this rule, but even with these plants the showiest part of the inflorescence is due to the coloured bracts that surround the flowers, and these are really modified leaves.

Temperate climates produce few plants with the characteristics that we require. The various ivies form an important exception to this statement, but, even so, the great majority of house plants come from the tropics. Plants are infinitely adaptable, as a general rule (there are, of course, exceptions and these are generally regarded as 'difficult' plants) and most tropical plants will adapt themselves to temperate conditions and even to the fluctuating lengths of daylight, which, even more than the alteration in temperature, mark the chief difference between tropical and temperate climates.

There are certain temperatures, varying from plant to plant, below which plant growth ceases. The plant may survive perfectly well, but it will neither produce fresh roots nor fresh leaves, until the temperature is raised. It is, obviously, more difficult to produce high temperatures when the outside temperature is very low and so it is most convenient to make our winter the equivalent of the tropical plant's dry season. The dry season in the tropics is generally very hot, but, owing to the lack of water, the plant makes no growth and stays in a dormant condition. This is one of the reasons why all house plant growers are recommended to keep their plants as dry as possible during the winter. How dry you can keep them, will depend on the type of plant you are growing and on how warm you keep your rooms.

The type of heating that you use and the temperatures you maintain in your various rooms during the winter will affect the types of plant you can grow. Some plants, notably begonias, are very intolerant of gas fumes, so that if your rooms are heated by gas, you will not be able to grow begonias satisfactorily. If you have really warm rooms, maintaining, perhaps, an average temperature of 70°F (21°C), they will be far too warm for such plants as ivy or x *Fatshedera lizei.* With high temperatures such as these, the plants will continue growing during the winter and more water will be required. The winter growth may not be very ornamental, as the lack of light will prevent the formation of good sized leaves.

Many house plants are 'stopped' in the spring: that is to say that the tips of the various shoots are nipped out, so as to induce the formation of secondary shoots that will give the plant a nice bushy appearance, and where this is done the weak winter growth can be removed. However, there are plants, such as most of the ficus, that are not stopped and, where these are concerned, it might be better to move them to cooler positions in the winter. However most of us, alas, cannot afford these high temperatures and it is more a question of keeping the room warm enough for our plants and ourselves. In any natural climate the highest temperatures are around midday, but many sitting rooms are kept cold during the day, when people are out at work, warm in the evening, when everyone is at home, but cool off during the late evening and the early morning after people have gone to bed.

Such a contradiction of natural rhythm is sufficient to disturb any plant and it is easy to see that keeping plants in good condition in the winter is less simple in the house than in a greenhouse. If you have some system of regular central heating, the problem is comparatively simple, but for rooms with only sporadic warmth, the matter is less straightforward. However, there are house plants to suit all conditions. It is as well to know what the average temperature of your room is during the winter, otherwise the problem can be resolved only by a system of trial and error, during which you might well lose the plants that you most prize. It is fairly safe to say that no plant will tolerate the conditions that are to be found on a mantelpiece above a coal fire. The atmosphere is far too dry and the alternations of cold and roasting heat are too much for all plants, except the toughest succulents. Even if the temperature is equable, plants that are put too near the window risk being chilled, or even frosted, when the weather is very cold and they should be moved further into the room during these periods.

Even when the temperature is satisfactory, the dry atmosphere that we like in our rooms is not beneficial to plants. This, however, can easily be overcome, by placing the pots in a larger container and filling this container with some moisture-retentive material. Peat is most frequently used, but moss or mica powder does equally well. Some people get perfectly satisfactory results with damp newspaper, which is topped with moss to look more elegant. By these means we can maintain a moist atmosphere in the immediate surroundings of the plant without either affecting the atmosphere of our rooms or the correct state of moisture of the soil ball. With this we come to the most crucial matter in the successful cultivation of house plants.

More house plants are killed by over watering than by any other cause. Like human beings, plants cannot live without water, but, again like human beings, they can be drowned. However, this analogy cannot be pressed too far. Human beings need water at regular intervals, but plants need water most when they are making growth. This is usually during the spring and summer. There is a correlation between the growth of the aerial portion of the plant, the portion we can see, and the growth of the roots which we can't see. If the plant is making new leaves and stems, we can be fairly sure that it is also making new roots. Unfortunately, the root growth is liable to precede the production of new leaves and so these latter may be prevented from developing if the soil is too dry at the appropriate period. On the other hand, if the soil is too wet, the roots cannot breathe and, far from developing, are liable to rot and, unless this process can be stopped immediately, the plant itself will succumb. We can guard against this to some extent by purely physical means. If we have an open soil mixture that drains rapidly and well, the risk of the soil becoming sodden and sour is reduced, although not, of course, obviated altogether. When to give water is only satisfactorily learned by experience, but the following hard and fast rules are generally acceptable.

1 When water is applied, it should be in sufficient quantity to moisten the whole of the soil ball. The water should be at room temperature. Rain water is preferable but not essential.

2 The soil should be allowed to dry out between waterings. This is not too easy to interpret. We do not want the soil to become dust dry, but on the other hand, we want to avoid saturation. A useful rule of thumb with clay pots and soil mixtures, is to strike the side of the pot with your knuckle. If the resultant sound is dull, watering is not needed, but if it is a ringing sound, water should be applied. With peat mixtures the weight of the pot is a more reliable indication. If it feels light, water is wanted, but not if it feels heavy. The same applies, but to a lesser extent, with soil mixtures in plastic pots. These are much the most difficult to gauge.

3 During cold weather plants make little or no growth and so require little water. Growth is also slowed down when there is little light. It is safe, therefore, during the winter to keep all watering down to a minimum, even though the room may be kept at quite a high temperature. Naturally plants in warm rooms will require more than those in cool surroundings.

4 From about mid-April it is probable that growth will start and so more water may be required. Be cautious, nevertheless, until you see new leaves appearing. It is possible to knock the plant out of its pot to see if new roots (characterised by their white tips) are forming and to replace the soil ball without disturbance. When growth is vigorous water will be needed more frequently. 'Stopping' checks growth temporarily and watering should be on a reduced scale until a resumption of growth is seen.

5 By the end of August it is advisable to discourage much further growth and encourage the plant to ripen its new growth. This is done by keeping the plant as dry as possible.

6 The type of leaf will give some indication of the plant's requirements. Plants with thick leaves or with succulent leaves (such as the large-leaved ficus and sansevieria) can tolerate longer periods without water than thin-leaved plants. These latter will probably wilt when they become too dry and they should be watered at once. The thicker leaved plants will not wilt and so should be inspected frequently. Drought, unless acute, will not kill them but may cause subsequent leaf drop.

If leaves turn yellow and fall off, it usually indicates over-watering. However some plants, such as *Ficus benjamina,* will naturally shed their year-old leaves in the autumn and most plants shed a few leaves in the course of the year. Excessive defoliation is almost certainly due to incorrect watering; although it can be caused by under-watering as well as by over watering. If the plant becomes unsteady in the pot, this is generally due to root-rot caused by excessive water and is very difficult to arrest. Some leaves will wilt in the summer if they are in direct hot sunlight. If the soil appears to be satisfactorily moist, a syringeing of the leaves with water will generally restore them to their normal turgidity, and in any case, they

A group of flowering house plants all of which add colour indoors in winter.

1 Maranta mackoyana must be protected from sunlight to keep its leaf colour.
2 A collection of Ferns in a bark container, with Helxine added in the front.

will resume their normal appearance as soon as the sunlight goes.

Once the question of watering has been mastered, there are few other problems. Rooms are very dusty which spoils the appearance of the leaves of house plants and also prevents them from functioning properly. It is advisable, therefore, to clean the leaves every two or four weeks. This is best done with cotton wool and tepid water and the leaves should be sponged on both sides. New leaves are soft and easily damaged and should be left until they are older. Some people use milk, or oil, or flat beer to give the leaves a more glossy appearance, but these mixtures do not do the leaves any good.

During the summer, when growth is most vigorous, the plants may be fed. A liquid feed is most easily applied and should be given according to the instructions on the bottle. Little and often is invariably better than doses in excess of those recommended. Unless the plant is really well-rooted, feeding should not be applied and is not necessary for plants that have been repotted. Repotting is done in the early summer. For the majority of house plants the John Innes potting compost No 2 is the best. Plants are usually potted on into a pot one size larger. Plants from 5-inch pots are put into 6-inch pots and so on. The only exception is that the 4-inch pot is very rarely used and plants are moved from 3-inch to 5-inch pots. Plants with very thin roots such as begonias and peperomias do better in a mixture of 2 parts of leafmould to 1 part of sharp sand, while epiphytes, such as the bromeliads, are usually given a mixture of peat, leafmould and sharp sand. However, it is only rarely that epiphytes require any potting on, as they use the soil as an anchorage only. After being potted on the plants should be kept on the dry side until the roots have penetrated the new soil. It is best to move plants from 2-inch pots to 5-inch pots after a year, as the 3-inch pots dry out so quickly, but after that most house plants will need repotting only every other year. The second year the plant will need feeding.

The epiphytic bromeliads (aechmea, neoregelia, nidularium, guzmania, tillandsia and vriesia) need rather different treatment from most house plants. They have a rosette of strap-shaped leaves which form the so-called 'vase'. This must be kept full of water, preferably rain water. The mixture in which they are potted may be kept moist, but this is of minor importance, as the roots serve little purpose except anchorage and it is from the leaves that nutriment is absorbed. During the summer the merest trace of liquid feed may be added to the water in the vase, but this must be done with great discretion.

Most house plants are easily propagated if you have a greenhouse, although some, such as the large-leaved ficus, cordylines and dracaenas, need a good deal of heat to get them to root. There are a few that can easily be propagated in the home. The various tradescantias and zebrinas will root easily in water and so will *Cissus antarctica* and *Rhoicissus rhomboidea*. Shoots of succulents, such as *Sedum sieboldii* and aichryson will root easily, either in ordinary soil or in a mixture of equal parts of peat and sharp sand, which is an ideal mixture for most cuttings. Shoots of the various ivies, taken when they are half ripe, that is neither too young nor too woody, will root easily although rather slowly. The peperomias, with single leaves rising from the base, can be rooted from leaf stem cuttings. The leaf with its stem is pulled off and inserted in the peat and sand mixture, when a new plant will form at the base of the leaf stalk. Sansevierias will produce new leaves on rhizomes, but they do not root until a year has elapsed and should not, therefore, be severed from the main plant before this time. If, however, you can find the new rhizome without disturbing the plant and cut half-way through it, it will hasten the formation of roots at the base of the new leaf. Many of the climbing aroids produce aerial roots and these can be induced to develop in soil. These climbing aroids (philodendron, syngonium and scindapsus), will grow more luxuriantly if they are given a cylinder of wire stuffed with moss up which they can grow. However, the moss must be kept damp and this is not easy in the home. They can also be trained on blocks of cork bark.

Chapter 10

PEST AND DISEASE CONTROL

Gardening may be an enjoyable hobby and it may give a great deal of pleasure, but at the same time it involves the expenditure of considerable effort, time and even money. Anything that tends to diminish the value, quality or quantity of the result of this expenditure is not only to be deprecated but avoided or prevented wherever and whenever possible.

Under this category come the pests and diseases which can undo in a night and waste for ever the hard labour of weeks. On the whole, however, we are comparatively fortunate in this country for with no more than reasonable care we can keep our crops clean and protected. Indeed, it is possible to carry this matter of pest and disease prevention and cure too far.

If we ourselves resorted to heavy doses of powerful drugs because of an insect bite, a minor cut or scratch, a touch of colic or a slight cold we would probably be doing ourselves more harm than good in the long run. In exactly the same way some gardeners take some of the minor and insignificant ailments of their plants too seriously. Again, if we rush for the spray each time we see a caterpillar we will no longer enjoy butterflies in the garden and if we try to kill at once all the aphids on our roses we may very well be killing at the same time armies of beneficial insects such as ladybirds and efficient pollinators such as the bees.

So the gardener would be advised to cultivate a sense of proportion, neither resorting to sprays, powders, puffers and potions at the least sign of trouble, nor accepting blindly some of the hysterical anti-chemical propaganda propounded by well-meaning but ignorant amateur ecologists.

Pest

Almost any creature which causes significant damage to plants may be defined as a pest. Most garden pests are insects and they cause many different kinds of damage. These include weakening the plant and spreading virus diseases by sucking the sap. Another form of damage by insects reduces leaf area, impairs the root system and allows the entry of disease, when the plant tissue is eaten away above or below the ground. They also kill shoots by tunnelling along them; and disfigure the plant by the formation of galls, discoloration, distortion, spinning up or mining the leaves, etc.

Pests include mites, which cause galls and yellowing of the leaves and damage to bulbs; slugs which rasp plant tissue above and below ground; millepedes which damage the underground parts of plants; woodlice which gnaw stems and leaves; springtails which attack seedlings, etc., and microscopic eelworms which attack roots, bulbs and foliage of various plants.

Larger creatures which sometimes become garden pests include mice, voles and squirrels which eat bulbs and corms; rabbits and hares which devour plants and bark fruit trees, especially in severe weather; moles which spoil lawns with their tunnelling; deer and sheep which occasionally break in and create havoc; domestic dogs and cats, which are occasional nuisances; and birds which destroy buds and berries.

But we do not necessarily wish to kill all these garden pests. It will be sufficient for us if we merely send them away or keep them out of our gardens.

Repellents

There are now a number of animal and bird repellents on the market. Commercial alum and quassia were often used against birds in the past but were not consistently successful. Now a number of proprietary repellents are available based on various substances such as aluminium ammonium sulphate. Success, however, depends on a number of factors, such as timing and number of applications made. Seasonal weather and food scarcity may also affect results. The maker's instructions regarding timing and frequency of application should be carefully followed.

Rayon cobwebs can be bought to enmesh the trees and bushes to keep away birds. Since the substance rots away within a few months, it can be used to give protection over a vulnerable period as an improvement on black cotton.

Animal repellents include rabbit smears which are often evil-smelling concoctions used to soak rags which are then placed in burrows or mole-tunnels to disconcert the inhabitants. Another use of the smears is to soak twine which is then fastened to sticks to form a fence a few inches from the ground round areas to be protected such as flower beds.

There are also aerosol repellents for use on such things as garden furniture and gate posts. These deter dogs from contaminating them. To repel cats and domestic pets from such places as seed beds there are repellents based on commercial pepper and other substances. Repellents of this kind need renewing after rain. There are even mouse repellents available under proprietary names.

There are occasions, however, when we have to take stronger measures.

Pest Control

Pest control in home gardens is not easy.

In general, it is best to use chemicals only when it is strictly necessary, taking into account whether the amount of damage done is sufficient to warrant spraying, or whether it is a small outbreak that can be tolerated without lasting injury to the plant. First, the pest responsible must be identified. The insect found on the plant is not necessarily the culprit. It may be innocent, while the pest causing the damage may be feeding at night or may have completed the feeding stage of its life cycle, or have migrated to another host plant.

A knowledge of the habits and life history of common pests is therefore useful for their correct identification, and for the correct timing of control measures. If necessary, the aid of experts may be called in and most gardening periodicals and some chemical firms run advisory services. The Royal Horticultural Society gives advice to members; commercial growers can consult the Agricultural Development and Advisory Service.

When choosing chemicals to control the pests, the home gardener is confronted by a huge range of proprietary brands offering a bewildering choice. There are insecticides to kill insects;

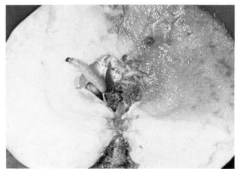

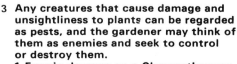

3 Any creatures that cause damage and unsightliness to plants can be regarded as pests, and the gardener may think of them as enemies and seek to control or destroy them.
1 Earwig damage on a Chrysanthemum.
2 Loganberry fruits attacked by the Raspberry Beetle.
3 A sectioned Potato showing damage done by the Keeled Slug.
4 The caterpillar of the Codling Moth.
5 Cabbage Aphid damage on Sprouts.
6 Slugs and Snails.
7 The female striped Hover Fly.
8 Ants can cause much damage.

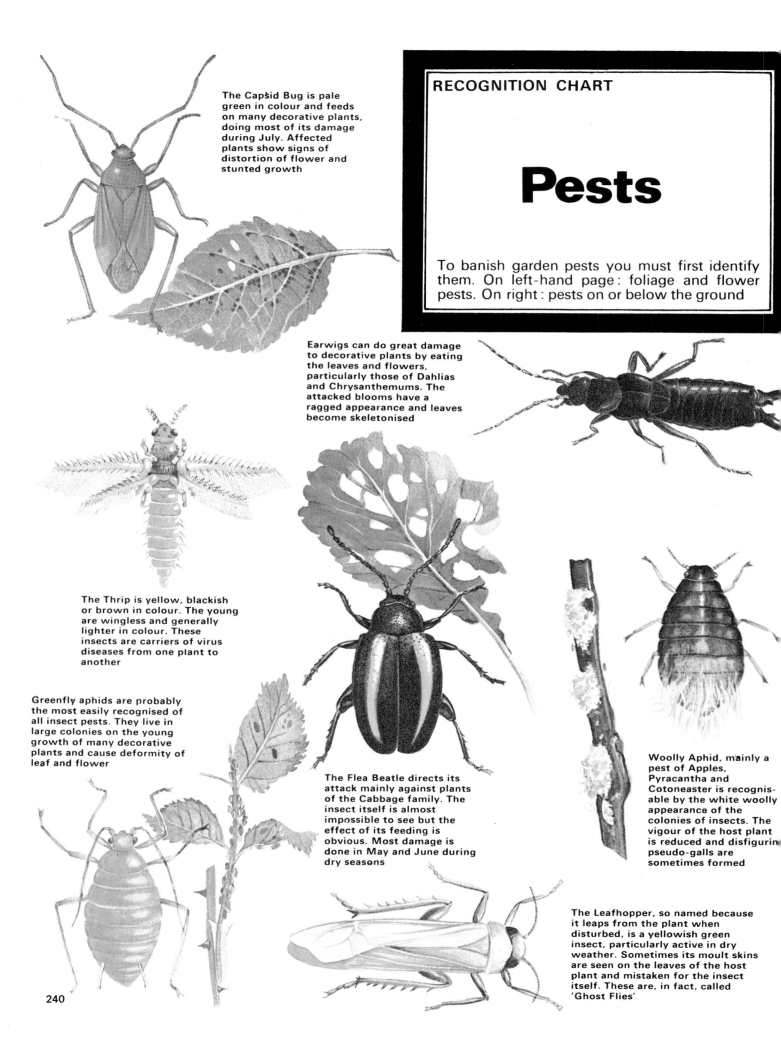

The Capsid Bug is pale green in colour and feeds on many decorative plants, doing most of its damage during July. Affected plants show signs of distortion of flower and stunted growth

Pests

To banish garden pests you must first identify them. On left-hand page: foliage and flower pests. On right: pests on or below the ground

Earwigs can do great damage to decorative plants by eating the leaves and flowers, particularly those of Dahlias and Chrysanthemums. The attacked blooms have a ragged appearance and leaves become skeletonised

The Thrip is yellow, blackish or brown in colour. The young are wingless and generally lighter in colour. These insects are carriers of virus diseases from one plant to another

Greenfly aphids are probably the most easily recognised of all insect pests. They live in large colonies on the young growth of many decorative plants and cause deformity of leaf and flower

The Flea Beatle directs its attack mainly against plants of the Cabbage family. The insect itself is almost impossible to see but the effect of its feeding is obvious. Most damage is done in May and June during dry seasons

Woolly Aphid, mainly a pest of Apples, Pyracantha and Cotoneaster is recognisable by the white woolly appearance of the colonies of insects. The vigour of the host plant is reduced and disfiguring pseudo-galls are sometimes formed

The Leafhopper, so named because it leaps from the plant when disturbed, is a yellowish green insect, particularly active in dry weather. Sometimes its moult skins are seen on the leaves of the host plant and mistaken for the insect itself. These are, in fact, called 'Ghost Flies'

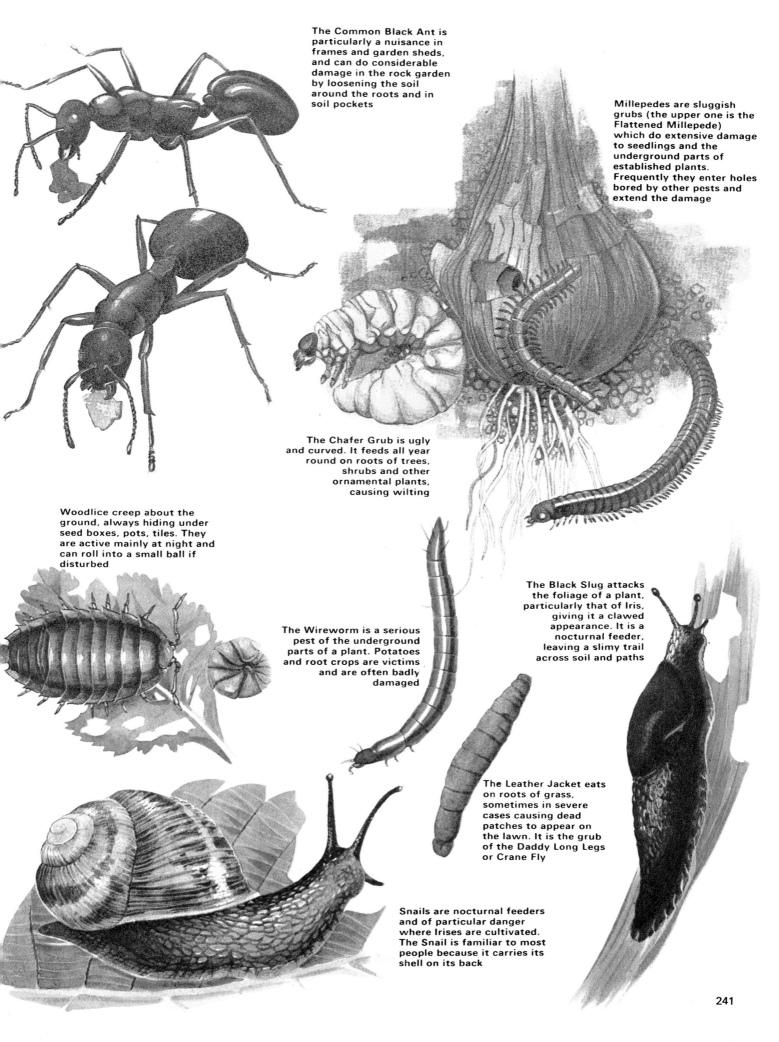

The Common Black Ant is particularly a nuisance in frames and garden sheds, and can do considerable damage in the rock garden by loosening the soil around the roots and in soil pockets

Millepedes are sluggish grubs (the upper one is the Flattened Millepede) which do extensive damage to seedlings and the underground parts of established plants. Frequently they enter holes bored by other pests and extend the damage

The Chafer Grub is ugly and curved. It feeds all year round on roots of trees, shrubs and other ornamental plants, causing wilting

Woodlice creep about the ground, always hiding under seed boxes, pots, tiles. They are active mainly at night and can roll into a small ball if disturbed

The Black Slug attacks the foliage of a plant, particularly that of Iris, giving it a clawed appearance. It is a nocturnal feeder, leaving a slimy trail across soil and paths

The Wireworm is a serious pest of the underground parts of a plant. Potatoes and root crops are victims and are often badly damaged

The Leather Jacket eats on roots of grass, sometimes in severe cases causing dead patches to appear on the lawn. It is the grub of the Daddy Long Legs or Crane Fly

Snails are nocturnal feeders and of particular danger where Irises are cultivated. The Snail is familiar to most people because it carries its shell on its back

241

acaricides to kill mites; nematicides to kill eelworms; molluscicides to kill slugs and snails; vermicides to kill earthworms; ovicides to kill overwintering eggs; repellents to deter birds and mammals, etc. There is also the formulation of the insecticide to be considered. It may be best to use a stomach poison, a systemic insecticide, or a fumigant. The insecticide may be in the form of a liquid, dust, a wettable powder, an aerosol, smoke, granules or seed dressings. It is necessary to consider what form would be most suitable.

The scientific world moves very swiftly. New formulations of greater efficiency and lesser toxicity are constantly being introduced and older preparations withdrawn or their use discouraged. If in doubt about which material to use to combat which pest or disease, information is always available at the better garden centres and stores, from gardening journals and from the advisory departments of the garden chemical manufacturers themselves.

Some years ago the Ministry of Agriculture introduced the Agricultural Chemicals Approval Scheme. Under this scheme the manufacturers of all types of garden chemicals can provide samples of their products for stringent official tests. If the products pass the tests (which are not only for efficacy but also for safety) they are granted the approval mark, a capital A surmounted by a crown. This sign will be found on the labels of tested and approved products and should be sought by the gardener.

Because a product has been approved does not mean that it can be used carelessly. Instructions must be read carefully and followed meticulously.

It may well be found, for instance where nicotine or malathion are concerned, that an insecticide that is of short persistence on the plant is extremely poisonous in the concentrated state before dilution. Containers should always be kept well out of the reach of children and animals and every care taken to ensure that they do not come in contact with sprayed plants or lawns within the period specified. Insecticides should *never* be put in other bottles, such as soft drink bottles, even after they have been diluted for use.

For preference, an insecticide of short persistence should be selected. A double dose of the insecticide will not do twice as much good as that recommended by the manufacturer and may result in damage to the plant. Whatever the chemical, there are almost always a few plants which react unfavourably to it. These will usually be mentioned in the

1

2

**1 Insecticides can be applied as a fine spray from a pressurised container. A fine spray wets the plant evenly.
2 A sprayer of the knapsack design with a long spray gun is useful for roses growing in beds.**

instructions if they are commonly grown plants, but where unusual plants are grown, it is as well to test chemicals on a few of them before spraying them all.

It is often possible to obtain control of more pests at one time by combining two or more compatible chemicals. These may be two insecticides designed to kill biting and sucking pests respectively. An insecticide and an acaricide may be combined or an insecticide and a fungicide, and so on. Many proprietary pest control preparations contain more than one chemical used in this way, or compatible substances can be made up at normal dilutions to form one spray, thus saving two applications. The efficiency of sprays may be increased by the addition of wetting compounds, where these are not already incorporated in the proprietary substance.

Probably the most frequently used mixture of two substances in the gardener's armoury is an insecticide and a fungicide. A proprietary rose spray which will control mildew, blackspot, aphids and caterpillars is now available.

Disease

The word disease in connexion with plants is considered to refer to any disturbance in the normal life processes which results in such things as (a) abnormal growth (b) temporary or permanent check to the development or (c) premature death of part or all of the plant. Plant diseases can be divided into two sorts (i) Parasitic, where the trouble is due to attacks of parasites such as fungi, bacteria or viruses and (ii) Non-parasitic in which the trouble is a result of faults in the environment (soil, temperature, moisture etc). The biggest group of diseases is that caused by fungus parasites (including bacteria) which are spread about by spores produced in the fruiting bodies (equivalent to seeds of higher plants but, of course, microscopic in size). Viruses are incredibly small in size and in nature are carried from infected to healthy plants by insects, mainly aphids, and also by trimming knives and hands (in glasshouses), by knives etc., (in propagating houses) and in a very few instances by seed transmission. It will be noticed that the great difference between parasitic and non-parasitic disease is that the former is infectious while the latter is not. Despite this, where a non-parasitic trouble begins, there is likely to be great loss unless the fault in environment is quickly corrected. The symptoms in either kind of trouble can be very similar and even almost identical so that to judge the cause it is often necessary to consult an expert to get microscopic examination and sound advice.

Disease control

The control of plant disease depends

on an accurate estimate of the symptoms shown by the affected plant so as to arrive at the exact cause of the trouble. Even with parasitic diseases the cause is usually microscopic, requiring a careful examination and often laboratory tests on the diseased tissues. Similarly with non-parasitic troubles the environment must be studied as well as the plants and the details of cultivation carefully considered. There may have to be a careful soil analysis as well as a study of the drainage and soil texture and there may also be an analytical test of some of the foliage or fruits which could reveal a shortage of some essential plant food.

Precautionary measures Before considering measures which have to be taken to check diseases in plant crops we may look at some of the things which can be done to guard against disease ever appearing. These can best be termed precautionary measures. They aim at building up the vigour of the plants to help them to resist any possible attack by a parasitic disease and they also include various precautions which can be taken to eliminate the possibility of disease being in the neighbourhood of the crop, more especially in the soil.

It is of the utmost importance to study the special requirements of any particular plant so that the soil can be prepared in order to ensure good drainage and also that it contains sufficient organic matter (humus) and the necessary plant foods. Where some plants are concerned, for instance camellias and rhododendrons it is important to ensure that there is no lime present in the soil. Everything should be done to get vigorous plants with robust stems and foliage. In glasshouses, proper light and ventilation must be arranged and in fruit trees skilful pruning helps to build up strong, healthy shoots and buds with good circulation of air among the branches.

Rotation of crops is intended to avoid growing the same kind of plant on the same spot year after year. If crops are grown on the same site year after year any disease of that crop is encouraged to build up and the soil can become heavily infected, addition to which the same plant foods are taken out of the soil. A different crop takes different amounts of the various chemical elements so that a balance can be easily kept. In glasshouses the same crop is very often grown each year but the disease build-up is checked by suitable methods of soil sterilisation. Other precautionary measures are weed

1 Watering Cheshunt Compound on to a seed box before sowing seeds, to prevent attack by damping-off disease. 2 Watering seedlings with Cheshunt Compound. 3 A chrysanthemum plant attacked by the disease powdery mildew.

eradication (e.g. wild celery harbours celery leaf spot disease and the common plantain can carry the virus of spotted wilt). Careful spacing is also helpful so that diseases are not provided with the humid and moist conditions between plants which they need to germinate their spores and infect the leaves.

The protection of large wounds is another obvious precaution and one which is very important where large specimen trees or even expensive fruit trees and shrubs are concerned. It is not suggested that small pruning cuts need to be treated but where a large branch is broken down by wind or snow or cracked during severe frosts it is wise to try to protect the broken or cut places. After any branch is removed the cut should be painted over with a suitable protective paint or a proprietary pruning compound to prevent the entry of fungus parasites. Not only are plum trees likely to be infected by the silver leaf fungus but many fine ornamental trees and shrubs can be lost by neglecting this simple precaution. Even after cutting out a canker from apple trees the wound should be painted.

Resistant plants An important method of avoiding plant disease is to use resistant plants. A plant immune to a particular disease is valued very highly by the grower if its quality is as good as those which are susceptible to the disease. Growing immune varieties is the simplest way of avoiding disease and such varieties are steadily increasing in number.

Soil sterilisation One of the most important precautions taken to avoid disease in horticultural crops is the practice of soil sterilisation. In this the soil in a greenhouse intended for tomatoes, cucumbers, lettuces etc., is treated by passing hot steam through it (a commercial practice) or by watering with chemicals (formaldehyde or a tar-oil emulsion) before the crop is planted so that any dormant spores of disease are killed. However, at the temperature used, the spores of beneficial bacteria such as the nitrogen fixers are not killed, so that after the process is completed these can begin to enrich the soil without any immediate competition from other organisms. For use in small pots and seed boxes sterilised soil made after the John Innes formulae can be bought for use by gardeners. Similarly, sterilised soilless composts are now available. Small glasshouses can be washed down inside with formalin or other disinfectants and the same sort of treatment can be given to garden frames, pots, boxes, seed trays and tools. Tar-oil emulsions are often used for this purpose and in some instances also for sterilising the surface of the soil, but there are several other good disinfectants available for the gardener.

Preventing the spread of diseases When,

Wounded tissues are susceptible to invasion by disease spores which are always present in the atmosphere. Where large cuts have to be made protect them at once with a proprietary pruning compound.

despite the precautions referred to, a disease makes its appearance it is necessary to act quickly and to take direct action measures. The chief of these is to cover the plant with a protective film of a chemical which will kill the fungus or at least prevent the germination of its spores. Diseased parts can be removed before treatment, but it must be remembered that in most diseases an affected plant is often doomed (except where the disease is superficial or where affected parts can be cut away). The object of the treatment is to protect still healthy tissues, so that it is wise to spray or dust early.

Various chemicals, known as Fungicides, which will deal with all types of disease, are widely obtainable on the market. These are applied as a fine misty spray or as dust (most people hold that spraying is more efficient than dusting). Many types of spraying and dusting machines are in use. There are also smokes which are lit to fumigate glasshouses, containing fungicides, and/or insecticides. Seeds, bulbs and corms are also treated by dusting or by immersion in a liquid fungicide to give them protection from soil-borne diseases, etc., after planting.

Fungus diseases

These are diseases which are caused through the attack of various parasitic fungi. Some fungi obtain food by living on the decaying organic matter which we

call humus in the soil, but some obtain their food by attacking living plants and injure or kill them in the process—these are called parasites. In general, the harmless saprophytes are large and easily seen but the parasites are very small and need a microscope for their proper identification, although their presence may be detected because of some whitish or greyish mould or furry growth (e.g. rose mildew). These parasitic fungi grow microscopically inside plants but some have also a smothering effect (mildews) and grow on the outside of leaves and stems etc. They reproduce and spread themselves by means of innumerable spores.

Fungicides

Fungicides are chemical substances which are used in the control of those diseases of plants which are caused by fungus parasites (see Fungus diseases). The ideal fungicide is a substance which will kill a fungus or prevent its spores from germinating, without doing any harm to the host plant. These substances are used in various forms and in various ways and many chemicals have been tried in the search for the most effective safe fungicide. Sulphur and copper are two of the oldest elements used for this purpose and in various forms are still used against some diseases. For instance, copper sulphate is used to make the well-known Bordeaux mixture which has been in use for a century, while sulphur probably dates from Biblical times.

In recent years many of these fungicides have been replaced by more modern ones as the result of much research and there is now a much greater choice. In general the modern fungicide is more specific, that is to say it will prove very effective against a certain disease but is not so generally useful against many others, whereas the older kinds had an all-round fungicidal effect and exercised a check on many diseases likely to attack the plant.

Fungicides are applied either as sprays or dusts on the foliage or in empty greenhouses as sprays or in the process of fumigation. They may also be applied as a 'smoke' from a special generator or tablet which is lit.

But although fungus diseases are those we most frequently come in contact with in our gardens, the viruses are also important.

Virus diseases

A virus is a minute particle, visible only under the electron microscope, which causes disorders or diseases in living cells. The presence of viruses may result in leaves developing yellow or brown spots, streaks or ring patterns. Other symptoms affecting the leaves may include dark green areas along the veins (vein banding), a loss of colour (vein clearing), complete yellowing, distortion and small outgrowths. Streaks and stripes may appear on stems. Other symptoms include witches' brooms (large numbers of side shoots), distortion, colour breaks or white flecks on flowers. A condition where flowers become green and leaf-like is called 'phyllody'. Fruits may be small, misshapen or bumpy. Less distinct symptoms of virus infection are a general stunting and reduction of cropping. Viruses can also change the internal structure and the metabolism of plants; for example, virus-infected tomatoes are said to have a better flavour.

A plant may contain a 'latent' virus without any visible symptoms. There may also be interactions due to the hidden presence of viruses. Indicator plants, which give a quick and characteristic reaction when inoculated with the sap of a virus-infected plant, are widely used in the identification of viruses. Good indicator plants include *Nicotiana* species, beans and *Chenopodium* species.

Non-persistent viruses adhere to the mouth parts of insects feeding on infected plants and are carried to healthy plants. The particle remains infective for up to about two hours. Persistent viruses are absorbed into the digestive system of the insect, and from there pass into the salivary glands where the virus multiplies. When feeding the insect injects saliva containing virus particles into plants and remains a disease carrier all its life.

Virus diseases may be mechanically transferred from one plant to another by man. Plants propagated from infected material will contain virus particles. This is important in all vegetatively propagated crops such as potatoes, fruit and bulbs.

Control Heat therapy kills or inactivates the virus, and apical meristem culture is another method of approach. As a general rule avoid the spread of virus diseases by regular spraying against the insect vectors. Clean cultivation prevents weeds acting as carriers of infection. Remains of the previous year's crop are another source of infection. Plants susceptible to the same virus should not be grown close together. Regular inspection and rogueing of obviously diseased plants is often effective. Seed should not be sown near an old infected crop. Barrier crops are sometimes grown by planting immune plants around those liable to a particular virus infection. Early sowings may enable plants to become established before the activity of disease-carrying insects.

Physiological disorders

In the study of plant diseases it is usually found that most diseases are due to the attack of some small organism such as a fungus, a bacterium, or one of the microscopic viruses. The work of the plant pathologist when confronted with a disease is to try to identify the parasite which is causing the trouble and then to take steps to combat it. Long ago it was realised that plants sometimes become sick and show symptoms of ill-health although they are not infected by any parasite. This type of trouble in plants is referred to as non-parasitic disease or physiological disorder. It can arise from a multitude of factors such as unsuitable soil, lack of lime, excessive moisture, drought, lack of some essential food element, spray, fume or fumigation damage, and so forth. There is no parasite present so there is no infection to spread but it is obvious that unless something is done all the plants will become affected and weakened.

The identification of a physiological disorder is not easy and, in general, must depend on finding the symptoms as it does with the parasitic diseases which are microscopic. In both groups symptoms from different troubles are so similar that it requires an expert to recognise them.

Attempts have been made to form a rough classification of symptoms and the most study has so far been given to the effects of shortages of essential food elements which are often referred to as mineral deficiencies. These include shortages of the major elements such as nitrogen, potash, phosphate, magnesium and lime, which plants absorb in fairly large amounts and the lesser known minor or trace elements, such as boron, copper, zinc, manganese and iron, which are needed only in very small amounts. Although some shortages, for example of potash, show as a reddish-brown scorching of the leaf margin, it is usually necessary to obtain an analysis of the soil or of the leaf tissues to identify such deficiencies using a soil-testing kit.

The absence of iron shows as a lack of green colour until the leaves are very pale yellow or even white and this condition often results from excess of lime and is called 'lime-induced chlorosis'. This, however, is easily tested by

1 Green petal on Strawberry flowers is a symptom of virus disease.
2 The attractive colour breaking of the Parrot Tulip is due to a virus.
3 A Bracket Fungus growing where bark has been stripped from a tree trunk.

one of the soil-testing field kits which will give the pH measurement of the soil showing its acidity or alkalinity. A quick remedy for iron shortage is now available by watering with a proprietary brand of iron chelate compound, which should be applied in January. A modern treatment for deficiencies is to use a proprietary foliar fertiliser, (many different types are now commercially available).

This is sprayed onto plants and supplies major and minor food elements through the leaves. It is the quickest way of getting foods into a plant which may be suffering from food deficiencies.

Plants suffering from bad drainage, wrong treatment, fume damage, etc., should be referred to the expert to judge from his experience.

From the foregoing it can be seen that in general a commonsense attitude to gardening, the cultivation of such good habits as cleanliness, proper attention to basic techniques and the swift diagnosis and treatment of any trouble should enable the average gardener to produce from his small plot crops of quality and quantity that make his work worth while. At the same time he has more friends than he sometimes knows and it will be worth taking just a little trouble to identify some of the common predators which will help him in the garden.

1 A female spider of species Aranea reaumuri, which feeds on other insects, most of which are plant pests.
2 The black and yellow striped Hover Fly, the grubs of which feed on colonies of Aphids.
3 The carnivorous Testacella Slug is one of the less conspicuous predators.

Predators

Garden pests have many enemies apart from gardeners. They must contend with smaller hunters of their own kind, apart from the parasites, fungi and viruses which beset them from time to time.

The predators catch and eat their victims. These hunters range from large creatures such as hedgehogs and birds, to extremely small insects and mites. A few of these creatures have been used in biological control, but it is not always as easy as it might appear to breed predators in sufficient numbers at the right time to control pests before severe damage is done. However, it has been done successfully in a few instances.

Perhaps the most familiar predators in our gardens are the ladybirds and their grey, torpedo-shaped larvae feeding on aphid colonies. The grubs of the yellow and black-striped hover flies feed on them too, as do also the sickle-jawed larvae of the lacewings. Fruit tree red spider mites are attacked by the antho-

corids and the black-kneed capsid. It is now possible for amateur gardeners to control the glasshouse red spider mite by introducing the predatory mite *Phytose iulus persimilis;* and the greenhouse whitefly by introducing the whitefly parasite *Encarsia formosa* (a parasitic wasp).

There are a number of general predators which may devour neutral or beneficial creatures as well as pests in the course of a day's hunting. Probably the best-known general predators are the long-legged carabid beetles and the sinister-looking devil's coach horse beetles. Some of the bigger water beetles are also vicious hunters and may occasionally tackle goldfish. Glow worms, unfortunately not very common these days, eat snails. Centipedes form another common group of predators.

Wasps may be seen carrying off great numbers of insects in the early part of the year and the hunting dragonfly is a familiar sight by the waterside. Spiders lay their traps and less conspicuous predators include the carnivorous testacella slugs, the red velvet mites, the larvae of certain gall midges and many other small creatures.

Many people are reluctant to use chemicals in the garden for fear of harming predators. The effects may be minimised by using insecticides of short persistence and systemics where possible.

1

2

4

3

5

6

7

Some of the most familiar predators which can be found in the garden.
1 The Southern Aeshna Dragonfly.
2 The Two-Spot Ladybird is a common garden species.
3 The male Demoiselle Dragonfly.
4 The Toad is especially active in gardens near water, and helps to keep garden pools clear of insects.
5 The Common Grass Snake.
6 The Carabid Beetle has long legs and moves quickly to catch its prey.
7 The Centipede, a relatively fast-moving and beneficial garden inhabitant.

Index

The letter references 'a', 'b', and 'c' after each page number indicate which column of the text should be consulted –
i.e. first (a), second (b), third (c).

Page numbers in italics indicate a relevant illustration and caption.

A

H

Hampton Court, Middlesex, formal garden, 44a
Hand hoe, *66p*
Hand saw, for pruning, *83p*
Hanging baskets, 174c, 175, 176
Harewood House, landscape garden, 41c
Haseley Court, Oxon., formal garden, 44a
Hedges, 149a
background for herbaceous border, 114a
conifers as, 155c
formal, at Hidcote Manor, Glos., *88p*
general cultivation, 89c
plants for, *90t*
pleached screens, 89b
preparation of site, 89a
roses as, 152c
trimming, 89c
watering, 89b
Helleborus foetidus, Stinking hellebore, poisonous plant, *36p*
Helleborus niger, Christmas rose, Black hellebore, poisonous plant, *36t*
Hemlock, *Conium maculatum,* poisonous plant, *37t*
Hemlock, *Oenanthe crocata,* Water dropwart, poisonous plant, *37t*
Herb gardens, 216c
borders, 216c
collections, 217a
designs for, 217b
natural orders, 217a
plants to include in, *217t*
at Sissinghurst, *218p*
Herbaceous borders, 113a
choice of plants for, 118a
hedges for, 114c, *114p*
as island borders, 118b
planting, 117c
prolonging the display of, 118c
supplementary dressings for, 114c
weeds in, 113c
Herbaceous plants, 121a, *121t*
Herbicides, in fertilisers, 21a, 92c
Herbs, drying, harvesting, etc., 218b
freezing, 219c
storing, 219b
Herringbone trenches, drainage, 29b
Hidcote, Glos., formal gardens, 44a
Hoes, 66a

Holkham Hall, Norfolk, formal gardens, 44a
Honesty, biennial, *112p*
Hoof and horn meal, 17b, *18t* *21t*
Hop manures, 27a
Hops, spent, analysis of, 27a
to add humus, 17b
Horse chestnut, terminal buds, *43p*
Horse manure, 23b
Horsetail, weed, *94-95p*
Horticultural Advisor, County, 13c
'Hot' manure, 23b
House, summer, as focal point in garden, 31a
House plants, 233c
a collection, *234p*
collection of ferns, *237p*
group of flowering, *236p*
Maranata mackoyana, *237p*
Hover fly, *239p, 246p*
Humus, 17a, 22b
suppliers, 27a
Hyacinth, basal bulbils, *43p*
Hyacinthus species, Hyacinth, poisonous plant, *37t*
Hydrangeas, blue, as indication of acid soil, 15b
Hydrated lime, 15a, 16a, 29a
Hydrochloric acid, soil test, 15b

I

Innes, John, base fertiliser, recipe, 19a
Innes, John, Horticultural Institution, 24b
Inorganic fertilisers, artificials, 17b
Insecticides, 242a, *242p*
Inter-cropping, in kitchen garden, 39c
Iris, Blue flag, *Iris versicolor,* poisonous plant, *36t*
Iris pseudacorus, Yellow flag, poisonous plant, *36p*
Iris versicolor, Blue flag, Iris, poisonous plant, *36t*
Iron, as deficiency corrective, *21t*
in over-limed soils, 16a
in soils, 12a
sulphate of, fertiliser, *20t*
Iron chelate, *21t*

J

Jekyll, Miss Gertrude, 44a
Johnston, Major Lawrence, 44a
Jonquil, Daffodil, Narcissus,

poisonous plant, *36t*

K

Kale, 206a, *206p*
Kalmia species, poisonous plant, *36t*
Keeled slug, attacks of, *239p*
Kingcup, Marsh marigold, *Caltha palustris,* poisonous plant, *37t*
Kingdon-Ward, Frank, plant hunter, 45c
Kitchen garden, 38c, 200c
design, 34b
at the RHS gardens, Wisley, *39p*

L

Labour saving gardening, 38c
Laburnum anagyroides, Laburnum, Golden rain, poisonous plant, *36t*
Laburnum seeds, poisonous, *35p*
Labyrinths, in formal gardens, 41c
Ladybird, two-spot, predator, *247p*
Lanceolate leaf, *196p*
Lanhydrock, Cornwall, formal garden, 44a
Larkspur, *Delphinium ajacis,* poisonous plant, *36t*
Laurel, Cherry, *Prunus laurocerasus,* poisonous plant, *36t*
Law and the gardener, 56c
Lawn(s), 70a
aerating, *74p*
clearing the site, 70a
construction and maintenance, 69b
diseases, 75b
drainage, 70b
seeding, 71c
turfing, 71a
watering, *74p*
weed control, 74b
Lawrence, W. J. C., of John Innes Horticultural Institution, 24b
Layering, 79c
strawberry runners, *80p*
Leaf portraits, *196-197p*
Leafhopper, pests, *240p*
Leafmould, 17b, *25p*
Leather jackets, pests, *241p*
and lime, 15b
Leaves, composted, *25p, 28p*
Leeks, 206b, *207p*
Lesser bindweed, weed, *94-95p*
Lettuce, 207a, *207p*